THE PSALMS IN
ISRAEL'S WORSHIP

SIGMUND MOWINCKEL

THE PSALMS
IN ISRAEL'S
WORSHIP

Translated by
D. R. AP-THOMAS
Lecturer in Hebrew & Old Testament,
University College of North Wales
Bangor

In Two Volumes — Volume I

ABINGDON PRESS
New York · Nashville

PRINTED IN GREAT BRITAIN

CONTENTS

Volume I

I, b

Volume II

Translator's Preface

I rejoice that at last one of the really significant works of our day on the biblical psalms is available to a wider circle of readers than could be reached by the original one-volume Norwegian edition. This book however is more than a translation of *Offersang og Sangoffer* as published in 1951 by H. Aschehoug & Co. of Oslo; it gives the reader a fully revised text. One chapter from the original has been dropped because the author felt that it was not fully relevant here; the material in another chapter has been redistributed; less immediately germane excursuses have been arranged as a series of Additional Notes appended to volume II; and most chapters show more or less extensive revision at the hands of the author, the final revisions having been incorporated at the proof stage, so that the present edition may claim to represent the author's latest views. These revisions, but still more the fulfilment of a lecturer's manifold tasks, have delayed the appearance of this book far beyond what had been expected. But the author has never once chided me for my slowness, and I am most grateful to him also for his careful reading of the proofs—which should guarantee that his views are nowhere seriously mis-represented in this volume. Where the author's technical terms seemed to me to carry overtones not present in the conventional English equivalents, I have not hesitated to translate more literally than elegantly.

References to the Old Testament follow the chapter (Psalm) and verse in Hebrew as given in *BH*[3]. (this means, as most will know, that for the psalms in English the verse number must usually be decreased by one). English renderings are based on the author's own Norwegian renderings in most cases. Where the Hebrew text is quoted, transliteration has been used, in spite of some complication in the chapter on metrics; the system used will, it is hoped, be obvious to the Hebraist and not too uncouth to the uninitiated.

I fear that consistency in such matters as abbreviation and form of reference has not entirely been attained, but it is hoped that intelligibility at least has been preserved. In addition to the many scripture references, all the bibliographical references given in the notes—with a few exceptions on account of inaccessibility—have been cross-checked for this edition, and my warmest thanks are due to Professor emeritus H. H. Rowley, who not only placed the splendid resources of his own library at my disposal but most generously helped me to track down and borrow books from other sources also. Wherever an English translation of a work referred to was known to me, a reference thereto has been added if applicable; but it should be pointed out that in some cases published translations are incomplete, consequently—and for the convenience of those possessing the original—the reference to the foreign work has been retained in every case.

In preparing the MS. for the press I have had every co-operation from my typists, Mrs F. G. Hughes and Miss Joan Yates. My friend the Rev. D. J. Williams and my wife, too, have helped me a great deal in checking the final draft of the MS.; in addition to these, I would like to thank the publisher for his continuous interest and readiness to discuss each stage of the work. Père de Vaux and L'école biblique at Jerusalem most graciously allowed me to use the resources of their magnificent library for some final checking while the MS. was in press.

D. R. AP-THOMAS.

Bangor,
October, 1961

Author's Preface to the English Edition

This book originally appeared in Norwegian dress in 1951; it has been revised in certain respects for the present edition. One chapter, which dealt with the use of the psalms in the Church, and which was strongly coloured by having been written during enemy occupation, has been omitted.

Scientifically speaking, the historical viewpoint from which I regard the psalms is that of form history—or, as it may better be termed, type history (*Gattungsgeschichte*)—a method of approach introduced by Hermann Gunkel. But when I began my *Psalmenstudien* I–VI (1921–24) it had become apparent to me that that point of view was not sufficient. In order to understand the psalms in their relationship to the religious life of Israel and of Judaism it is necessary also to use in addition the cult functional approach. They must be viewed and comprehended in their relationship to the congregation's devotional life. The great majority of the psalms which have come down to us do not simply derive, as a matter of form history or literary history, from ancient cult poetry—they are real cult psalms composed for and used in the actual services in the Temple. Private and more personal psalm poetry first occurs in the late Jewish period. In the Psalter such psalms constitute a minority.

The Norwegian edition bore the title *Offersang og Sangoffer*—'Song of sacrifice and Sacrifice of song' or 'Offering song and Song offering'. This was meant to suggest one of the avenues through the history of psalm poetry in the Old Testament. What I mean by that will appear in the chapter entitled 'The Learned Psalmography' (Chap. XVI).

One result of my work in connexion with the psalms—which has even surprised myself—is to see to how great an extent the piety and image of God which grew up within the official cult religion in the Temple at Jerusalem is presupposed by, and not a result of, the activity of the great classical prophets. Within the Christian Church the Psalter has always been the most used and most beloved book of the Old Testament. The biblical psalms have been the *fons et origo* of Christian hymnody, and they have still much to teach us about the real essence of writing hymns for divine service; for they provide a corrective to the often only too subjectively lyrical in more modern religious poetry and song.

The chapter on The Psalms at the Enthronement Festival of Yahweh was delivered as the Dale Lectures at Mansfield College, Oxford in 1953. I frequently think back with joy and gratitude to that occasion.

I would also express my thanks to the translator, Mr D. R. Ap-Thomas for his unwearying patience and care; the work has not been easy. My thanks go likewise to the publisher for his kindness in undertaking to publish the English edition.

SIGMUND MOWINCKEL.

Oslo,
October, 1961

CHAPTER I

The Psalms and the Cult

I

No book of the Old Testament has been read so much throughout the ages as the book of Psalms, 'the Psalms of David' as they are popularly termed.

The sense of the actuality of the prophets has often fluctuated; in evil times, in war, and in great disasters men have felt their significance more easily than under other conditions. But in the psalms the human heart has found its own counterpart at all times, in sorrow and in happiness, as an individual and as a member of God's People.

Hence it is natural that the psalms have been more often examined and interpreted than any other part of the Old Testament. Both the theologian and the historian of literature are interested in this poetry, and desire to know what are the conditions for understanding it, the soil from which it has sprung, the background against which it must be seen. Who are the men who are here pouring out their hearts and in whose words we are still doing the same? When did they live, under what conditions did they strive and suffer, sorrow and rejoice? What have they experienced, and what have they to tell us of their faith and hope, and of the reality on which that faith and hope are founded?

We wish to become acquainted with the psalms as they really were, namely, as real prayers uttered by men of flesh and blood praying in actual situations at a definite period. And with that background we also wish to see what is common and representative in them—that which makes them live to this day.

We must therefore try to understand them historically, on the basis of their own times. But this also means that we must try to find their place and function in the religious life of ancient Israel, or in early Judaism, if a critical historical examination should show that we have both pre-exilic and post-exilic psalms in the Psalter. Incidentally, in my view, this difference in time has not been of any great importance for their real place and function in the religious life of the congregation.

It is against this background of the historical and religio-phenomenological understanding that the real and lasting qualities of the psalms will appear.

What then, is the right view of the psalms? What are they essentially?

Neither the Greek word *psalmós* nor its Hebrew equivalent *mizmōr* necessarily means a cultic song only, but they are mostly used in this sense.

And by the word 'psalm' (Norwegian 'salme' is used also for hymn) we nowadays as a rule mean, in contrast to other spiritual songs, not a religious poem generally, but one which is connected with the worship of the congregation.[1] In any case it means a poem which arises from, or is related to, that experience which is expressed in worship, a worship which expresses the ideas and sentiments of the worshippers and their common attitude to the Godhead; such a poem therefore makes a more or less marked use of language which has already been shaped by worship.

Closer investigation has proved that in all religions, Christianity included, religious poetry has originated in connexion with congregational worship, and has been subordinated to it. Then the question arises: was this also the case in the Israelitic-Jewish religion, and does it thus apply to the poetic pieces collected in the book of Psalms?

It is quite clear that many psalms in the Psalter have been *used* in the cult of the Second Temple. Scholars have often called the Psalter 'the hymnbook of the Second Temple' meaning that it was collected just for this purpose. In this form the thesis is not quite correct: the Psalter may have *become* the cultic hymnbook, but was scarcely made with that end in view. Of the cultic use of many psalms, however, there is much evidence.

2

The title of the book of Psalms in Hebrew is *Tĕhillîm*, which means 'cultic songs of praise'.[2] This tallies with the indications we have that the songs and music of the levitical singers belonged to the solemn religious festivals as well as to daily sacrifices in the Temple. Such evidence is found both in the book of Chronicles and in Ecclesiasticus.[3]

In this connexion we must also draw attention to the technical terms in the psalm headings. Though the meaning of most of them is uncertain, there can be no doubt that many of them refer to liturgical practice in the temple service, some having reference to the cult-ritual acts for which the psalms in question have been used, some to the manner in which they were used, and some with other connexions. (See below, Chap. XXIII.)

In addition to this we have the Rabbinic tradition preserved both in Mishna and Talmud regarding a series of psalms which were used on different occasions in the temple cult.[4] Some of these traditions are supported by the titles in the Hebrew text. Thus we are told that Ps. 92 was used 'on the Sabbath'. No doubt what is referred to is the singing after the

---

[1] The word has received this sense through the usage of the Church. Greek *psalmós*, used in Greek Bible tradition about the Psalter (*psalmói*), in itself has no particularly religious meaning, but is used about a song accompanied on strings, and therefore in G (see note 5 below) as a rule renders Hebrew *mizmôr*, which has the same meaning and an analogous etymology, and may also be used of secular poems.

[2] See Additional Note I.

[3] See for instance 1 Chron. 16; Sir. 50.16ff.; 1 Mac. 4.54.

[4] The sources will be found in Buhl, *Psalmerne*,[2] pp. VIIIf.; Bentzen, *Indledning til Salmerne*, p. 29; likewise in the article on 'Psalms' in *The Jewish Encyclopedia*, X.244.

drink offering at the daily morning sacrifice (*tāmîdh*) in the temple. Notes in the Septuagint (the oldest Greek Bible translation)[5] and in the Mishna and Talmud[6] add information as to the psalms for the other days of the week.[7] Ps. 44.24 belonged to the *tāmîdh* sacrifice also for some time, whether every day or on certain occasions only we do not know. The Maccabean high priest and king, Hyrcanus I (134–104), who probably reformed the service, abolished this rite.[8]

Other psalms were sung at the special 'additional' festival offerings (the Musaf sacrifices) during the seven days of the feast of Tabernacles.[9] The special 'festival psalms', 120–134, were sung at the water-pouring rite on 'the great day of the festival', i.e.' the eighth day of celebration. According to the Targum, the old Aramaic synagogue translation of the Biblical texts, Ps. 81 was sung at the Musaf on new year's day (the feast of trumpets), the first of Tishri (that is September–October). Ps. 47 was also used as a new year hymn. At the feast of Dedication (of the Second Temple) which was instituted during the time of the Maccabees, Ps. 30[10] was sung—as corroborated by its title. The same psalm was used when the first-fruits were presented.[11] The so-called 'Egyptian Hallel', i.e. Pss. 113–118, was sung both at the slaying of the Paschal lamb[12] and at the feast of Tabernacles[13] and according to other sources also at the feast of Weeks (Pentecost) and at the feast of Dedication.[14] A very late source[15] mentions psalms also in connexion with the feast of Dedication, Purim, the first six days of the Passover and the seventh day, at Pentecost, and at the Lamentation on the eighth of Ab.[16] A title in the book of Psalms itself says that Ps. 100 was used at a special sacrifice, 'The Sacrifice of Thanksgiving'.[17] Probably also another of the titles (*Lĕhazkîr*), points to a specific sacrifice, the so-called *'azkārâ* offering.[18] This interpretation is supported by Sir. 38.9, 11.

[5] Hereafter shortened to G (=Graeca); often also shortened to LXX. On the true nature of the Septuagint see now Kahle, *The Cairo Geniza*, pp. 132ff.

[6] Mishna Tamid VII 4; cf. Talm. Bab. Rosh hashshana 30b, 31a; Sopherim XVIII 1.

[7] Ps. 24 on Sundays (G), 48 on Mondays, 82 on Tuesdays, 94 on Wednesdays (G), 81 on Thursdays (L), 93 on Fridays (G).

[8] Mishna Sota IX 10 (47ab); Tosephta to the passage; Sota 48a. cf. B. Jacob in *ZATW* 16, 1896, p. 141.

[9] Pss. 29; 50.16ff.; 94.16ff.; 81.7ff.; 65. See Bab. Sukka 55a; cf. G, for Ps. 29, referring the latter to the eighth day of the festival.—At the musaf-sacrifice on the Sabbath, according to Bab. Rosh hashshana 31a they would sing out of Deut. 32, and at the evening sacrifice Ex. 15 and Num. 21.17ff. See Snaith, *Studies in the Psalter*, p. 47. This, however, probably refers to the synagogue service. See Mowinckel, *Z. isr. Neujahr u. z. Deutung der Thronbesteigungspss.*, pp. 41f.

[10] Talmud. Sopherim XVIII.

[11] Mishna Bikkurim III 4.

[12] Mishna Pesahim V 7; Tosephta Pesahim III 11.

[13] Mishna Sukka IV 1. Cf. Büchler in *ZATW* 20, 1900, pp. 114ff., and the essay of Jacob (note 8 above).

[14] Tosephta Sukka III 2.

[15] Talmud Sopherim XVIII.

[16] Respectively Pss. 30; 7; 135; (according to other Rabbis, 83), 'the Egyptian Hallel' (see ch. XXII 2 j), 29 and 137.

[17] See Lev. 7.12ff.; 22.29; 2 Chron. 33.16.

[18] Pss. 38.1; 70.1; Lev. 2.2, 9, 16; 5.12; 6.8; Num. 5.26; Sir. 38.11; 45.16. Cf. Jacob, *ZATW* 17, 1897, pp. 48ff.

Some scholars have held that these items of information in the tradition do not refer to the service in the Temple, but to that in the synagogue.[19] But that is impossible. The synagogue is on the whole later than the period of biblical psalmody. The earliest mention of a synagogue is found in an inscription from Egypt from a time after 247 B.C. and all the evidence shows its introduction to have been later in Palestine than in the Dispersion. As an institution for worship the synagogue was not created to supplant the temple service, but to gather the congregation for the reading and teaching of the law and for common prayer at the appointed hours. The synagogue service was in ancient times always songless. It is quite another matter that in the course of time portions of psalms came to be used as lessons and prayers at the service in the synagogue. That only happened after the psalms had become 'Holy Scripture', and has nothing to do with hymn singing. We are here concerned with the recital by the synagogue 'recitator' (miqrē') who at certain intervals asks the congregation to answer with an 'Amen'! Not before mediaeval times did synagogal poetry and singing come into existence.[20]

The traditional use of the psalms in the temple service is confirmed by the fact that when the Chronicler in 1 Chron. 16 uses quotations from the so-called 'Enthronement Psalms' for the description of a certain cultic occasion, this tallies with the idea of the festival of 'Yahweh's enthronement' and with the ideation of these psalms and the situation from which they in fact must have sprung (see below, Chap. V).

But does (later) cultic use demand cultic origin? No. It is quite possible that poems which were not originally composed for cultic use, may later have been thus applied—as is also the case with so many hymn tunes. There are several instances of this in the hymnbooks of most Protestant denominations. And so it may have been in the Psalter, at least with some psalms.

---

[19] So for instance Duhm, Die Psalmen, p. XXIV; Staerk in S.A.T. III 1² p. 88. Quell, Kult. Probl. d. Pss. p. 5, also seems to attach little importance to the traditions about the use of psalms in the Temple. Cf. also Jacob in ZATW 16, 1896, p. 145 about the information in Sopherim XVIII.

[20] On the age of the synagogues see Hölscher, Gesch. d. isr. u. jüd. Religion, pp. 177f.; Schürer, Gesch. d. jüd. Volkes II⁴, pp. 497ff. Theological handbooks keep telling us that the synagogues originated during the Exile, that is to say shortly after the carrying off to Babylonia (for instance Wellhausen, Isr. u. jüd. Gesch.,⁶ pp. 149f.; 196f.), but this is nowhere justified by the sources, and the idea is as unlikely as it could possibly be. J. Morgenstern's arguments in support of A. Lods' suggestion that the Josianic reformation, 621 B.C., called forth the synagogue ('The Origin of the Synagogue' in Studi Orientalistici in honore G. Levi della Vida II, pp. 192ff.) are not convincing—especially not when it is recognized that the basis of Josiah's reform cannot have been Deuteronomy—which is most certainly an early post-exilic book. As to the synagogue in Palestine see for instance Oesterley, A Fresh Approach, pp. 153ff. The synagogue originally without singing: see Jacob in ZATW 16, 17, 18, 1896–98; Moore, Judaism I, pp. 241, 296; III, p. 65. Reading (!) parts of the psalms in the synagogue a 'Biblicism': see Oesterley, op. cit. pp. 106ff.; Hirsch's article 'Psalms' in JE X: the usual psalms were Pss. 105-107 ; 111-114 ; 116-118; 135 ; 136; 146-150. On the later poetry and singing of the synagogues (piyyutim and hizanoth), see Elbogen, Jüd. Gottesdienst, pp. 206ff. What Oesterley says (op. cit., pp. 106ff.) about the singing of psalms in the synagogue is partly hypothesis based on testimonies which actually refer to the temple service, and partly a reference to the use of psalms or psalm verses as prayers ('Biblicism', see above).

The possibility cannot be denied. There is at least one psalm whose attested liturgical use, according to the heading, does not correspond to its original purpose: Ps. 30, once used 'at the Dedication of the House', i.e. the temple dedication festival, instituted in 164 B.C., was no doubt composed for a quite different use, being concerned with a single individual, and not with the congregation as a whole. But this does not—even in this case—mean that Ps. 30 was composed for non-cultic use.

The prevalent opinion among both ancient scholars and the older generation of modern critical psalm interpreters has been, that both psalmody as such and our extant psalms originated as private individual lyrics, and only at a later stage were given a secondary use as songs for the temple service. For this opinion they seem not to have felt it necessary to give any proof.

Among modern interpreters, there have always been some, e.g. B. Duhm and Fr. Buhl, who were inclined to admit that this or that psalm was originally composed for liturgical purposes, even if they very seldom made any attempt to find the definite 'liturgical' or cultic situation of the psalm in question; especially in psalms composed wholly of set formulas, as e.g., Ps. 136, they were inclined to see 'merely liturgical compositions'. One has the impression that these interpreters were less interested in a psalm that was made for 'liturgical purpose' only, and that this of itself was a sign of a certain inferiority in such a psalm. In their opinion—so it seems—the good psalms were individual poetry, the poor ones might be made for liturgical (cultic) purpose. But why should only poetically poorer products have been made for the cultic service? Both Christian and 'pagan' cult lyrics offer many examples which demonstrate that even poems of the highest poetical and religious quality have been made for the cultic use of the congregation in question.

3

So we have to look for more scientifically founded criteria for the cultic purpose of psalms. And such criteria can be found.

Even at a first glance there are psalms, apart from those composed of set formulas and more or less clearly liturgical phrases, which must have been composed for some liturgical and ritual purpose, and which at the same time are of high poetical quality and great originality. To give some concrete examples, we have psalms that obviously presuppose, and are made for, a festal procession, such as Pss. 24; 68; 118; 132. They can only be understood in connexion with a vision of the procession itself and its different acts and scenes. The interpreter has to use both the descriptions of such cultic processions and the allusions to them in other Old Testament texts, and his own imagination, to recall a picture of the definite situation from which such a psalm cannot be separated. Only thus is it possible to find the inner connexion between the apparently incoherent stanzas of, e.g., Ps. 68.

Ps. 24 divides into three main parts which were used during the procession on the way to the Temple, before the gates, and when the procession winds in through the gates.

Ps. 118 also starts before the Temple and resounds while the 'procession' (*hagh*) marches through 'the Gate of Righteousness' and encircles the altar of burnt-offerings in the temple court.

Ps. 132 is (part of) the text for a dramatically performed procession, where we meet both the reigning king, playing the role of 'David', and his men who have been searching for Yahweh's holy shrine (the ark) and now are bringing it back to its proper place in the sanctuary of Zion. We hear the song of the priests who carry the shrine, the intercession for the anointed descendant of David referring to the merits of his ancestor: 'for thy servant David's sake', and at last the promise in Yahweh's name from the temple prophet to the king, if he keeps Yahweh's commandments.

In other psalms we find allusions to what can only be understood as definite ritual acts.

So the worshipper in Ps. 5.7 says that he has now 'come into Yahweh's house and will worship toward his holy Temple'. In Ps. 66.13 the worshipper comes into Yahweh's house with burnt offerings to keep the vows he has previously made. In Ps. 63.2–4 he comes at the dawn of day to the sanctuary to obtain proof of God's power and his glory and to get help in his distress. In Ps. 26.6f. he draws attention to the fact that he has 'washed his hands in innocency, and compassed God's altar', 'that he may publish with the voice of thanksgiving, and tell of all his wondrous works', i.e., sing the thanksgiving psalm when the prayer has been granted and the distress ended. It is an affirmation of innocence, alluding to the fact that the worshipper has been through the prescribed rites which gained him purgation from sin, and testified that he was now pure and blameless and worthy of help. Ps. 51.9 also alludes to such purification, e.g., the sprinkling with a hyssop wand and holy water, as we know it from the ritual prescriptions for purification and purificatory sacrifices. In v.8 the same psalm probably alludes to previous omens and signs which the priest (or the temple prophet) has interpreted for the suppliant. Ps. 86.17 prays for such a 'token for good'.

Probably it is an augural sacrifice, a sacrifice which accompanies the 'scrying' for the oracular answer, which is alluded to by the rare verb *biqqēr* in Pss. 5.4 and 27.4.

Ps. 84 gives a resounding testimony both to the psalm's inner bonds with the holy place and to its living connexion with the cult:

> How amiable thy dwelling is,
>   O Yahweh, Lord of Hosts!
> My soul has (long) been panting, pining
>   for the temple courts of Yahweh,
> Now soul and body thrill with joy
>   over the living God.

The bird has found her home at last,
    a nest to lay her young,
at thine own altars, Lord of hosts,
    my King and my God!

These random samples do not stand isolated. We shall not here anticipate the systematic research into psalm types. At this stage of our
inquiry we shall only draw attention to a number of definite allusions which
show the close connexion which both psalms and poets had with the Temple
on Mount Zion and with its rules and rites.[21] Very often they describe the
pious as already in or going towards 'Zion', 'Jerusalem', 'Salem', 'The
City', 'the Gates of the Temple', 'Mount Zion', 'the Holy Mount',
'God's Mountain', 'Yahweh's tent', his 'house', 'abode', or 'palace', his
'dwelling place', 'the Place', 'the Sanctuary'. The suppliant stands before
God's 'choir', 'before God', and prostrates himself before 'his Holy
Shrine' (the ark) which is his 'footstool', or before the 'Throne' 'on the
cherubim'. There are allusions to the 'Holy Feasts' and 'Processions' and
to the 'walking round about the altar' or the 'city walks', to the cultic
dance, and to the 'via sacra'. And now and then the action is performed
in such a way as to make it quite clear that the psalm in question belongs
to one or other of these particular rites. We have mentioned above, the
procession psalm 118 with its allusions to the circumambulation of the
altar. We may note 'the procession' to the temple gates in Ps. 24 as well
as the walking round about the city walls in Ps. 48. Allusions to the
festal processions are also found in Pss. 42.5 and 68.25f.

The 'New Moon and the Full Moon Feasts' are mentioned, and also the
'New Year Festival' (Ps. 81), the latter being alluded to as the beginning
of the new 'Time of Grace' (Ps. 65). The suppliants speak of the 'vigils' in
the Temple (Isa. 30.29; Ps. 134.1), 'evening offerings', 'the night-(service)'.
They present themselves both in 'the beauty of holiness' and in the 'sackcloth' of the penitent. They exhort to adoration the holy ones, 'the priests,
Yahweh's servants' and others 'dwelling in Yahweh's house', 'standing
in his palace'. Again and again the suppliant declares that he presents
himself at the 'altar of Yahweh' and 'prepares' offerings of all kinds:
'sacrifice' (of animals, zebhaḥ), 'sin-offerings' (better: 'sacrifice of purification'), 'meat offerings', 'incense', 'voluntary offerings', 'votive offerings',
'burnt-offerings', 'whole burnt sacrifice', 'fat offerings', 'drink offerings';
'with bullocks, rams, and he-goats' he will 'meet Yahweh'; he will 'prepare
an augural sacrifice' and 'look for Yahweh's answer'. He often alludes
not only to the sacrifices[22] but also to many ritual ceremonies connected
with them.[23] He testifies that he is 'pure', 'pure both in heart and hands',
he 'washes his hands in innocency and walks around the altar' (28.6), or

---

[21] For this section see Quell, *Kult. Probl. d. Pss.*, pp. 149–156, with systematically arranged
references to the sources of all these cues and many more.

[22] Pss. 22.27; 20.4; 27.6; 66.13ff.; 116.17, and other places.

[23] Cf. Pss. 51.19; 73.13; 116.13; 118.27.

asks to be 'purified', or 'redeemed', and 'purged with hyssop that he might
be clean' (51.9). He asks for a 'blessing' and himself utters both 'blessings'
and 'curses'. At times he comes in 'mourning' or 'sackcloth'. He 'kneels'
and 'prostrates himself' 'before Yahweh', 'lies on the threshold of God's
house', 'stretches out his hands' in 'humble prayer' and 'laments' or 'cries
out' his 'praise', and employs all the usual cultic expressions.

He does all this, not when alone in his closet, or in the fields, but in
'the midst of the Great Assembly', in the 'congregation', 'before his brethren', i.e. his fellow believers. In these exercises he feels himself a member
of the 'house of Jacob', of 'Israel', of 'the sons of Zion', of 'the flock of
Yahweh', as one of 'his chosen', his 'righteous', his 'servants' i.e. worshippers, his 'faithful' or 'devotees'—ḥăsîdhîm, the Hebrew word, might
perhaps be translated 'bondmen' or 'covenanters' or 'devotees'[24]—as one
of the 'brethren', one of 'the Sons of Yahweh'.[25]

In all ancient cults *song, music and dance* play an important role. So they
do in the psalms, and we shall therefore examine this characteristic somewhat more in detail.

There can be no doubt that the psalms were meant to be sung. They
contain a number of allusions to singing,[26] and they are often described
in the titles[27] as 'songs' (*šîr*) rendered to music, or as 'hymns' (*mizmōr*). But
it is a very doubtful exegesis for scholars to interpret a number of the titles as
directions about the tunes,[28] as was formerly, and is sometimes still, done.

As we shall see below, a song is a quite common feature of the cult.
This springs from a universal psychological law. The frequently repeated
invocation of the deity,[29] which belongs to the older religions and cults,
grows of itself into a rhythmical call, a short invocational song with some
kind of melody, be it ever so simple. When a human being is 'moved' by
the 'holy' he cries aloud. The cry grows into ecstatic song, a primitive
hymn of praise. Hymns belong to the oldest cultic utterance everywhere.[30]
The lament also calls for repetition, and grows into entreaty.[31] The same
prayer is repeated again and again, and the emotional crescendo and
decrescendo between despair and confidence, with the exhalation and
inhalation, create a rhythm and a rising and falling tune, however simple.

Even the primitive *ex opere operato* formula is full of awe and ecstasy[32]
and grows into a metric chant, which is 'sung'.

[24] Cf. Nelson Glueck, *Das Wort hesed* (*BZATW* 47).
[25] See the statistics given by Quell, *op. cit.*, pp. 154ff.
[26] The words 'song' (singing) and 'sing' occur 38 times in all in the psalms; *zāmar*, 'accompany
the singing', 43 times. For these and other terms for singing and music and doxology etc. see
Jacob in *ZATW* 17, 1897, pp. 266f., 273, and Quell, *Kult. Probl. d. Pss.*, pp. 152f.
[27] For these two terms see *Ps. St.* IV, pp. 2f. and below, Chap. XXIII 1–2.
[28] Cf. *Ps. St.* IV, pp. 22f. and below, Chap. XXIII no. 2.
[29] See van der Leeuw, *Phänomenologie*, pp. 345, 401f.
[30] *Ibid*, p. 406; Heiler, *Das Gebet*,[4] pp. 157ff.
[31] Hebr. *taḥănûnîm* = entreaty for indulgence and mercy. It is a significant fact that the word
is mostly used in the plural.
[32] Cf. what is told of the Australians, that they are often moved to tears, when performing
their 'magical' ceremonies, Söderblom, *Gudstrons uppkomst*, pp. 184, 190.

In many languages the word for 'song' originally betokened the power-full ritual word.[33]

In the psalms we constantly hear the poet, and through him the worshipper or the congregation, declaring their intention to 'sing' or 'praise' or 'sing and play' for Yahweh. The poet will recite his hymn 'to psaltery and harp', and so on. The psalm will be a song sung to Yahweh, either in praise and thanksgiving, or with prayer for help and deliverance. In this respect its connexion with the cult is clear enough.

We know nothing about the tunes in Israel's temple cult. But if we are to judge from analogies in more recent oriental music, we may assume that they were quite simple. It is a safe supposition that as the 'period' (the verse) was the proper rhythmic unit, it was also the melodic one. The 'tune' was limited to the single verse, perhaps with a marked rise or fall at the end of the last line in a 'stanza' or 'strophe'.

According to what we know and can conjecture from later times in the East, music was not based on the octave scale. As far as we can judge, the tune was extremely simple, hardly to be called a tune, but more like a sort of recitative.[34]

The first task of the muscial accompaniment was undoubtedly to stress the rhythm, to 'keep time'. We may draw that conclusion both from analogies in the present,[35] and from the old oriental and Israelite instruments of music.[36] The psalms mention the tambourine, the cymbals, the horn, the trumpet, different kinds of lyre (R.V. harp and cithern), flute and castanets.[37]

At all periods all kinds of cult have made use of instrumental music.[38] Like rhythm and tune it is a way of expressing the sense of rapture and sublime abandonment. It is a reaction to the encounter with the holy. By means of the rhythmical sound made by his own voice and the instrument, the individual 'shapes' this reality which affects his inner being, and thereby makes it his own; he objectivizes it and is in turn filled and used by it. Music is an expression of the soul, and affects the soul intensely. As in so many other religions, the rhythmical noisy music of ancient Israel was also used to induce that ecstasy in which the cultic experience culminates, and which is the form and medium of the inspiration in the holy men, the prophets and seers.[39]

[33] This applies for instance to Latin *carmen* as well as to Arabian *sa 'r* and *saj'*, probably also to Hebr. *shir*.
[34] Cf. Eerdmans, *Hebr. Book of Pss.* (*O.T.S.* IV), pp. 51ff. See below, Chap. XV 2.
[35] Besides Eerdmans (n. 34 above), see also Sachsse in *ZDPV* 50.
[36] Gressmann, *Musik und Musikinstrum. im. A.T.*; Bentzen, *Indledn.*, p. 95; Galling, article 'Musik (und Musikinstrumente)' in *BRL* col. 389ff.; Kolari, *Musikinstrumente und ihre Verwendung im A.T.*; R. Follet u. P. Nober, 'Zur altorientalischen Musik', *Biblica* XXXV, 1954, pp. 230ff. Murray in *Verbum Domini* 32, pp. 84ff. Wegner, *Die Musik-instrumente der alten Orients*. For a fuller list of literature see Schürer, *Gesch. d. jüd. Volkes*[4] II, p. 334 n. 83.
[37] Pss. 57.9; 92.4; 149 .3; 150.4; 68.26; 71.22; 81.3f; 98.5f; 150.3–5; Ex. 15.20; 2 Sam. 6.5; Jer. 31.4; Neh. 12.27; 1 Chron. 15.16ff.; 2 Chron. 5.12; 20.28; 29.26f.
[38] Van der Leeuw, *Phänomenologie*, p. 431; Heiler, *Das Gebet*,[4] pp. 165f.; for Oriental and Israelite cult, see Oesterley, *A Fresh Approach*, pp. 91ff., 106ff.
[39] 1 Sam. 10.5; 19.24; 2 Kgs. 3.15. See Lindblom, *Profetismen i Israel*, pp. 131f.

It is repeatedly alluded to in the psalms themselves, and expressly told in the Chronicler's description of the divine service and in his account of the temple ritual, that instrumental music had its place in the hymn singing. As is well known, the Temple in Jerusalem had its own guild of singers and musicians (see Chap. XV). When the Chronicler describes the work and the equipment of the temple singers he usually dwells on the musical instruments. The temple music had no independent significance. It was meant to accompany the song, the chanting recitation of prayers and hymns.[40] All the words for 'singing' and 'playing' in the Old Testament really signify the musical expression as a whole, the unity of song and instrumental accompaniment.

As to the point in the service at which, in old times, the song occurred, little is known. One thing is certain, that it was supposed primarily to belong to the sacrificial act.[41] This also applies to the private offering (Ps. 116.17). So we may suppose that also at the private and congregational sin and purification sacrifice those lamentation psalms and prayers which belonged to the ritual were offered together with the sacrifice or in immediate succession to it.

Together with cultic song and music goes the *dance*,[42] which is a common way of expressing the encounter with the holy. The dance is a spontaneous human expression of the sense of rapture, and hence it is regarded and utilized as a means to bring about this rapture and an experience of holy power and the presence of the divine. It is well known that the dance is associated with the fertility cult, because the dance may also be an expression of sexual elation. In the cult it is an expression of, and a means to produce, that feeling of strength which guarantees fertility, victory, success in hunting, and daily bread; it is 'work', 'cult'. At a higher religious level it develops into an expression of the joy at the encounter with the Holy One, an act for the glory of God (2 Sam. 6.20ff). It behoves one to give such visible and boisterous expression of 'the joy before Yahweh'.

Israel too had the cultic dance[43] as a means to produce ecstasy and that fullness of power to which it testified.[44] It was a part of the regular congregational cult, a testimony to the 'joy in Yahweh', and a mark of honour to him. We find both the whirling and leaping dance practised by more or less ecstatic individuals,[45] and the calmer kind, termed cult processions and circumambulation. The cultic festal procession in Israel must not, however, be visualized as anything like a grave and solemn march of the

---

[40] See Schürer, *Gesch. d. jüd. Volkes*[4] II, p. 335.

[41] Ps. 100.1; 2 Chron. 29.26ff.; Sir. 47.9; 50.18f.; Mishna Tamid VII 3. Cf. Schürer, *op. cit.*, pp. 350, 355.

[42] Cf. van der Leeuw, *op. cit.*, pp. 351f.; Oesterley, *Sacred Dance*; Backman, *Religious Dances*; Johs. Pedersen, *Israel, its Life and Culture*, III–IV, pp. 436ff.; Bentzen, *Indledn.*, pp. 98ff.; Heiler, *Das Gebet*[4], p. 159.

[43] Ex. 15.20; 2 Sam. 6.5, 12ff.; Pss. 30.12; 87.7; 149.33; 150.4; Judith 15.13.

[44] Lindblom, *Profetismen* p. 132; cf. index *s.v.* 'Dans'.

[45] 1 Sam. 10.5ff.; 2 Sam. 6.14ff.; cf. the Syrian name of the god *Ba'al marqod*, 'the Baal of the (ecstatic) dance'.

citizens. It has always something of the character of the folk dance. We can see this in Assyrian and Egyptian pictures of cultic processions[46] which display something of the original conception of the procession as a power-increasing and strength-conferring ambulation with holy powerful objects, as e.g., the holy ark of Yahweh. The idea of circling is preserved in the Hebrew word *ḥagh* which means circling, ambulation. In Pss. 48 and 118 the circling of the city wall[47] or the altar is itself the procession and the dance. Of course not all processions had the character of circum-ambulation. The grand procession which served as the enthronement procession of Yahweh held a prominent place at the great feast (see below, Chap. V.7). We may judge from the description of the procession with the ark in the second book of Samuel (ch. 6)—a description which is of course no contemporary 'reportage', but is modelled on the feasts of the writer's own time—that even the procession at the Throne Ascension of Yahweh had something of the elated mood of the dance.

Both music and song belong to the festive dance. When the warriors come home with victory they are met by dancing, singing and playing virgins (Jdg. 11.34; 1 Sam. 18.6), and that is how the legend imagines the people as celebrating and worshipping after the crossing of the Reed Sea (Ex. 15.20), and a festival psalm declares:

> We are seeing thy processions, O God,
> The processions of my God and my King in the sanctuary,
> Singers in front, musicians behind,
> Between them girls with tambourines.   (Ps. 68.25.)

The psalms often mention the cultic parade dance, or dance procession, in a way which shows it to have been the characteristic form for the festival cult, and that this was where many of the psalms were used.[48] At the cult place on Mount Zion 'start-up the springs of life of the singers and dancers' (Ps. 87.7).

The cultic dance went on right down to the last days of the Temple. Rabbinic tradition speaks particularly of a torch dance by night at the water pouring ceremony at the feast of Tabernacles: 'It was said that the gladness there was above everything. Pious men danced with torches in their hands and sang songs of joy and praise, while the Levites played all sorts of instruments. The dance drew great crowds of spectators for whom grandstands had been erected. It did not end until the morning at a given sign, when water from the spring of Shiloh was poured over the altar'.[49] This is certainly not the invention of later Jewish times, but a very old tradition.[50]

---

[46] See illustrations in Bentzen, *Indledn*, pp. 99 and 101.
[47] Cf. Neh. 12.31ff.
[48] Pss. 30.12; 87.7; 149.3; 150.4; Isa. 30.29.
[49] After Bentzen, *Indledn*. pp. 98f.; see Mishna Sukka IV 9, cf. V 5; Talmud Sukka 51a.
[50] Cf. Oesterley, *Sacred Dance*, p. 94.

The testimonies to the connexion of the psalms with the cult and its ceremonies, its sacrifices and lustrations, its song, music and dance are thus both numerous and strong, and certainly not to be found only in such psalms as are composed of 'set liturgical formulas'; the quotations given above are fairly equally dispersed over the whole Psalter.

4

Here one might object: those positive relations to temple and cult may be valid for the personal religion of the psalmists, but do they prove a cultic aim for their poems? They are at least more valid proofs than the unproved supposition of a mere private, individual origin for the psalms—a supposition that in fact is only a traditional prejudice.

It is, in fact, surprising that a cultic interpretation of the psalms has not been suggested long ago.

The traditional Jewish and Christian interpretation, however, took it for granted that the psalms were originally private, individual poetry. They were of course bound by the theory that most of the psalms had been composed by David and some of his supposed contemporaries, such as Asaph, Heman, etc. This exegesis was concerned to discover what events in David's public or private life had occasioned a particular psalm[51]—a point of view that is reflected already in the Massoretic headings of many psalms (see Chap. XV.5). Even the older, critical, historically orientated type of interpretation represented by scholars such as de Wette, Ewald, Wellhausen, Duhm, Buhl, Briggs, etc.,[52] was primarily interested in finding references to contemporary historical events in the psalms, and trying to discover the historical background and the date of the single psalm. In the main, these scholars believed that the psalms had sprung from the life and experiences of individual persons, and sometimes they even tried to find the historical person who had 'written' this or that definite psalm. Wellhausen went so far as to declare that without the prophetic activity and personal experiences of Jeremiah, the psalms would never have been composed.[53]

Smend shared the common presumption, but thought that the poets had spoken in the name of the congregation; in the 'I' of the psalms he found a poetical personification of the Jewish congregation—the theory of the so-called 'collective I'. But even Smend and his followers did not take the next step, to discuss a real cultic destination of the psalms; even to them 'the congregation' meant the pious 'private' lay circles supposed to exist within it, and to which they applied the expressions, the 'ănāwîm, the hăsîdhîm, the ṣaddîqîm, occurring in the psalms.

---

[51] Cf. Ps. St. VI, pp. 76–94, particularly pp. 84ff. An example from later times of this method of interpretation is J. S. H. Storjohann, Kong David, hans liv og salmer, Kristiania, 1900.
[52] See additional Note II.
[53]. Wellhausen, Isr. u. jüd. Geschichte⁶ p. 149f.

The more or less conscious presupposition on which these opinions rested, was the interpreters' personal low estimate of cult and liturgy, at which I have hinted above. 'Cult religion' was adjudged bad and primitive religion, and 'liturgical psalms' were poor psalms. The Roman Catholic exegetes might have shown more insight, but they were bound by their dogmatic presupposition of Davidic, Asaphite, etc. authorship—as was also the oldest Protestant exegesis. The modern, critical Protestant interpreters, in fact, had no real understanding of the cult either in Biblical religion or in religion in general. More or less consciously they all shared that contempt of ordered ecclesiastical worship which was common to pietism, revivalist movements, rationalism, and liberalism. Often coming from pietistically influenced circles themselves, they took it for granted that such groups had existed in Judaism as well, and found there the birthplace of psalmody.

In the meantime, the comparative study of religions had brought to the fore the important place of the cult in religion in general. The rediscovery of the old oriental cultures showed biblical scholars that exactly the same was true of the religions of the peoples that surrounded Israel, from whose culture and religion Israel had taken over many important customs and conceptions. Even in Protestant Christianity a better understanding of the value of ordered worship has emerged—although in some circles it is still branded as a 'high church' tendency. This change in the scholarly and spiritual situation has necessarily influenced also the interpretation of the Old Testament and especially of the psalms.

The man who pioneered the way for a new understanding of the psalms, and laid the foundation for a cultic interpretation, was Hermann Gunkel.

By his 'form-critical' or 'form-historical' (*formgeschichtliche*) and 'type-critical' (*gattungsgeschichtliche*) methods he has proved beyond doubt that in Israel also the origin of psalm poetry is to be found in the public cult: the different types of psalms have come into existence in connexion with different cultic situations and acts to which they originally belonged.

By tracing the peculiarities of the different types back to the attested or supposed cultic situations from which they have sprung, light falls both on the type and on its style as a whole, and on all its motifs and its formal peculiarities in their relation to one another. This is very important; Gunkel has by his method laid the foundation for a real historical and literary understanding of psalm poetry. In the following chapter we shall discuss the full content of his discovery.

On the basis of Gunkel's discovery of the cultic origin of the oldest Hebrew psalmody as such, the present author has for decades urged the cultic interpretation of the psalms and tried to show that this includes both a revision of many points in the older critical view of Old Testament religious history and a revaluation of the disparaged 'cult religion' of the Old Testament. The number of adherents to the cultic interpretation has increased, and in some circles there has lately appeared a tendency even to exaggerate the cultic aspect in the interpretation of the Old Testament.[54]

But Gunkel himself thought that the direct cultic connexion was true only with regard to the original, now mostly lost, psalm poetry; the now extant psalms were to be considered as a later evolution, a free, 'private' poetry, unconnected with the cultic situations, but imitating the style and the motifs of the older one. In this case we should have the following evolution of psalm poetry: from the cultic origin to private individual poetry, and back to the cult again.

It must be admitted that it is conceivable and confirmed by historical experience, that cultic poetry can engender a freer, so to speak, 'private' religious poetry, which will, to a great extent, use the old cultic forms and images, but can express more individual and private needs, moods and experiences. Both from Jeremiah and from Deutero-Isaiah[55] we can see that there have been non-cultic imitations of the style of the cultic psalms and that, moreover, in Israel. In later Judaism a religious poetry sprang up, independent of the cult, but to a great extent making use of old forms,[56] frequently enough in a very loose way.

But in the imitations by the prophets there are always sure indications that these poems are, and are intended to be, something other than cult songs, namely prophecies, or prayers springing out of the prophet's consciousness of a personal calling and its problems. Late Jewish psalm poetry moreover betrays its detachment from the cult by many obvious signs, both by an individual personal note, and by a breaking up and mixing of the old typical cultic psalm styles.

This seems to me to be a fairly strong argument against Gunkel's theory that the greater part of the psalms were 'private' imitations of old cult songs.

And what are Gunkel's arguments for this departure from his own sound fundamental position? They are, in fact, just the same as with the older critical school: the asserted incompatibility between the personal religious note in so many of the psalms, and the 'impersonal' character of the 'liturgical formula'. In other words: the newer Protestant lack of understanding of the importance of the cult and of its real essence. If Gunkel and his followers were right at this point, exactly the same argument should be valid against the psalmists' strong dependence on all the conventional forms of the old cultic style.

We shall in a later chapter see that there is no real incompatibility between 'traditionalism' and 'personality' in religious poetry. Here I only want to remark that traditional 'sacred' forms and expressions may often carry a richly personal content. True enough, they can become worn out and petrified by use. But through all the various experiences and emotions associated with them through generations, they may also be able some-

---

[54] See below, Chap. XVIII.2; cf. Chap. XVI.3.
[55] See below, Chap. XVI.
[56] See below, note 28 to Chap. V.

how to store the religious experience of the generations and become symbols and 'ideograms', 'words saturated with experience', as V. Grön-bech calls them, words which only need to be mentioned to release a series of associations, of thoughts, experiences, and emotions. The words convey more than they seemingly contain. The stereotyped phrase may express a personally experienced and genuine religion, both for the poet and for those who use the psalm in worship.

The task which psalm exegesis then has to face, is to try whether a consistent cultic interpretation can be applied to them in a natural way.

Having put this question, our duty is to obtain a right understanding of the meaning of 'cult' in religion, especially in the religion of Israel.

5

What is meant by cult? It has been said that religion appears in three main aspects, as cult, as myth and as ethos. Or, in other terms, as worship, as doctrine, and as behaviour (morals). This does not mean that religion can be split up into three sharply divided 'parts' or 'sections'. The three words signify forms of expression and manifestations, aspects of religion. The whole living content of a religion is present in all three. One and the same phenomenon may be seen from any of these three points of view. But the picture will be different according to which viewpoint we adopt. In the cult both doctrine and morals are expressed, and both draw power and new life from the cult.

The cult is thus a general phenomenon appearing in all religions, even in the most 'anti-cultic' Protestant sects and groups. It is indeed an essential and constitutive feature of a religion, that in which the nature and spiritual structure of a religion is most clearly manifested. It may take many forms, though a closer examination reveals the same main features in all religions. Like everything living, the cult has its history—a necessary evolution which is specific for each individual religion and is structurally determined by that which is peculiar, essential, and central in the religion in question.

Cult or ritual may be defined as the socially established and regulated holy acts and words in which the encounter and communion of the Deity with the congregation is established, developed, and brought to its ultimate goal. In other words: a relation in which a religion becomes a vitalizing function as a communion of God and congregation, and of the members of the congregation amongst themselves.

It stands to reason that inside a common field of culture like the ancient East, where all the nations have lived for thousands of years in the closest connexion with one another, in war and peace, at the same cultural level and with their ways of thinking and their sense of reality in common— interchanging hundreds of cultural forms and ideas—many elements and

forms of the cult will be the same or similar, being variations of the same
basic types. *A priori*, we could expect Israel, which after entering Canaan
adopted the material culture of the natives, and therewith also a good deal
of its modes of thought and spiritual culture, to have a cult whose basic
elements would be the same as those of the neighbouring peoples. That
this was so is proved at several points both by texts and archaeological
findings.[57] We may be sure that several of these conformities are the result
of direct borrowing. In many cases then, where the Old Testament texts
contain only casual and vague allusions to a cultic custom or rite, the
picture can be successfully completed by analogies from the cults of neighbouring peoples, which throw light on the allusions of the Old Testament.
The same holds good where certain allusions in a group of psalms, or the
situation to which they refer, seem to point to a cult ritual in connexion
with which the group of psalms must be understood. Such conclusions are
corroborated by the fact that a similar ritual and cultic situation is to be
found among other oriental peoples with whom Israel has been in close
connexion. There is no doubt that allusions here and there in the Old
Testament and the later Jewish and Rabbinic literature to certain ideas
and customs connected with the great annual festival—that of the New
Year—are explained and amplified by a comparison with the annual
festival of neighbouring peoples (see further, Chap. V).

The picture of the Israelite cult which we may draw from allusions in
the sources, and which may throw some light on the psalms and give them
their right setting, is conditioned by the extent of our general understanding of the nature and basic elements of the cult. It will, therefore, be
better to say a little more about the cult in general, in order to amplify
the short definitions given above.[58]

The cult is, as mentioned above, the visible and audible expression of
the relation between the congregation and the deity.

It may often look as though the initiative lies with the congregation,
on the human side. But seen from the point of view of cult and religion
it is rather the other way round: the initiative lies with God. True enough,
it is man that 'searches for God', 'seeks God', but he can, and does so,
because the deity has first 'revealed himself' and taught man where and
when and how to seek him. That is a fundamental idea in all religion, and

---

[57] Cf. R. Dussaud, *Origines Cananéennes du sacrifice Israelite*²; Lods in *RHPhR* 1929, pp. 199ff.;
W. F. Albright, *Archaeol. and the Relig. of Isr.*, pp. 70ff., 90ff., 127f., 165 etc.; Cook, *The Relig.
of Anc. Palestine in the Light of Archaeology*; Burrows, *What Mean these Stones?* Our knowledge of
the conformity has been strengthened and extended through the Ugaritic texts, see Dussaud,
*Origines,*² pp. 325ff., cf. Hooke, *Origin of Early Semit. Ritual*, p. 66; the general view of Dussaud
has not been seriously invalidated by Gray in *ZATW* 62, 1950, pp. 207ff., even if the specific
technical meaning of a term may have changed during the centuries. Gray is not right in
concluding from the silence about the sacrificial terms in the Patriarchal tales that the Patriarchs
as semi-nomadic immigrants are not representative of the culture of Canaan proper, Gray,
however, is right in criticizing Dussaud's theory of the common South-Canaanite ('Negebite')
origin of the 'Hebrews' and the Phoenicians. Cf. also Rowley, 'The Meaning of Sacrifice in the
O.T.', *BJRL* 33.1. (1950), pp. 74–110.

[58] For the following, see Mowinckel, *Religion und Kultus*, pp. 10ff., with the necessary references
to sources and literature.

not least in Israel. The deity represents a reality and a power which is different from the human, and belongs to a sphere termed '*the holy*', he is experienced as something 'different' and 'separate'—which is the original meaning of the word 'holy', 'sacred', in many languages—and imparts powers and effects which are holy. This holy sphere is inaccessible to man in his normal condition; it is 'taboo', and requires certain rules and forms of association, and a 'holy', or 'purified' quality in the person who desires to approach it. It is full of 'power' or *mana*—the Polynesian word which is often used by the science of comparative religion. Through the cult this effective and wonderful 'power' is imparted to the partakers, the congregation or the society. It may well be that at some stage, somewhere, sometime, 'the deity' has been construed quite indefinitely in the form of holy powers or influences, more or less impersonally conceived. But after all, it is not 'something holy', but 'The Holy One'—more or less clearly conceived—to whom the congregation turns in its cult. We can also trace the notion that through the words and acts of the cult, not only the congregation, but the holy forces and powers themselves are increased and fortified. The 'glory and power' of the deity waxes by the cult. But usually the deity is conceived of as the personal will and power that comes to the congregation through the cult, and creates and gives it what it needs, through the sacred acts and words. This is quite evidently the case with the cult in Israel.

At all events it is a mutual relation which is set up and developed in the cult. The acts and words express and produce this mutuality. Hence there are acts and words directed, so to speak, upwards from below, from the congregation to the deity—'sacrificial' acts and words—and also such as are directed downwards from above, from the deity to the congregation—'sacramental' acts and words. But the boundary between them is not sharply defined.

In the cult something happens: a relationship is established and developed which is of vital importance to the congregation, and the acts and words express what happens.

What the congregation wants to achieve through the cult, and what the 'power' from God is to create, is *life*—in the most comprehensive sense of the word, from the fundamental material need: rain, sun, fertility, the continuation of the race, the strength and victory of the tribe, and so on, up to the spiritual, religious and ethical values that are the life-blood of the society—life for everything that belongs to its 'world'. The Israelites expressed the same idea by the word 'blessing'.[59] Blessing is to be created, increased, and secured through the cult; the office of the priest is to 'bless in Yahweh's name'. Both life and blessing have their ultimate source in the deity.

One of the most important means to increase and secure blessing and life, in Israel also, was the *sacrifice*. Through the changing ages the various

[59] See Pedersen, *Israel* I–II, pp. 182ff.; III–IV, pp. 299ff.

I, 2

religions have had numerous and changing ideas about that. Such was
also the case in Israel. It might be seen as a gift or present to Yahweh, or
as a potent, sacramental meal, in which both Yahweh and the congregation take part, where the congregation are guests of Yahweh, and where
fellowship and covenant both with him and amongst the members of the
congregation are renewed and strengthened. By sanctifying and giving to
Yahweh part of the herd or the harvest, the remainder is 'sanctified' and
strengthened, and man is given blessing and life. Later the gift point of
view is more prominent. The congregation gives to Yahweh a present of
beasts and fruits, and in return he blesses them. The mental attitude may
be emphasized: it is not the gift in itself Yahweh desires, but the humble
or grateful mind of which it is an expression.[60] The sacrifice may also be
the means of purification and expiation, ordained by Yahweh in order to
have the sin and uncleanness obliterated and forgiven. This may be conceived in a more physical way ('magically'), blood being a 'magic' substance which 'cleanses' and 'redeems'; or in a more spiritual way: the
rites purify and create goodwill and forgiveness, when they are enacted
in obedience to what Yahweh has ordained.

That life is thus *created* through the cult means salvation from that
distress and destruction which would befall, if life were not renewed. For
existence is an everlasting war between the forces of life and death, of
blessing and curse.[61] 'The world' is worn out if it is not regularly renewed,
as anyone can see by the annual course of life and nature. Thus it is the
'fact of salvation' which is actualized in the cult.

This actualization of the fact of salvation is repeated as often as necessary. There are certain climaxes in life, crises when such a renewal is
specially needed: all the important transitions, birth, maturity, death,
spring, autumn, mid-summer, mid-winter, seed-time, and so on. The cult
therefore follows the course of the natural year, and takes shape in ritual
festivals, at certain climaxes of life. Some of these have a more private
character (birth, marriage, death), others are for the whole society in
common: the great annual festivals at sowing time and harvest time, new
year and solstice, passing from the dry season to rain, and so on. The main
festival of earliest, semi-nomadic Israel, was Passover, at the vernal
equinox. It was connected with the breeding of sheep and goats. By that
time the lambs were big enough to be sacrificed and eaten; the rains had
ceased (it was now a question of the pastures holding out); what little
barley and other grain the flock-rearing nomads grew, was ripe. In
Canaan the Israelites took over the three agricultural festivals already in
force there: the barley harvest festival (*maṣṣôth*, or barley cake feast),
which coincided with the Passover; the feast of weeks, or wheat harvest
festival, seven weeks later; and the wine and fruit harvest festival or feast
of Tabernacles, at the autumnal equinox, before the rains started. The feast

---

[60] See Pss. 50; 51, and for more details below, Chap. VIII. 11; X. 2.
[61] Cf. Pedersen, *Israel* I–II, pp. 453ff.

of Tabernacles was the greatest of these, the real 'festival of Yahweh', or 'day of Yahweh'; and it was in olden times celebrated as the new year festival (see Chap. V).

Through the acts and words of the festal cult, laid down in fixed, sacred *ritual*, the reality which is to be created—the renewal of the herd, of the field, of the forces of life, of righteousness, of blessing and life—is portrayed ('acted') in visual and audible form. The actualization takes place through the representation. This does not mean that the representation, the acts and words, are seen as 'magic' which by itself creates life and renewal. It is the 'powers', or the deity, Yahweh, who acts and creates through them; to that extent they are 'sacramental'.

The representation may be *either*, more or less realistic, *or*, more or less symbolic—more often the latter, i.e. the rites stand for something; they symbolize and represent that for which they stand.

Their inner meaning is that the powers of death are overcome by the powers of life, by the Life-giver himself, by Yahweh, the living and life-giving God. Thus they symbolize a *struggle*. In the festival Yahweh comes and *conquers* the evil powers, and establishes 'the world' of his people anew, with 'peace' (*šālôm*), new life and blessing and happiness.

Hence the festival cult invariably has a more or less dramatic character; it is a sacred drama, representing the salvation which takes place. This dramatic character tallies with the fact that the cult is a mutual act on the part of God and of the congregation, with address and answer, action and reaction.

The fact that the cult is a repetition and a renewed creation leads to the view that the salvation which takes place is a *repetition* of a *first salvation* which took place in the dawn of time.

The very fact that the cult is creative led to this first salvation being generally conceived as the first creation of life and blessedness, of the 'land/world' (the Hebrew word *'ereṣ* meaning both). Creation *is* salvation. This idea of the cult at the great festival as a reiteration of the creation is the general one all over the ancient East. Israel, also, was quite familiar with it. But in Israel a new thought was added, the idea that the people itself had been created by the *election* which even for the earliest Israelites was manifested primarily by the Exodus from Egypt and the accompanying miracles, and in the making of the covenant. Ever since then it has been a basic element in Israel's religion that Yahweh acts and manifests himself in the actual history of the people. He is the *God of history* no less than the God of creation. Hence it is especially the historical facts of salvation which are 'remembered', and thereby turned into new effectual reality by Yahweh's presence at the festival. All he formerly did, gave, and secured, he does and gives and secures again when he 'appears' at his festival.

The epic story—or the allusions in the songs of praise—that recites the deeds of salvation which are 'remembered' and repeated at the cultic festival, form its *festal myth*. The myth expresses what happens in the cult, and what once happened for the first time. There is consequently no disagreement between myth and reality. The nucleus of Israel's festal myth was the remembrance of that historic reality: the Exodus, the election, the covenant, the immigration.

In the cult, action and words belong together. The acts—the rites—represent, symbolize, and are agents for what happens. When water from the holy spring Gihon in the valley of Kidron is poured over the altar at the autumnal festival, this signifies that the rainy season will bring rain in plenty. A sacrifice is similarly effective. The sacrificial meal creates and demonstrates community and covenant. The imposition of hands conveys the blessing. The fact that Yahweh, represented by his holy ark, enters the Temple in a solemn procession, means and shows that he now comes as the victorious king, conqueror of all evil powers, of Israel's and his own enemies. The fact that he is there, in his Temple, means that earth is once more firm, in spite of the furious uproar of the primeval ocean; earth is once more created as in the beginning, cf. Ps. 93. It is the rites which symbolize the struggle and victory of the deity that more especially provide the clear stamp of a real cult drama. In the same way, in Egypt, the death of Osiris and the struggle of Horus, his son, against his enemies, and his victory over them, and the resurrection and enthronement of Osiris, are produced in dramatic form, and thus experienced as reality. An analogous case was Marduk's triumph over the dragon of the primeval ocean in Babylon, and, in Assyria, Assur's fight and victory. In Canaan, the content of the cultic drama was Baal's defeat in the fight against Môt (Death), followed by his resurrection and victory over Môt, his ascension to the throne as ruler over gods and men, and the re-creation of the world and of the Temple. In Israel, too, Yahweh's royal entry, the festal procession, had much of this dramatic character, with a representation of Yahweh's fight, victory and accession, as will be demonstrated in Chap. V.

The *words* of the cult seem originally to belong to the acts as interpretation and complement—that also being one side of the cult's dramatic character. The power inherent in the act is also concentrated in the word; the holy word is effective and creative. Word and act co-operate in the creation of reality. We find many instances of this in Israel's cult, both in the old clan and tribal cult as well as in the temple cult of the people.

Before Isaac can communicate the force of his own and his clan's blessing to his son, a ritual meal must be prepared and celebrated—this is the act. Thereby his power is strengthened and the communion deepened. Then he lays his hands on his son's head—the act again—and blesses him—the words (Gen. 27).

When the clan's daughter is to be given in marriage to another house, the clan gathers round her and gives her the blessing which is to make her fruitful and increase the power and glory of her new clan in the days to come. It says:

> Our sister, be thou thousands of myriads,
> may thy seed possess the gates of their enemies.
>
> (Gen. 24.60.)

No doubt this took place accompanied by the imposition of hands and other ritual ceremonies.

When the tribe is threatened by a mighty enemy, or arms itself to go to war, a great sacrifice is held, and (as we can read in the legend of Balaam) a curse, which is to break the power of the enemy and lodge defeat in his soul (Num. 22–27), is composed and uttered, to the accompaniment of very specific ceremonies.

Other rites bring us to the temple cult in Jerusalem, to the holy processions with the ark of Yahweh. When the priests lifted the ark to carry it in the procession[62] or in battle (1 Sam. 4) it signified that Yahweh himself on his throne headed his 'hosts'. So they used to lift the ark with a short song calling upon Yahweh himself to march:

> Rise up, Yahweh, and let thine enemies be scattered,
> let them that hate thee flee before thee!

and when the army pitched camp, or the procession reached its destination and the ark was put down, the words were:

> Take thy seat, Yahweh, among the myriads of Israel.
>
> (Num. 10.35f.)

On the festal days, when the service was over, the high priest concentrated the essence of the whole in an act which was visibly and audibly to convey to the congregation the blessing gained by it. He reached out his hands over the people and pronounced the well known 'Aaronic blessing', 'The Lord bless thee, and keep thee', etc. (Num. 6.22–27.)

Also the older type, the word which explains the act and is intended to increase its effect, was long preserved in the temple service. We see this among other things, from the words accompanying the 'ordeal' which the priest imposed upon the wife suspected of adultery. (Num. 5.19ff.)

In most of these cases the words express what is to happen to the congregation or to an individual member by an act of the deity. They are 'sacramental' words. This applies also to the cultic *oracle*, the augural and future-shaping answer from Yahweh, or his 'directions' or 'guidance' as to what the inquirer should do, e.g. in case of war and in impending danger generally (see further below, Chap. XII). The word may also express the *demand* and direction of the deity addressed to those who come to the place to partake of the blessing of the cult, and thus may become a vehicle for the religion's moral demand on the worshipper, 'the holy law' of the deity and the place (see below, pp. 177ff.).

But the words may also be the congregation's words to the deity (sacrificial words). They then express the congregation's reaction to and acceptance of what happens, as when the appearance of the deity in the pro-

---

[62] The journeyings through the desert in Num. 10–11ff. are described on the model of a cultic procession; cf. Ps. 132.

cession is greeted with hymns of praise, or the congregation gives thanks for the benefactions received. But they may also contain the congregation's prayer for help, salvation and blessing.

Prayer has not, as such, sprung from the cult, but in all higher cults it gradually takes precedence over everything else. Invocation and prayer are older than any cult, and independent of it. They are the primary expressions of religion.[63] That is why they have their place in the socially regulated intercourse with the divine, and may in the cult both be connected with, and have embodied and displaced, more magically significant and effective words which have their origin in the primitive 'magical' conception of life, which may be the background, but is not the 'origin', of religion. But on the other hand, the prayer may be overgrown by magic and, in a petrified religion and cult, sink down, to become a more or less magically conceived formula. But normally prayer is a petition to a powerful, willing and personally acting God, and is intended consciously to support, underline and express what the acts in their way express and effect. What is performed is accompanied by prayer and praise. It has been thus in all oriental cults, and without doubt also in Israel. The psalms are the actual proof of it.

It appears to be a universal law that the words in the cult take on a rhythmic form. In the rhythmic poetic form the 'force' of the words is more obvious both to perception and to emotion, and is further heightened by the music. The natural form of the cultic prayer is the *psalm*. Hence the large place in the cult which is given to the psalm in all the ancient oriental religions—in India, Iran, Babylonia-Assyria, Egypt, by the Hittites in Asia Minor, and by the Canaanites before the invasion of Israel, not to mention the many later developments during the Hellenistic age, in Manicheism and the Gnostic sects. Christian hymn-writing also grew out of worship, as is seen from the New Testament (cf. 1 Cor. 14.26).

Accordingly we find that psalms—hymns of praise, supplications, thanksgiving psalms, etc.—have in the different religions been connected with almost every one of the above cultic acts and ceremonies. From Babylonia-Assyria, Egypt, the Hittites in Asia Minor, India, etc., we have long series of psalms with indications of the definite cultic performance at which they were to be recited. The Ugaritic texts give strong reason to believe that the same was done by the Canaanites.

From Am. 5.23 must be concluded that hymn-singing at that time was a normal part of the Israelite cult, as well (cf. 6.5, and see below, Chap. XVIII.2).

It is therefore at least a very strongly founded working hypothesis that the biblical psalms are to be interpreted as cultic texts.

If this interpretation can be applied to the psalms individually there is no reason to look for any other explanation. It is the non-cultic character of a psalm which has to be proved, the contrary being the more likely supposition.

[63] Cf. Heiler, *Das Gebet*[4], pp. 157f.

CHAPTER II

The Method of the Cultic Interpretation

I

It follows from what has been said in Chap. I that a cultic interpretation—and a real understanding—of the psalms means setting each one of them in relation to the definite cultic act—or the cultic acts—to which it belonged.

All scientific research demands a proper arrangement of material, a classifying and a grouping, so that the things which belong together may be seen in their mutual connexions and illuminate one another. But the principles and criteria of classification must be derived from the material itself, not from disparate fields or modern interests and points of view. Not seldom the 'catchwords' for classification have been taken from the loci of Christian dogmatics, e.g. from the different divine attributes. But the ancient Israelites did not shape their thoughts to the pattern of Christian dogmas and morals. Nor can a classification according to the religious ideas represented in the different psalms be considered satisfactory: we cannot be sure that the idea which to us seems most prominent was so for the poet. It is quite unsystematic to group together 'nature psalms', 'creation psalms', 'psalms on the majesty of God', with 'prayer psalms', 'thanksgiving psalms', 'penitential psalms', etc.[1] The creation and the majesty of God, etc., may well be mentioned both in a 'prayer psalm' and a 'thanksgiving psalm'; the question is: why, and with what aim? There is no psalm which does not accept God's majesty and his power to intervene everywhere and all the time, or which does not acknowledge him as creator; the question is: why does, e.g., *this* special psalm speak at greater length and in more detail about creation than is usual in the psalms? It is misleading to speak of a 'nature psalm', because 'Nature'—this modern conception—plays no independent part in the psalms at all, but only occurs as an example of God's creative work. But why do certain psalms call 'heaven and earth, mountains and oceans, trees and fields, beasts and birds', etc., to praise the Lord, whilst the regular call to praise in the psalms is directed to the congregation of Israel, or the like?

All this modern grouping only leads us to ask the poets about things which interest *us*, but to which *they* often have no answer; instead of trying to see things from *their* point of view, and asking what is in *their* mind, e.g. when they appeal to God's omniscience, or call upon nature to praise

[1] See Additional Note III.

Yahweh. The usual interpretations of Pss. 90 and 139 are examples of such a mistaken way of putting the question. We read them as contemplations of the eternity or the omnipresence of God—but that is not what the poems seek to convey. They speak out of a definite situation, and it is in order to make God intervene in this situation that they speak of his eternity and omniscience. We must first listen to the emotion in the psalmist's own heart, and to be able to do that we must try to find the actual situation in which he is placed. Only then can we ask what he— and God through him—has to say to *us* in *our* situation.[2]

A proper classification must try to find the different fundamental types or species of psalms according to their own rules. How can these rules be recognized and described?

This is where Gunkel's 'form-critical' ('form-historical', *formgeschichtliche*) or 'type-critical' (*gattungsgeschichtliche*) method comes in.[3]

Even a superficial consideration shows that, in form and in details of content and structure, the psalms largely fall into a certain number of markedly different groups, which usually show a close conformation in form and matter within each individual group.

A number of psalms, for instance, are immediately recognizable as praises of Yahweh and of his great works and attributes. We soon discover that certain fundamental elements recur in such psalms with great regularity, and that in regard to their structure also the psalms of this group have certain traits in common. Another group consists of prayers and lamentations, in which a 'we' or 'I' voice their distress and beg Yahweh's help. Here too we meet with a number of characteristic details and common formulas both of prayer and lamentation, and with particular motivations for granting the prayer (*Gebetserhörungsmotive*), which in many variations constantly recur. Thus we are here confronted with special 'kinds' or 'types' of psalm whose peculiarities of content and form are amenable to description and explanation, and in which the agreement between form and content can be studied. These conformities cannot be accidental.

The first task is to classify the different forms and styles, thoughts and moods, of the psalms which are more or less distinctly alike in all these respects, and which thus form a special group or 'type' (species), for the moment leaving the dubious cases aside. Thus we become able to give a more or less complete description of the characteristics and peculiarities of every single group or species, each one containing those psalms which

[2] For this statement see Mowinckel, *The Old Testament as Word of God*, pp. 120ff.

[3] Gunkel presented the programme of his investigations in his *Israelitische Literaturgeschichte*; see further the article 'Psalmen' in *RGG*[1] and *RGG*[2]; followed up concretely in *Ausgewählte Psalmen*[4] and in the commentary *Die Psalmen* (in *HKAT*) as well as in Gunkel-Begrich, *Einleitung in die Pss*. Further references in *Einleitung*, p. 20. Even earlier B. Jacob (*ZATW* 17, 1897) and Matthes (*ZATW* 22, 1902), among others, had stood up for the principle of a cultic interpretation of the psalms. Bickel already saw and—without stating any reasons for it—declared that the psalms had been composed with a view to the public worship (*Dichtungen der Hebräer* I, p. VI). But only the historical method of studying form and type has been able to provide a safe basis for this theory.

show a fund of common forms, thoughts and moods. The work may be compared with that of the botanist, who decides the species of the individual plant and its place within the system on the basis of such objective criteria as the form and number of stamens, petals and sepals, and the place of these organs above or below the ovary.

We have to do with fixed style forms, where the similarities between the individual pieces within the group cannot be due to one poet having imitated the other, but to the fixity of a traditional and conventional style.

In a closed cultural orbit, both in a primitive culture and in the ancient high civilizations, the power of tradition and custom over form was much stronger than in modern times, when both an open exchange of cultural values and a much higher appreciation of the individual and his peculiar qualities have broken up the formerly closed and uniform circles of culture. The durability of form, and the power of convention over what is to be thought and said and done in the different constantly recurrent typical situations of life, we Norwegians, for example, until quite recently have had the opportunity of studying in our own remote valleys and communities. The conditions in ancient Israel were very much the same. Thus the hold of style over the poet was very great; from one point of view poetic composition was a thing which might be learned by anyone who cared to familiarize himself with the ideas and forms which custom demanded on typical occasions. Poetry, then, exists in definite traditional types or kinds, each with its own special rules as to content and form.

Content and form belong together. There exists no form without a content, and no content without a form. The psalms are poetry, and poetry is an art, and in art both content and form are determinants. Good art means a work in which there is unity of content and aim on the one hand, and of form and style on the other—where the form serves and adequately expresses the content, makes it living and allows it to appear with its full weight and to exhibit its real character. But especially in a remote culture, the forms are easier to detect, and they are often more fixed and more durable than the content. A form may live, even if the content has become more or less incomprehensible, and the ideas connected with it have changed, or have got a different emphasis. It goes without saying that in the classification of the psalms due attention must be paid to the motifs or themes included in the different form elements and thus recurring in several psalms as characteristic of the group. Essential parts of the content lie concealed in the form elements. Each motif or theme must be followed up in the different psalms and its quality be determined by comparison.

But even so, the fixed forms provide the easiest point of departure, and that is just what Gunkel has seen. So he came to call his method the *formgeschichtliche*, the form-historical, or form-critical method. The term is not quite adequate, and has given rise to misunderstanding. We might better call it the 'type-critical' or 'type-historical' method.

The fixed form elements will usually begin to appear in the opening words of the psalm.[4] Any one could at once classify a piece of writing that began: 'Once upon a time', or 'Dear Friend', or 'We are in receipt of your favour' . . . . In the same way we find that a certain group of psalms, a 'psalm-type', quite regularly starts with 'Praise Yahweh', or 'Let us praise', and so on. Another starts with a mention of Yahweh's name (the 'invocation') and a supplication, 'LORD (i.e. Yahweh), I cry unto thee', and so on.

Just as important as the opening words are the closing ones. Compare 'and they lived happily ever after', or 'Yours faithfully'. In the psalms we very often find that the closing words, in some form or other, re-iterate or correspond to the opening ones.

But even the central portion or main part has its typical elements of form and content. Religious experience and custom had long ago decided what details of content, what thoughts and formulas in the cult were 'right' and 'appropriate' in each type of psalm and situation in the cult. And these forms persist, even where the individual poet does not think consciously of a purpose any longer, or of gaining anything by his prayer. Thus we see that with the exhortation to praise God in the opening words there usually goes an enumeration of Yahweh's great and glorious works, his těhillôth. Very often a description of the sorry state and need of the suppliant corresponds to the opening invocation and prayer, and an appeal to the attributes of Yahweh or his deeds which make it likely that help may be given.

The realization of which elements of form normally belong to a certain type not only makes it possible to define the individual psalm and the cultic situation from which it originates, but is also of considerable importance for the exegesis, and for the interpretation of any obscure passage. The problem is frequently solved when we find out to what fundamental type the psalm in question belongs. It is also important when solving the question of how to divide a psalm into stanzas. The form may decide whether a verse belongs to the preceding or to the succeeding part. The determination of type can also answer the question we often meet with in the commentaries as to whether a psalm is a unit or should be divided into two; in the light of form criticism we can tell which subject matter and elements of form regularly belong to, or may belong to, a certain type.

Gunkel also realized that there is a close connexion between the fixed forms and contents on the one hand, and certain typical, more or less regularly recurring situations in the life of the community in question. Each 'literary' type has its special *place in life*, from which it has sprung.

As hinted above, there are in the life of every society, and especially in a closed cultural orbit, like that of the Hebrews, certain ever recurrent situations where certain things have to be done and certain words to be said. That applies both to what we call secular life, and to the sacred, cultic life. That means that even what we call secular, but important,

[4] For further details see Gunkel-Begrich, *Einleitung*, pp. 25f.

situations in life tend to become hedged by fixed 'rituals'. In his book
Rites de passage, A. van Gennep has demonstrated this as a very important
side of man's culture and cult. In the decisive situations of life, in life's
supreme moments, it is necessary that something vital be created and
obtained; and the means by which it was to be attained were the efficacious rites and words. As an element in these acts and words art has always
found its place, from the cave paintings of the Mousterians to the cultic
poetry, song, and music of the higher religions.

Poetry, like all other sorts of art, may have come into existence by the
eruptive expression of what filled man's soul, without any other aim and
purpose than just to express, to give birth to what demands expression,
just because it 'presses on' the soul. But even this is an 'aim', although
perhaps an unconscious one; man at once experiences that he has gained
something by the expression, and that what he has created is useful to
obtain certain results. What he expresses makes an impression on the
others. It can and shall be used.

To primitive man art and poetry have their aim and purpose, their
'tendency' in the good sense of the word. The ancient civilizations do not
know of poetry which is not 'tendentious'. Even the fairy-tale has its
purpose: to entertain, to move, to excite and to release. No ancient oriental
could have conceived of 'Art for art's sake'. Art and poetry are individual
and personal, but also social. Primitive poetry has its place in definite
situations in life, and aims at expressing what then happens and should
happen, what is felt and should be felt; what should then be said, because
the situation demands a lofty form of expression. Poetry itself was an
expression of a sociological function. Certain emotions, thoughts and words
were to be expressed so as to bring about a certain result, important for
the life of the community, and the form had to be the 'impressive', creating,
efficacious form of poetry. At the marriage ceremony the rhythmic blessing
was meant to induce fertility in the bride and numerous offspring for the
husband and his clan, as in the narrative of the betrothal of Rebekah.
Before the battle a curse was flung against the enemy to break his 'luck',
put 'bane' and evil 'charms' into his soul, to enable them to stand up to
him and drive him away, as in the Balaam story (Num. 22–24). At the
holy places, when the council sat and cases were brought forward, the
priests gave their directions from Yahweh in traditional forms. Before the
battle they and the prophets give oracular answers. When the army comes
home, the women sing paeans. At a burial the 'mourning-women' sing
their dirge, the *qînâ*. Each of these 'literary categories' has its traditional
form and its traditional subject.[5] No chance words were then spoken, but

[5] See the survey in Gunkel's fundamental *Israelitische Literatur* (above, note 3). Since then the
individual types have been thoroughly examined in a great many special works. For the *tôrâh*
or instruction in sacral law and 'oracle of the priest' cf. for instance Alt, *Urspr. d. isr. Rechts*;
Begrich, 'Die priesterliche Tora' in *Werden u. Wesen d. A.T.* ed. Hempel, *BZATW* 66, pp. 63ff.;
for the funeral wail, Jahnow, *Das hebr. Leichenlied*; for the prophetic oracle, for instance,
Mowinckel in *GTMMM* III, pp. 38ff.; cf. Begrich, 'Das priesterliche Heilsorakel', *ZATW* 52,
1934, pp. 81ff.

words of a defined content, worked by a poet or poetess into a poem according to set rules governed by a long tradition. The content was determined by the aim, and the aim, again, was dictated by the situation.

In the same way the situations also determined the form. The form is the one which, in each case, was felt to be the most natural and most suitable means of expressing the word to be said and of reaching the goal to be attained. This consideration consciously or unconsciously decides the choice of the details to be included, the expressions and imagery employed, the fundamental mood, and the composition as a whole into which the details have been fitted.

This general principle must also be applied to the psalms. The classification into different groups, each with its specific peculiarities as to style, form and content, is no subjective arrangement of the material, based on aesthetical considerations and feelings. By taking the fixed forms as a starting point, the form-critical method shows that it is founded on something objective and amenable to control, dependent on external observations, which it classifies, systematizes and explains. In the forms—here taken in the widest sense of the word—some essential information is found. The study of the formal criteria of the different stylistic 'types' shows the way to the different situations in life from which they have sprung. To each of the main psalm types corresponds a definite situation; they have all their definite setting or place in life. It then becomes quite clear that all these situations are cultic situations.

The content and the style of the 'public psalm of lament', such as, e.g. Pss. 44; 74; 79; 80; are just those which can be singled out from the description in 1 Sam. 7 of what was done and said as the Philistines oppressed the Israelites and the latter 'gathered together to Mizpah, and drew water, and poured it out before the LORD, and fasted on that day, and said there, We have sinned against the LORD . . . and the children of Israel said to Samuel, Cease not to cry unto the LORD our God for us, that he will save us out of the hand of the Philistines. And Samuel took a sucking lamb, and offered it for a whole burnt offering unto the LORD: and Samuel cried unto the LORD for Israel'. What, at a similar celebration 'in the time of dearth' (according to Jer. 14), used to be said to Yahweh is, as to content and form and style, in the closest correspondence with the same psalm type. What, according to Isa. 38 or Jonah 2, a man used to say to Yahweh when bringing his thanksgiving gift after being saved from great danger—sickness or the like—has also its close parallels in a definite type of psalm represented by Pss. 32, 116, and others. When the Chronicler describes a cultic celebration of some sort, he often lets the singers sing a hymn of praise which, in all essentials, often even in the wording, has its formal and material parallels in the Psalter.

So Gunkel could confidently draw the conclusion that psalm poetry as such, all the main psalm types with their formal and material characteristics, have sprung from definite cultic situations. Every psalm type as such has been created to serve cultic performances in a definite cultic situation with its own specific aim—hence its typical content, its structure and its formal expression.

With an objective inner logic the cultic situations demand a particular content in a particular form. Within the framework of a divine service of worship nothing is accidental. Everything has its significance and its purpose, which we must try to fathom. All the formal and material peculiarities of a type are explained by that origin and that purpose. To find these definite cultic situations was to Gunkel an integrating part of his form-historical research. So far, he was, in principle, absolutely right, as has been acknowledged by most recent interpreters,[6] and all further investigations of the psalms must be based on the foundation thus laid by him.

2

But, as already mentioned, Gunkel has not drawn the full consequences from his own fundamental discovery. His commentary on the psalms (*Die Psalmen*) and the Gunkel-Begrich 'Introduction to the Psalms' (*Einleitung in die Psalmen*) have gone only half-way. His method led him to see that psalm poetry as such was old in Israel, and that many psalms must be dated to pre-exilic times; but in the main he kept to the opinion ruling at the beginning of this century, that the greater number of extant psalms were post-exilic and came from small, more or less private 'conventicles' of pious laymen—for the existence of which he has given just as little proof as did his predecessors. The majority of extant psalms were in Gunkel's opinion no real cult psalms; they were 'spiritualized' imitations of the old, now mostly lost, cultic psalm poetry. In the many allusions to cultic rites and performances (see above, Chap. I) he would see only metaphors, and in this supposed emancipation from the cult, in the psalmists' 'freedom from the cult religion', he saw just that religious 'progress' which gave the psalms their religious value. The psalms had, so to say, to apologize for their cultic origin. He clung, like most of the older psalm interpreters, to the curious prejudice that direct cultic destination—as 'cult formulas', as they said—was more or less incompatible with deep personal feeling and experience—and the presence of these latter traits in many psalms they of course could not deny.

From this position, however, arose a serious problem which neither Gunkel himself nor his nearest followers perceived, or which, at least, they left unsolved. Both the titles of the psalms and express notes in the Jewish tradition in the Mishna and Talmud show—as we have seen—that several psalms have definitely been used in the temple service. But since we know that Judaism, like all other ancient cult religions, always demanded that everything concerning the cult should rest on old and sacred

[6] See Additional Note IV.

heritage and tradition, and that the cult should be a kind of closed world which no 'profane' influence might enter, it is inconceivable how any younger, private, lay poetry could possibly have made its way into the cult, and even supplanted most of the genuine old ritual poetry.

If the many psalms in which 'the suffering ones' or 'the hapless ones' ('ŏnîyîm, 'anāwîm) complain about their oppressors, originate from the 'suppressed' lower classes in the congregation—as the long prevailing theory of Rahlfs and others would have—how can it then be explained that they later on found their way into the official cult, which was in the hands of the supposed oppressors of the authors, the mighty and wealthy priesthood and the rulers of the congregation? In fact those 'oppressed ones' are the nation of Israel itself, suffering under the oppression of its heathen neighbours or the oriental world empires. Or, to take another instance, if the Korah psalms, Pss. 42–44, as Snaith has tried to demonstrate, originated in the circles which Nehemiah drove out from Jerusalem, and Pss. 50; 73–83 from the Jewish rigorists at that time, can it be conceived that this private polemical poetry has been taken up into the official cult, at a time when its true nature must still have been known to everyone?

To this problem there is only one satisfying answer: the psalms are—with very few exceptions—real cult psalms, made for cultic use.

Another consideration points in the same direction.

We do have a Jewish psalm poetry which came into existence as 'private religious lyrics' without any connexion with the temple cult, and without cultic destination. This psalmody emanated from certain 'pious circles', which really existed in later Judaism, after the days of the predominance of the written law on the one hand, and the Hellenizing influences among the upper classes before and after the Maccabean revolt on the other. It is to be found in the so-called Psalms of Solomon, and the newly found Essenian Hodayoth from the Qumran caves. Owing to the emancipation from the temple cult and the individualistic spirit of the poets concerned, they demonstrate a far-reaching disintegration of the old fixed forms and a mixture of elements from different styles and types not found in the biblical psalms, where in all essentials the old fixed formal and stylistic rules predominate.

What strikes us in the biblical psalms is the uniformity and formality which characterize most of them. One is often so like another that they are difficult to differentiate. The personal, individual element is pushed into the background. Imagery and phraseology are often the stereotyped traditional ones. Rarely is there a clear allusion to the poet's personal situation, rarely anything definite and concrete, almost invariably only what is typical of a whole circle, in the most general terms. This cannot be explained as only the usual lyric dependence on a particular style with its partiality for that in which everybody can join; for even then there can be room for personal variations, as may be seen from the dirge over Saul and Jonathan in 2 Sam. 1.19ff., compared with the usual stereotyped dirge. The set formality of the psalms can only be explained on the basis that they are not primarily meant to be personal effusions, but are, in accordance with their type and origin, ritual lyrics. It is of the nature of the cultic psalm that it cannot express the individual's definite, once-for-all, experiences and emotions. It voices those moods and experiences which have common currency within the cult community. Hence everything which is too concrete and individual is pushed into the background.[7] In its original form the cultic psalm springs from set formulas, suiting all occasions. We meet the same formality to a much higher degree in Babylonian-Assyrian cultic psalms.[8]

This does not imply that the personal element has been cut out, or that type analysis pays no heed to it. We shall return to this point in a special chapter.

But also in another respect Gunkel—and after him many of his followers —went only half-way. He often stuck too much to the mere formal registration and labelling of the single elements of a psalm and did not see clearly enough that his own form-historical method demanded that it be developed into a real *cult-functional method*.

The form may be overrated so as to arrest one's vision and understanding through purely formal limitations, and make one overlook important inner correspondences between psalms which outwardly appear to belong to different groups, but which are governed by the same ideas, and thus prove to belong together, perhaps as psalms for some specific festival.

In course of time an old form may have become the bearer of new contents in a new situation.[9] That also must be taken into consideration.

On the other hand, an alien form may have been used as an effective means of expressing the content. Thus although the prophets often used the psalm-style to underline and emphasize their message; nevertheless their utterances are prophecies and neither hymns nor lamentations. And the psalm-writer may use the form of the 'wisdom-poetry' for his personal expression of the praise of God, or thanksgiving for a blessing received— without his psalm becoming a wisdom or problem poem.

Occasionally we meet with 'compound' psalms, whose different parts use two completely different form types, e.g. hymn of praise plus lamentation, or thanksgiving plus lamentation. In such cases the older critical psalm interpreter often solved the problem by declaring that here two different psalms had been joined together 'by chance'. This was possible when the psalms were still viewed from a purely literary and aesthetic point of view, and one did not raise the question about their background

---

[7] Cf. my treatise 'Salmeboken' in *NTT* 1927, pp. 153f., where this peculiarity even in Danish and Norwegian psalmography ("hymnology") is briefly commented on.

[8] Cf. Jastrow, *Relig. Babyl. u. Assyr.* II, pp. 10f., 61f., 116; Weber, *Liter. d. Babyl. u. Assyr.*, pp. 116f.

[9] Gunkel is of course fully aware of this, for instance, when he maintains that a new sense has been 'spiritually' assigned to the cultic psalms of illness, so as to change them into individual cult-free prayers. But this theory of a new reading is itself untenable.

in an actual cultic situation. Even Gunkel's interpretation, which on principle took its point of departure from the latter point, sometimes failed here and was content to classify and establish the facts instead of explaining them. An instance of such a failure is his treatment of Pss. 9–10, which form *one* psalm bound together by 'the alphabetical scheme', that is, each new stanza starts with another letter, in alphabetical order. The first part of this, the letters *aleph* to *kaph* (*a–k*) make a hymn; while the second part, the letters *lamedh* to *taw* (*l–t*), is a lament. Gunkel's explanation is that when the poet reached *lamedh* he could not, on the spur of the moment, find any other word starting with an 'l' than *lamma* 'why', and hence he plunged into the lament style, where the lamenting phrase 'Why hast thou forsaken me?' and the like, frequently recur, and continued in this lamentation style! This is a curiously superficial explanation, poorly corresponding with the firm and conscious style of the poem, and is only possible because Gunkel with regard to the individual psalms usually betrays his own cultic principle, maintaining that they are not real cult psalms, but only 'literary' imitations.[10]

Sometimes Gunkel stressed the formal identity between the psalms of a definite species at the risk of drawing too narrow limits for the species in question, thus failing to see an important idea that at least has some inner connexion with that species. There can be no doubt that Gunkel is wrong in excluding Ps. 95 from the category of the 'enthronement' psalms 93; 96–99. Ps. 95 has all the characteristics of the others, *plus* something more: and this plus in fact opens the way to a deeper understanding of the enthronement psalms, and widens the number of psalms belonging in the same ideological connexion. We then see that the narrow group of enthronement psalms, in the strictest sense of the word, tells us very little about religious experience, life and thought in ancient Israel, compared with the great complex of experiences and ideas that we grasp when we put the real cult functional question: to which cultic occasion must this psalm group have belonged, and what has the congregation experienced and felt on that occasion? The definition 'enthronement psalms' must be made not only from the formal literary, but also from the cult functional point of view, and the latter is the more important.

That the psalms belong to the cult will in many cases mean that they belong to some definite cultic festival cult to the ancient Israelite meant primarily 'festival'.

But the experience, thought, and mood involved in a particular cultic festival are generally many-sided, and complex enough to cover the whole range of religious content and experience. The ritual of a festival service is in fact a very complex affair with many subdivisions, each intended to express a certain aspect of the experience and of the 'cultic drama', and

---

[10] A much more organic understanding of the connexion between the two parts of the psalm is found in Bentzen, *Fortolkning til de gt. lige Salmer, ad loc.*, cf. also Junker in *Revue Biblique* 60, 1953, pp. 161ff. Bentzen is right in his criticism of the present author in *Ps. St.* I 172.

the corresponding religious need and mood. Corresponding to these different aspects are different kinds of style, evolved to express each of them. So to the same festival there may have belonged both plaintive prayers for help in distress and need, and joyous hymns to the living God, thanking him for salvation promised or 'seen' and grasped by the believer in the symbols of the cult. The festival cult involved a number of very different acts and ceremonies. This point Gunkel of course had seen, when he recognized a 'sacramental' element, an oracle of Yahweh, in some psalms, and defined a group of psalms as '(compound) liturgies'. But each festival also has its main idea, with many varying notions and conceptions. This main idea and the conceptions which accompany it will of course characterize most of the appertaining 'words' and psalms. With us, for instance, the main idea of Easter or Whitsun, and the reality of salvation which these festivals express and revive, will in many ways stamp all true Easter or Pentecost hymns, and appear in prayer and confession as well as in hymns of thanks and praise. There is no Christian Easter hymn—of whatever style—that does not in some manner refer to Christ's victorious resurrection and its power and hope. It is not sufficient then, to define a psalm as a lamentation or prayer-psalm, if its main idea suggests in addition a connexion with the idea and experience of a particular festival. This must become perfectly clear, and we shall have understood neither the psalm nor its place in actual life, its cultic situation and its aim, until we have connected it with the festival in question, and with its idea and cultic forms.

In other words, the purely form-historical classification and interpretation of Gunkel, the pure 'examination of types', and grouping of the psalms according to the form categories found by the form critic, has to be enlarged and replaced by proper cult-historical ones. The formal point of view is only a provisional help.

This point of view, then, will lead us to a modified division of the psalms and to another principle of interpretation than that of Gunkel, viz. to the form *and* cult-historical one. If we take this seriously at the same time remembering the old Israelite 'collective' (corporate) view of people and community, as it appears in the cult (see below, Chap. III. 1), we shall see that a purely formal classification often has only a relative value. We shall not have reached our goal by, e.g., dividing the 'lamentation-psalms' into 'we-psalms' and 'I-psalms', and imagining that we have in that way reached two really different categories and cultic situations. The I-form in reality includes psalms of two very different cultic types, each with its own cultic and historic background and causation. One of these groups—the so-called public (congregational) lamentations—is objectively and cult historically much more closely related to the 'we-psalms' than it is to the proper 'I-psalms'. There is a series of 'I-psalms' where the 'I' is not the single, private member of the congregation, but the social, political and cultic representative of the people—that is to say, the king. In this case the occasion and the corresponding cultic situation is, as we shall see below, a public matter, not the experience and situation of a single private individual.[11] This leads both to somewhat of a return to older positions in the interpretation of the 'I' in the psalms,[12] and to a view of the so-called 'royal psalms' diverging from Gunkel's (see Chap. III).

In practice the form-critical and the cult-functional method cannot be separated from each other, but must work hand in hand when we arrange the psalms in groups or species, according to such common forms, thoughts and moods as are in accordance with that cultic situation, or that special festival, which is supposed to be the background of the species in question. True enough, the common elements must be the essential ones in the psalms in question; but if a whole coherent complex of ideas is included in the supposed cultic festival, it may well happen that one of the components of this complex is predominant in one psalm, another component in another. Here it will be necessary to bear in mind the old Israelite way of 'thinking in totalities': if one note of a chord is struck, all the others sound in his mind; one important component of a complex of ideas being mentioned, the others are recalled in his consciousness.

The present author has for a good many years in his studies on the psalms endeavoured to apply a really cult-functional interpretation, and to bring out all these features in the psalms and in what we know about the Israelite and Jewish cult which help to prove that the psalms of the Psalter, on the whole, are real cult-psalms and an expression of that experience of God which the cult seeks to further.[13]

The cult-functional method includes the attempt to understand every surviving psalm as a real cult psalm, made for a definite cultic situation. The foundation has been laid by Gunkel's explanation of the cultic origin of the different types. But in trying to trace the consequences for the surviving psalms, we shall find ourselves concerned with more of such situations than he thought, and realize that the connexion between psalm and cult is much closer than he imagined.

To understand a psalm means to see it in the right cultic connexion. This is, in fact, a quite elementary truth. Everybody will agree that a Christian baptismal hymn or a communion hymn acquires full significance only when seen in connexion with the holy act to which it belongs.

---

[11] See Chap. VII.

[12] This applies for instance to the view of the so-called 'collective ego', which has more of truth in it than the purely form-historical school has been willing to admit. It also applies to the view of the political background and the events occasioning the I-laments, which are actually 'national' (royal) psalms, as has been demonstrated especially by Birkeland (*Feinde d. Indiv.*); he shares this interpretation with earlier critical psalm interpreters like de Wette and Fr. Buhl; cf. Bentzen's remark on the book by Birkeland: 'Many of B.'s arguments, when read today, half a dozen years after the appearance of the book, look like a "repristination", a return to earlier criticism' (Bentzen, *Sakrale kongedømme*, p. 39). This is true, as far as it goes, but no real objection. Even earlier critics may sometimes be in the right!

[13] Cf. the summary in my essay in *NTT* 1924, pp. 1ff. As far as some groups of psalms are concerned this point of view has been followed up in my *Ps. St.* I–VI; but the conception in *Ps. St.* I especially is in need of the thorough re-examination carried out in the present book.

From the cult new light falls on the psalms, and from the psalms light falls on new sides of the cult. There is no first and last here. In the actual process of research these two points of view must be kept in a constant reciprocity.

The best proof for the correctness of our method will be when we succeed in explaining the whole extant material in this way. This the following chapters will try to do.

But our method will also afford a possibility of distinguishing between real cult psalms and a 'private' psalmody which partly uses the old styles and forms, but in many ways points to another 'place in life'. There *are*, even in the Psalter, some non-cultic psalms, but they are few.

A true interpretation of the psalms must try to form as complete and vivid a picture as possible of the old Israelite and Jewish cult and its many situations and acts.

3

Apparently we are quite well informed about the cult in Israel. The whole central part of the Pentateuch consists of cultic and ritual laws. But these are mostly to be found in a relatively late form and system, such as the 'Priestly Document' (P), the latest of the Pentateuchal sources, collected in post-exilic, Jewish times. As is shown by a comparison with the allusions in older sources and in the historical books, the view taken of important ritual acts (e.g. of the importance of the sacrifice), has changed and developed; so that it would be a mistake to base our conception of the psalms on the later stages of Israelitic-Jewish cultic development. The psalms are to a very great extent much older, and date from the time of the monarchy (before the exile). Further, the picture which the priestly source gives us of the cult is both one-sided and fragmentary. It presents ritual and other features of the service from the priests' own technical point of view. The laws (priests' agenda) speak of the kind and number of beasts to be sacrificed, and how the priest is to conduct himself in the course of the sacrificial act. We are also told what sacrifices and contributions the lay people are to offer, and the rituals at certain purifications and sacrifices are described from the point of view of the officiating priest. But they never give a living picture of a ritual festival as a whole. We hear practically nothing about the part played by the congregation, e.g. in the great festal processions which, from other sources, we know belonged to it. Nor do they say anything about the words which belonged to the cult, the prayers which were prayed, and the psalms which were sung. But from other sources, e.g. the book of Chronicles, we know that they formed part of the service. Only very rarely do the laws record a cultic prayer (Deut. 21.7–9; 26.1ff.), and we hear very little about hymn singing, even though other sources contain allusions to ritual acts where hymns were sung.[14]

[14] Cf. Am. 5.23; Job 33.27; 2 Sam. 6.5; 1 Kgs. 8.12; 1 Chron. 16.8ff.; 2 Chron. 6.1f.; 6.41f., and other places.

In addition to what is given in the laws, we find, in historical and legendary accounts and in the prophets, more incidental remarks and allusions which may serve to amplify the picture.

But, to a certain extent, the situations can and must be pictured from hints in the psalms themselves. When once we have grasped that each situation creates its own formal language around a definite subject-content, then we are able, from the characteristics of the content and form in a certain group of psalms, to reconstruct the precise cultic occasion which has produced them, and which also supplies their natural explanation. In this way Gunkel and others after him re-discovered important parts of the ancient Israelite cult which were not mentioned in the laws. We shall look more closely at this when treating of the particular types of psalms and their origin.

This process of induction from the types of psalms to the underlying cultic situation of course becomes increasingly convincing as it can be confirmed by analogies from neighbouring oriental civilizations. We must realize that in matters of the framework of the cult, and incidentally, of many of the ideas expressed through it, the partially Canaanized Israelites took as models the temple cults of neighbouring peoples. The Yahweh religion in the period immediately following the immigration (and especially after the blending with the indigenous population had been achieved with the rise of the monarchy), had been deeply influenced by Canaanite religion, that is to say by oriental religion generally. The religious history of Israel in the following period largely consists of a dramatic struggle to expel the obviously syncretistic, and to work out the peculiar historical significances of the Yahweh religion. Israel's cult places were to a great extent the same as those of the ancient Canaanites, and there followed, as a matter of course, the adoption of many Canaanite cultic traditions. The three great annual festivals are characteristic agricultural festivals, which Israel adopted from the natives and adjusted to the religion of Yahweh, giving them a new, historically orientated interpretation. The first of them, the festival of the barley harvest, the Maṣṣôth festival, corresponded in time to the old Israelite cattle-breeding festival of Easter (Pesaḥ), and could be combined with it. The very Temple in Jerusalem was built according to Canaanite patterns. To worship Yahweh in temples was a novel custom. In Jerusalem, Yahweh was 'identified' with the ancient deities, and inherited their names and titles of honour. There can, for instance, be no doubt that the name El Elyon, 'The Highest God', which in the Old Testament means Yahweh, originally signified the chief god of Jebusite Jerusalem. There are even signs that point to a connexion between the new priestly family to whom David entrusted the Yahweh cult in the Temple—the Zadokites—and the ancient dynasty of priest kings in Jerusalem.[15] Israel had no tradition as to the framing of a temple cult which went back to the period of desert wander-

[15] See below, n. 87 to Chap. V.

ing. That was adopted from outside. Another very important case of influence from oriental cultic ideas and customs will be demonstrated in Chap. V.

Hence it goes without saying that the knowledge of other oriental cult rituals—as Gunkel has already shown[16]—will throw light on much in the cult of Jerusalem, and thereby yield important contributions for a correct location of the psalms in the cult—not least because they so often support the conclusions one can draw from the psalms themselves.

In several respects—e.g. in the way we look at the collective element in many of the 'I-psalms'—our presentation will mean a return to older positions in psalm-interpretation,[17] but in new connexions and in a new light. Such is often the way of science.

In spite of a definite and fundamental cult-historical view we shall, in what follows, resist the one-sided exaggeration of this view which has cropped up in certain quarters lately, where it has even been suggested that all psalms and all details in them allude to cult-mythical happenings and experiences, leaving no room for an historical background or for allusions in any of the psalms to historical events. This can be understood as a reaction against older interpretations which paid no heed to the cultic side, and of each psalm asked first of all, 'what historical occasion is here alluded to, and who can the author of this psalm be?' That is an untenable position; but the reaction goes too far. Even though the lamentation-psalms belong to a cultic situation, there can be no doubt that they have for their background and cause historical events in the life of Israel, such as a definite national catastrophe or defeat in the fight against known enemies. Sometimes this is expressly stated. The duty to take this into account in the interpretation cannot be put aside by speaking slightingly of 'historicism', and the like.

4

A classification of the psalms must—like every understanding of them—be in accord with the 'divisions' in the cult itself, its different occasions, situations and acts.

At the present stage there is only the question of a rough classification, according to the main features.

What main types of divine service were there in ancient Israel and in Judaism? From what points of view can we classify them?

As we have already mentioned, the service is always essentially a communion, a matter that concerns both God and the congregation. To ancient Israel this was a matter of course, in accordance with the 'collective' or 'corporate' view of the relation between the society and the individual (see further, Chap. III). From the human point of view, the

[16] This applies to the whole 'religio-historical school' and was an important point in the scientific programme of the latter.

[17] See note 12 above.

protagonist in the cult, the one in whose name the action and speaking takes place, is the congregation.

But the congregation is also positively interested in the individual members, regardless of the degree in which they represent the whole. There are cultic actions on behalf of the individual, in which he or she is the centre. From our own divine service we may mention baptisms, churchings, weddings and funerals. But here too it is the congregation which is the real actor. The individual is regarded as a member of the congregation. To us, therefore, the natural form of the cultic psalm is the first person plural, 'we'. But the I-form, too, may be the right one, either when the cultic act in question is performed for the sake of the individual, or when he is so representative a person that he appears on behalf of the people, and in such a way that what is done to him is also done to the whole. The last train of ideas is characteristic of ancient religions, including that of ancient Israel.

In the psalms we meet with both the we-form and the I-form. How is this to be explained?

The simplest solution would be to say—like Gunkel and others—that the I-form means there is an individual who is speaking, a Mr So-and-so who is in need of that special cultic act, or a certain person who has composed the psalm or has had it composed to express his personal situation and experience. Only the psalms in the we-form are then congregational psalms proper.

There can be no doubt that this view contains a substantial truth. The psalms may be divided into those which concern the congregation or the people, that is *national* psalms or *congregational* psalms, and such as are connected with the individual's, possibly a private person's, religious and ritual need, that is, *personal* or *individual* psalms.

But the problem is not solved yet. The matter cannot be decided simply on the basis of I- or we-forms. There are also psalms where there is no doubt that the 'I' in question speaks on behalf of a plurality (as in Ps. 118), or where a 'we' appears together with and in the same sense as an 'I' (e.g., Ps. 44). There are also 'I-psalms' where the matter that caused the supplication to Yahweh obviously is a public one, concerning the whole people, and not only a single person (e.g., Ps. 66).

To this may be added that it is only to us moderns that it seems a matter of course that the natural form of plurality should be 'we'. In reality this 'we' presupposes a mental attitude and outlook which is individualizing compared to the old corporate one—a mental attitude proper to each individual person who has begun to be conscious of his own individuality, the congregation being a sum of 'I's (a 'we'). In the religion and common prayer of ancient peoples and civilizations the I-form is the usual and natural one, because there it is the whole and not the individual that is given reality, a 'corporate personality' which may act through a representative personality who 'incorporates' the whole. According to such an attitude it will be natural for the representative of the collective prayer to use the I-form. We see this for instance in Babylonian hymns,[18] and it has persisted through the ages.

An apparent I-psalm therefore may be really a congregational psalm, because the 'I' is the national and cultic representative of the congregation. Below (Chap. III) we shall see that the full appreciation of this fact helped on the study of the so-called royal psalms.

But there are also real I-psalms where the suppliant is the single member of the congregation. They belonged to cultic acts performed on behalf of the individual as a 'private' person—no matter who he was, a king, or a nobody. That Israel had such cultic acts is seen from many of the ritual laws of the Pentateuch.

There is, then, after all, a reality in the distinction between congregational or national psalms, and individual or private psalms. This distinction must be the point of departure in psalm interpretation, even though it is only of relative value, and cannot be carried through in all its details in this chapter.

Another division is that between joy and thanksgiving festivals, and days of penitence. They demand each their own type of prayer and psalm. From these two principles of division spring the *four main types* of psalms in the Psalter, the praises and thanksgivings of the congregation, private (that is, individual) thanksgivings, and besides them both congregational and individual lamentation and prayer psalms.

The praise and thanksgiving psalms of the congregation divide into two kinds: the common praises or hymns, about God's excellence and benefactions in general (Chap. IV), and the special thanksgiving psalms, giving thanks for a particular, just experienced, salvation (Chap. IX). This may be a special historical act of salvation, or one renewed at regular intervals.

In the same way we can distinguish between the common prayer psalms of the congregation (see Chap. VI.5–6) and lamentation and prayer psalms on a special occasion such as a catastrophe or a threatening danger (see Chap. VI.1–3). Within the latter group we can distinguish between real lamentations, when a catastrophe has already taken place, and 'protective psalms' where the event is as yet only a threat (Chap. VI.4). The last-mentioned distinction of course also obtains for the 'I-psalms' which are really royal or congregational psalms (see Chap. VII).

Besides these six or seven important types there are a certain number of less frequent kinds and types of psalms.

In the following chapters an account will be given of the most important kinds of psalm, and the cultic situations to which they belonged. I want to underline again that the foundations for such an investigation were laid by Gunkel, even if I, on many points already hinted at, disagree with his results.

[18] For examples, see Birkeland, *Die Feinde d. Individ.*, pp. 352ff.

5

In this form- and cult-historical investigation of the psalms it is important that *all* the material be taken into account. There are psalms outside the Psalter, and whether these have been composed for the same purpose as the others, or are only literary imitations, they are nevertheless dependent on traditional style and thus contribute to the explanation of the types.

This other material is to be found in several places in the Old Testament and in post-canonical literature. The narrative books, both the historical and the legendary ones, quite frequently let their dramatis personae utter a psalm or a prayer in the psalm style: e.g. Hannah's thanksgiving, king Hezekiah's thanksgiving, Jonah's prayer, Tobiah's and Judith's thanksgiving.[19] Or they may record parts of psalms that were sung at the festivals they describe.[20]

Poems in the style of the dirge, which may be regular cultic lamentations, have come down to us in Lamentations, Chaps. 3 and 5.

In addition to this we have the literary imitations in the book of Job, where Job himself often laments his afflictions in phrases typical of the psalms,[21] and the friends praise God's greatness, power and righteousness in the hymn style.[22]

In the prophets too we find many psalm-like passages. Sometimes the collectors of their prophecies, the later prophet-disciples, have given expression to the song of joy which the congregation is to sing, when once salvation has become a fact.[23] Sometimes they themselves exhorted the congregation to break into praise for the salvation which already sends its rays into the age.[24] More often they used the psalm form as an effective garb for the prophecy. Jeremiah laments on behalf of the people, or lets the people itself lament the disaster as if it had already happened—an effective way of driving the prophecy home. Deutero-Isaiah fashions his salvation prophecy as a hymn to Yahweh who works such great things, or opens his prophecies with such a song of praise. In the style of the 'personal lamentation', Jeremiah laments to Yahweh over the sufferings which the prophetic calling has brought on him, and prays for help.[25]

Wisdom poetry, too, like the proverbial philosophy of Ecclesiasticus, has many touches of the psalm style.[26] The sages felt that they were spiritual guides, *pneumatikoi*, the heirs of prophets and psalm writers. They saw a proof of their inspiration in the very fact that they were able to formulate a worthy prayer to God and to praise him in lofty psalms.[27]

[19] 1 Sam. 2; Isa. 38.9ff.; Jonah 2; Tob. 13; Judith 16. See Chap. XVI.6.
[20] 1 Chron. 16.8ff.; 2 Chron. 6.41f.; Ezra 3.11.
[21] Job 10; 13.23–14.22; 16.6–17.9; 19.7ff., etc. Cf. Mowinckel, *Diktet om Ijôb*, pp. 115ff.
[22] Job 5.9ff.; 9.3–13; 12.13ff.; 26.5ff.; 36.26ff.; 38.4ff. Cf. Mowinckel, *op. cit.* pp. 120ff.
[23] Isa. 12; 25.1ff.; 26.1ff.
[24] Isa. 42.10–12; 49.13; 52.9f., etc.
[25] See Baumgartner, *Klagegedichte des Jeremia, BZATW* 32; Mowinckel in *Edda* VI, 1926, pp. 276–304; Gressmann 'Die literarische analyse Deuterojesajas' in *ZATW* 34, 1914, pp. 283ff.
[26] Cf. Baumgartner, 'Die Literar. Gattungen i. d. Weisheit d. Jesus Sirach', *ZATW* 34, 1914, pp. 169ff.
[27] Cf. H. Ludin Jansen, *Spätj. Psalmdichtung*, pp. 55ff. See below, Chap. XVI.1–3.

From late Jewish times we have a collection of psalms called, 'The Psalms of Solomon', which show that the sages were still composing psalms in the old style, though no longer for cultic use.[28]

The old style psalm-poetry of Israel and Judaism reaches right down into the New Testament. We may instance the songs of Zacharias and Mary in St Luke[29] and the hymns in the book of Revelation.[30]

Lastly we find strong elements of psalm poetry—both in style and subject matter—in the prose prayers which are to be found in several places in the Old Testament. This is only natural, for the psalms are prayers, and experience shows that so-called 'free prayer' is to a large extent dependent on the pattern set by the prayers and psalms of public worship.[31]

All these imitations illuminate the various forms of style and individual peculiarities of the psalms.

6

In conclusion it must be mentioned that we have valuable material for comparison in other *ancient oriental psalm poetry*—the Babylonian-Assyrian, the Egyptian, the Canaanite and Hittite—which throws light on the style-forms and types of biblical psalm poetry.

It becomes evident that most of the stylistic and formal elements, and quite a number of details of content in general oriental cult poetry are either the same as the biblical ones, or at least show many great similarities to it. Undoubtedly there is here a great common cult-historical connexion. As the Babylonian-Assyrian psalm poetry is many centuries older than the Israelite, there can be no doubt that the latter has taken over a very great part of its style and form of expression, partly also its ideas and thoughts, from the older religious forms of expression common to the East. This, too, Gunkel has clearly seen, and duly underlined. The special characteristics of Israel's religious poetry developed against a background of general oriental culture. This is all the more probable as the Israelite liturgy to a large extent adopted the older cultic patterns of the East, with Canaan as intermediary.[32]

A thorough comparison between Israelite and other oriental psalm poetry, both from stylistic and cult-historical points of view, as well as from that of the contents, should be of the greatest interest. It would throw light on the types of psalms and their cultic connexion, not only on the biblical ones but also on the others. Such a comparison would also help to draw into a clearer and sharper focus the peculiarities of biblical psalm poetry and religion in relation to that of neighbouring civilizations, and to show what the religion of revelation has made of the foreign material it has adopted in expressing its own peculiar nature. Such a comparative examination has only just begun. (See below, Chap. XXI.)

[28] See Jansen, *op. cit.*, and below, Chap. XVI.6.
[29] Lk. 1.46ff.; 1.67ff., and below, Chap. XVIII.7.
[30] Rev. 4.11; 5.9ff.; 11.17f.; 15.3f.; 19.5f.
[31] Cf. Wendel, *Das freie Laiengebet*, which, however, includes much material belonging to cultic prayers in verse. Ample material for comparison is given by Heiler, *Das Gebet*.[4]
[32] See above, p. 16 with note 57 to Chap. I; and further, below, p. 134 and Additional Note XX.

CHAPTER III

'I' and 'We' in the Psalms
—The Royal Psalms

I

How the corporate view of reality and society in ancient Israel determines the relation between 'we'-psalms and 'I'-psalms has already been mentioned.

The basic reality in human life is, for the Israelite, not the individual, but the community.[1] The individual had his real existence in the tribe. Outside of that he was nothing, a severed member, one without rights, 'whom everyone that findeth him shall slay', as Cain said. But this community was not only an external and judicial one, it was even more a spiritual one. To the Israelite, a species, e.g. an animal species, was not a combination of individuals, an abstraction, or a sum. The species was the original entity, which manifests itself in the single specimen. Likewise with human beings: the tribe—'Israel', 'Moab', etc.—was not looked upon as a sum of individuals who had joined together, or who enjoyed an existence of their own apart from the whole to which they belonged; it was the real entity which manifested itself in each separate member. We might, with Johs. Pedersen, say that 'the individual Moabite is not a section of a number of Moabitic individuals, but a revelation of "Moabitehood" '. To the Israelite this was the reality, it was in no wise an abstraction. One sees this from the general attitude to the traditional blood revenge. The responsibility lay on all, not so that each one had a part in it, but placing the whole responsibility on each individual. To those who had the grievance, every single member of the manslayer's clan or tribe would at a given moment represent the whole tribe.

We may also see this clearly in the view taken of the founder of the tribe. Each tribe, or group of tribes, has a common ancestor, 'the Great Sheikh' as the Bedouins call him today, and the tribe is named after him. All the historical memories of the tribe, besides all sorts of legends and stories are centered in his person. Traditions about the life and wanderings of the tribe, its social and religious institutions, its borders, rights of possession to wells, and so on, are usually in some way or other connected with the person of the ancestor;[2] he is the one who has experienced and

---

[1] For the following statement cf. Johs. Pedersen, *Israel* I–II, pp. 263ff. and Index *s.v.* Individual, Individualism; Wheeler Robinson in *Werden u. Wesen d. A.T. (BZATW* 66), pp. 49ff.; id., *The Group and the Individual*. Cf. also Bräunlich in *Islamica*, 1933, 1–2.

[2] After J. Lindblom, *Israels religion*, pp. 13f.

achieved it all. This is important for the understanding of Israel's patriarchal traditions. The ancestor represents the clan or tribe, and embodies
its life in himself. Quite naturally, therefore, he is often looked upon as
the deity of the tribe—or in other cases he may bear the name of the
tribe. Side by side with such tribe-names as Gad, Asher and Edom we
have the divine names Gad, Ashera and Edom. The character and will of
the ancestor, his 'soul', lives in all his descendants; they all bear his stamp,
are revelations of him and of the sociological unity which he represents.
He is the 'father' of each one.

The tribe is a living corporate personality which to the mind of the
Israelite naturally presented itself as an 'individual'. For him this was not
a conscious artificial act of the imagination, a poetical personification, as
when we speak of 'Mother Norway', or 'Mother England', but the self-
evident way of seeing and thinking. The whole was a greater 'I'. Hence it
came quite naturally to an Israelite story-teller to relate the origin of the
conquest in this way: 'Judah said to his brother Simeon, "Come up with
me into my lot, that we may fight against the Canaanites, and I likewise
will go with thee into thy lot" '.[3] This refers to the *tribes* of Judah and
Simeon, and not to the persons.

In all important situations the paterfamilias, the chief, or the king,
represents the whole. He is not merely a casually chosen 'representative'
in our modern sense of the word. He could not be replaced by anybody
else. He is the 'representative' because the 'soul', the history, the honour,
the vigour and the blessing of the whole are concentrated in him. And,
the other way round, all the others participate dynamically in what he
represents. Because the clan, outwardly as well, constitutes a community,
having not only 'flesh and blood' in common, but nature, blessing, soul
and honour too, everything flows from the one to the other, from the representative to the whole, and vice versa.

Normally a similarity between all the separate members in feeling, will
and thought corresponds to this mode of thinking. To be 'original', someone apart, a 'personality', whose right of existence depended on being
different, would not to the ancient Israelites have appeared as an ideal
or an end to attain, but on the contrary, as a madness, an arrogance,
something abnormal, or, in their own words, an 'unrighteousness' and a
'folly'.

This does not mean that the single member was not conscious of himself
as an individual and a personality. He was; but he found himself, his
'personality' and his 'rightness', in being an ideal expression of what was
common to all, of what was his clan's 'nature' and 'blessing' and 'honour'.
Of course the individual distinguished between himself and the one who
on public occasions 'represented' his clan in its unity; but he identified

---

[3] Jdg. 1.3. Many other references in Smend's paper 'Über das Ich der Psalmen', *ZATW* 8,
1888, pp. 61ff. Balla's explanation, *Das Ich der Psalmen*, pp. 118ff. is here too modernizing and
rationalistic.

himself with him too. They were one in nature and feeling and will. And the representative knew that he carried them all within him, that the honour and blessing and 'peace' of all depended on him, and that what he could win flowed to all by the law of community, and gave to all honour and power.

Within the nation the king is the representative of the whole. Israel is his 'house' and he is its father. The covenant between Yahweh and Israel and between Yahweh and David is one and the same thing.[4]

This unity of the whole and its proper representative becomes particularly clear in the cult. The single person who then steps forward is one with the history of his people from his first ancestor onwards. When the individual Israelite brought the first-fruits to the holy place he said a prayer beginning like this, 'My father was a wandering Aramean' (Deut. 26.5). He is thinking of his progenitor, Jacob. And he goes on, 'The Egyptians afflicted us with burdens and made us to serve with rigour'. The suppliant is identified at the same time both with the progenitor and with the Israelites in Egypt; he is a part of the body everlasting and incorporates it within himself. Likewise, the priest or the king contains the whole and all its members, when he appears as the leader of the cult. He really represents—in the old meaning of the word—the whole people. When he says 'I' it is the whole Israel, who speaks through him and who appears in his person 'in the presence of Yahweh'.

In course of time this old way of thinking has been tempered and modified by a much more individualizing one. The 'we'-form in the mouth of the congregational leader is a proof of that. It proves that the whole is also conscious of being a number of individuals. But all cult is conservative, not least in its forms. Both in its experiences—common experiences binding all together—and in its forms, the old way of thinking lives on.

On this basis it will be seen to be quite natural that the congregation through its cult-representative or representatives appears as a 'corporate personality' speaking in the first person singular, 'I'; and is answered with a 'thou'. The prayer with the first-fruits mentioned above is introduced by a statutory provision beginning thus: 'When thou hast entered the land which Yahweh, thy God, gives thee in possession, and thou hast subjected it' (Deut. 26.1). The ritual legislator is here really speaking to the whole people—the one which was contemporary with Moses, and that which *is* today. The single suppliant is looked upon as if he were the whole people. The commandment and the prayer-rubrics have regard to 'the unity, Israel' and to the single Israelite.

We find the same thing in the Decalogue. 'I am Yahweh, thy God, which have brought thee out of the land of Egypt, out of the house of bondage. Thou shalt have no other gods before me. Thou shalt not make unto thee any graven image . . . .' It is Israel as a whole, and hence the

---

[4] Cf. Isa. 55.3f. and see Mowinckel, *He That Cometh*, pp. 89, 98ff., 158.

single Israelite also, that is addressed. It is in the public cult of the people that Yahweh alone is to be worshipped. It is in the cult, that is, in the community, that there shall be no graven image. In the following commandments the individual point of view is more prominent, as in prohibiting theft, homicide, adultery, the bearing of false witness, covetousness. When the priest in the cult pronounces the Aaronic blessing (Num. 6.22–27): 'Yahweh bless thee and keep thee', etc., the 'thee' is not primarily the individual Israelite, but the congregation, and only through it the individual member, as it is also expressly stated in the introduction: 'With these words shall you (i.e. the priests) bless the children of Israel' (i.e. the congregation). In the utterances of the prophets we meet with many echoes of such cultic modes of speech.[5]

Thus it would be quite natural to find this mode of speech in the psalms as well. When the historian makes 'Moses and the Israelites' burst into a song of praise for the miraculous crossing of the Reed Lake—no doubt a congregational festive psalm-beginning like this: 'I will sing unto the Lord, for he hath triumphed gloriously. . . .' (Ex. 15.1–2) he no doubt means that it is Israel who here praise their God, the God of their fathers who has just saved them from distress and proved himself a mighty 'man of war'. Moses, or, according to another reading, Miriam (Ex. 15.20f.) is the singer, but cultically they represent Israel with the whole of its history. When the saga-writer lets them say 'I' and 'me' they are not speaking on their own behalf, but on behalf of the congregation. The singer represents the 'corporate, greater I' of the congregation.

Examples of this form of speech may also be found in the Psalter. In Ps. 129 it says:

> 'Cruelly have they harried me from my youth'—
> > may Israel now say,
> 'cruelly have they harried me from my youth,
> > yet they have not crushed me.
> The plowmen plowed upon my back,
> > and long they drew their furrows'.

This 'I' is not a unique exception, nor a casual 'poetic personification' demanding the line 'may Israel now say', in order to be understood, but normal ancient, Israelitic cult style.

It is not surprising therefore that investigators have felt this question of the 'I' and the 'we' in the psalms to be a problem. It was impossible not to see that at times 'I' and 'we' alternate in the same psalm, without apparent reason—as e.g. in Ps. 44. Nor could it be overlooked that many 'I'-psalms really spoke about matters concerning the people and the congregation.

---

[5] See Balla, *op. cit.*, pp. 122ff. But here we are dealing not with 'poetical personifications', as Balla thinks, but with remnants of ancient modes of expression in the cult.

Smend gives the explanation that the 'I' in the psalms is *always* a 'personification of the congregation'.[6] This view is both exaggerated and distorted. There is no question of personification as a form of art. Smend has not been able to see that we are dealing with an ancient Hebrew conception that is bound up with their view of the community and the individual, and with the whole psychology of the Israelite. Nor was he aware of the fact that the representative in the cult spoke on behalf of the whole, and that, so far, the 'I' was a reality even from a modern point of view. In fact the 'I' is very often the king or another cultic representative of the congregation. And there are also many psalms in which the 'I' is really a single individual speaking about strictly personal matters.

But Balla's refutation[7] of Smend and the other supporters of the theory of 'the collective I' (as it was misleadingly termed) goes much too far when he maintains that the only instance of such a mode of speech is presented by Ps. 129. Balla, like Gunkel, has seen that an alternating 'I' and 'we' often means that one person is speaking on behalf of the whole. But he was not aware that there is nevertheless a much more intimate relationship between the individual and the whole than our modern individualizing psychology takes into account; and both Gunkel and Balla are definitely wrong when they deny that many of the 'I-psalms' deal with congregational and national matters. They greatly exaggerate the private, individualistic point of view.

The explanation of the problem is to be found in the ancient conception of 'corporate personality' and in the fact that there is, in the ancient meaning of the word, a *representative* person in the cult speaking on behalf of the congregation. Because he embodies it in himself, he is the congregation, and the congregation is he himself—as we have endeavoured to show above.

But this representative personality in the royal Temple in Jerusalem was the king himself. Our way to full certainty in this matter lies along a path indicated by Gunkel, namely the conviction that there are in the Psalter a number of psalms where the king clearly and definitely stands as protagonist. And this brings us to the royal psalms proper.

2

According to the traditional theological view, most of the psalms should indeed be royal psalms, to the extent that they were supposed to have been composed by king David, and dealt with his relationship to his own and the nation's enemies, and with his difficulties as a king. But in its earlier phase modern scientific study of the psalms tended to deny the presence of any royal figure in the psalms, and it was maintained that they had been largely composed in Jewish times, after the Exile, out of

[6] Smend in *ZATW* 8, 1888, pp. 56ff.
[7] Balla, *Das Ich der Psalmen.*

the private experiences of ordinary people in the joys and sorrows of daily life, and through impulses from certain individual prophets (cf. above, p. 12). About the group of psalms, 93 and 95–99, which has so many traits in common with the sayings of Deutero-Isaiah, the general opinion even of conservative theologians was that they had been composed in imitation of the style and thoughts of Deutero-Isaiah.[8] Where we do meet a royal figure, as in the so-called 'Messianic' psalms, this figure was interpreted as a personification of the people of Israel.[9] Gunkel was the first to re-conceive of the royal psalms as real king psalms, and place this interpretation on a sure scientific foundation.[10] The present author has tried to give the interpretation a broader foundation by connecting the picture of the king drawn in these psalms, not only with the general oriental one, but also with the actual religion and cult of ancient Israel,[11] and this work has been continued by younger investigators.

Now, what do we mean by the expression 'royal psalms'?

These psalms are not a special 'kind' or 'type' (*Gattung*) from the point of view of the history of style or literature or liturgy. They comprise nearly all kinds of psalms, both hymns of praise and lamentations, thanksgivings and prophetic sayings, and several other types. Common to them is the circumstance that the king is in the foreground. He is the one who prays or the one who is spoken of, or who is prayed for. They include Pss. 2; 18; 20; 21; 45; 72; 101; 110; 132; 28; 61; 63; 89; and quite a number of others.

That these psalms concern a real king, a definite individual person, and not a poetical personification of the people or the congregation is quite clear. The congregation talks about him as 'our shield', and intercedes for him.

The supposed prophetic poet could not have let Yahweh say to the people of Israel that he has begotten him 'today'. That will fit only one person who 'today', that is at the moment that the psalm is being sung, becomes what he is—Yahweh's 'son' and king (Ps. 2.7). Israel, on the other hand, became Yahweh's 'son' when Yahweh called him out of Egypt (Hos. 11.1). The congregation is not 'Yahweh's king', as is the king in the psalms, but on the contrary, Yahweh is 'the king of Israel'.

It is also beyond question that the kings in these psalms are Israelite or Judaean kings—not, as older psalm critics sometimes held, foreign kings, the Ptolemaic and Seleucid rulers of the Jews. The king in Ps. 2 reigns in Zion (v. 6), the same is the case with the king in Ps. 110.2 and in Pss. 20.3; 132.15; he is a descendant of David, Pss. 18.51; 89.15; 132.10, 17; his friends are 'the faithful of the land' (101.6); the king's people is

---

[8] E.g. the psalm commentaries of both Delitzsch and Buhl.

[9] E.g. Wellhausen, Buhl[1], Gray.

[10] Gunkel, 'Die Königspsalmen', *Preuss. Jahrb.* 1914.

[11] Mowinckel, *Kongesalmerne; Ps. St. II* pp. 299ff. Neither in the treatise in *Preuss. Jahrb.* nor in *Einleitung*, pp. 140ff. have Gunkel and Begrich realized the extent of the royal psalms and their significance for the understanding of psalm problems; cf. Birkeland, *Feinde des Indiv.*, pp. 144ff.

'Jacob', 'Yahweh's people and heritage', he is 'our'—that is Israel's—
'shield' (20.2; 28.8f.; 72.2; 84.10). He is 'the Lord's anointed'. The king
in Ps. 20 is a Yahweh-worshipper; he and the people ('we') worship the
same god. The king's victory forms the greatness and triumph of Israel.
Likewise in Ps. 21, the king 'joys in the strength of Yahweh', 'he trusteth
in the Lord', and he lives and reigns 'before the countenance of Yahweh'.
In Ps. 45.8 Yahweh is the god of the king. When Yahweh saves the king
from distress, in Ps. 28.9, it is at the same time the salvation of the people
of Yahweh. In Ps. 63.12 the cause of the king and the Yahweh-worshipper
is identical. In Ps. 61.4f. the praying king says that Yahweh has always
been a shelter to him, and he will abide in God's tabernacle for ever, that
is, in the sanctuary on Zion.

Nor is the alternative explanation possible, which was used to maintain
that the psalms belonged to a later time, namely to interpret the king as
one of the later Maccabean priest kings. John Hyrcanus (134–104 B.C.)
was the first to call himself a king, but at that time the compilation of the
Psalter had long since been finished. Nor can the royal psalms allude to
any of the earlier Maccabean princes. These were not considered as 'the
Lord's anointed', like the king in Pss. 2; 20; 45; 28; 89; 39. Nor were they
the sons of kings, like the king in Ps. 72, or David's descendants, like the
king in Pss. 18 and 132.

So they must be real Judaean or Israelite kings in these psalms.[12]

We must also make it clear at once that these psalms refer not to a future
king, the 'Messiah', but to the reigning king, who is a contemporary of
the poet.[13] In Ps. 110 the situation is that the poet-prophet stands before
the king, who is sitting on his throne, addresses him as, 'My Lord', and
pronounces an oracle from Yahweh. The situation in Ps. 45 is of a similar
kind. The king sits by the side of his queen on their wedding day, and the
poet recites his ode to them. Ps. 18 is a thanksgiving in which the king
thanks Yahweh for the help he has given him on the battlefield, and for
the victory he has already won. In Ps. 89 the king laments about the defeat
he has suffered in the fight against his enemies, who have pulled down his
castles and wasted his land. In Ps. 132 we meet the king as the leader of a
religious festival play in remembrance of the time when David brought
Yahweh's holy shrine up to Zion, and the king is here playing the part of
David. In Ps. 28 he asks for help in sickness; in Pss. 61 and 63 for salvation

[12] The historical interpretation of the royal psalms has actually been accepted not only by
such interpreters as accept the cultic principle of interpretation (see above note 6 to Chap. II)
but by most modern exegetes. Cf. Cosgrave, 'Recent Studies on the Psalms', *Canadian Soc. of
Bibl. St. Bulln.* No. 5, July 1939, pp. 11ff., Barton in *The Haverford Symposium*, pp. 66ff.; Johnson
in *O.T. and Modern Study*, Index *s.v.* 'Royal Psalms'.
[13] A detailed refutation of the messianic (and eschatological) interpretation is given by König,
Die Psalmen, pp. 453ff.; Nötscher (*Die Psalmen*, pp. 4f. and *seriatim* in the interpretation of Pss.
2, 72, 110 and others) represents an intermediate view-point between directly messianic and
historical and typological interpretation, which is quite vague and untenable; he shares the
fallacy of the 'religio-historical school', that even before the kingdom there existed a messianic
theology after the image of which the king of any particular age might be pictured. Further
discussion of the often recurring messianic interpretation of this or that psalm is from the point
of view of scientific research unnecessary.

from other dangers. In Ps. 63 he is moreover present in the Temple to pray for Yahweh's help. In Ps. 20 allusion is made to the gifts and burnt-offerings which the king has already presented or will present to Yahweh, and the singer points to the fact that he has just learned—through a divine promise in connexion with the sacrificial act—that Yahweh will now help his anointed. Pss. 20; 21; and 72 are intercessions for the king, and invocations of blessings upon him. A Messiah needs no intercession. When it is a question of a Messiah the congregation prays that he may come; but in these psalms the king is already there, and needs the intercession and good wishes of the congregation to be able to fulfil his high vocation.

The kernel of truth in the Messianic interpretation is, as we shall see, that it is ultimately the same common oriental mythologically conceived superhuman king-ideal, which underlies both the psalm-poets' descriptions of the present king in David's city, and the prophets' description of the future king. Historically considered, the idea of the Messiah is derived from the same king-ideal that we have presented in the royal psalms. True enough, there is a great difference between what the poets have made of this traditional king-ideal, and what the prophets have made of it. The poets thought that the ideal was realized, or hoped that it would be realized, in the earthly king, seated before them on the throne. The prophets were not satisfied with anything which the present reality could offer, and looked hopefully forward to a new king, whom God would send 'in his own good time', and who would be the realization of the ideal which the present kings did not appear to fulfil, because it was beyond human power. Thus both the psalmists' and the prophets' conception point beyond themselves, and are only realized in a figure of a totally different kind, in the Messiah Jesus who was both 'King' and 'Son of Man', and the suffering and expiating 'Servant of the Lord'. To this extent the Church is right in taking the king in the royal psalms as a presage of Jesus, the Messiah.[14] But, historically considered, the king in the psalms is not a future figure, but a contemporary one.

The title 'the Lord's anointed' is the actual title of the reigning king of Israel, and is in the Old Testament never used of the Messiah.[15]

Then how are we to explain the fact of the appearance of the king in the psalms?

[14] The typological-Christological interpretation of the king on the basis of a consistent historical exegesis is different. On this question see Coppens in *Ephemerides Theol. Lovanienses* XXXII; *De Messianische verwachting in het Psalmboek.*

[15] See the complete list of passages in Gesenius-Buhl[16] *s.v. Mashiaḥ,* p. 468, item 3. Buhl's remark here: 'where, however, partly at any rate, a collective interpretation about the people of Israel would naturally suggest itself', is false and a remnant of the interpretation which was fashionable before the part played by the king in the psalms was realized. In Judaism the position of the king, and so the anointing, had passed to the high priest, cf. Lev. 4.3, 5, 16; 6.15; therefore the term 'an anointed' (but not '*the* anointed') is used on one occasion of the high priest, Dan. 9.25f. (or: 'the anointed priest'). Sometimes even a prophet was anointed: therefore in later times the patriarchs who were then all considered to be prophets, might in poetical usage be called 'the anointed (of Yahweh)' (in the plural); cf. Ps. 105.15; 1 Chron. 16.22. However, '*the anointed*' or 'the anointed of Yahweh' in O.T. always indicates the reigning king.

The fact that, in a collection like this, which to a considerable extent contains cult psalms, we also find several psalms about the king, is to be explained by the ancient Israelite view of the king and his position in public worship.

3

The conception of the king held in Israel was fundamentally the same as in the rest of the ancient East[16]—quite naturally, since Israel according to the testimony of the Old Testament itself had adopted kingship in direct imitation of the Canaanites (1 Sam. 8.5), who had in turn obtained ideas, forms and etiquette from the great kings of the Nile and the Euphrates-Tigris.[17] Ultimately these ideas go back to the general primitive view of the chief as the powerful 'great-man', 'mana-man', the bearer of some superhuman quality. But we must not forget that the ancient oriental ideology of the great king, the divine sovereign on earth, is a product of civilization, a special development of the primitive thoughts with the absolutist oriental Imperium as a background, where the king's power and legitimacy are supported by the theory that he is the divine representative of the god, called and enthroned by him, and given authority as his deputy among men. Nor may we overlook the very essential difference between, e.g., the Egyptian and the Babylonian-Assyrian view of the king.[18] There never existed a homogeneous 'general oriental king-ideology', to which the view of the king as held by all Eastern peoples conformed in all details—as has been supposed by several modern scholars.[19]

The most important elements in the ancient oriental view of the king are as follows: the king was more or less clearly and consistently looked upon as 'divine'. In Egypt he was held to be a god incarnate, begotten of the queen by the god, who took the guise of the reigning king; he was metaphysically one with all the great gods, who in him reveal themselves on earth, and rule with divine power over the universe. He is a god from birth, and at his death he becomes one with Osiris, the god of death and life, and partakes of the eternal life of the gods.

In Mesopotamia and Asia Minor the king is a man made divine. He is chosen for the kingship by the gods, sometimes from his mother's womb, but sometimes he is even predestined for it from the beginning of time.

[16] See Mowinckel, *He That Cometh*, Chap. III with references to literature. The chief works are Labat, *Le caractère religieux de la royauté assyro-babylonienne*; Frankfort, *Kingship and the Gods*. Cf. also Gadd, *Ideas of Divine Rule in the Ancient East*; Fish, *Some Aspects of Kingship in the Sumerian City and Kingdom of Ur*. Less reliable—on account of his tendency to identify likeness in words with likeness in thought and belief—comes Engnell, *Studies in Divine Kingship in the ancient Near East*. Cf. the critical remarks against the methods of Engnell in Frankfort, *Kingship*, p. 405 n. 1; p. 406 n. 35; p. 408, n. 67, n. 69; and de Langhe in *Bibliotheca Orientalis* X, 1953, pp. 18ff.

[17] This was already acknowledged by Gressmann, when he spoke of the influence of 'court style' on the Messiah picture, see *Ursprung d. isr.-jüd. Eschatologie*, pp. 250ff. For further details Gunkel-Begrich, *Einleitung*, pp. 150ff.

[18] This is rightly emphasized very strongly by Frankfort, *Kingship*, pp. 3ff.

[19] Especially in works by Widengren, Haldar and others. Cf. Mowinckel, *He That Cometh*, Chap. III. The theory of the common uniform 'king ideology' is mostly connected with the idea of a common Oriental 'cult pattern', the king being always supposed to represent the suffering, dying and rising god. See Additional Note XX.

'The Kingship'—i.e. the superhuman endowment and quality and majesty, the 'mana' of the king—'descends from heaven' and fills him from his mother's womb. Or it may be conferred on him, strengthened and preserved by the sacramental rites at his accession, and the annually repeated enthronement of him as king at the new year festival, and by the close union with the deity. This he especially experiences by joining with the mother goddess in the 'sacred (cultic) marriage', a fixed part of the fertility cult in the religions of the East. He is the 'son' of the god, adopted, nursed, reared and educated by the different gods and goddesses. Thus he is endowed with divine faculties and power, and is a 'superman' (Sumerian: *lugal*, 'great man'). He is 'holy' and a partaker of divine qualities, e.g. 'life', 'eternity', 'splendour', 'glory', and so on. He is 'like a god', and using religious terms he can be compared with different gods, with the sun god, the national god and the resurrected fertility god.

The king is thus the representative of the gods on earth, the steward of the god or the gods. Through him they exercise their power and sovereignty, and he is the channel through which blessing and happiness and fertility flow from the gods to men. 'He rises like the sun over humanity'. With the right king, in whom the gods have pleasure, all material and spiritual welfare is secured. Speaking poetically and devotionally, he may be said to create all this for his people.

But he is also man's representative before the gods. In him the people is one. According to the corporate view of those times the people was somehow incorporated in him, and the strength and blessing which he receives from the gods were partaken of by the whole country and people.

This double position of the king as the link between gods and men is expressed and made effective through the cult. He is the high priest—in Egypt he is theoretically the only one—and as a 'governor' he is also 'priest-king'. In the cult he represents the gods before men and men before the gods. In Egypt the main stress is laid on the former capacity, in Mesopotamia and elsewhere on the latter. Through his performance of the effective cult acts the re-creation of life and blessing which is the purpose of the cult is realized. In Egypt in the cultic drama which presents and actualizes the struggle and the victory of the life powers over the powers of death and chaos, and the resurrection of life, the king is the god himself who appears bodily, fighting, conquering, and creating. In Mesopotamia he is the champion and helper of the gods, 'representing' them in that way. At the same time he is the representative of man, who by his intimate connexion with the gods experiences their victory and revival of the 'power' (*mana*) and through the mystical fellowship with his people, the 'congregation', transmits the power to them and to their world. As the representative of the congregation he is the lord of the sacrifice and the intercessor, the vicarious penitent, purified and redeemed on behalf of the whole congregation. At the same time—as a priest and the representative of the gods—he conveys these blessings to the congregation. This is particularly obvious when the king is chosen by the goddess to be her partner in the cultic marriage. By mystical union with the goddess he is filled with the forces of fertility and resurrection, joins in the experience of the resurrected fertility god (Tammuz, etc.), and is charged with divinity, life and blessing, which flow on from him to the congregation (the people).

In Egypt the king does all this because he is the god himself, he himself is the embodiment of all the gods. In Mesopotamia, as the representative of mankind, he experiences it in the cultic mystical union. Regarding Egypt we can speak of a really lasting and essential 'identity' between the king and the different gods which he represents, because he *is* and comprises them all. In Mesopotamia the king may occasionally call himself a god and place the divine ideogram before his name; also sometimes an oath may be taken in the names of the gods and the king. But that is something he has become, and it does not abolish his humanity. In Egypt the king is— as 'the good God', as Horus, Re, Osiris, etc.—the object of direct worship in the cult, not least after his death. In Mesopotamia we may at most speak of sacrifices to the king's statue, which in the temple represents him as his intercessor with the gods. The king's 'name' and 'life' in the image must be maintained by sacrificial gifts. We cannot rightly speak of identity of king and god in Mesopotamia, or the countries influenced by its culture, either essentially or as a result of anything which took place in the cult. Even in the cult he is not really the god himself, although he is in a cultic-mystical way imbued with the god's destiny, experience and revived strength, imparting it in his turn to the society of which he—in like 'mystically-corporate' manner—is the visible manifestation.

As we shall see, some of these most characteristic traits are to be found also in the Israelite view of the king.

But although Israel has adopted a number of ideas, functions and style forms of oriental monarchy, the basic conceptions have been fundamentally altered under the influence of the Yahweh religion. There were certain features in the conception of the king—'the king-ideology'—which were incompatible with the belief in Yahweh, as that belief had been shaped already by the time of David. And the history of Israel may from one point of view be seen as a constant tension between the ancient ideas from the desert and the new Canaanite (general oriental) ones. The old ideal of the chief, or sheikh, stemming from the patriarchal conditions of desert life never died. On the contrary it constantly impressed its stamp on the king ideal; and in spite of certain common fundamental features, the semi-nomadic and Bedouin chief ideal is a different type from the oriental king-god ideal.

It is therefore just as important to point out the features which are characteristic of Israel's view, and find what it is that unites them into one characteristic Israelite king ideal, as it is to point out what is common to Israel and the other peoples' view of the king. The general Eastern 'king-ideology' is only the background, throwing its light on and explaining many single features of the Israelite king idea, not only on those which Israel adopted, but indirectly also on those which are different. It is important also to see what Israel did *not* adopt, but on the contrary rejected as something incompatible with its cult and religion.

Fundamental to the king's position is his relation to Yahweh. The king is Yahweh's anointed, and as such he is endowed with the spirit of Yahweh (1 Sam. 10.6, 9ff.; 11.6f.; 16.13) and with supra-normal faculties and powers (Ps. 89.22; Mic. 5.3; Num. 24.17). He is chosen by Yahweh (1 Sam. 10.24; 16.1ff.; 2 Sam. 7.8; Pss. 45.8; 89.21), adopted and fostered by him (Pss. 2.2; 18.35; 89.27f.). He is the son of Yahweh. The filial relation may be expressed in pure mythopoeic form: 'This day have I begotten thee' (Ps. 2.7). 'I have borne thee from the womb of dawn on the holy mount' (Ps. 110.3.G). He stands in a closer relation than other people to Yahweh. 'Yahweh thy God' is said, referring to his and Israel's God.[20] In a special sense he is 'Yahweh's servant',[21] performing his commissions and enjoying his particular favour. He is endowed with 'eternity' (1 Kgs. 1.31; Pss. 21.5; 72.5) i.e. superhuman life-force, even divinity (Ps. 45.7).[22] His person is sacrosanct ('holy'). It is a mortal sin to lay hands on him (1 Sam. 24.7; 31.4; 2 Sam. 1.14). By the anointing, which was a sacred, cultic act, he becomes 'another man', he has 'another heart' (1 Sam. 10.6, 9), that is, he has obtained a special 'holiness', a superhuman quality. He has obtained those faculties and gifts and powers which he needs to be the rightful king. He is the people's source of strength, its 'breath of life' (Lam. 4.20), 'equal to ten thousand of us' (2 Sam. 18.3), 'Israel's lamp' (2 Sam. 21.7), the bearer of divine forces, without whom Israel cannot live (Hos. 3.4), the protector in whose 'shadow' it lives (Lam. 4.20). He is endowed with an extraordinary quality of success (Pss. 20.5f.; 72.6, 17; 2 Sam. 23.3f.), with victory and glory (Pss. 110.2, 5ff.; 72.9; 45.4–6), with righteousness (Pss. 72.1, 4f., 12–14; 45.7f.; 101), wisdom (2 Sam. 14.7; 1 Kgs. 3.5ff.), and piety (Pss. 20.4; 72.1; 18.21ff.). As the son of the highest god, Yahweh, and his viceroy on earth he is entitled to world sovereignty (Pss. 2.8; 72.8–11; 89.26ff.). This is the style in which he speaks, like one of the great rulers on the Euphrates or the Nile.

The attributes and equipment of the kings and of the kingship show that the prevailing ideas, or at least the ideas which these customs are

---

[20] See for instance 1 Sam. 25.29; 2 Sam. 14.11; 18.28; 1 Kgs. 1.17, 47. Cf. Birkeland, *Feinde d. Individ.* pp. 125f.; cf. also Eissfeldt in *ZATW* 61, 1945/48, p. 11.

[21] See for instance Pss. 18.1; 36.1; 89.4, 21; 132.10; Hag. 2.23; Zech. 3.8; cf. Jer. 25.9; 27.6; 43.10. For details, v. Baudissin, *Kyrios als Gottesname im Judentum* III, pp. 176ff., 196ff., 524ff., 529ff.; Birkeland, *Feinde d. Individ.*, p. 124; Lindhagen, *The Servant Motif in the O.T.*, pp. 285ff. When used about an individual the term 'Yahweh's servant' always indicates a special relationship between Yahweh and the person in question; cf. Smend in *ZATW* 8, 1888, p. 134. The religious use of the word *'ebhedh* is of course older than the kingdom and it is therefore quite false when Lindhagen thinks that this epithet, when used about Abraham, Moses and others, has been transferred from the 'king ideology'.

[22] Cf. 2 Sam. 14.20. In Ps. 89.28, David is 'Elyon', i.e. (like) the supreme God, among the kings of the earth.

derived from, placed the king beside the deity, high above ordinary people. He sits on Yahweh's throne, at the right hand of Yahweh (Ps. 110.1). The king's throne in Jerusalem symbolizes the world-mountain,[23] the king is figured with horns (1 Sam. 2.10; Pss. 89.18; 132.17; Deut. 33.17), the usual symbol of the gods (Num. 24.8; cf. Ps. 89.24). The diadem also, 'the crown' (2 Sam. 1.10; 2 Kgs. 11.12; Pss. 89.20, 40; 132.18) is a divine symbol (2 Sam. 12.30.G), and it is not unthinkable that similar ideas have been linked with the sceptre (Pss. 110.2; 45.7; 2.9; Mic. 7.14) as a 'divine staff' (cf. Ex. 4.17, 20).[24]

To nearly all these special traits closer or more distant 'parallels' in other Eastern civilizations may be found.[25]

Both in Egypt and in Mesopotamia the king is held to be the son of the deity. In Egypt the case is conceived physically and metaphysically; the king is the product of a physical act of generation by the god incarnate. In Mesopotamia also, where the adoption idea is the prevailing one, the king's filial relationship may be represented in mythical forms, as the result of a divine begetting or as the birth of the new sun god on the unknown mountain of the east.[26] Both in Egypt[27] and in Mesopotamia[28] the god addresses the king with the adoption formula, 'thou art my son'. In Egypt this also includes the literally implied 'I have begotten thee'.[29]

That such expressions, when they are sometimes met with in Israel, are there formed upon alien patterns, is seen, among other things, from the fact that phrases which were originally intended to be taken literally have in Israel been transformed into expressions of adoption: 'Today have I borne you'. This conclusion is obvious from the fact that the expression 'I have borne you' is originally to be imagined as spoken by a female deity. In Israel it is turned into a saying of Yahweh.[30]

When the king in Ps. 18.34 says about Yahweh that 'he teacheth my hands to war, so that I can bend a bow of bronze', this may be illustrated by an Egyptian picture of the God Seth teaching Pharaoh Thutmose to use a bow.[31]

In Egyptian pictures we can also see the king sitting in the place of honour at the right side of the throne of the god, as the poet-prophet says to the king on Mount Zion in Ps. 110.[32] In the same psalm Yahweh places the king's enemies 'under his feet'. To symbolize their submission the king

---

[23] Gressmann, *Urspr. d. Eschatologie*, pp. 257f.; cf. Johs. Pedersen, *Israel* III–IV, pp. 79f.

[24] On the attributes of the kingdom and the enthronement of the king, see Pedersen, *Israel* III–IV, pp. 77ff.

[25] For details see Gunkel-Begrich, *Einleitung*, pp. 150ff.; for the different royal psalms Gunkel, *Die Psalmen* (2; 18; 20; 21; 45; 110, etc.); Mowinckel, *He That Cometh*, Chap. III; Pedersen, *op. cit.*

[26] See Engnell, *Div. Kingship* Topical Index *s.v.* 'son of the god'; Frankfort, *Kingship*, pp. 36ff., 159ff., 299ff.; Labat, *Royauté*, pp. 53ff.; Gunkel, *Die Psalmen*, pp. 6f.

[27] Roeder, *Urkunden*, pp. 158f.

[28] *KB* IV, pp. 4f., 320; Law of Hammurabi ¶ 170f.; Meissner, *Bab. u. Ass.* I, p. 390.

[29] Roeder, *Urk.*, p. 159.

[30] Gunkel, *Die Psalmen*, p. 7.

[31] Erman-Ranke, *Aegypten*,[2] p. 325; Gunkel, *Die Psalmen*, p. 65.

[32] Gunkel, *Die Psalmen*, p. 481.

set his foot upon the neck of his enemies, who prostrated themselves before him.[33] Egyptian pictures show Pharaoh enthroned with his foot on the neck of the vanquished.[34] The foot-kissing (Ps. 2.12, cf. Isa. 49.23) as a sign of subjection and homage was a general oriental custom, known both from Egypt, and Babylonia-Assyria.[35]

When the king in Ps. 2 is 'ideally' promised world sovereignty this is of course not to be explained as realistic political aspiration, but is a religious postulate founded on the belief in Yahweh as the Lord of the world. But this idea has much older prototypes both in Egypt and in Mesopotamia, where it belongs to the fundamental 'king-ideology'; Pharaoh is 'king of the two countries', that is to say the bipartite universe.[36] The gods expressly promise him the sovereignty of all countries and peoples.[37] The Babylonian-Assyrian kings also with divine sanction use the title 'king of the lands', 'king of the universe', 'king of the four quarters of the world'.[38] It is worth noting that when the Israelite psalmist wishes to express the king's universal sovereignty, he does so in images which are formed from the Babylonian point of view, and which originated there. 'He shall rule from sea to sea, from the river to the utmost boundaries of the world' (Pss. 72.8; 89.26). 'From ocean to ocean' is a set Babylonian phrase for the whole of the known world: 'from the upper sea in the West (the Mediterranean) to the lower sea in the East' (the Persian Gulf). 'The streams' are the ocean which, according to the ancient conception of the world, lies like a ring round the earth-disk. 'The river' is here, as everywhere in the Bible, the Euphrates. The first expression mentions the extension of the realm from east to west, the other from its centre on the Euphrates to the 'ocean' or 'the ends of the world' on the periphery.

That the king is the 'life-breath' of the people (Lam. 4.20) is a common Canaanite-Egyptian idea, which we often meet with in the letters to Pharaoh from the vassal princes in the Amarna-letters.[39] To the Egyptians Pharaoh is 'the air of all noses', 'the one by whom one breathes'.[40] As in Israel, the people of Egypt and Babylonia live in the 'shadow' of the king (Jdg. 9.15; Lam. 4.20), that is to say, under his cool and pleasant protection.[41]

---

[33] Josh. 10.24; cf. 1 Kgs. 5.17; Isa. 51.23. For parallel modes of expression in the Amarna letters see Knudtzon in *VAB* II No. 84.4; No. 141.40.

[34] After Gunkel, *Die Psalmen*, p. 482 with reference to illustration in Riehms, *Bibl. Handwörterbuch* art. 'Krieg'. Cf. Gressmann, *AOB²*, Abb. 59.

[35] Gunkel, *Die Psalmen,*p. 8, with reference to Erman-Ranke, *Aegypten,²* p. 82; Jastrow, *Relig. Bab. u. Ass.* I, p. 514; Jensen in *KB* VI, 2, pp. 108f.; Klauber, *Assyr. Beamtentum*, p. 15.

[36] See Frankfort, *Kingship*, pp. 19ff.

[37] Cf. Roeder, *Urkunden*, pp. 158ff.

[38] Labat, *Royauté*, pp. 5f., 10, 13f., 18ff.; Frankfort, *Kingship*, pp. 227, 229f.

[39] E.g. Knudtzon in *VAB* II No. 141.2, 7, 10, 13, 37, 43; 143.15, 17; 144.2, 8.

[40] Roeder, *Urkunden*, p. 74; Grapow, *Bild. Ausdrücke der Aeg.*, p. 122.

[41] In Egypt: Erman, *Literatur der Aeg.*, p. 234; Oppenheim in *BASOR* 107, pp. 7ff.; in Mesopotamia: Frankfort, *Kingship*, p. 304.

In Canaan and Mesopotamia also the king is the special 'servant' of the god, his trusted man who stands in a specially close relation to him.[42]

Just as Yahweh chose David to be 'the shepherd of his people',[43] so 'shepherd' is a standing attribute of the king in Mesopotamia. It is his calling to 'tend the black-headed' (i.e., men). Hammurabi is 'the beneficent shepherd' (re'u mušallimu),[44] and so likewise in Egypt.[45]

As was the case in Israel (see below, pp. 6of., 63f.), so in Egypt and Mesopotamia the king was also a priest.[46]

In the same way as the king in Ps. 20, the Egyptian and Babylonian-Assyrian monarchs plead their abundant offerings and pious acts.[47] The king's prayer for 'life' and 'length of days for ever and ever' in Ps. 21 often recurs both in Egyptian and Mesopotamian royal inscriptions.[48]

The king's vow in Ps. 101 to rule Yahweh's people wisely, which has obviously belonged to the great annual feast (see below, pp. 65f.), has, both as to style, content and cultic form, a model in the Babylonian king's confession on the day of penitence at the new year festival, that he has kept Marduk's law and reigned well in Babylon.[49]

Finally we may mention the hymns praising the divine king, of which we have at least one example in the Old Testament, in Ps. 45 (see below, pp. 73f.). They occur somewhat more often in Babylonia[50] and very frequently in Egypt.[51]

But phenomenological 'parallels' are liable to be elusive. If an expression, an image, or a particular idea is found in two different places, in two civilizations and religions, it does not follow that they mean the same, even if there is a direct historical borrowing or influence on one side or the other. Each detail obtains its significance from the whole structure in which it has been incorporated, and of which it is a part. It is not first of all a question of proving that this or that Israelite idea is also found in Babylonia or Egypt or has been 'borrowed' from there. The essential question

---

[42] As for Canaan, see Mowinckel in *NTT* 1942, pp. 24ff.; Engnell, *Div. Kingship* Top. Index *s.v.* 'servant of god'. For Mesopotamia cf. Gadd, *Ideas of Div. Rule*, pp. 3, 34. The king often names himself the *wardu*, 'servant', 'slave' of such and such a god; cf. names of kings like Waradsin, 'Sin's servant'.

[43] Ps. 78.71; cf. Jer. 3.15; Ezk. 34.23; 37.24; Mic. 5.3f.; Nah. 3.18; 2 Sam. 5.2; 7.7; for 'bad herdsmen': Isa. 56.11; Jer. 2.8; 22.22; 23.1, 4; 50.6; Ezk. 34.2ff.; Zech. 11.5; a people without a king is like 'sheep which have no shepherd', Num. 27.17; 1 Kgs. 22.17; Zech. 10.2.

[44] Cf. Gadd, *Ideas of Div. Rule*, pp. 38f.; Jastrow, *Relig. Bab. u. Ass.* I, pp. 48f.

[45] See A. Jeremias, *Ausserbiblische Erlösererwartung*, pp. 108ff.; idem, *D. Alt. Test. im Lichte d. alt. Orients,*[4] p. 653.

[46] The king as priest in Egypt: Erman-Ranke, *Aegypten*,[2] p. 73; Erman, *Die Religion der Aegypten*, pp. 186f.; in Mesopotamia: Meissner, *Bab. u. Ass.* I, pp. 49, 63, 67ff.; Jeremias, *Handbuch*, p. 284; Jastrow, *Relig. Bab. u. Assyr.* I, pp. 211, 217, and especially Labat, *Royauté*, pp. 131ff.; Frankfort, *Kingship*, p. 221; Gadd, *Ideas of Div. Rule*, pp. 39f.

[47] Ps. 20.4; cf. Erman, *Lit. d. Aeg.*, p. 379 (E.T., p. 307); Jastrow, *Relig. Bab. u. Ass.* I, p. 409. Cf, Heiler, *Das Gebet,*[4] p. 85.

[48] Ps. 21.5. Egyptian and Mesopotamian examples with references to sources in Gunkel-Begrich, *Einl.*, pp. 162f.

[49] Frankfort, *Kingship*, pp. 319ff.; Labat, *Royauté*, p. 168.

[50] See Engnell, *Div. Kingship*, p. 45 with references to sources.

[51] See Erman, *Lit. d. Aeg.* pp. 35f.; 44f., 179ff., 318ff.

is, what significance has been imparted to it in its new context; what has the religion of Israel made of it?[51a]

In Israel as in Mesopotamia there are two important sides to the idea of the king. He is the representative of the people, incorporating its 'greater I', and he is the representative of the deity and more than a human being—he has something of the 'divine' in him. We must first make clear that in Israel, the oriental type of divine king has never quite been able to supersede the old, more 'democratic' chieftainship of desert days, when the chief was also priest and the bearer of the blessing, and 'father' and 'holy' and yet held his authority by virtue of his corporate identity with the tribe, and not from any special relation to the great gods. The god of the tribe was his 'father', but so was he to the whole tribe. Many ideas and forms were taken over by Israel from the great kingdoms, but they were considerably modified by the old chiefdom ideology.

If we are to realize what the king's divinity meant to Israel, we must find out what the Israelite meant by 'god', and how the Old Testament understands the king's relationship to Yahweh. The Old Testament uses the word 'god' for all sorts of lower 'supernatural' beings, such as the dead soul, the ghost (1 Sam. 28.13) or a 'demon of sickness' (Job 19.22). 'The divine beings', (literally 'the god-sons'), signifies the lower heavenly beings round Yahweh's throne who are sent forth as his messengers,[52] corresponding to the 'angels' in later usage. Even about man the poet may say that Yahweh 'has made him little less than a god' (Ps. 8.6). But it is just such an expression that shows us the essential difference between such a 'god' and Yahweh. What characterizes a 'god' is a superhuman and supernatural power, wisdom and insight. A 'god' is in a special degree a 'holy' being[53] and partakes of all the faculties and attributes of 'holiness' (cf. above, pp. 54f.). The 'godlikeness' of man in Ps. 8 consists above all in his sovereignty and power over all other beings, in his godlike 'honour and glory' compared to them.

Then how do all these 'gods' differ from the only true God, Yahweh, who 'is', who alone has creative and saving power both as to nature and history?[54] We see the answer most clearly in Ps. 82, where Yahweh passes judgment on all other gods. 'Ye are gods, and all of you are children of the most High. But ye shall die like men, and fall like one of the (earthly) princes'. Any other 'god' can die, and this also applies to the 'divine' king, but Yahweh is 'the living God', 'the holy God who does not die' (Hab. 1.12).

Consequently nowhere in the Old Testament do we meet with a 'meta-

---

[51a] Alt ('Der Königtum in den Reichen Israel und Juda', *Kleine Schriften* II, pp. 116ff. = *VT* I, 1951, pp. 2ff.) has stressed too strongly the lack of adjustment of the ideological and political content of kingship to the old Israelite ideas and ideals. Cf. my review of Alt's book in *ThLZ* 80.4, April 1955, esp. col. 204.

[52] Pss. 29.1; 89.7; Gen. 6.2, 4; Job 1.6; 2.1; 38.7.

[53] Pss. 16.3; 89.6, 8; Deut. 33.3; Zech. 14.5; Job 5.1; 15.15; Dan. 4.5, 6, 10, 15, 20; 5.11; 8.13; Sir. 42.17.

[54] Isa. 41.4; 43.10f.; 48.12; cf. 43.12f.; 44.6.

physical' unity of Yahweh and the king, or a really 'mythological' idea of
the king's relation to Yahweh. Clearly and plainly the king's filial relation
to Yahweh is based on an adoption (see above, p. 54). His divinity depends
on the endowment he has received at his election and anointing and on
the power flowing to him through the holy rites of the cult, by Yahweh's
free will, and depending on the king's loyalty and obedience towards
Yahweh's commandments.[55] The wish that the king may 'live for ever'
(see above, p. 53) contains no thought of immortality. It is not David nor
the individual king personally but the royal race which is promised eternal
life and which shall sit on David's throne for ever.[56] In spite of all, the
relation between Yahweh and the king is no kind of equality, but a
relation which shows a distinct superiority and subordination. The king is
'Yahweh's servant', his 'slave',[57] in all respects dependent on Yahweh's
allegiance and help and power.[58] Compared to Yahweh the king is a
'mortal man', 'a man of the people' (Ps. 89.26), whom Yahweh 'has
lifted up and crowned' and 'placed on high'.[59] In spite of all 'divinity'
the king is a human being, and there is an enormous distance between
man and the real God.[60] Thus it is not wholly without reason that some
have spoken of 'oriental court style' in connexion with the royal psalms'
expressions about the king.[61] Many a phrase has been borrowed from the
general oriental ritual king style without taking over its original sense,
and without giving it greater significance than that which agreed with the
Yahweh religion's view of the relation between Yahweh and man, even a
superman.[62]

There is then no doubt that the Yahweh religion has radically transformed the general oriental idea of the king, and consequently those forms
of the cult which are connected with these ideas. Here we must note the
increasing criticism of the kingship which developed in Israel.[63] It arose
from religious motives and finally led to the kingship being regarded as

---

[55] Pss. 89.31–33; 18.21–25; 20.4; 132.10; 2 Sam. 7.14f.

[56] 2 Sam. 7.12–16, 19, 26–28; Pss. 89.29–38; 132.11f.; 72.17; Jer. 22.1–5.

[57] Pss. 18.1; 36.1; 89.4, 21; Zech. 3.8 and other places; this expression is even used about
pagan kings: Jer. 25.9; 27.6; 43.10. Cf. above, note 42.

[58] Though with somewhat exaggerated one-sidedness, this has been rightly maintained by
North in *ZATW* 50, 1932, pp. 8ff.

[59] Ps. 89.20; 2 Sam. 23.1; 7.8; cf. 1 Sam. 15.17; 2 Sam. 7.18f.

[60] Cf. Seierstad, *Die Offenbarungserlebnisse*, pp. 82ff.

[61] Gressmann, *Urspr. d. Eschatologie*, pp. 250ff.

[62] This is even admitted by the investigators who most strongly emphasize the dependence of
Israel on common oriental 'cultic patterns' ('ritual patterns'), when they speak of the disintegration of the ritual pattern, see e.g. Hooke in *Myth and Ritual*, p. 6. But they often seem to
content themselves with admitting this in general without entering into the details of the question as to what the Israelite author himself in the concrete instance means by the style pattern
and the terms he is using. Thus Widengren in his treatise on Ps. 88 finally declares that he would
be misunderstood if his opinion were interpreted to the effect that he 'was supposed to look upon
the text of Ps. 88 as it has been handed down to us, as a rendering of the original cult text as it
was delivered by the king at a point of the ritual when mythically he was supposed to find himself in the underworld'. Cf. also Engnell, *Div. Kingship*, p. 50. An ordinary exegete would be
inclined to think that the exegetical problem starts here, and that what really concerns the
exegete is to learn what the author of the psalm himself thought about the worshipper and his
actual conditions.

[63] Cf. Johs. Pedersen, *Israel* III–IV, pp. 89ff., 97ff.

contrary to Yahweh's sovereignty.[64] Then gradually a new king ideal grew up, placing the main stress on the righteousness and justice of the king, and on his will to help the suffering, the poor and oppressed and to give them their rights, and on the divine wisdom and wonder-working power he is endowed with to do this, to 'reign in Yahweh's strength'. It is by the help of Yahweh, and because the king humbly relies on his allegiance to Yahweh and his loyalty to Yahweh's covenant, that he can do this. It is really Yahweh who does it for him.[65]

That the king in Israel should have been regarded as identical with Yahweh, or in the cult have played Yahweh's part is thus wholly improbable; nor is there any proof whatever that this was ever the case. The polemics of the prophets give us a clue. They never suggest that the king has made himself a god. The book of Ezekiel is probably the prophetical writing which most violently upbraids the historical kings of Judah for their sins. The climax of the attack is where the prophet points to the blasphemy which the kings have committed by placing the king's palace next door to the temple, and even placing the kings' graves there, thus 'fouling the holy name of Yahweh with their idolatry and their corpses'.[66] It is then easy to imagine what Ezekiel would have said if the king had really made himself equal with Yahweh, and comported himself like God and received worship in the cult. In the cult the king sings and dances 'before Yahweh' at the head of the procession, and in the cultic drama he plays the part of David, while Yahweh is represented by his holy shrine, 'the footstool' before the throne, where he sits invisible.[67] Even in Ps. 110 where the king sits on Yahweh's own throne at his right hand, a clear distinction is made between Yahweh and the king.

Nevertheless it is clear that the notions about the nature and essence of the kingship which reach their climax in the idea of the king's divinity, in Israel too were more than a matter of mere form and 'court style'. They expressed a reality in Israel's belief and cult. When the poet, even after the fall of the country and the kingdom, can speak as he does in the book of Lamentations about 'The breath of our nostrils, the anointed of the Lord, of whom we said "Under his shadow we shall live among the nations" ' (4.20), this means more than just a lyrical expression of lost glory. It shows what was actually expected of the king, even after bad experiences with real kings, such as Judah had had with the last kings before the fall of the kingdom. The king's close relation to Yahweh, his

---

[64] Judges 8.22f.; 1 Sam. 8, 6ff. A comparison with the original versions—made possible by a traditio-critical investigation—brings out very clearly that we have here a legendary back-dating of the attitudes of a later age. Buber's attempt in *Königtum Gottes* to trace this idea back to the earliest history of Israel is not convincing; B. does not really seem to have an eye for the natural and historical value of the different sources.

[65] Cf. Isa. 9.5f.; 11.1–5; 16.5; Mic. 5.1, 3, 9f.; Jer. 22.15f.; 23.1–8; Zech. 9.9f; Ezk. 22.6; 34; 37.24f.; 49.9f.; Pss. 18.21, 25f., 28; 20.8; 21.8; 72.1f., 12–14; 101; 2 Sam. 23.3.

[66] Ezk. 43.7–9. See likewise *He That Cometh*, p. 61.

[67] 2 Sam. 6.5, 14ff.; cf. Pss. 42.7; 132.1–10. For the throne in the Temple see Isa. 6.1ff.; cf. Johs. Pedersen, *Israel* III–IV, pp. 247ff. H. Schmidt in *Eucharisterion* (*Gunkel Festschrift*) I, pp. 120ff.

endowment with divine strength, the experience and assurance of this in the festal cult, the king's appearance there as the visible pledge of the existence and permanence of the covenant, were realities for the religious belief and experience of Israel.

This links up with the other side of the king's being and position. Though Yahweh's representative towards the people, he is even more the representative of the people towards Yahweh. Figuratively speaking he is the channel through which the blessings of the deity flow to the people. But he is also the 'corporate representative' through whom the people approaches Yahweh to partake of the blessing. If the empires of the East have occasionally made a divine being of him, the Yahweh religion with its different idea of God has, in spite of it all, put him back in his right place as the first representative of men towards the deity. He has become a real 'mediator', and the religion of Israel developed a tendency to make his human position more and more clearly marked. As we have seen, he became a 'man of the people' (Ps. 89.26) whose duty it is to mediate the blessing of Yahweh to 'his brethren'. All the great deeds ascribed to him depend on his obeying the will of Yahweh and adhering to him (see above, p. 58).

The old corporate way of thinking keeps on asserting itself. As the 'father' and first man of the people the king 'incorporates' it in himself. In the great crises of the people the king *is* the people. Its 'breath of life' and its 'happiness' are in him and depend on him. Its 'blessing' has its earthly source in him. The king and the people are inextricably bound together. His piety and greatness constitute the righteousness and happiness of the people. If the king is godless disaster strikes the whole people. In his person the people approaches God, and through him God speaks to the people. Thus he is also a priest[68] and has prophetic gifts.[69]

Thus it is in the cult that the king's part as a mediator and his divine qualities and near relation to the deity and his position as the incorporating representative of the people, are most obvious. The day of the king's enthronement (his anointing), was a festival laying the foundation for the future of the people. As far as we can see, the king's enthronement was celebrated each year in a feast not only in Egypt, Babylonia, Assyria, and the other Eastern empires[70] but also in Israel. Ps. 132 shows that this annual enthronement of the king was also felt to be a repetition of David's legitimization as Yahweh's king at Zion, and was accompanied by promises to the royal house corresponding to those which at that time were given to David. In the psalms, e.g. at the procession on the great festival

---

[68] I Sam. 13.9; 2 Sam. 6.17; 7.18; 1 Kgs. 8.5; Ps. 110.4. More fully Gunkel, *Die Psalmen*, p. 484.

[69] 2 Sam. 23.1f. Cf. also 1 Kgs. 8, the prayer of Solomon at the consecration of the Temple, when the saga-writer makes him—hypothetically, certainly—predict all the punishments to overtake Israel, even including the carrying away of the people and the diaspora.

[70] See Dürr, *Reichsgründungsfeiern im antiken Orient*; Böhl, *Nieuwejaarsfeest en konigsdag* (*Opera Minora*, pp. 236–281); Johs. Pedersen, *Israel* III–IV, pp. 746ff. For the special part played by the king in the cult see also Johs. Pedersen, *op. cit.* pp. 428f.

days, the intercession for the king had its place (Ps. 84.10; cf. 63.12), corresponding to the prominent part which the king himself took in the procession.

It is, then, a matter of course that the king at important moments should act as the leader of the festal cult, as we hear of David doing when Yahweh's shrine was taken to Jerusalem, and of Solomon at the consecration of the temple. The king has direct access to Yahweh and arranges the details of the service himself.[71] He holds, at least theoretically, the same position in the cult as the high priest held later. He officiates at the sacrifice. He prays on behalf of the people and he pronounces the blessing on the congregation. He also receives the revelation from Yahweh, e.g. by staying over night in the holy place.[72]

He is responsible for the people towards Yahweh. Through the 'righteousness' of the king, fertility of people, cattle and land is secured (cf. Ps. 72.1–7). The righteousness of the king is the righteousness of the people, his sin is the people's sin (2 Sam. 21.1; 24.1ff.). The whole of the book of Kings is written in accordance with this view of the connexion between the king's relation to Yahweh and the fortunes of the people.

When the king appears in the cult in such a way he is more than what we nowadays mean by the word 'representative'. In a mystical way he *is* what he represents. The people acts, receives, and lives in and through him. The ancient idea of the people as a 'greater I', which at important moments is manifested in an individual, comes to the fore here. We may say that the king at the same time both incorporates and represents the people. It is the old Israelite 'collective' and 'corporate' way of thinking which has produced and formulated these ideas. The king receives the promises of blessing and the power of blessing which are to benefit the whole congregation.[73] And in the rites of penance he appears as the vicarious bearer of all the misfortunes and sufferings which have hit the people, and subjects himself to the rites of expiation which have to be performed, and prays for help and salvation.[74]

Whether the king in such a capacity says 'I' or 'we', on behalf of the people, does not matter. The 'I–form' may seem to be the more exact and original, corresponding to the thought of the 'greater I'; the 'we form' being the later and disclosing a more individualizing and differentiating way of thinking: the totality as a sum of independent units.

4

Starting with this view of the king and his place in the cult we can now understand the royal psalms. The king stands at the centre of the religious festivals. And from the power and blessing he there obtains from Yahweh,

[71] 2 Sam. 6; 1 Kgs. 8; 21.9, 12; 2 Kgs. 16.10ff.; Isa. 37.14ff.; 3 Macc. 6.1ff.
[72] 1 Kgs. 3.5ff., and cf. above, note 69 and Ehrlich, *Der Traum im A.T.*, pp. 19ff.
[73] Pss. 132.11–18; 72; cf. 20.8; 21.14; Isa. 55.3.
[74] See Ps. 102, probably a royal psalm, see Birkeland, *Feinde d. Indiv.*, pp. 311f., 328f.

vital force and blessing radiate to the people. There is a great difference
between the kingdom of David and the ancient chiefdom of the time of
Moses and the Judges, with which Saul was more closely related. The
chief as well was a central figure at the old cult festivals. But there he sits—
as Saul did—on his own estate or in the local sanctuary; 'his men and his
family are gathered around him, their blessing is centred in him'.[75] It was
the clan as a whole that met Yahweh and was active in the cult. After
David, the king was the master of the cult: he arranged it, and it took
place primarily for his sake. He marches in the procession to the 'king's
sanctuary'. He provides and presents the offerings. The priests perform the
rites on his behalf. The people are spectators. From his blessing, blessings
overflow on to the others.

The royal psalms may thus be grouped about the king festivals. Of
special importance are the psalms which have belonged to the anointing
and enthronement festivals, both because they give so clear a picture of
the 'king ideology', and because they throw light on the religious ritual of
the festival.[76]

We can see from the descriptions which by chance have come down to
us (1 Kgs. 1.33ff.; 2 Kgs. 11) that the festival was divided into two main
parts, the anointing in the Temple and the enthronement in the king's
palace. Seated on his royal mule[76a] the king is led to the holy place and
anointed by the priest. He stands on a high platform or pediment in view
of all the people—we hear of that in Egypt too—and the priest anoints
him, 'places the diadem, the crown, on his head and gives him the edict
($h\bar{a}'\bar{e}dh\hat{u}th$)[77]. It is the same ceremony which is alluded to in Ps. 2: 'I will
declare the decree' ($h\bar{o}q$). According to the Egyptian ritual of enthronement the reference here is to a written document expressing the divine
legitimacy of the king, his calling and enthronement by the deity, and the
further destiny and 'name' that will thereby be his. The 'decree' or 'edict'
is thus a confirmation of the covenant with David. In other words the
'covenant' and the 'crown' constitute Yahweh's gifts to his adopted royal
son.[78]

The decree is based on Yahweh's own word, not only on old promises
to the ancestor David, but on the expressly renewed promise at each new
enthronement. At the installation the prophet also has his place and the
prophetic legends generally intimate that it is the prophet who performs
the anointing.[79] In any case the seer-priest[80] and later on, the temple

---

[75] Johs. Pedersen, *Israel* III–IV, p. 429.
[76] For the ritual of anointing and coronation and its reflection in the psalms, see Mowinckel,
Ps. St. II, pp. 6ff.; Widengren, *Psalm 110 och det sakrala kungadömet i Israel* (*UUÅ* 1941: 7, 1);
v. Rad, *Das judäische Königsritual*, (*ThLZ* 4, 1947, also in his *Gesammelte Studien*).
[76a] See Jdg. 5.10; 10.4, and Mowinckel, *He That Cometh*, p. 176.
[77] 2 Kgs. 11.12. This word is often falsely changed into *hasse'adhôth* 'the bracelets', after 2
Sam. 1.10; so also in *GTMMM* II, p. 401; but see v. Rad, *op. cit.*, col. 213f.
[78] See Pss. 132.12; 89.40; for this idea cf. also Ps. 105.10.
[79] 1 Sam. 16.1ff.; 1 Kgs. 1.32ff.; 19.15f.; 2 Kgs. 9.6.
[80] This is the picture of Samuel in 1 Sam. 9; cf. Mowinckel, *Ps. St.* III, pp. 9ff.

prophet[81] proclaims Yahweh's oracle at the anointing; that which gives the anointed one the legitimate foundation of his kingship. In Pss. 2 and 110 and in allusions in Ps. 89.20ff. such enthronement oracles have come down to us, and it is the style and content of such anointment oracles that furnish the material which the tradition used when, in the legend of Nathan, it makes Nathan pronounce such promises to David.[82] The historical core here is that Yahweh's covenant with the king and his 'decree' at the anointing was expressly understood to be a renewal of 'the favours promised faithfully to David' and of the covenant with him.[83]

The fixed contents of these anointment and instalment oracles embraced also the allusion to the king's filial relation to Yahweh by adoption, the promise of everlasting rule for his family and the allusion to the covenant with the progenitor, as well as the promise of sovereignty over the nations and an allusion to the great 'name' in store for the king.[84] The mention of the king's 'name' contains an allusion to the fact that the oracles and 'decree' really contained those names of honour which the deity gave to the king on the day of his anointing, his 'regnal-name' which expressed both his close relation to Yahweh and the promise of the happiness and honour he was to gain for himself and for his people.[85] We know this to be the case in Egypt, and both in the East generally and in Israel the custom prevailed that the king should take a new name at his accession.[86] The divine conferring of royal names of honour is what the prophet is alluding to in the promise to the newborn royal child in Isaiah 9.1ff.[87]

Several of the traditional royal psalms have their place within the framework of the anointment ritual. This applies, e.g. to Ps. 110. It evidently belongs to the moment when the king is led forth to ascend his throne. The king's throne was in the East looked upon as a symbol of the throne of the deity. It is on a throne flanked by winged lions (cherubs), like that of Solomon, that the deity himself sits in Syro-Canaanite pictures. Such a winged lion throne (empty!) stood in the Temple in Jerusalem also, and it was supposed that 'Yahweh who sits upon the cherubim' was seated on it invisibly. When the king as the 'son of Yahweh' seats himself

---

[81] Cf. *Ps. St.* III, pp. 12ff.; A. R. Johnson, *The Cultic Prophet.*

[82] 2 Sam. 7. See *Ps. St.* III, pp. 35f., 110; 'Natanforjettelsen 2 Sam. Kap. 7', *SEÅ* XII, 1947, pp. 220ff.

[83] Isa. 55.3f.; Pss. 132.11ff.; 89.20ff. On the Davidic covenant see Pedersen, *Israel* III–IV, pp. 87ff., 654ff.; on its identity with the covenant with Israel, see Mowinckel, *He That Cometh*, pp. 89, 98ff., 158.

[84] Sonship: Pss. 2.7; 89.27f.; 2 Sam. 7.14. Everlasting kingdom: Pss. 89.29f., 37f.; 110.4; 2 Sam. 7.18; Isa. 55.3; 2 Sam. 23.5. Covenant with David: Pss. 89.31–34; 132.10–12, 17; 2 Sam. 23.5; 7.12–15. In Ps. 110.4 the promise is based on the idea that the house of David is the righteous successor to Melchizedek. Empire: Pss. 2.8–12; 89.26, 28; 132.18; 110.2, 5f.; Isa. 55.4f. Name: 2 Sam. 7.9; Pss. 72.17; 45.18; cf. 1 Kgs. 1.47.

[85] See von Rad's treatise (mentioned above, n. 76), col. 215f.

[86] See 2 Kgs 23.31 (Shallum-Jo'ahaz); 23.34 (Elijakim-Jehoiakim). 2 Sam. 12.24f. probably also has to be interpreted to the effect that David's son Jediah as king took the name Solomon. See Honeyman in *JBL* LXVII, pp. 13ff. For the names of Egyptian kings see Erman-Ranke, *Ägypten,*[2] pp. 58ff.; for Babylonian-Assyrian names see Meissner, *Babyl. u. Assyr.* I, p. 398.

[87] See v. Rad, *op. cit.*, col. 215f.

on his throne, this is a symbolic expression of the fact that he, as Yahweh's appointed governor, sits on the Lord's own throne, i.e. wields sovereign power in the name of Yahweh. That is the background of the oracle in Ps. 110. There reference is made to the holy robe in which the king has been arrayed for the anointing, to the life-giving water from the holy spring—probably the waters of Gihon—with which he has been purified and strengthened, and to the procession from the brook to the king's palace.[88] And at the moment when he ascends the throne, the temple prophet stands forth and proclaims for him in the name of Yahweh that to the king belongs the seat of honour on the right hand of Yahweh, and the priest kingdom 'after the order of Melchizedek'—or, 'for Melchizedek's sake':

> This oracle hath Yahweh for my lord:
> 'Sit thou throned at my right hand,
> Until I shall have made
>   Thine enemies thy footstool' . . .
> Yahweh hath sworn an oath,
>   and never will repent it;
> 'Thou art to be a priest for ever,
>   (a priest) as once Melchizedek was'.

Yahweh shall send the royal sceptre out from Zion, and go at the king's side in the battle,

> And he shall crush the (peoples') kings
>   in the day of his burning wrath.

The union of royal and priestly power was the main characteristic of El Elyon's kings in ancient Jerusalem, whose realm David and Solomon had inherited and maintained as the foundation of their position of power. But the increasing influence of the priests soon threatened the ecclesiastical power of the king. So it was important to have Yahweh's promise of the old right. Apart from this the warrior-ideal is strongly marked in this psalm. By the eternal 'youthful force' which the king—like the Canaanite fertility god *Tal*, 'Dew'—in that day receives from Yahweh, he shall 'strike through' all his enemies.

When the king had mounted the throne, and received the 'king's homage' (*těrû'ath melekh*), it is part of the ceremony that he is to make a speech to his people and his vassals. In so doing he points to the legitimate foundation of his sovereignty and to the way he intends to exert it. He produces, so to speak, his 'political programme' of which we also hear in connexion with Rehoboam, 1 Kgs. 12.14. This is the background of Ps. 2. In its form it is the king's first proclamation to his subjects, and it is the

---

[88] See Widengren, *Psalm* 110.

king himself who speaks.[89] He imagines the following situation: the subdued vassal kings are planning rebellion—a normal situation at practically every new accession in the Eastern empires—but he warns them, it will be in vain,

> for *I* have (now) been set as His king
> upon Zion, His holy hill.

And in proof of this he points to the legitimizing oracle he has just received through the cult prophet: 'I will declare the decree of Yahweh'; and then follows the oracle of appointment ('initiation oracle') verbatim:

> He said to me: 'Thou art my son,
> this day I have begotten thee.
> Ask, and I make thee master of the nations,
> lord over all the ends of the earth.
> Thou canst maul them with an iron mace,
> and shatter them like potter's ware'.

So the kings have nothing else to do but to 'be wise' and submit to Yahweh and his anointed, if they wish to save their lives.

Two things are noticeable in this proclamation. The first is the idea of the world sovereignty of the king of Zion. Ideally he has such a claim because he is the anointed one and Yahweh's governor, and Yahweh is the God of the world. The other point is the basis of the argument for this close relation between Yahweh and the king. He is 'Yahweh's son', adopted by Yahweh 'today'. It is the election, the anointing and the installation which are viewed as an adoption. Thereby the king is, ideally speaking, world-ruler; and all other kings are his vassals, whose duty it is to pay him homage by 'kissing his feet'—the usual sign of homage to the liege sovereign in the East.[90]

In Ps. 101 the new king proclaims his 'charter' before Yahweh and promises to 'behave himself wisely in a perfect way'. This psalm being

---

[89] If we keep to the text of G and H in v. 6, supported by verbatim parallels from the Ugarit texts, we shall avoid the constant unstylish changing of the person speaking, see Hvidberg, *Graad og Latter i det Gamle Testamente*, p. 34 n. 1–2. For the understanding of the presupposed situation in Ps. 2 see my discussion with Bentzen 'Urmenschen u. "Königsideologie"' in *Studia Theologica* II, pp. 87f. (cf. n. 100). Daiches (*Studies in the Pss.*, pp. 27ff.; 38ff.) maintains—though without any real exegetical basis—that *gôyîm* and *lĕ'ummîm* do not indicate 'nations', but something like 'great people' or 'nobles', and that *mĕlākhîm* in Ps. 2 and other places does not mean (foreign) 'kings', but native 'magnates', 'great noblemen', 'governors' and the like; Ps. 2, then, is supposed not to deal with the relationship between the supreme king and the other nations and kings, but to be a warning to the Judaic magnates that they do justice. D.'s concept of Israelite 'ideas' seems rather rationalistic and modernizing. Cf. also Kaminka (*MGWJ* 71, 1927, p. 296), who finds that Ps. 2 belongs to the poetry 'die Israels geistige Sendung glorifiziert' Morgenstern ('NŠQW BR' in *JQR* XXXII, 1941–42, p. 385) thinks that Ps. 2 (like Ps. 48) has for its background the Messianic expectations at the time of Zerubbabel, supposed to have been terminated very abruptly through some catastrophe in the year 485. The hypothesis is unnecessary—as nothing decisive can be said against a pre-exilic dating—and so is his textual conjecture in v. 12.

[90] See Gunkel, *Die Psalmen*, p. 8 (*ad* Ps. 2.12).

typologically quite unique and not to be classed under any of the greater types ('Gattungen') we take the opportunity of analysing it here.

It starts as a hymn, but in a personal form: 'I will sing', and then continues as a vow made by the worshipper before Yahweh. The contents of this promise quite obviously prove that the speaker is supposed to be a king; his 'house' is the people and land of Israel, and the promise has for its object that he is going to rule the kingdom according to 'justice' and the 'goodwill of the covenant'.

From the point of view of form-history, elements from hymn and psalm of lament and prayer are here combined to make a new unity: the hymnal (self-) invitation to praise, and the 'promise' in which lament and psalm of prayer usually end. But there must be a special reason for this combination; it must be a consequence of the fact that this psalm—or psalms of this type—had a definite place in the liturgical framework of religious life. What, then, can possibly be the cultic 'place' for such a solemn promise on the part of the king before Yahweh?

It can hardly be anything else than the religious cultic part of the enthronement of the king, in connexion with the ceremonies of anointing, and in that case, before the proclamation to the vassals in Ps. 2. As we have seen above (p. 64, Chap. III.3), there is every reason to presume that the official festival of anointing, at any rate in the later monarchy, would take place in connexion with the new year festival, and that it would be commemorated as an annual festal day in connexion with the latter. No doubt the pattern from the Babylonian enthronement festival has had its influence here, directly or indirectly.

Now we know it to have been one feature of the enthronement of the king in Babylonia, that the king, by way of a confession before the god, would account for the way he had ruled his kingdom. This was a consequence of the fact that the new year festival was a festival of penance and purification, the king had to play the part of a penitent, humbling himself and laying his dignity at the feet of Marduk, to receive it again from his hand.[91] The confession of sins was always part of the penance. But as we shall see, confession of sins and declaration of innocence go together in the Babylonian as well as in the Israelite psalms of penance. It is not difficult to understand that in a ritual, aiming at the re-instatement of the king into his office, the main emphasis would have to be put on the declaration of innocence. From Babylonian and Egyptian sources we know that it was often part of the rituals of penance for the priest to make use of a kind of 'confessionary mirror'; he would ask the penitent: 'hast thou done this, has thou done that?', and so on. And because, as has been said, in such rituals we have a re-instatement, a 'justification' of the person in question, the answer to the question would usually be: 'I have not done this, I have not done that'. Such a 'negative confession of justification' is for instance made by the dead pharaoh, before he is admitted into the

<hr>

[91] See Frankfort, *Kingship*, pp. 318ff.

realm of Osiris.[92] In Babylonia the confession of the king has the same form: 'I have not sinned, thou Lord of the commandments, I have not failed to honour thy divineness, I have not depraved Babylon', and so on.[93]

It is on behalf of the deity that the priest puts his questions. And in putting them he also gives instruction as to the will and the demands of the deity with regard to the king, as to the religious and moral standards and commandments, according to which he is to rule. The instruction of the deity is answered by the 'confession' of the penitent, but also of the king who is to be installed.

The promise of the king on the day of his anointing must be seen against this background. As we shall discuss in detail below in Chap. XII, the king on his festal day is confronted not only by the promises of Yahweh but also by the religious and moral pre-conditions of such a promise: the promise is dependent on his submission to the commandments and laws of Yahweh. And if the official installation of the king was identical with the great new year festival (Chap. V), and was celebrated every year in connexion with the latter, then king as well as people had to face Yahweh's demands at many points during the festal ritual.

The psalm of promise, Ps. 101, is the answer of the king to these demands from Yahweh, the promise made by him on the day of his election and anointing as king of Yahweh's people. It is, so to speak, his religious 'charter'. It is the counterpart of the intercession for the king in Ps. 72, to the effect that Yahweh may give him 'righteousness' and 'judgments' (pp. 65f). And, as already mentioned, we have reason to believe that it was repeated every year as a regular part of the great new year festival, at which the kind used to play such a prominent part. We may even say that it expresses the thanksgiving of the king to Yahweh for his gracious election, for the 'rightness' and 'faithful goodwill' to David and his house, which Yahweh has shown by electing him king of his people.[94] The king promises to repay all this 'rightness' and 'goodwill' on the part of Yahweh by ruling the 'house' of Israel and the 'city of Yahweh' in conformity with them.

Therefore the psalm starts by paying homage full of awe to Yahweh and his goodwill, and naturally this would take the form of a normal hymnic introduction:

> I will sing of goodwill and righteousness
> and play unto Thee, O Yahweh.

And it agrees with the fundamental idea of Israelite religion, that the king is conscious of receiving the 'rightness' and 'goodwill' needed in his high office, and of having to learn it from Yahweh, as we are told in Ps. 72.1;

---

[92] See Galling in *ZATW* 47, 1927, p. 130. That the rituals of the 'Book of the Dead' were originally concerned with the passage of the king into the world of Osiris is evident. Cf. Frankfort, *Kingship*, pp. 110ff.

[93] See Frankfort, *op. cit.*, p. 320.

[94] Cf. Isa. 55.3: *ḥasēdhê dhāwîdh* = 'the covenant promises of mercy to David'.

it is something for which the king must ask God:

> May I get insight in the perfect way—
> when wilt thou come to me?

In this introduction the tone of the hymn and of the psalm of prayer harmonize perfectly.[95]

The king promises to rule Yahweh's people righteously, and according to the covenant, and to exterminate all the wicked, the deceitful and proud, together with the sorcerers, and to surround himself with only true and honest men.

> Mine eyes shall be upon the faithful of the land,
>   that they may dwell with me;
> he that walketh in a perfect way,
>   he shall be my servant . . .
> Every morning I will destroy
>   all the wicked of the land,
> that I may cut off all evil-doers
>   from the city of Yahweh.

Such was the ideal; according to the Yahweh religion the king *ought to be* like this. That everyday reality was very often quite different can be seen both in the speeches of the prophets and in many of the historical records.[96]

The ethical strain in the Yahweh religion and its king-ideal is also clearly expressed in Ps. 72 which constitutes the congregation's petition and good wishes for the new king:

> Inspire the king, O God, with thine own justice,
>   endow the king's son with thine own equity,
> that he may rule thy people aright,
>   and thy poor with just judgment.

It is the lowly and the helpless among the people who are the special object of Yahweh's care: they are *his* poor, and the king's first task is to see that they are not oppressed. The king who does that shall live long, he lives in his race 'as long as sun and moon exist'. The petition becomes a

---

[95] Danell, *Psalm* 139. Danell places Ps. 139 in the context suggested by Solomon's vigil at Gibeon, 1 Kgs. 3.5ff., and thinks that it was used as 'the king's declaration, his profession to Yahweh after his enthronement during the New Year Festival'—i.e. in a cultic situation analogous to that of Ps. 101. Danell has given no tenable argument for this opinion. In Ps. 139 the worshipper is probably a leading person in the congregation but no king; the linguistic Aramaisms cannot be overlooked. The cultic background of the psalm is not an installation, but a casual distress; the psalm is a psalm of lamentation with a broad hymnic introduction, the purpose of which is the assertion of the innocence of the worshipper. What form a king's proclamation may have taken can be seen from Pss. 2 and 101.

[96] See above, pp. 59f. and n.63.

description of the blessings that shall befall the people:

> He shall come down like rain upon the mown grass:
> > as showers that water the earth.
> In his days shall welfare flourish;
> > and abundance of peace so long as the moon endureth.

The hills shall bear peace and happiness, and right order (i.e. welfare and good things) fill the valleys. Then shall his realm reach over the whole earth and 'all kings shall fall down before him: all nations shall serve him'. The most distant kings shall bring tribute:

> For he shall save the forlorn who cry to him,
> > the poor, and him that has no helper;
> he shall pity the poor and needy,
> > and shall save the life of the weak.
> He shall rescue them from outrage and oppression;
> > and precious shall their blood be in his sight.

When 'righteousness' rules the land, material blessings shall flow as a fruit of the king's probity and divine favour—his 'kingly luck' as the ancient Scandinavians would have said, his 'blessedness' the Israelites termed it:

> May the corn be abundant in the land
> > and sprout on the top of the mountains;
> the fruit thereof bloom like Lebanon,
> > and flourish like grass of the earth.

The psalm becomes a formula of blessing which reminds one strongly of the promises of the prophets as it oscillates between blessing and prediction. The officiating priest who recites the psalm, to begin with speaks on behalf of the congregation and in the form of a petition. But he is also the representative of Yahweh and pronounces strong and effective words with a ring of certainty. Through these he, so to speak, conducts Yahweh's own blessing to the king:

> May he be blessed for ever,
> > his name be confirmed as long as the sun.
> All nations envy his bliss,
> > the tribes of the earth hail him as the Blessed.

Before the king marches to war he offers sacrifice to Yahweh in order to gain his help. In the name of the congregation ('we') the officiating priest pronounces the words of blessing which are to bring fortune and victory, whilst they have at the same time also a note of petition. Thus in Ps. 20:

> May Yahweh answer thee on the day of trouble,
>   the name of the God of Jacob protect thee;
> sending thee help from the sanctuary,
>   and reinforcing thee from Zion.
> May he remember all thy offerings,
>   and be pleased with all thy sacrifices!

And having received Yahweh's answer through the oracle, he can with complete assurance proclaim:

> Now do I certainly know
>   that Yahweh grants victory to his anointed;
> he will hear him from his holy heaven
>   with the saving strength of his right hand.

Ps. 21 begins as a thanksgiving for the blessings which Yahweh has already bestowed on the king: protection, the fulfilment of 'his heart's desire', 'blessings of welfare', 'a golden crown on his head', 'length of days for ever and ever', glory, honour and majesty, and 'joy of thine own presence'; all this is the reward for the king because he has trusted in Yahweh. The second part of the psalm is a promise of victory over his enemies, Yahweh's 'answer' through the officiating priest.

> Thine hand will catch all thine enemies
>   thy right hand will crush those that hate thee ...
> When they intend evil against thee
>   and plot a device, they shall not perform it.
> For thou wilt make them turn their back,
>   aiming thine arrows at their faces ...

The situation seems to be similar to that in the previous psalm.

Ps. 89 is a lament, attributed to the king on a day of penance and prayer after lost battles. It starts in hymnal form with praise of Yahweh's mercy and faithfulness, his mighty power which he proved in the victory over the monsters of the primeval sea and in the creation, and of his previous 'deeds of righteousness', his victorious help for Israel and its king throughout the ages. Then the king mentions Yahweh's covenant with David and his promises never to forsake his seed; he may indeed chastise them 'if they forsake his law and walk not in his commandments', but he has sworn never to fail them:

> His seed shall endure for ever,
>   and his throne as the sun before me.
> It shall be established for ever as the moon,
>   as the faithful witness in heaven.

However—here starts the lament—Yahweh has now 'cast off and

abhorred' his anointed, the reigning king, and 'profaned his crown to the ground':

> Thou hast broken down all his walls
>> and laid his strongholds in ruin . . .
> thou hast also turned the edge of his sword,
>> and hast not made him to stand in the battle.

And at last the prayer: 'How long, Yahweh?'

> Remember, Yahweh, the taunts thrown at thy servants,
>> how I do bear in my bosom the insults of the tribes,
> how thine enemies, Yahweh, have insulted,
>> insulted the heels of thine anointed.

The last line hints at the flight of the defeated king.

But the king may also have reason to celebrate a festival of thanksgiving, and let psalms of thanks be sung after a victory gained and deliverance from death in the battle. Such a royal psalm of thanks is Ps. 18 with its grandiose description of how the king was already in the jaws of death, surrounded by enemies on every side. He saw himself swallowed up by 'the breakers of Death' and 'the floods of (the land of) Destruction'. Then in his distress he called upon the Lord, and Yahweh revealed himself as when he went to fight against chaos and the primeval sea:

> Then the earth shook and trembled,
>> the foundations of the heavens moved . . .
> He rode forth in his cherub [chariot], flying,
>> and swooped with the wings of the wind . . .
> And from heaven Yahweh thundered,
>> the Most High gave his voice.
> Yea, he sent out his arrows and scattered them,
>> he shot out his lightnings, and discomfited them.
> The bed of the ocean then appeared,
>> the earth's foundations were laid bare,
> at thy threatening menace, Yahweh,
>> at the blast of thy nostrils' breath.
> He stretched from on high and took me,
>> he drew me out of great flood;
> he freed me from my foes so strong,
>> from haters far too strong for me . . . .

Thus did Yahweh save him and reward him 'according to his righteousness and the cleanness of his hands', 'his faithfulness to the covenant and his perfection', and the psalm now gives thanks for this help. In the following stanzas he returns to the description of the danger and of the deliverance in the same grandiose style, this time without mythological images, so that one clearly sees that it is a question of war and political enemies.

> Thou gavest me the shield of thy salvation,
>   thy granting my prayer made me strong.
> Thou enlargedst my steps under me
>   and my ankles did not slip.
> I chased my foes and overtook them,
>   I did not turn till they were killed,
> I smote them through, that they could not rise,
>   they fell under my feet.

Thus the king has again been able to secure ascendancy over his enemies:

> Thou deliveredst me from the rage of nations,
>   thou rescuedst me from violent foes,
> thou liftedst me up above mine enemies
>   and madest me the head of (foreign) peoples.
>
> Peoples whom I do not know, become my servants,
>   once they hear of me they render homage,
> strangers yield feigned obedience to me,
>   come trembling out of their hiding places . . . .
>
> And therefore now I thank thee, Yahweh,
>   sing praises to thy name before the nations,
> to him who hath given his king great victories
>   and showed loving kindness to his anointed,
>   to David and to his seed for ever.

It has long been known that this psalm of thanks, both in its construction and its details and the whole conception and description of events, has many analogies with the hymn with which Pharaoh Ramses II celebrated the god Amon in Thebes, after his escape from a critical situation in the battle against the Hittites at Kadesh in the Orontes valley.[97] Of all the psalms this is the one which has the most Egyptian style, and reminds one most directly of hymns to the 'god' Pharaoh, with their highflown descriptions of his majesty's overwhelming victories over all the wretched and wicked 'foreign' nations—poetical descriptions which are not always in accordance with the historical results of the 'victories'. One suspects the composer of Ps. 18 of having studied the poetical art of Egypt, and that he too lays more stress on grandiose description and ebullient enthusiasm than on actual facts.

That the king's wedding with a foreign princess was a religious act to be celebrated with cultic ceremony goes without saying. And the ritual words of blessing and good wishes for bride and bridegroom which belonged to the common man's wedding in the times of the patriarchs and the semi-

---

[97] Translation in Erman, *Lit. d. Aegypter*, pp. 329ff. (E.T., pp. 260ff.).

nomadic state, were surely still more in place at a royal wedding. It is therefore not surprising to find a royal wedding-hymn in the book of Psalms —Ps. 45. The psalmist stands forth as an inspired proclaimer of power-filled, effectual words of blessing:

> My heart bubbles over with luck-bringing words,
> > I recite my (powerful) poem to the king,
> > > my tongue is like the pen of a quick writer.

It is characteristically oriental that he says little about the bride, but much more about the king:

> Kings' daughters are among thy 'jewels',
> > at thy right hand stands the queen in gold of Ophir ...
> The king's daughter is all glory,
> > her clothing (decorated with) corals set in gold,
> > in broidered work she is led unto the king.
> Behind her come virgins, her companions,
> > they are brought unto thee with gladness and rejoicing,
> > > they are led and they enter the king's palace.

The poet has also a word to say to her, a word of counsel from an experienced sage:

> Listen, O daughter, and bend thine ear:
> > forget thine own folk and thy father's house,
> > > then will the king desire thy beauty.
> For he is thy lord, render homage to him.
> > Then the Tyrian traders shall come with gifts,
> > > the richest of the nations shall seek thy favour.

Behind the commonplace sentiments of the counsel there is also a suggestion of the Israelite temple poet's recollections of the evils ensuing for the faithful when a foreign princess like Jezebel was unwilling to forget her father's house, seeing it as her duty to introduce the cult of Baal among Yahweh's people: that must not happen again.

But the greater part of the poem takes the shape of a hymnal description of the king himself:

> Thou art fairer than all the mortals;
> > charm is playing on thy lips
> > > because God hath blessed thee for ever.

The poet describes him as the bold warrior whose 'right hand shall teach him deeds of dread', who 'rides forth prosperously' in his war chariot, and whose 'arrows are sharp in the heart of his enemies'; he is addressed as a god; his sceptre is a 'sceptre of right'; 'thou lovest righteousness and hatest wickedness'; therefore Yahweh has elected him among all his brethren and 'anointed him with the oil of gladness'.

Here too there are marked analogies with other royal hymns of the East, particularly with those of Egypt; but by contrast, in Egypt we often meet with hymns of praise to the divine king, who upholds the world order, creates and secures life and fertility, defends his people against all his enemies, 'rises' (as the sun) over the earth, etc.[98] Ps. 45 is the only example in the whole of Israelite psalm poetry of a true hymn to the king.[99] As regards form it remains within the framework of those effectual words of blessing pronounced according to Yahweh's commission which from the beginning had a place in Israelite cult and ritual, and which had a natural tendency to become a laudatory and promising description of the honour and fortune which will befall the one blest.

It is obvious when we consider this conception of the king—his significance as the people's source of blessing and centre of power, and his place in the cult—that all that concerned him and his house also concerned the people; nothing which happened to him was a purely private affair. The people had the greatest interest in all that concerned him. Everything must be done from the point of view of the official cult to support him as the centre of blessing and prevent anything from happening which might injure his 'soul' and his royal strength and fortune. All misfortunes and dangers which demand divine help become occasions for cultic activities. In case of sickness, sacrifices and prayers were offered up for him along with the ritual purifications which also were necesary. Ps. 28 is, in all probability, a psalm referring to the king's sickness, although it may be uncertain whether this psalm was originally made for this definite occasion or whether an older psalm has been adapted. The suppliant presents himself as 'Yahweh's anointed', and it is suggested that Yahweh by saving his anointed would manifest himself as the 'saving strength' of his people. Hence the petition for the recovery of the king, and the confidence expressed in it, concludes as a prayer to 'save thy people and bless thine inheritance'.

We also learn that when the king has recovered from sickness a thanksgiving is celebrated and a psalm sung, as recorded of king Hezekiah. The hymn of thanks sung on that occasion is preserved in Isa. 38.9ff. At all events the psalm belongs to a cultic thanksgiving festival.[100]

These royal psalms, as we have seen, have arisen out of the prevailing concept of the ideal king which was fundamentally the same throughout the whole of the East—a view of the king which was in no wise primitive, and which differs considerably from the old view of the chief, and which yet has its roots far back in primitive ideas of the powerful 'mana'-being. These royal psalms had their fixed place in the national religious service,

[98] See Erman, *Lit. d. Aegypter*, p. 320 (E.T., p. 256); *ANET*, pp. 373f.

[99] It is worth considering whether the original text of Ps. 21.14 may not have been speaking of the king instead of Yahweh. See note in *BHK*[3] ad loc.

[100] See Begrich, *Der Psalm des Hiskia*. De Boer (*OTS IX*) comes to the same conclusion.

and expressed the generally accepted ideal of the king. They contain therefore no realistic description of the individual historical king and his particular situation. They present the royal ideal, the typical king as he exists in religious theory and in the people's mind and imagination, and as he should be when he appears before God in the cult. The psalms presuppose and describe typical, constantly recurring situations, e.g. the situation at the death of the old king who is represented as a universal king. Before the enthronement of his successor, the vassals might be preparing insurrection (Ps. 2)[100a] or the enemies have overrun the country (Ps. 89), but the deity arises to save his royal son (Ps. 18), etc.

That traits from the old myths here blend in as poetical elements in the picture is quite possible; thus when distress is seen as an actual descent into the realms of death, as in Ps. 18, this goes back finally to accounts of the death of the vegetation god (see below, Chap. VII.5); but one cannot conclude from this that the king here appears in the form and role of the god. The royal psalms give us the idealized portrait of the king even in the normal kingly situations where the king is identical with his people. We see the king as he should be according to the view obtaining in the circle of the psalmist—and, we may add, in the leading religious circles.

But one must also add: it is not simply a copy of the general oriental king-ideal and king-pattern that we find here.

The foregoing short review of some of the prominent royal psalms has again and again given us occasion to point out special Israelite variations and accentuations of the king ideal, and these modifications are the result of the influence of Israel's own particular religion on the borrowed style. As stated above, both in Babylonia and in Egypt the direct 'hymn to the king', who is more or less clearly described and praised as a god, is quite common,[101] but of this type of poem we have only one actual example in the book of Psalms—the wedding psalm, Ps. 45. With this exception the hymn is in Israel reserved for Yahweh himself. And even Ps. 45 is no purely royal hymn; the glorifying description is rooted in the word of blessing which generally takes the form of a description of the glory and fortune which it calls forth for the one blest. It is Yahweh's glorious gift to the king that the psalmist is painting; for it is Yahweh who has provided him with this grace, power and glory. But thus has Yahweh in his wonderful mercy equipped all mankind, says the poet in Ps. 8.

And just because the royal psalms describe the ideal in the light of

---

[100a] It therefore seems like conceding too much to the extreme exponents of a common oriental god-king-ideology in Israel, when Bentzen in his *Sakrale Kongedømme* is willing to accept that the situation given in Ps. 2 as the background of the enthronement of the new king has been taken over from the conception of the rebellion of the powers of chaos against the god. The situation of Ps. 2 was regularly repeated at the death of practically every Assyrian king. See note 89.

[101] See Steindorff and Seele, *When Egypt Ruled the East*, p. 83; Erman-Ranke, *Aegypten*,[2] pp. 72, 76, 466, 469, 471, 473. On Sumerian royal hymns see Kramer, *Sumerian Mythology*, p. 13; see also Zimmern, *König Lipit-Ištar*, pp. 3ff. We often meet with loud echoes of royal hymns in the I-form in the introductions to the Assyrian epigraphs of kings; cf. Mowinckel, *Statholderen Nehemia*, pp. 140ff.; 'Die vorderasiatischen Königs—und Fürsteninschriften' in *Eucharisterion* I, (*Festschrift Gunkel*), pp. 297ff.

religion, it is not without justification that later Judaism has given them a Messianic interpretation, and the Church has taken the psalms' pictures of the king as prophecies of Christ. They sprang from the need for a super-human helper and saviour, the fulfilment of which is Jesus Christ.[102]

5

According to this view of the king and his relation to the deity and to the people and of his position in the divine services, there is no sharp distinction between public and private psalms—those of the congregation, and those of the separate individual. From one point of view the king is a single person who, for instance in a lament, may speak of his ('my') sickness, or of other distress and danger; but still he is something more. It is really the congregation's, the people's fate that is involved when the king, 'our shield', is in distress and danger.

It goes without saying then, that the king played a prominent part at a number of national cultic festivals, as, for instance, on the days of prayer that were arranged before a war or after a defeat (Chap. VI.1) or at a thanksgiving after victory (Chap. IX).

Thus, when in national hymns of thanks or lamentation, as e.g. Pss. 44 and 66, we meet with a narratory 'I', there can be no doubt that this is the king, or at best a high ranking representative of the congregation— the high priest or the provincial governor or the president of the pro-vincial council—who is here speaking on behalf of the community.

The *royal psalms* in this extended sense are thus really *congregational psalms*. This is the grain of truth in Smend's theory about the so-called 'collective I', which simply took the narratory 'I' as a personification of the congregation (see above, pp. 45f.). In this form the theory is in-correct; there are plenty of cases in which the speaker ranges himself, as an individual person, alongside 'his brethren' in 'the great assembly', that is to say, he is plainly not identical with 'the great assembly', i.e. the congregation, but is a single person in the midst of the congregation. But on some occasions he represents all the others and speaks on their behalf and is in so far one with them. In most of these cases this person is the king.

6

What has been said above has really a much wider bearing.

Many of the set phrases and images which recur in the formally pure 'I'-psalms, are of such a nature as to exclude the possibility of their having been connected with any private person; they evidently refer to some king or great chieftain. The frequent war pictures,[103] to begin with, point in this direction. The matter is still plainer when the petitioner speaks of how 'the peoples', 'peoples and kings', 'all the nations', are interested in his

---

[102] Cf. for this von Rad in *ZATW* 58, 1940–41, pp. 216ff.
[103] See for instance Pss. 3.7; 27.3; 55.22, and many other places.

welfare.[104] It is the royal and divine symbol that the petitioner borrows when he speaks of 'lifting his horn'.[105] Also the near relationship in which many psalms place the petitioner to Yahweh—as e.g. that he is Yahweh's particular 'servant'—go beyond what the private individual in the old times could take it upon himself to say. It was the king—or the priest and the prophet[106]—who stood in such a particular servant relationship to the national god.

All this points to the fact that in Israel, as in Babylonia and Egypt, the psalms—together with the corresponding august cultic dispositions—were originally intended, not for all and sundry, but for the king and the great.[107] The style of the psalms in all these places shows clear traces of the original conditions.

This is really what was originally meant by the heading *lĕdhāwĭdh*, which is usually translated 'by David'. In Israel it was in later times undoubtedly taken as an indication of authorship; this is, among other things, seen from the twelve psalms where to this note has been added information as to *when* David composed or sang the psalm in question. But this interpretation is in many cases impossible; for the expression is also found above psalms which must be more recent than the time of David, since, for instance, they refer to the Temple in Jerusalem (Pss. 24; 64, etc.). In Ps. 18 the petitioning king describes himself as the descendant of David, and in Ps. 132 he begs for Yahweh's blessing 'for David's sake'.[108] The linguistically natural translation of *lĕdhāwĭdh* is 'for David', cf. the heading in Ps. 102: 'a prayer of the afflicted' (i.e. for the use of someone in such a situation), 'who poureth out his complaint before the Lord'. The psalms were composed for the use of, and were in due time used by 'David'—that is to say, in most cases, by a king of the house of David. Such information was a good recommendation for the psalm; a psalm which helped a man of good fortune, like David, must needs be pleasing to God and effective, a useful prayer. This interpretation of the expression[109] was thought to be confirmed by recent discoveries at Mari, where the word *davidum* was said to occur as the title of a chief or king, used in particular among semi-nomadic tribes.[110]

---

[104] Pss. 7.7, 9; 9.5; 18.50; 56.8; 57.10;.59.9; 138.4.
[105] Ps. 92.11; 1 Sam. 2.1; cf. Pss. 75.5, 11; 148.14; 89.18; 132.17.
[106] See Lindhagen, *The Servant Motif in the O.T.* L. thinks that the use of the epithet is everywhere due to a transfer from the 'king ideology'. But being originally cultic, its connexion with the priest is sure to be older than that with the king.
[107] See Jastrow, *Relig. Babyl. u. Assyr.* II, pp. 106f., 117; Meissner, *Babyl.-assyr. Literatur*, pp. 37ff.; *Ps. St.* VI, p. 74.
[108] For details see *Ps. St.* VI, pp. 2ff.
[109] See *Ps. St.* VI, pp. 72ff. Eerdmans likewise arrived at this conception of *lĕdhāwĭdh*, see *Hebr. Book of Pss.* (*OTS* IV), pp. 36ff.
[110] See Dossin in *Syria* XIX, 1938, pp. 109f.; Bentzen, *Sakrale kongedömme*, pp. 54f. [But Tadmor in JNES XVII, 1958, pp. 129ff., refutes this suggestion.] In Ugarit the king 'sealing a contract in which he participates, or one that he witnesses and so guarantees, does not seal in his own name, but in that of the founder of the dynasty'. 'This practice had already been noticed in the neighbouring city of Alalakh' (N. Nougayrol in *Academie des Inscriptions et Belles-Lettres*, see *Manchester Guardian*, April 18th, 1952, p. 5).

In later times the expression was taken to refer to the author, and naturally to David himself; a notion which in its turn led to the descriptions of situations contained in the headings of several psalms, which have been deduced—as a rule not very convincingly—from the contents of the psalm itself (see below, Chap. XVI.5).

We must consequently look upon many of the 'I-psalms' as really royal psalms, and therefore psalms of the people and the congregation. In numerous other cases however it is very difficult to decide definitely what they are, the reason being that the description of the Psalmist's situation and of his enemies is usually couched in such general and in part stereotyped imagery that it is far from easy—at times impossible—to judge whether it is a question of national or private need and trouble. We shall return to this later (see Chaps. VII, VIII.5, 6).

The view that the narratory 'I' in the psalms mainly represents the king is supported by the fact that this has been proved to be the case in Babylonian-Assyrian (and Egyptian) psalms. There too the elaborate cultic ceremonies with hymn singing, etc. were originally intended for the king and his family and high officials, and the style and imagery of the psalms are completely coloured by this intention. Many of the preserved texts give the name of the king for whom they have been composed or by whom they have been used; others have come down in several versions, of which one mentions the name of one king, another that of a different one. In some copies we read: 'I, N. N. the son of N. N.'. This suggests that these royal psalms might at a later stage be used by or for other persons in connexion with cleansing from sin or sickness or some other evil. In other words, it would seem that a democratization of the cult and the religion had taken place.[111]

7

There is every indication that such a democratization—and individualization—of religion did take place in Israel. Yahweh has gradually become, not only the god of the whole people as in the earliest time, and the god of kings, chiefs, priests, and prophets—as official and cultic representatives of the whole—but the god of the common man and woman as well. This, of course, does not imply that Yahweh was not also from the first the god of the common member of the tribe and the people. Abraham's servant prays to the god of his master Abraham (Gen. 24.12) and Samuel's mother approaches Yahweh with a prayer regarding so private a matter as that of being granted a son (1 Sam. 3). But in the official religion during the monarchy it was the king and the great officials and the cultic ministrants who stood in a particularly near relation to Yahweh and acted as intermediaries between him and the common people. To them the layman generally applied, begging for their intercession, if he wished to obtain

[111] See Additional Note V.

some favour from Yahweh.[112] But a change gradually came about. Whereas in the remoter times the layman spoke to the king and the other great men, or to special men of religion like priests and prophets, of Yahweh, as 'thy God',[113] he can in later times speak of 'our' or 'my' God.[114] The thought gradually gains ground that Yahweh especially cares for the lowly, the widow and the fatherless and the stranger, who have no other help.[115] An important part in this 'individualization' of religion was without doubt played by the personal prayer life of the great prophets with their prayers both intercessory[116] and personal;[117] in at least some measure this life of prayer would be adopted by their disciples and adherents. This fact has been of importance for the Jewish conception of the relation between Yahweh and the individual.

With this development the old royal psalms of the temple service took on a new meaning.

The Temple in Jerusalem was, to begin with, what we might call a royal chapel, a 'royal sanctuary' (Am. 7.10). It is most probable—considering, among other things, the prophets' dislike of pretentious cultic and ritual ceremonies—that in Israel, ritual acts that took place on behalf of a common individual were of a much simpler kind. As a rule they were probably enacted in the local sanctuary, or still more simply in the village. Here the ritual no doubt had a much more ancient and less elaborate form than in the temple rites of Jerusalem, a fact which can be faintly discerned behind the cultic and ritual legislation of the Priestly Code. The local rites took over many forms from older Canaanite and other oriental cults.

A decisive epoch in the history of the temple cult of Jerusalem was introduced with the restoration of the Jewish congregation after the fall of the kingdom. The cult was restored in the old forms, according to old rules and ritual, as is evident from the wealth of old tradition and material which became included in the ritual laws of the priestly code, and also from late psalms in which the old style has been faithfully followed. But the central figure itself—the king and his house—has gone. His place has been taken over by the high priest, partly also by the governor. The Temple becomes a place of pilgrimage and worship[118] for Jews and proselytes from many lands, who come with their purely personal needs and submit themselves to the prescribed rules of the place. The private individual becomes a more important member of the congregation than he had ever been as a member of the corporate national body; his participation or non-participation now depends much more upon himself. Far more than

[112] Gen. 20.7; Ex. 14.5; 15.25; 17.4; 32.11ff.; Num. 11.2; 21.7; 1 Sam. 2.25; Isa. 37.4; Jer. 42.1ff.; 37.3ff.
[113] Ps. 89.27; 2 Sam. 24.3; 14.11, 17; 1 Kgs. 18.10.
[114] Neh. 1.6, 11; 2.8, 12, 18; 5.19; 13.14, 22, 29, 31; Ezra 7.6, 28; 9.6; Sir. 51.1f.; Tob. 3.14; 13.13; Judith 9.4; 16.2; Esth. 13.15 (G).
[115] See for instance 1 Sam. 2.5, 7f.; Pss. 10.14, 18; 18.28; 68.6f.; 113.6f.; Prov. 15.25; Deut. 10.17f.; 24.17f.
[116] Am. 7.2, 5; Jer. 17.16; 11.14; 14.11.
[117] Isa. 8.17; Jer. 11.18f.; 12.1ff.; 15.10ff.; 17.17ff.; 18.18ff.; 20.7ff.
[118] Isa. 56.7; 60.7 (GTMMM III); cf. 1 Kgs. 8.31ff., 41ff.

before Yahweh becomes the god of the individual person. What previously only a priest or a prophet or a king might say to Yahweh is adopted by the common man. The elaborate ritual which in Jerusalem was originally designed for the cleansing of the king or the high officials from their sin and sickness, was in the ritual rules of Leviticus made applicable to any Jew—though occasionally with a certain distinction between rich and poor (see e.g. Lev. 5.7ff.). The book of Job contains direct evidence that the common man and woman in Jewish times presented themselves in the Temple in sickness and distress, and after recovery and other mercies received, in order to offer the various sacrifices and have the appropriate psalm sung.[119] We see the same in Ps. 107, which recounts the different categories of members of the congregation who have made their vows in distress and are now bearing forth offerings and singing psalms of thanksgiving (see Chap. X.3).

It is therefore quite possible—nay, probable—that use was made in ritual acts of texts and psalms which were originally composed for the king, and that furthermore new psalms were composed in the same style, but now for the use of Everyman. The fixity of the stylistic tradition and poetical language led to the old expressions—originally connected with the king—being taken over and continued even where new hymns were composed. This is a further reason for caution when seeking to distinguish between congregational and personal psalms.

[119] Job 33.24-25; cf. Duhm, *Das Buch Hiob*, p. 162. It is interesting to notice that Duhm is here actually anticipating Gunkel's cultic psalm interpretation and that he has seen the connexion between the thanksgiving psalm and the ritual thank-offering. Only it is a pity that so little of this is to be found in Duhm's own psalm commentary.

CHAPTER IV

The Hymn of Praise

The first of the main types to be described is the hymn or song of praise.[1] The Psalter contains many examples of this kind, e.g. Pss. 8; 19; 29; 33; 46; 47; 48; 76; 104; 135; 136; 145–150, which are all typical. To these we may add the three fragments of a hymn of praise which are now embedded in the book of Amos, as 4.12f., 13; 5.8f.; 9.5f.[1a]

I

The core of the hymn of praise is the consciousness of the poet and congregation that they are standing face to face with the Lord himself, meeting the almighty, holy and merciful God in his own place, and worshipping him with praise and adoration. He is in their midst, and they are his chosen people, who owe him everything. Therefore they now meet him, with awe and trembling because he is the Holy One, but also with a sure trust, love, jubilation and overflowing enthusiasm, while remembering all the great and glorious things that he has done. From the encounter with the Holy One, from the reverence and trust, the gratitude, joy and enthusiasm, the song of praise thus rises to the Lord of Hosts, to express what the congregation is seeing and feeling, and to increase his glory in the world. This is the fountain-head from which all the characteristic features of the hymn, too, all its elements of matter and form, must be conceived as taking their rise.[1b]

The hymn opens with the exhortation to sing unto the Lord, to praise,

---

[1] See Gunkel-Begrich, *Einleitung*, pp. 32–94, as also for the sources and evidences of the characteristic individual features of the hymn style; Gunkel gives fairly complete statistics, but Westermann's painstaking analysis (*Das Loben Gottes im A.T.*) does not give much of importance beyond Gunkel.

[1a] These verses have no connexion whatever, either syntactically or logically, with the context of the sayings of Amos; they obviously belong to the same set and are fragments of a 'psalm' in which each stanza ended with the refrain 'Yahweh, the God of Hosts is his name'. The collectors of the book of Amos have inserted a stanza or two in such places as speak of Yahweh's appearing for judgement with the intention of underlining His majesty and power. Cf. *GTMMM* III, pp. 634f.; H. Schmidt, D. *Mythos vom wiederkehrenden König*, p. 29; *Thronfahrt Jahwes*, p. 22.

[1b] Westermann's idea (*Das Loben Gottes im A.T.*) that the origin of the hymn of praise is to be found in some vague urge to praise God for the experience of His interference in history is gainsaid by the fact that this type is found in all religions, even those in which the thought of God's work and witness in history has no place. And when W. considers this urge to be the 'Sitz im Leben' of the hymn of praise, he at any rate gives to this term another meaning, quite different from the one ascribed to it by Gunkel and form-critical and cult-historical research. That the hymn of praise has its setting in the cult cannot be denied, see below, p. 136. The religio-psychological problem is a different question.

thank, exalt and bless him, to fall down and worship him, to proclaim him, to 'clap your hands and shout unto God', etc.—usually in the imperative plural.[2] It is in fact the precentor's exhortation to the choir which re-echoes in this 'introit'.[3] Occasionally the exhortation is inclusive: 'O come, let us sing',[4] or still more personally: 'I will praise the Lord', and similar expressions. The 'I' may originally have meant the leader of the choir or the cultic act, the spokesman of the congregation. But it was also appropriate to express the poet's personal and emotional relation to his theme, his identification of himself with what he had to say.[5] The introit may be repeated before every new subdivision or stanza of the hymn, and is reflected in the responsory 'Hallelujah'.

Then those to whom the exhortation is directed are mentioned, generally in some expression or other referring to the congregation: Yahweh's servants (i.e. worshippers), Jacob's or Zion's sons, Yahweh's faithful, 'the righteous', 'they that fear the Lord', etc., that is: Israel as a cultic congregation.[6] At times it is even, with poetic enthusiasm, directed to the whole earth, to all that lives, to peoples and kings and princes,[7] heaven and earth, woods and rocks and sea,[8] even to the heavenly powers ('sons of God'),[9] or to the dead.[10] The personal note in the exhortation finds its complete realization when it is directed to the poet's own 'soul'.[11]

In the exhortation Yahweh's name is always mentioned.[12] To this is sometimes added a series of laudatory (hymnal) attributes: 'The most High', 'Israel's God', or 'King' or 'Creator', 'our King', 'our Defence', etc.[13] This may be varied in such a way that the poet exhorts his hearers to praise 'the name of the Lord',[14] his glory, his power, his deeds, and great works, his wonders, his mercy and faithfulness, in a word, his great and glorious qualities.[15] In such wise is the theme and the aim of the hymn set forth.

[2] See references in Gunkel-Begrich, *Einl.*, p. 33. Instances: Pss. 33.3; 96.1, 2; 98.1;– 113.1; 117.1; — 32.2 (thanksgiving psalm); 105.1; 106.1; — 99.5, 9; — 96.2; 134.1f.; — 29.2b; —47.2; 81.2; 100.1 (*hārı̄'û* indicates the shout of homage *tĕrû'â*); 33.1; 81.2; 98.4.
[3] Cf. Pss. 118.2–4; 134.1; 135.19f.
[4] Pss. 95.1, 2; 11.24; 79.13 ('promise' within a psalm of lamentation, see Chap. VI. 3); 115.18, etc.; see Gunkel-Begrich, *Einl.*, p. 34.
[5] Ps. 111.1; Ex. 15.1; Pss. 9.2f.; 104.33; 22.23, etc.; see Gunkel-Begrich, *Einl.*, p. 38.
[6] Pss. 113.1; 134.1; 135.1; — 105.6; 149.2; — 145.10; 149.5; — 33.1; — 22.24, etc.; see Gunkel-Begrich, *Einl.* pp. 35f. For the sense of the terms, 'the righteous', 'the godly', etc., see below, pp. 242ff.
[7] Pss. 33.8; 96.1, 9; 98.4; 100.1; 145.21; 150.6; — 22.28; 96.7; 47.2; 68.33; 138.4; 148.11; see Gunkel-Begrich, *Einl.*, p. 36.
[8] Ps. 96.11f.; cf. Isa. 44.23 (prophetic imitation of the style).
[9] Pss. 29.1; 103.20ff. (thanksgiving psalm in hymnic style); 148.2.
[10] Ps. 22.30 (rd. *kol-yĕshēnê 'ereṣ*; hymnic 'promise', see n. 4).
[11] Pss. 104.1; 146.1; cf. 103.1 (a thanksgiving psalm). See Gunkel-Begrich, *Einl.*, p. 39.
[12] For instance Ps. 27.6 (hymnic introduction to a psalm of lamentation, see below, IV. 4); 33.1; 66.1; 81.2; 95.1; 96.1, etc.; see Gunkel-Begrich, *Einl.*, p. 40.
[13] Pss. 9.5 (hymnic introduction, see IV. 4); 92.2 (thanksgiving psalm); 150.1; — 71.22 (hymnic thanksgiving in a psalm of lamentation); 81.2; 149.2; — 47.7; 66.8; 81.2; 95.1; 144.1 (hymnic introduction), and other places; see Gunkel-Begrich, *Einl.*, p. 40.
[14] Pss. 9.3 (see n. 13); 22.23 (see n. 10); 29.2; 92.2; 96.2; 113.1; 135.1, etc.
[15] Pss. 9.12 (see n. 13); 71.8, 18 (see n. 13); 89.2 (hymnic introduction to a lament); 92.3; 96.2, 3; 145.4, 10, 11, 12; 150.2 and other places, see Gunkel-Begrich, *Einl.*, p. 41.

Frequently the mode which the praise is to take is also indicated: 'with harp', 'with the psaltery and an instrument of ten strings', 'with dance', etc.[16] All the significant elements of the introit to the hymn are found together in Ps. 149.1–3.

> Sing unto Yahweh a new song,
>> his praise in the congregation of covenanters!
> Let Israel rejoice in his creator,
>> the sons of Zion be joyful in their King!
> Let them dance in praise of his name,
>> make melody to him with timbrel and lyre!

It is interesting to see how many variations the poets have been able to produce by combining these traditional elements in different ways, and how rich and varied the traditional hymn-style has thus become. The whole of Ps. 150 is, from the point of view of form, just one richly varied introit; praise is implicit throughout the very exhortation itself.

The theme is then further developed in the main body of the hymn. It generally begins with the ground for the exhortation, introduced by a 'for', 'because', e.g. Praise the Lord, 'for he is good'.[17] In this short motivatory section the whole hymn is contained as in a nutshell. The oldest hymns were, it seems, constant repetitions of the reasoned exhortation to praise and jubilation, such as: Praise the Lord, 'for his kindness endureth for ever'. The germinal cell of the hymn is just this again and again repeated jubilant mention of Yahweh's deeds and qualities, such as the short reverential cry of joy that recurs like a refrain in the Greek Dionysos-hymn: 'Worthy bull!'[18] The main body of the hymn gradually grew by the addition of further motivations with more and more praiseworthy works and qualities (těhillôth). Beside the motivated main clause the appositional nouns or participles[19] which we usually translate by relative clauses—'(he) who does so and so'—or explanatory relative sentences are often used.[20]

This interplay between repetition and accretion is clearly demonstrated in Ps. 136, where the first part of each period consists of a praising participle in apposition to 'Yahweh', and the second part of the reiterated motivation, 'for his kindness endureth for ever'.

In consequence of this development the main body of the hymn usually consists of a series of short sentences each of which mentions some praiseworthy deed or quality. Yahweh is as a rule the subject in these sen-

---

[16] Pss. 33.1; 149.2f.; 150.3–5, etc.

[17] Ps. 135.3; Ex. 15.21; cf. Ps. 13.6 (hymnic 'promise', see n. 4).

[18] Cf. Heiler, Das Gebet,[4] pp. 160f. Cf. the short paean of victory of the Ama-zulus, consisting of two constantly repeated lines, see Blessing-Dahle in Festschrift Meinhof.

[19] See Gunkel-Begrich, Einl., pp. 43f., 33ff.—See, for instance, Pss. 18.2; 65.6; 89.8 (see n. 15); — 9.12 (see n. 13); 103.3–5 (see n. 9); 114.8; 136.3–7; 147.8, 9, 14–17, and other places.

[20] For instance Pss. 46.9; 66.20; 124.6 (public thanksgiving psalm, see Chap. IX); 135.8; 136.23; cf. Gen. 24.27; 1 Sam. 25.32, 39. See Gunkel-Begrich, Einl., pp. 43f.

tences,[21] but sometimes it is his name, his arm, his right hand, or one of his qualities or works: his voice, his word, his dominion, his honour and glory, his mercy, his throne.[22]

These short sentences generally speak of Yahweh's qualities, his permanent divine attributes; consequently they mostly have the form of appositions, relative clauses and nominal clauses. Besides these we have sentences that describe what he is regularly or repeatedly doing, with the verb in the participle, perfect or imperfect. E.g. 'Yahweh looks from heaven, beholding all mankind: from his abode he scans all the inhabitants of the earth' (33.17f.). 'Yahweh sets the captives free, Yahweh gives the blind their sight, Yahweh raises those who are bowed down, Yahweh preserves poor foreigners, the widow and the orphan He relieves' (146.7–9).[22a]

A prominent place in the hymns of praise, however, is taken by such sentences as speak of Yahweh's special deeds in history—and to the minds of the ancient Israelites even creation, the victory over the primeval monsters, belongs to history. Such sentences have the form of statements (narrative clauses), with the verb in the perfect, imperfect, narrative imperfect, or consecutive imperfect. Examples: 'for He spoke, and (things) came into existence, He commanded, and it appeared' (33.9). 'The world and the fullness thereof, thou hast founded them, the north and the south, thou hast created them' (89.11f.). 'Yahweh hath chosen Jacob to be his, and Israel as his prized possession' (135.4).[23] Besides such short examples we also find longer descriptions, as e.g. in Ps. 104.6ff.:

> Once the primordial ocean covered (the earth),
>   the waters rose over the mountains:
> but they retired by thy rebuke,
>   scared at the sound of thy thunder . . .
> never to pass thine appointed bounds,
>   never to cover the earth again.

[21] As a rule in 3rd person: 24.1f.; 29; 33.1–2; 46; 47; 81.2–6; 95.1–7; 96; 98; 100; 103; 105; 111; 113; 117; 134; 146; 147; 148; 149; 150;. Very seldom in the 2nd person throughout the whole psalm: 8; 65; 139.1–18; cf. Isa. 25.1–5. More often a mixture of 3rd and 2nd person: 9.6–13; 48; 66.1–12; 67; 68; 76; 77.14; 84; 89.2f., 6–19; 92; 97; 99; 104; 135; 145; Ex. 15. See Gunkel-Begrich, *Einl.*, p. 47.

[22] His name: Pss. 8.2; 9.3; 75.2; 76.2; 96.2; 102.13; 111.9; 113.3; 135.3, 13; 148.13. His arm or hand: 48.11; 49.14; Ex. 15.6. His voice: Ps. 29. His words: 12.7; 18.31; 33.4. His testimonies (i.e. promises): 93.5. His commandments: 19.8ff. His eyes: 11.4; 33.18; 34.16; 66.7. His face: 34.17. His plans and thoughts: 33.11; 92.6. His deeds: 33.9; 66.3; 86.8; 92.6; 104.24; 111.2, 3, 7. His wonders: 9.2; 96.3. His ways: 18.31; 25.10; 77.14; Deut. 32.4. His judgments; Pss. 36.7; 48.12; 97.8; 105.7. His dominion and empire; 103.19; 45.13. His throne: 11.4; 93.2. His highness and glory: 8.2; 68.35; 138.5; 145.3; 148.13. His *tĕhillôth* (praises): 48.11; 111.10. His 'mercy and grace and slowness to anger': 103.8; 145.8. His goodness and faithfulness: 31.20; 36.6, 8; 57.11; 63.4; 86.13; 89.3, 15; 100.5; 103.11, 17; 136. His justice (i.e. his saving activity): 36.7; 111.3. His wisdom: 147.5.

[22a] Other instances: Pss. 5.13; 9.9; 11.4–6; 25.8f.; 29.3, 5f., 8; 33.5, 7, 10; 36.7; 68.7, 20, 36; 84.12; 90.3, 5; 97.10; 103.6, 9f., 13f.; 111.5; 135.6, 14; 138.6; 145.14, 16, 19f.; 147.6, 11, 18; 148.14.

[23] Further examples: Ex. 15.2, 21; Pss. 16.7; 22.25; 24.2; 28.6; 31.22; 52.11; 54.9; 59.17; 66.20; 86.13; 92.5; 95.5; 100.3; 102.26; 103.19; 111.4, 6, 9; 147.13; 1 Sam. 2.8c. See Gunkel-Begrich, *Einl.*, pp. 51f.

Cf. also the description of the crossing of the Jordan in Ps. 114, or the struggle against the primordial dragon in Ps. 74.13–17—in itself a national public psalm of lamentation, but with hymnal motivations of the prayer.[23a]

At times there may also occur the more sentimental, admiring, rhetorical questions: 'Who is like Yahweh?' or an exclamation,[24] or the indicative statement,[25] 'There is no one holy as Yahweh, no rock like our God'. The last form may also become a juxtaposition of Yahweh and other deities: 'For all the gods of the nations are idols: but Yahweh made the heavens'.[26]

It may be due to later developments that hymns occasionally give a more graphic and epic description of one of Yahweh's great works—particularly of the creation, as in Pss. 8; 29; and 104—or of one of his qualities, for instance his superiority over all cosmic and terrestrial enemies. In such cases where the epic-mythical tendency comes to the fore, it presents Yahweh's superiority in the guise of one great mythico-historical victory over all enemies at once, as in Pss. 46; 48; and 76. This is particularly in evidence in the epiphany and enthronement psalms (see below, Chap. V).

But in this epic-mythical form there remains also an original trait from the cultic experience: the hymn concentrates on the praise of that particular act of salvation which Yahweh has now come to the festival to renew; and the description of this circumstance is introduced as an epic strain in the song. At this point, the brief, enumerative style with the independent quasi-detached single sentences is replaced by a broader, more graphic description.

There thus arise *two main types* of hymns: first, the more general one which simply enumerates or points out God's lasting qualities and glorious deeds, a form which may suit any cultic occasions, both daily and festal; secondly, the more special one, which more fully depicts one particular feature of divine activity, a single fundamental act of salvation, a single situation in his both self-assertive and protective struggle. The second type appears to belong to one particular kind of cultic festival, and celebrates Yahweh for the salvation, or the great work, which is to be remembered. Hymns of this type are e.g. Pss. 46; 48; 76; 114.

A representative sample of the first type is Ps. 136:

> O give thanks unto Yahweh, for he is good:
>> for his kindness endureth for ever . . .
> to him who alone doeth wonders,
> to him whose wisdom made the heavens,
> to him who stretched out the earth above the waters,
> to him who made the great lights . . .

[23a] Further examples: Pss. 31.8f.; 44.3f.; 66.10–12; 71.19f.; 77.16–21; 80.9–12; 89.11–13; 99.6–8; 135.9–12; 148.5f.; see Gunkel-Begrich, *Einl.*, p. 52. Several of these psalms are psalms of lamentation with hymnic 'motivations of the prayer' (see below, Chap. VI. 3).

[24] For instance Pss. 8.2, 10; 36.8; 66.3; 92.6; 104.24; 106.2; 113.5; Ex. 15.11. See Gunkel-Begrich, *Einl.*, p. 54f.

[25] 1 Sam. 2.2; Deut. 33.26; Ps. 86.8; see Gunkel-Begrich, *Einl.*, p. 55. On the psalm Deut. 33.2–5, 26–29 see Mowinckel, *Der Achtundsechzigste Psalm*, pp. 75ff. and below, Chap. V, n. 136.

[26] Pss. 96.5; 146.5ff.; Gunkel-Begrich, *Einl.*, pp. 55f.

to him who killed Egypt's firstborn,
and brought out Israel from among them . . .
to him who divided the Reed Lake in sunder
and made Israel to pass through it . . .
who giveth food to all flesh!
o give thanks to the God of heaven!

Each line is here marked by the antiphonic 'for his kindness endureth for ever', two choirs—or a choir-master and a choir—alternately singing a line.

Another typical sample of the appositional style may be found in the book of Amos, in the fragments of a hymn of praise about Yahweh as creator and ruler of the universe: He

who formed the mountains and created the winds,
    who reveals to man what is in His mind,
who made the dawn and the darkness,
    who marches over the heights of the earth . . .
who made the Pleiades and Orion . . .
    who turns the darkness into dawn
and darkens the day into night,
    who calls upon the waters of the sea
        and pours them out on the surface of the earth.

The other type is more varied and often employs the traditional forms in a free manner. The introductory exhortation may be lacking, and the psalm may open with a revering and glorifying exclamation:

O Yahweh our Lord, how excellent
    is thy name in all the earth (Ps. 8.2.)

Or with a statement:

In Judah has God made himself known
    his name is great in Israel (Ps. 76.2.)

Great is Yahweh, and greatly to be praised
    in the city of our God (Ps. 48.2.)

God is shelter and stronghold for us,
    as a help in trouble he is always found (Ps. 46.2.)

The praise itself, the principal part of the hymn, may take the form of a series of declarations of confidence, with more or less detailed and graphic reference to the relevant acts of salvation. Thus, for instance, in Ps. 46, which goes on as follows:

Therefore will we not fear, though the earth be removed,
   though the mountains move in the midst of the sea.
May the sea roar and its water be troubled,
   may the mountains shake by its haughtiness:
Yahweh the Almighty[27] is with us;
   the God of Jacob is our refuge.   (Ps. 46.3–4.)

Following this reference to the victory over the primeval sea is a mention of the wondrous 'river of God' which is now safeguarding and sanctifying Jerusalem; further, we hear of the Lord's presence in his Temple—the victory over all the peoples of the earth which his coming will secure, the subjugation of all evil powers, and the peace which he establishes on earth. The psalm ends with Yahweh calling his enemies to submission and declaring that he alone is God:

Be still and know that I am God,
   high over the nations, high over the earth.   (v. 10.)

The final refrain sums up the conclusion and repeats once more the chief subject of the psalm: the people's unshakable trust in the only, almighty God, who has again shown that he 'is with us'. Higher praise than the confession that it builds its whole existence on this trust, the congregation cannot give.

At times these special festal hymns may contain an almost epic description of the divine act of deliverance which is praised, as for instance the account of 'the king's' advance on Jerusalem in Ps. 48, and of the annihilation of the enemies on the appearance of Yahweh. See also the description in Ps. 114 of how the sea fled and the Jordan was driven back, and 'the mountains leaped like rams', when Yahweh led Israel out of Egypt and made a covenant with her on Mount Sinai, and the poet's ironical triumphant question: 'What ails thee, sea, that thus thou fleest? Thou Jordan, that thou makest way?' Or the description of Yahweh's victory over the nations in Ps. 76.2–7.

The praising clauses may be varied by an exhortation to the congregation to come and see the great work which the Lord has now accomplished:

Come and see the deeds of Yahweh . . .
   who maketh wars to cease unto the ends of the earth,
breaking the bow and snapping the spear
   and burning the shields in the fire.   (Ps. 46.9–10.)

Or, by a statement:

As we have heard, we now have seen
   in the city of our God.   (Ps. 48.9.)

---

[27] For this interpretation of *yhwh ṣĕbā 'ôth* see Eissfeldt, 'Jahwe Zebaoth' in *Miscellanea Academ. Berolin.*, 1950, pp. 126ff. Maag ('Jahwäs Heerscharen' in *Köhler-Festschrift*, p. 50) sees in *ṣĕbā'ôth* 'die depotenzierten mythischen Naturmächte Kanaans'.

In the background we find everywhere the traditional elements and forms of the hymn; but the composition itself is very far from following any set pattern or schedule.

The subject of the hymn of praise is, as already mentioned, Yahweh's glorious qualities and his great works, both those which he regularly repeats in nature—including the creation, which at an early stage became a main subject of the hymn of praise—and his great deeds in history, especially in the history of Israel. Particularly in later psalm-poetry, which is influenced by the wisdom-poetry and its didactic, admonitory tendency (see below, Chap. XVII), the wonderful works of Yahweh in ancient times, the election at the time of Moses and at the occupation of Canaan, became a favourite subject, as in Pss. 78 and 105; here there is a marked admonitory strain.

But Yahweh may also be praised more indirectly, by exalting all that belongs to him: his Temple, his holy city, and the blessings which flow from that place where the fountain of life is and where strength is to be found.

> Blessed are they that dwell in thy house:
> 　　they shall ever be praising thee.
> Blessed the man whose strength is through thee,
> 　　in whose heart are the paved ways . . .
> They are the stronger as they go
> 　　till they see the God in Zion.　(Ps. 84.5, 6, 8.)

And of Zion it is said:

> The singers like the dancers (are praising thee):
> 　　'All my springs are in thee'.　(Ps. 87.7.)

But beneath the praise of the hymn lingers something of the old idea that Yahweh in the festal cult repeats his great works and acts of deliverance; the congregation praises him for what they have themselves experienced; the particular great deed that he has come to the festival to perform again becomes an important subject for the praise. This is particularly clear in the epiphany hymns (see below, pp. 92, 94f.).

The song of praise endeavours to glorify Yahweh to the utmost, to increase his power and renown. Joy, enthusiasm and adoration are its dominant moods. They refer to God himself, not to the needs of man; hence the hymn rarely ends with a prayer (see below, p. 89). Man falls down in worship of the only God, the Holy One.[28] From this, however, faith gains new power. The hymn of praise 'gives power' to Yahweh (Ps. 29.1), but it also provides the congregation with new strength and faith.[29] In the first beginnings of the hymn the naïve idea of flattering the

---

[28] Cf. also Eissfeldt, ' "Mein Gott" im A.T.', *ZATW* 61, 1945–48, p. 11.
[29] Ps. 84.8. Cf. Ex. 15.2; Isa. 12.2.

deity, of 'smoothing the face of Yahweh' and mollifying him, no doubt played a part; but the deepest motif is the adoration of the Holy One, the experiencing of him as the 'terrible' and the 'glorious', he that humbles and raises up, that 'abases and exalts'.

The hymns of praise express the consciousness of standing before Yahweh personally and of experiencing him as he really is. At the festivals—and particularly at the harvest and new year festival, the chief annual festival (see Chap. V), all Yahweh's great deeds and acts of deliverance were recalled; then the coming of Yahweh and his 'salvation' was experienced; it is the eventuating God, the God who 'reveals himself' and 'saves', to whom the festal hymn is addressed. He, indeed, proves 'terrible' to all enemies, both his own and those of Israel, but is full of kindness and faithfulness and 'saving justice' towards his loyal folk. The hymn greets him as he returns at the festal service to abide with his people and work all his wonders anew. Hence trust becomes one of the dominant moods of the hymn.

Occasionally the hymn closes with a brief wish or *prayer* for the future prosperity of the congregation (Pss. 29.11; 104.31f.; 135.19), or of the poet himself (Pss. 19.14f.; 138.8). As a rule it is couched in general terms. Stylistically this is a relic from the mixed, less pure types of older times (see below, pp. 95f.), rather than evidence of a later mixture of styles. But this kind of conclusion does express a deep and original religious need: to give up oneself and one's cause to such a glorious and mighty God, and to know oneself safe in his care. We find it in some of the most characteristic and personal hymns, e.g. Pss. 84; 104; 125. We meet, in Israel, too, with a phenomenon which is very common in the cultic songs of Babylonia and Assyria, in which a fully formed hymn of praise is used as an introduction to a lament or a petition. A good instance is Pss. 9–10, really one psalm. It is natural that the trust here comes markedly into prominence beside the praise, as is also the case in Pss. 90 and 139. In the same way a psalm of thanksgiving and trust may be used as introduction to a psalm of petition, as in Pss. 27 and 40.

The hymn was recited to the playing of stringed intruments, cymbals and the flute, to which there is frequent reference (see Ps. 150 and above, pp. 8ff.). It often goes together with the cultic dance as we have seen above. Both accompaniments are common in the most widely differing religions,[30] and distinctly belong to the cult.[31]

On the whole the hymn clearly shows its place of origin to be the holy place, to which there is frequent reference. The hymn belongs to the cultic festival[31a] where the people gathers and experiences the Lord's presence and the repetition of all his great works, and remembers what he has done

---

[30] Cf. Heiler, *Das Gebet*,[4] pp. 159f.
[31] Cf. Oesterley, *The Sacred Dance*.
[31a] Allusions to the holy place and the Temple: Pss. 65.2; 76.3; 84.3, 5; 87.7; 95.2, 6; 100.2, 4; 134.1; 135.2; 138.2; cf. 48.2f.; 89.13. Hymn singing at the sacrifice: Amos 5.21–23; Ps. 96.8; cf. 1 Chron. 23.30f.; 2 Chron. 23.18; 29.27f.; 1 Macc. 4.52ff.

and constantly does. Later on it was also used in the daily service which was gradually evolved in the great temples.[32] Particularly in connexion with the daily morning sacrifices—as generally with sacrificial acts—hymns were sung.[33] But also with the processions to the Temple or round the altar there was singing, as we see from Pss. 24 and 118. Still later on perhaps also the pilgrim crowds sang, when they marched in through the gates of Jerusalem.[34]

In the official congregational service of Israel, the hymn of praise always had a prominent place. To praise God was more and more regarded as a main feature of the cult; its aim and intention was to 'give to God the glory'. The collectors of the book of Psalms looked upon all psalm recital as praise of the Lord and his works, his righteousness, faithfulness, and loving kindness; they accordingly gave to the whole book of Psalms the title: 'Hymns of praise' (*tĕhillîm*).

2

It was not unusual to praise Yahweh in a more indirect way by a more detailed laudation of separate benefits which he had bestowed on his people: the Temple, the holy city, etc.[35] In this way there arose several varieties of the hymn of praise.

In the first place must be mentioned the so-called 'Zion-hymns' (as Gunkel called them, using an expression from Ps. 137.3). Instances are Pss. 48; 84; 87 and 122. The type is never unmixed; the 'Zion-hymn' is a motif among others, interchanging with the direct praise of Yahweh. For, of course, it is God himself to whom these hymns give the glory; it is because *he* is there and reveals himself and does his beneficial works of victory and deliverance that 'glorious things can be spoken of Zion'. The most characteristic Zion-hymn is Ps. 87. A special place is taken by Ps. 122 with its deeply personal tone and its free treatment of motifs from other types of poetry, namely, the pilgrim song and the benediction.

Another variety is the hymn to the Law of the Lord, e.g. Ps. 19B. To later Judaism the law appeared as Yahweh's greatest benefaction to his people, as is also expressly said by one of the psalm poets (Ps. 147.20). Through the law Yahweh bestows his blessings on the people and on the individual; Ps. 119, which is intended as a petition, is largely a hymn to the law.[35a]

It is characteristic of the composer of Ps. 19 and his attitude to the law that he has chosen to associate his praise with an evidently very old hymn to the Creator and to the sun; and has used the latter as an introduction to his poem. The thought is clear: in the same way as the sun is the most

[32] Ps. 89.17; 1 Chron. 9.33; Sir. 47.8.
[33] Ps. 100.1; Am. 5.22f.; Sir. 47.8.
[34] This may perhaps be concluded from Ps. 122.1. See, however, below, Chap XVI. 2, p. 311.
[35] Even in Egypt we find this 'indirect' hymn, eulogies of the sanctuary, the royal crown, and so on. See Erman, *Lit. d. Aegypt.*, pp. 337ff., 365ff. (E.T., pp. 270ff.; 295ff.)
[35a] See Mowinckel 'Loven og de 8 termini i Sl. 119', *NTT* 61, 1961, pp. 95ff.

glorious gift of the Creator to his creatures, as regards their physical and material life—no life without sun—thus is the law, with regard to their spiritual life, the 'wisdom' without which a man can neither lead a worthy life nor enjoy it. As the sun illuminates the world from one end to the other, so the law illuminates man both religiously and morally. As nothing is 'hidden' from the rays of the sun, so the law is 'a light to the mind', so that even the 'simplest' becomes 'wise' and can distinguish between right and wrong.[36] For the law of the Lord is not merely statutes, arbitrary regulations, commandments which might have been otherwise: it is a revelation, full of grace, of that fundamental law of all existence which lies in the plan of creation, which must be followed if one is not to collide with the basic laws of life and perish; God's moral and religious law is—to use a modern term—as essentially 'biological' law as the 'natural' laws of physics and chemistry. Hence it is a special mercy that God has revealed this law of life to Israel—'which he has not done to any other people'.

Meditation also hit upon the hymn as its most natural mode of expression. Thus the introductory part of Ps. 90 has become a song of praise to God's everlastingness as a background to a prayer for mercy towards short-lived man:

> Lord, thou has been our dwelling place,
>   in all generations art thou, O God;
> Before the mountains were brought forth,
>   before the earth bore and the continent brought forth.[37]
>
> Thou turnest man back to the dust,
>   and sayest: 'Return, ye children of men'.
> For a thousand years when they are past
>   are but as yesterday unto thee.   (Ps. 90.2–4.)

In the introductory part of Ps. 139 the poet dwells on God's inscrutable wisdom, his omniscience and omnipresence, in dogmatic parlance, and describes it in terms of praise and adoration, borrowed from the thoughts and language of the hymn of praise:

> Yahweh, thou dost explore me throughout,
>   (thou knowest me and all within me):[38]
> Thou knowest me, my sitting and rising,
>   my very thoughts thou readest from afar.
>
> Thou measurest my path and my lying down,
>   and thou attendest to all my ways.
> For the word is not yet on my tongue—
>   thou, Yahweh, knowest it altogether.

---

[36] For details on Ps. 19 see Additional Note XL.

[37] On the idea of 'Mother Earth', who has borne the mountains, as well as living beings, see my paper in *Lehmannfestskrift*, 1927, pp. 130ff. MT vocalization *wattĕhŏlēl* (passive) is correct; the subject of the clause is 'ereṣ wĕthēbhēl.

[38] As the psalm is written in regular stanzas, a 'colon' is missed after v.1, the remnant of which is 'attâ in v.2.

Thou besettest me behind and before,
   and layest thy hand upon me (ever).
(Thy) insight is too wonderful for me,
   too high—I cannot comprehend it.

Whither should I go from thy spirit,
   whither should I flee from thy presence?
If I climb up to heaven, thou art there,
   if I make my bed in She'ol, thou art there.

If I could take the wings of the dawn,
   and dwell on the other side of the ocean,
Even there thy hand should hold me,
   thy right hand take me even there . . .

For thou, thou hast made my reins,
   thou hast woven me in my mother's womb,
I praise thee, Yahweh, for thou art awful
   and wonderful, thy works are wonders.

Thou knowest my soul even since that time,
   my bone-structure was not hid from thee
At the time when I was made in secret,
   and wrought in the depths of the earth.

Thine eyes did see all my days,
   and in thy book they all were written.
The days were found (and destined for me)
   while yet there was not one of them.   (Ps.139.1–10, 13–16.)

In Babylonian–Assyrian psalm poetry we frequently meet with a variety of the hymn, which we might term the *I-hymn*: the god comes forth and tells his name and reveals his character in hymnal form, enumerating his mighty deeds and his divine qualities. This form, of course, arises from the idea of the self-revelation or 'epiphany' of the deity.[39] The book of Psalms contains no such hymn; but that it was known and used also in Israel in connexion with the epiphany of Yahweh, is evident, from, among other things, the hymnal expressions in the self-presentation of Yahweh in a psalm like 81.7–11; cf. Ps. 50.7b. We see it also from the poet's and prophet's imitation of this hymnal form; the whole of Yahweh's speech in the book of Job, chaps. 38ff., is a grand 'I-hymn'; Deutero-Isaiah, too, every now and then lets Yahweh present himself in like manner to his people in order to stir up their faith in his power and will to save them.

---

[39] For details see below Chap. V.3, 8, pp. 109ff. and 140f. The 'I-hymn' may be found also in the Egyptian-Hellenistic religion; see, for instance, the rendering of the Isis-hymn from Kyme by Schubart in *AO*, XXXV, 2, p. 27. There is also an echo of this mode of composition in the royal inscriptions with their introductory 'I am' and their self-praising enumeration of the great achievements of the king; cf. Mowinckel in (*Gunkel Festschrift*) *Eucharisterion* I[*FRLANT* 36], pp. 278ff.

In this way Deutero-Isaiah emphasizes the position of Yahweh as the only God, the creator of the world and the governor of history and the absolute superior of all strange gods.

The hymn has also been used as an expression of the *individual man's worship* of Yahweh, the Exalted, the Almighty, good and merciful. Such a poem is the 'alphabetic' hymn, Ps. 145.

The creation hymn, Ps. 104, has the same form. It starts with a 'Bless the Lord, O my soul' (i.e. with a song of praise), and ends in a similarly personal manner:

> I will sing unto Yahweh as long as I live,
>> touch the strings to my God while I have my being—
> May then my recital be sweet unto him,
>> that I may have my joy in Yahweh. (Ps. 104.33–34.)

Also in the hymn to the law, Ps. 19, the poet concludes with a reference to his poem, and a wish that it may incline Yahweh to mercy.

It has been supposed that this I-form is more recent than the We-form,[40] but this is disproved by the fact that the I-form practically holds the field in both Babylonian and Ugaritic hymn poetry. From the point of view of style the I-form is really just a variation of that I-form which is implied in the introductory exhortation to praise the Lord: it is the poet-singer himself who in the capacity of choir-master and reciter, exhorts the choir to join in the praises with antiphonies and shouts of homage; the poet imagines himself as precentor and choir-master. This does not prevent there being something consciously personal in the occasional use of this form in Israelite psalm poetry; the very fact that it is so rarely used shows that it has such an intention: the poet desires to give expression to his personal religion and to come under the eye of the deity, whom he worships, and upon whom he knows himself to be wholly dependent.

In other cases the I-form is due to the fact that the psalm in question is not really a congregational hymn, but a personal song of thanksgiving (see Chap. X). In Ps. 103 it is a single individual who makes use of a hymn and its general terms, to express his thanks for the help that he has received from God in sickness and distress—in other words, it is a psalm of thanksgiving in the style of the hymn of praise.

This personal stamp, then, does not imply that the psalm was not meant for cultic use. The poet knows that the whole congregation can and will join in. The composer of Ps. 104, as well, speaks on behalf of the cultic congregation. That is the reason for concluding with the wish for the destruction of the 'sinners', the 'ungodly', all Yahweh's and Israel's enemies, who do not acknowledge the Lord.

---

[40] Gunkel-Begrich, *Einl.*, p. 92; cf. Baumgartner 'Ugaritische Probleme u. i. Trageweite f.d. A. T.', *ThZ* III, p. 94.

3

Is it possible to connect the different individual hymns with definite festivals? This is not always easy, but in certain cases it can be done.

In Judaism the Exodus from Egypt was particularly associated with the *Passover*. This association existed even in early times. As we know, the Passover was the chief religious festival of the semi-nomads before the Entry into Canaan, and there is every reason to believe that it is a true historical tradition which—already in the most ancient records—connects the Exodus with the Passover.

It is, then, natural to conclude that the hymns which dwell on the Exodus belong to this festival. But in the period immediately after the Occupation the Passover seems to have played a less important role, and there is much that suggests that the recollection of the Exodus and the making of the covenant in earlier times was connected with the harvest and new year festival as well (see Chap. V.6).

That many hymns belong to the harvest thanksgiving which, after the settlement and down to a late period, was the main festival, stands to reason. The feast of Tabernacles, held from the fifteenth to the twenty-first of the seventh—in older times the eighth—month,[41] at the beginning of the rainy season, was for long, purely and simply 'the feast of Yahweh'. This feast was distinguished by Yahweh 'appearing', 'making himself known', revealing himself, and being personally present in the midst of his chosen people, visible to the opened eye of faith, and to the outward eye as well, through his visible symbol, the ark of the covenant. There the congregation gathered 'before the face of Yahweh' and 'he came to them and blessed them' (cf. Ex. 20.24). This happened at all festivals, but especially at 'the feast of Yahweh'. The harvest festival was, above all, the feast of Yahweh's *Epiphany*, to use the Greek expression for the same idea, later adopted by the Church.[42] Psalms which speak of Yahweh having manifested himself in Judah (76.1) or having 'shined out of Zion' (50.2) belong to this festival, or have at least sprung from this group of ideas and present the thoughts and experiences which originally belonged to it. The feast of harvest and tabernacles was above all a festival of harvest home, with special reference to the olives;[43] it was therefore also termed 'the feast of ingathering' or 'feast of harvesting' (*hagh hā'āsîph, hagh haqqāṣîr* Ex. 34.22; 23.16). Thanks were then given for the year's crops, and they were made available for human use by sacrifices and

[41] This may be concluded from 1 Kgs. 12.32.

[42] See Pfister, art. 'Epiphanie' in Pauly-Wissowa, *Real. Encyclop. d. Class. Altertumswiss.* Supplementband IV, cols. 277ff. The term is used rather comprehensively of any 'appearance' of a deity, whether in the myth or in the oracle or in dreams or through powerful deeds, etc., but especially indicates the appearance and presence and powerful revelation of the god at the cultic festival; whether literally 'visible' to the senses, or visible in symbols or in the experience of faith, is of little importance. The Greeks often looked upon the epiphany day of the god as the 'festival of his birth', where they experienced that marked appearance of which the myth relates.

[43] See Albright in *BASOR* 92, 1943, p. 22, n. 30.

ceremonies. On the same occasion the foundation of the blessing for the new year was also laid; efficacious rites were intended to ensure rain and fertility and new life; the 'coming' and 'appearance' of Yahweh at the feast was a promise of a good 'year of grace'. Prayers in which this fertility aspect of the feast appears are preserved in Deut. 26. 1–15. And there were certainly also psalms giving expression to the same feature. To this festival belong hymns of thanksgiving for the harvest of the year, like Pss. 65 and 67—probably also such psalms as dwell, not only on the appearing of Yahweh, but also on the work of salvation which he has thereby repeated, e.g. Pss. 29; 76 and several others.

Ps. 81 is a new year psalm. In early times the harvest feast (Tabernacles) was also the new year festival; in later Judaism a specific new year's *day* was established, namely, the first day of the seventh month (*Tishri*). To this day belonged the new year psalms proper. But the feast of Tabernacles always retained a strong impress of the new year festival and of the thoughts and ideas associated with it, namely the epiphany of Yahweh, the creation, the 'turning of fortune', and its fixing, i.e. the determining (*šāphaṭ* in the original sense of 'determining', 'establishing', 'fixing')[44] of that which was to happen in the coming year, the renewal of the covenant, and the re-living of memories from the Exodus. We shall examine this many-sided festival further in the next chapter.

4

The hymn of praise has also left its mark on other psalm types. It is not unusual for the psalm of petition or lament to commence with a laudatory introduction, which to us moderns may appear quite independent of the following lament and prayer. See Pss. 9–10; 27; 40; and compare also 90 and 139, which have been mentioned above.

That here it is not a case of a fortuitous collocation or coupling of two independent poems—as some scholars have been inclined to think[45]— but of deliberate composition on the part of the poet is proved, i.a. by Ps. 9–10, which is linked together by the 'alphabetic' scheme formed by the initial letters in each line.

The laudatory introduction has a double purpose, or perhaps rather, a double root. Firstly it is a primary expression of one aspect of the fundamental feeling in the person who is approaching the deity: the attraction, enthusiasm, confidence of him or her who 'knows God'. But then it is also the expression of a more naïvely utilitarian attitude: the suppliant

---

[44] Cf. the original meaning of the Old Norse *døma*, Ags. *dôman* = express an opinion, a decision, determine, establish, fix.

[45] So, for instance, Duhm, *Die Psalmen*, both as regards the psalms mentioned and many others. Even Gunkel treats Ps. 27 as two quite independent poems, and his explanation of 'the context' in Pss. 9–10 (see above, p. 32) is most superficial, just as he does not display any really organic understanding of the idea and intention of Pss. 90 and 139. On the unity of Ps. 27 see Birkeland, 'Die Einheitlichkeit von Ps. 27', *ZATW* 51, 1933, pp. 216ff.

tries to gain Yahweh's favour and induce him to grant the following petition; it belongs to the 'motivation of the prayer' (see below, Chap. VI.3),
appealing to Yahweh's sense of honour, and his obligations in regard to
the petitioner's trust in him; or, as in Ps. 90, the appeal may be to the pity
which the Eternal must feel for mortals; or, as in Ps. 139, to his complete
knowledge of the petitioner's life and thoughts.

Looking at it from the point of view of the form alone, the opinion has
often been expressed that this composite type was a secondary development: the pure hymn of praise was here supposed to have influenced other
types, or to have been subjected to their influence.[46] But this is not correct.

Both the element of prayer which we occasionally find in the hymn of
praise proper, and a comparison with the hymns of the other oriental
nations, and with the ritual songs of primitive peoples prove that the
hymn as a pure type has been brought about by the development of a
single element in the preceding, more complicated prayer songs.[47] The
oldest ritual songs are properly prayers which are introduced by, or framed
and interwoven with, laudatory elements. These latter have a practical
aim in that they are to help to make the deity favourably disposed towards
the suppliant. But they have also, as mentioned, another, purely religious
root. The praise of God's greatness and glory, goodness and care is the
immediate reaction of the soul to all this; it emerges spontaneously from
the encounter with the Holy One, inconceivable and yet revealed, who at
the same time isolates himself and attracts, who excites reverence and fear,
but also enthusiasm, joy and gratitude. Because this response is so essential
an element in religion generally, ritual prayer tends to produce a special
form for this aspect of the approach to the deity: the *hymn of praise*, from
which the other elements—the lament, the prayer, the persuasion, supplication—are suppressed or even eliminated, to form their own type of
prayer psalm, the psalm of lament and petition.

The blend of praise and prayer is thus a survival from an older stage.
In Babylonian and Assyrian psalm poetry it is almost the rule.[48] That the
praise should be used to support the prayer corresponds to a more primitive
and naïve stage of religion; it is the higher stage and purer state of religion
which feels the praise and the adoration as a, so to speak, independent
and necessary religious act, and which adores and praises God for his own
sake without selfish motives.

Actually it is a common law of evolution that the unmixed, simple
forms are later than the composite and undifferentiated ones; in the
history of art also, 'pure' forms are often later than the 'mixed' and undifferentiated ones. 'Mixture of styles' may often be a misleading expression when applied to those types which have grown spontaneously and are
therefore many-sided; that there may also come about a really secondary

---

[46] This is the opinion of Gunkel, see *Einl.*, pp. 84f., cf. 92f.
[47] See Heiler, *Das Gebet*,[4] pp. 157ff.
[48] See Cumming, *Accadian Hymns of Praise*, who has also seen from this standpoint that the
puristic style belongs to a later, distinctly Israelite phase of development.

mixture of originally pure styles is a circumstance that we shall return to later (Chap. XIV.3). The oldest and most characteristic, the most artistically superior and poetically powerful hymns in the Old Testament— e.g. Jdg. 5; Pss. 8; 19A; 68—are those that are most difficult to subject to the general rule of style described above. The great poet is often heedless of conventional rules.

But there are also instances where we can rightly speak of literary influence from the laudatory style. The laudatory form has been used both by other poets and by the prophets to express their views of God and their relation to him. In the book of Job the three friends are constantly proclaiming in hymnal terms God's power and justice and peerlessness and the duty of man to subject himself to his judgments; and they instance, as a proof of his might and power, creation and the struggle with chaos and his judgment of the ungodly. Passages like Job 9.3–13; 12.13–25; 25.2–6; 26.5–14 are, both with regard to style and to content, pure hymns. When Deutero-Isaiah proclaims the shortly forthcoming salvation with his 'Thus saith Yahweh', he frequently adds to this introductory formula a series of hymnic elements, painting God's power and faithfulness, which are to convince the Jews that it is Yahweh and he alone that rules the world, and that he both can and will save his people. Occasionally the prophet is carried away by his enthusiasm so as to give expression to his personal joy and gladness in ecstatic hymnal exclamations.[49]

5

It is particularly in the hymns of praise that we meet with that conception, or perhaps better, that picture of Yahweh as he lived in Israel's consciousness. Thus it will be well to look more closely at the conception of God which is to be found in the psalms.[50] In the hymns of praise we find all the elements of the complete picture. In these Yahweh is praised, thanked and adored for those qualities to which the laments and prayer psalms appeal.

It is really surprising to see how homogeneous the picture of the divine is in the psalms. The inner tension of the historical 'development' in Israel's religion and its conception of God, is little felt in the book of Psalms. The struggle against the Canaanite element is only faintly reflected. Nor is it the contribution of the prophets that we find here. The Yahweh of the main stock of psalms is absolutely superior to all other gods and powers, the only one worthy of the name 'God'. But he is not the only one; the other gods are there as realities, partly as his adversaries whom he conquers and triumphs over and then annihilates, partly as his

---

[49] See Koehler, *Deuterojesaja*, pp. 120ff.; cf. *GTMMM* III, pp. 52f., 190.
[50] For the following cf. Gunkel-Begrich, *Einl.*, pp. 71ff.; T. H. Robinson in *The Psalmists*, ed. Simpson, pp. 23ff.; P. Synave in art. 'Psaumes' in *Dict. Theol. Catholique*, Paris, 1936, XIII, col. 1115ff. (highly systematizing, according to dogmatic categories).

heavenly 'council', his servants, who pay homage to him, and who, either jubilantly or in fear and trepidation, do as he tells them. It is not the monotheism of the later prophets, and even less the abstract intellectual monotheism of Greek philosophy, that we meet with in the psalms. In a way it is the pre-prophetic Yahweh we find here, as he appeared to the experience and belief of those circles which gradually came to put their spiritual and intellectual stamp on the official cult in Jerusalem. In that way it provides one of the main grounds for the appearance and work of the major prophets. But the activities of the prophets assisted in at least touching up the image of Yahweh presented in the psalms. We shall in later chapters see how the Yahweh of the psalms has, so to speak, defined his relation to the other gods, and how the prophetic institution and the particularly Israelite prophetic movement had their connexion both with the cult and with the psalm poetry; and we may at once state that a not inconsiderable part of the psalm poetry chronologically follows the great classical prophecies, the work of the prophets both of judgment and of restoration, and that certain features of the latter may also be seen in the psalms. There *are* also psalms which are marked by the spirit of early Judaism and its whole conception of God after the full victory of monotheistic thought (115.1ff.; 135.15ff.; 96.6; 97.7). But in these younger psalms it is not the struggle against Canaanite influences which we face; it is the spirit of self-conscious Judaism, feeling its superiority over the stupid polytheism of the surrounding 'idolaters'. On the whole the psalms speak about the Yahweh of the cult of Jerusalem, as he had come to be conceived already before the time of Amos and Isaiah, etc. It means that without the religious development here attained, the appearance and spiritual type of the later prophets would have been unthinkable.

What we can see clearly from the psalms is what Yahweh became in the conception, thought and experience of believers, as a result of the collision between the historic Israel and the Canaanites, and the religio-historical victory of the historic Yahweh, over the gods of Canaan. The people, the *cultic congregation* which stands behind the psalms, is the historical Israel, the result of that full amalgamation of Israel and the natives which reached its final stage with the reign of David and Solomon. The religion behind the psalms is the one that developed as a result of the work of David when he introduced the Yahweh cult as the cult of the royal house and the realm in Jerusalem, founded on both the historical traditions of Israel and the inheritance from the pre-Israelite cult of 'El-'Elyôn, 'The Supreme God' in Jerusalem. It is the 'God of the fathers', the God of the election and the covenant and the historic revelation, whom we here meet, he who has chosen Israel as his people and demonstrated by great historical deeds, in real historical experiences, that he is the one 'who is' (Ex. 3.14). He is active and powerful, and acts in real events. He is superior to all other gods, and orders other peoples' fates as he thinks good to attain his aims for his chosen people. He is the God whose 'rights' and 'laws' go back to the practice and tradition of the time of Kadesh and Sinai, the mighty historical God of the time of the desert wandering and the invasion.

But he is also the God of Canaan, the promised land, the settled country and the kingdom, who has seated himself on the seat of Baal and El-Elyon and the Lord of Heaven. The Yahweh of the psalms and of the cult of Jerusalem is the God who has taken over everything of value, everything great and elevated in the whole previous religious development, all the ideas of the divine, and all the higher religious feelings among the people whose culture Israel took over. But then we must immediately qualify this by adding: in so far as this culture could be united with the religion of the times of Moses and the settlement and with the historical traditions about Yahweh. The Yahweh of the psalms is the God both of creation and the life-force, of the rain and the sun, of fertility and expanding life, of war and justice, and law and order; in a nutshell: for Israel, he is the God of the 'world'. But he is also the god who represents the opposition to and negation of all those features in the conception of the deity in the neighbouring countries, which made the god into a nature god, a vegetation and fertility god, a representative of the changes in nature beyond good and evil, a dying and rising god of fertility and sexuality. The Yahweh of the psalms has no female partner. Nor is he one with the life and force of nature. He is above it and controls it and gives his blessings through it; or keeps them back, according to his own will, which again means: according to the attitude which his people shows towards his holiness, and his will and his 'right'. If there is reason to believe that in Jerusalem, at the time of David and Solomon, Yahweh still had a more 'syncretistic' and 'Canaanite' or 'Baalized' stamp than the texts of the Old Testament now give direct proof of, this has certainly been much modified in the picture now presented by the psalms, where it can be traced only in figures of speech and poetical embellishments.

If it be the case that some psalms are remnants of recast Canaanite ones as e.g. the description of the sun as the youthful 'hero' and the 'bridegroom' in the picture of the sun in Ps. 19, this has in the extant Israelite version become purely poetical imagery, used as testimony to Yahweh's absolute dominion over sun and stars, heaven and earth. If it be the case that in the time of David and Solomon there still existed cultic images of Yahweh after Canaanite patterns, and that for instance his holy shrine, 'the ark', might have contained such an image,[51] there are in any case no traces of this in the psalms other than traditional pictorial expressions like 'seeing the countenance of the Lord', 'seeing his beauty' etc. If it be the case, once more, that the image of the fertility goddess Asherah, which king Asa removed from the Temple at Jerusalem (1 Kgs. 15.13) was intended to represent Yahweh's female partner, then the view of Yahweh contained in the psalms must on the whole belong to a later time.

[51] Cf. Gressmann, *Die Lade Jahves*, pp. 17ff.; Mowinckel in *RHPhR* IX, 1929, pp. 197ff.

It is the view of God which we find in the psalms which led to exactly that kind of cleansing of the Temple that Asa undertook, and this conception itself has been further developed and fixed through such acts of reformation. The Yahweh of the psalms is the Yahweh who, following the 'Yahwistic' tradition and reaction in the religious history of Israel, has taken from the gods of Canaan all that was worth taking, and who has rid himself of all that could keep him down on their level and make him into just one among the crowd of deities. More than anything else the conception of Yahweh in the psalms bears testimony to the high religious level, the purity and promise of further growth 'in the true line' of the religious history of Israel, and renders historically explicable the fact that it was against the background of this so often unjustly criticized cult religion that the major prophets were able to arise and become instruments for further progress in the history of revelation.[52]

Even though the psalms may know of other gods, Yahweh is after all, the only one who is *the* god, God, comprising all the perfection of divinity (cf. Ps. 50.1)—that which is expressed in the plural form '*Elōhîm*, an abstract plural summing up what makes for divine majesty. It is in perfect agreement with the conception of God in the psalms that Deutero-Isaiah repeatedly hears the Lord say: 'I am He', and in this evidently finds the original sense of the name 'Yahweh'. Yahweh is from everlasting to everlasting,[53] the eternal One who has been before all things and whose years are without end, 'the first and the last' in the words of the second Isaiah. He is the Holy One,[54] raised above the earth,[55] who is unique, powerful and dangerous, but also 'the Holy One of Israel'[56] 'the strong one of Jacob,[57] and sure defence of his people. The two chief aspects of holiness: the awe-inspiring and dangerous on the one hand, and the gloriously attractive and confidence-inspiring on the other,[58] are both included in the idea of God as expressed in the psalms.

He is the one that inspires fear,[59] the majestic and glorious,[60] the most

[52] See below, Chap. VIII. 11 (II.18) and Chap. XII. 7 (II.68). That the cultic religion of the psalms is independent of the prophets and older than classical prophecy, roughly speaking, has been realized by Weiser as well, 'Theophanie in d. Pss. u. im Festkult' *Bertholetfestschrift*, p. 526.

[53] Pss. 9.8; 10.16; 29.10; 66.7; 90.1ff.; 93.2; 102.13, 26–28; 103.17; 104.31; 135.13; 145.13; 146.10. The following section after Gunkel, *Einl.*, pp. 71ff.

[54] Pss. 22.4; 89.19; 99.5, 9; 105.3; 111.9.

[55] Pss. 46.11; 97.9; 99.2; 113.4.

[56] Pss. 71.22; 78.41; 89.19; Sir. 50.17. Even in Ps. 22.4 some genitive such as 'Jacob's' is likely to have been dropped after 'Holy'—according to the necessities of the metre. See further Isa. 1.4; 5.19, 24; 10.17, 20; 12.6; 17.7; 41.14, 16, 20; 43.3 and other places; here as in so many other cases the ideas and language of the cultic psalms have been adopted by the prophets.

[57] '*abbîr yiśrā'ēl* Ps. 132.2, 5, cf. Gen. 49.24; Isa. 1.24; 49.26; 60.16. Actually the 'bull' of Israel is a term which has probably been adopted from Canaanitish religion. There Baal is the 'bull', *ibr* in the Ugaritic texts, the hump-backed bull, the bison, see Gordon, *Ugaritic Handbook* II, p. 151, Text 75.30–32, and Anat is the 'cow', see Albright, *Archaeology and the Religion of Israel*, pp. 84ff. In Israel, from being an expression for the fertility of nature, it has become an indication of power.

[58] Cf. Otto, *Das Heilige: mysterium tremendum et fascinosum.* (E.T. *The Idea of the Holy.*)

[59] Pss. 42.3; 66.3; 76.5 (Theod., T); 76.13; 89.8; 96.4; 99.3; 111.9.

[60] Pss. 8.2; 57.6, 12; 66.2; 96.6; 104.31; 108.6; 111.3; 113.4; 145.5; 148.13.

wise,[61] the wonderful,[62] great in deeds and thoughts,[63] the omniscient who searches and knows everything (Ps. 139). And yet he is the caring and loving, the faithful and merciful Lord of his people, and the preserver of all his creatures.[64] All these qualities are attributed to Yahweh by the poets, not as abstract philosophical 'categories' fitting systematically into one another, but as something demonstrated in action by a personal God of whom they have themselves had experience in their national history, in the wonders of nature, and in their own lives.

Yahweh is the peerless one, with whom no other gods can be compared.[65] He is 'the God of gods'[66] and 'King of the gods'.[67] He is 'enthroned in heaven',[68] but all the same near; he 'becomes manifest', 'lets himself be found' in his temple[69] where he 'dwells'[70] and helps those that dwell 'in the low places'.[71] First and last he is the only one, who 'alone' is God, and 'alone' has created all things.[72]

A theme which constantly recurs is that of the creation, in which Yahweh has demonstrated his omnipotence, his wisdom and his loving kindness.[73] We shall in the following chapter see how the psalms look at this, and what it means for their piety. That he is the creator also means that he is the mighty Lord of nature, who 'hath done whatsoever he hath pleased' (Pss. 115.3; 136.6), who governs the whole course of nature, the stars and the rain, the thunder and lightning, and who created growth and fruitfulness and opens his hand and satisfies all that lives, upholds all his creatures, gives them the breath of life, and renews the surface of the earth.[74] 'The Lord killeth and maketh alive', he bringeth down to the grave, and bringeth up, maketh poor and enricheth.[75] In everything man is dependent on his lovingkindness and care.

Yahweh reveals himself especially in all that is striking and extraordinary in nature—in the storm, thunder and lightning, fire and earthquake.[76] Here he reveals his awful majesty, his merciful care and his flaming wrath when he comes to judge his enemies. His mighty 'voice', which once subdued the primeval sea, and which yet rings out in the

---

[61] Pss. 40.6; 104.24; 139.17.

[62] Pss 77.12; 139.14.

[63] Pss. 77.13; 92.6; 104.24; 111.2; 135.5; 145.3; 150.2.

[64] For instance, Pss. 103.11–13; 36.6–8; 89.2f., 6.

[65] Ex. 15.11; 1 Sam. 2.2; Pss. 18.32; 35.10; 71.19; 74.14; 86.8; 89.7, 9; 113.5; 135.5.

[66] Pss. 84.8 (voc. 'ēl 'ĕlōhîm); 50.1; cf. Josh. 22.22; Dan. 11.36.

[67] Pss. 95.3; 136.2.

[68] Pss. 103.19; 113.5f.; 11.4; 14.2; 33.13f.

[69] Pss. 46.2; 76.2f.; 50.1f.; 53.3; 66.7; 138.6.

[70] Ps. 135.21; cf. 24.3; 15.1.

[71] Pss. 113.5; 11.4.

[72] Pss. 72.18; 83.19; 86.10; 136.4; Deut. 32.12; Sir. 18.1f.

[73] Pss. 33; 104; 115.15; 121.2; 134.3.

[74] Ps. 8.4; Am. 5.8; Pss. 147.8; 76.10–12; 67; 147.8, 16f.; 104.27–30; 145.15f.; 139.13ff.; cf. Job 9.6.

[75] 1 Sam. 2.4–6; Pss. 75.8; 107.35ff.; 113.7ff.; 146.9; 147.6; cf. Job 5.11ff.; 12.17ff.; 36.5ff.

[76] Judges 5.4f.; Pss. 18.8ff.; 68.34; 97.2ff.; 135.7.

thunder, works both destructive and creative miracles in the earth, as described in Ps. 29.

That these thoughts clothe themselves in the imagery of myth is a matter of course; this means only that the poets are speaking the language proper to religious views of nature and reality. He covers himself with light as a garment, the clouds are his chariot, the winds and lightning his messengers.[77] 'He looketh on the earth and it trembleth: he toucheth the hills, and they smoke' (Gunkel; Ps. 104.32). 'The hills melt like wax at the presence of the Lord' (Ps. 97.5). The mythic forms in which the conception of creation appears will be further treated below, in Chap. V.8.

The psalms dwell frequently on Yahweh's acts in history, in the life of Israel from the election and the Exodus onwards,[78] and on his dominion over all kingdoms and nations.[79] This thought, too, gets its particular formulation in the experience and belief of the festal cult, as we shall see later (Chap. V.8).

As Creator, King and Lord of the Covenant, Yahweh is the almighty; and mankind, and particularly his chosen people, owe him absolute obedience.[80] Life and death depend on him. He is the giver of all good gifts. But he may also hide his face. All the same, God does not appear as an arbitrary tyrant. When we see him in his wrath it is because man has in some way sinned against him and awakened his anger. It is then a question of discovering the transgression and of making expiation. Then Israel may reckon on the bestowal of his grace again.

For the main characteristic of Israel's faith in God as seen in the psalms is that this almighty Lord God and Lord is *Israel's* particular God. He has, through a special historical act in the course of actual history, selected this people, and made his covenant with it—that is the foundation of the creed of Israel. This covenant the psalmist is able to claim on his own behalf and on that of the people, through this old 'historical credo'—to speak in the terms of G. von Rad[81]—has been varied in many ways in the cult poetry. The Lord's revelation to his people is determined by his mercy or faithfulness, his 'lovingkindness'—or whatever word one uses to translate *ḥesedh*,[82] that most important element in the Israelitic conception of God. This lovingkindness he has shown throughout the history of the people, and therefore they can point to his 'lovingkindnesses' to the fathers and expect similar ones towards themselves. The psalmists too know that Yahweh is merciful and gracious, slow to anger, and plenteous in active love, 'a God who forgives sins'.[83] They often speak of his love and faithful-

---

[77] Gunkel, *Einl.*, pp. 73f. with references to Ps. 104.2–4. See likewise Pss. 18.8ff.; 68.7.

[78] Pss. 105; 114; Ex. 15.2ff.; Pss. 22.5f.; 44.2–4; 66.6; 77.16ff.; 80.9ff; 99.6ff.; 103.7f.; 111.4,6,9; 119.138; 135.8ff.; 136.10ff.; 147.19.

[79] Pss. 2; 46; 48; 75; 7.8; 44.3; 59.9; 47.10; 99.1; 118.10ff.; 135.8–12.

[80] Cf. T. H. Robinson in *The Psalmists*, ed. Simpson, pp. 32ff.

[81] G. von Rad, *Das formgeschichtliche Problem des Hexateuchs*, BWANT 78, pp. 3ff., 8ff.

[82] Cf. Glueck, *Das Wort hesed*; cf. J. Pedersen, *Israel* I–II, pp. 309f.; A. R. Johnson, 'Hesed and Hasid' in Mowinckel Festschrift (*Interpretationes ad V.T. Pertinentes*, pp. 100ff.

[83] Pss. 86.5; 103.8ff.; 99.8.

ness towards Israel, towards the 'righteous', the 'brethren of the Covenant' (*ḥasîdhîm*),[84] and not least of his pity toward all those that are oppressed and suffering.[85] The psalms appeal to this pity and mercy.[86] These can be equated with his power and honour; for if he allows his people to perish, the other nations will believe that he is unable to carry out his promise and protect his chosen, and that other gods are stronger than he (Pss. 42.4; 79.10; 115.2).

This confident and warm, emotionally tuned relation of the worshipper(s) to Yahweh often finds its expression in the phrase 'our God', or 'my God' when a single person is speaking on behalf of the congregation or of himself. The phrase may be a more or less unaccented formula, antagonism against other gods not being intended; but the confident consciousness of the close relationship to Yahweh always lies implicit in the word.[86a] But his mercies have their conditions. Against sinners he rises in all his wrath. If a sinner—whether the whole people or an individual—is to have hope of divine forgiveness, he must confess his sins, humble himself and do penance.[87] His mercies are dependent on Israel's obeying and serving him, keeping his laws and commandments,[88] the content of which is, in a word, 'the right', 'what is correct and just' (*ṣedheq, ṣĕdhāqâ*). Yahweh is a god who 'loves righteousness' and 'has established right order and righteousness in Jacob', 'the foundation of whose throne is righteousness and justice.'[89] Only he who has clean hands and a pure heart may dwell on his holy hill (Pss. 24.4; 15). The worshipper in the psalms always appeals to the justice of Yahweh for help against his enemies.

But here there is one point in which we notice a difference between the psalms and the prophets of doom. The word which is rendered 'justice', 'judgment' or 'righteousness'—*ṣĕdhāqâ* or *ṣedheq* is not in the first place a moral concept in our sense of the word. It signifies Yahweh's 'right doing' and is based on the covenant. It is one with his lovingkindness (*ḥesedh*) and faithfulness (Ps. 89.2f., 6, 9). Yahweh's 'righteousness' is his power and will to maintain himself, and his covenant, and his promise to obtain the 'right' conditions for his people. In the first place it is used of his positive saving action for the benefit of Israel.[90] Even when the idea of his just government, which rewards and punishes according to deserts, plays a part, the emphasis is laid on the fact of his saving his people.[91] That is exactly why the prophets of doom rarely, if ever, speak of Yahweh's *ṣĕdhāqâ*. In their eyes the Lord is essentially just and righteous, when he

---

[84] Pss. 33.18; 34.16, 20, 22; 68.36; 97.10; 100.3; 103.8ff.; 135.3f.; 145.10; 148.14; cf. Jer. 14.8; Mic. 7.18; Nah. 1.3, 7f. See below, pp. 174ff.
[85] Pss. 34.19; 68.6f.; 103.6; 107.41; 113.7ff.; 145.14, 19; 146.7ff.; 147.3, 6; 1 Sam. 2.8; cf. Job 5.11.
[86] See below, Chap. VI. 3; VII. 4 (pp. 195, 229ff.).
[86a] See Eissfeldt in *ZATW* 61, pp. 3ff. See, however, n. 12 to Chap XVI.
[87] Pss. 32; 65.4; 103.9f.; Sir. 17.29.
[88] Pss. 81.9ff.; 95.7ff.; 50. For details, see Chap. V. 6, p. 130f.
[89] Pss. 99.4; 76.3; 97.2.
[90] Cf. Leivestad, *Guds straffende rettferdighet*, pp. 21f.
[91] *Ibid.*, pp. 40ff.

upholds the ethical law of his own being by punishing his sinful people.[92] Here the prophets of doom rise above the view which is most prevalent in the psalms.

This, however, does not mean that the ethical element is missing in the conception of God presented by the psalms. On the contrary, 'Yahweh loves those who hate evil', or in another reading: 'Those who love Yahweh hate evil' (Ps. 97.10, cf. 11.5). It is on account of the unjust and immoral government of the other gods on the earth that Yahweh pronounces judgment on them (Ps. 82). To the psalmists it is a sign of Yahweh's righteousness that he helps suffering Israel, whom evil-minded enemies have subjugated. They implore his help against 'deceit' and 'falsehood', 'lies', and 'violence'.

It is implicit in the nature and function of the psalms as cultic psalms that they have no particular reason to enlarge on the ethical aspect of the image of God. All the same, the idea of Yahweh as the maintainer of justice frequently appears. In comparison with their enemies Israel are the 'righteous' ones and it is 'right' that Yahweh should both secure for his people its rights and provide just recompense for the deeds of man.[93] Against injustice Yahweh must interfere.

Here the ideas of justice and injustice are yet, as already mentioned, in part nationally coloured, and this again influences the conception of Yahweh's justice. The psalms hardly get beyond the stage that God's righteousness is proved in the first place by his saving Israel—even though this salvation gradually acquires a deeper content than the politico-nationalistic. But there are also attempts at a more ethical individualistic conception of Yahweh's righteousness. In some of the later psalms—as Pss. 1; 91; 112; 128; 34; 37—we find the thought of just individual recompense: Yahweh rewards or punishes the individual according to his acts and attitude to Yahweh's commandments. But also in the older psalms we see the ethical projecting itself into the ritual, and determining the type of piety, and thence the conception of God. When it is a question of formulating conditions for those who can be allowed a part in the blessing and 'salvation' of the sanctuary, moral demands are stressed besides the ritual and the purely religious ones; see Pss. 15; 24; 50. In Ps. 50 we see that Yahweh watches over righteousness in Israel not only by seeing to it that Israel wins her 'right' in the struggle with her outward enemies, but also by ensuring that injustice does not get the upper hand within the nation.[94] It is obedience to the simple moral commandments that Yahweh here demands from both the individual and the congregation as a whole; the congregation too has to show moral discipline. But this psalm evidently belongs to the later period and has been influenced by the

---

[92] *Ibid.*, pp. 118ff.
[93] Pss. 11.5ff.; 33.5; 66.7; 89.15; 92.10ff.; 97.2, 10; 98.9; 99.4; 103.6; 111.5; 145.20; 146.9; 147.6.
[94] Leivestad, *op. cit.*, p. 57.

teachings of the prophets of doom. 'The people' is here obviously the small Jewish congregation.

And it is just this psalm that bears witness to that rationalization of the conception of God which always takes place when the ethical aspect comes to the fore. It then forces the mythopoeic view of Yahweh into the background. It is true that Ps. 50 still has some of the old colours in its description of Yahweh's theophany: 'From Zion the God of gods is flashing . . . in front of him devouring fire, encircling him a mighty storm'. But this Yahweh is principally the Lord who 'will take no bullock out of thy house, nor he-goats out of thy folds', and who 'will not eat the flesh of bulls nor drink the blood of goats'. It is by right moral behaviour and by proper discipline that the congregation will honour him.

It is a rich and varied picture of Yahweh that the psalms show us. It has practically all the single features of the prophets' conception of God. But it lacks the ethical passion which characterizes the Yahweh of the prophets, which even leads him to crush his own people, so that justice may prevail. Hence the God of the psalms is not yet the universal God. Yahweh is the God of the world, but he *uses* his universal power as the God of Israel. In practice no wider circle is envisaged, as a rule, than the worshipping cultic congregation; nevertheless there are still some elements which do bespeak the God of the universe.

CHAPTER V

Psalms at the Enthronement Festival of Yahweh

I

The fact that the 'Epiphany psalms', mentioned above in Chap. IV, are connected, at least ideologically, with the harvest festival, is evident from the close relationship between their underlying mood and ideas and those of the so-called *enthronement psalms*. That these psalms are connected with the harvest and new year festival, the present author has tried to show in his *Psalmen-Studien II*, and we shall take up the question further below.

Characteristic of this group is that they salute Yahweh as the king, who has just ascended his royal throne to wield his royal power. The situation envisaged in the poet's imagination, is Yahweh's ascent to the throne and the acclamation of Yahweh as king; the psalm is meant as the song of praise which is to meet Yahweh on his 'epiphany', his appearance as the new, victorious king. Hence the name: enthronement psalms.

This applies, in the first place, to Pss. 47; 93; 96; 97; 98; 99. But Ps. 95, as well, belongs in its first part to the same type, even though it be not purely a hymn, but also contains other important liturgical items. A clear parallel with 95 is 81, with the same construction and the same poetical (and liturgical) vision. This fact indicates that Yahweh's enthronement is ideologically and in the religious consciousness of the Israelites connected with other complexes of ideas and liturgical situations.

It cannot, therefore, be our task solely to give a description of the forms and contents of the enthronement psalms in the narrow sense from the point of view of *Gattungsforschung* and the history of literature, but we must also seek to find the cultic situation which lies behind them, and to give a picture of this in all its ideological and liturgical complexity. Then, granted that there *is* such a cultic situation, Ps. 95 shows that it contained other ideas and liturgical situations besides the idea of the enthronement alone. And that is only what is implicit in the nature of the matter and of the cult. In the cultic festival the whole orchestra of the life and experience of the religion can be heard playing. No single psalm type nor any unbalanced typological treatment can reveal the whole content of the cultic festival. The fact that the second part of Ps. 95 expresses an idea other than the mere enthronement, and that the psalm, from the point of view of *Gattungsforschung* is a 'liturgical composition', gives no right to exclude it from the group of the enthronement psalms and from the scope of our investigation, as Gunkel, and more recently Kraus, have done. This means that we are at once forced outside the narrow circle of the enthronement hymns proper. Among other things the above mentioned epiphany psalms will be seen to have close ideological and liturgical connexions with the ideology and the cultic situation of the enthronement hymns of praise.

But first we must see how far we can advance through a consideration of these latter alone.

2

The characteristic phrase in the enthronement psalms proper—one which often appears in the introduction—is 'Yahweh has become King', *Yahweh mālakh* (93.1; 97.1; 47.8; 96.10). It is not a lasting condition that the poet describes with this expression, and the older translation 'The Lord reigneth' is misleading.[1]

The poet's vision is of something new and important which has just taken place: Yahweh has now become king; hence the new song of joy and praise to be sung. What the poets have seen in their imagination, and describe or allude to, is an event and an act which was linked with an enthronement, Yahweh's ascent of the throne. They see and describe it, of course, in the forms and the colours of the myth; but this mythical event is none the less a real event to them. The myth is the genuine form of the religious conception. We shall see later on how the conception of Yahweh's *becoming* king is related to his eternal kingship.

Other expressions, as well, proclaim his reign[2] or rule ('judgment').[3] The picture seen by the poets is that of a great celebration which they present with the same features as that of the enthronement of a terrestrial monarch,[4] only on a magnified mythical scale and with unearthly splendour. Yahweh himself 'comes' (98.9), 'makes himself known' (98.2), 'goes up' (47.6) in solemn procession to his palace, the Temple, seats himself on his throne (93.2; 97.2; 99.1) and receives his people's acclamation as king (*tĕrû'â*, 47.2). 'Yahweh has become King' is just such a cry of acclamation as 'Absalom has become king!', 'Jehu has become king!' (2 Sam. 15.10; 2 Kgs. 9.13). Before beginning his rule, or in immediate connexion with his enthronement, he performs great deeds (47.4f.; 93.2ff.; 96.10; 97.2ff.; 98.1ff.).

Not only of Israel but of the whole earth, has Yahweh become king. The songs exhort all peoples to acclaim him (47.1, 8ff.; 96.1, 3ff.; 97.1, 6, 9; 98.3f.); all other gods tremble before him and worship him (95.3; 96.4; 97.7, 9; 99.2f.).

---

[1] On the grammatical and ideological meaning of the expression see Additional Note VI.
[2] Pss. 47.3; 95.3; 97.6; 99.4.
[3] Pss. 46.10; 96.7, 13; 97.8, 10–12; 98.9; 99.4.
[4] Cf. 1 Kgs. 1; 2 Kgs. 11.12; 2 Sam. 15.10ff. Cf. *Ps.St.* II, pp. 8ff.; Gunkel-Begrich, *Einl.*, p. 97. See also G. von Rad in *ThLz.*, 1947, col. 211ff.

This universalistic idea is connected with the conception of those psalms regarding the great deed on which the kingdom of Yahweh is founded, namely, the Creation (93.1b; 95.3–5; 96.5), therefore all created things are exhorted to praise him (96.11f.; 97.6a; 98.7f.). As often in the psalmists and the prophets[5] the creation is pictured as a victorious struggle with the primeval dragon or the primeval sea (93.3f.) and its monsters. We have here a mythical conception of creation which may be termed the Primeval Struggle Myth or the Fight with the Dragon Myth, which is alluded to in the mention of the 'victory' (98.1ff.).

The victory of Yahweh is also a catastrophe for all the *other gods*; they are now confounded, stricken with terror (96.7; 97.7; 99.3f.); Yahweh's victory is also a victory over them. But together with the other gods, stand the heathen: them, too, has Yahweh conquered with his coming (47.7f.; 97.7, 10; 99.1). More pointed mention—with reference to history —is made of the Lord's victory over the nations of Egypt and Canaan (47.4f.).

Occasionally the idea of Yahweh's struggle and victory is combined with that of an act of *judgment*: the Lord comes to judge his enemies, either the gods or the whole earth (97.7f.; 98.9; 99.4). But this is not, as a rule, clearly worked out as a concrete judicial act with regular indictment and verdict (a 'forensic act'). For 'to judge' is in Hebrew just as much to rule, or to account for one's enemies in battle, or to save one's friends, as to pronounce judgment; the last is only one of many ways of 'judging'. As a rule, it means setting conditions on earth in the right order; that is the meaning of Yahweh's 'judgment' as a king. But there was also the determination of events for the following year, which, for instance, both the Babylonians and the Jewish tradition in the Mishna speak of as one of the deity's deeds on mounting the throne, and which both refer to the new year festival.

Besides the Creation, and the fight and victory which it represented, there is also mentioned an historical foundation for the Kingdom of Yahweh, namely, *the creation of Israel*, as the Lord's chosen people, *the election* as it was manifested in the Exodus from Egypt, the miracle of the Reed Lake, the revelation of Kadesh and Sinai with the making of the *Covenant*.[6] The sea where the Egyptians perished becomes the primeval sea (cf. Ex. 15.5, 8), Egypt is turned into 'Rahab', the primeval dragon.[7] Some poets declare expressly that it was on the occasion of the Exodus and the making of the covenant that Yahweh became king;[8] in that case the kingship is usually limited to Israel, whereas it is, as a rule, universal

---

[5] Pss. 74.12ff.; 89.10ff.; 104.5ff., 25f.; 44.20; 65.7f.; 18.16ff.; 46.4; 68.31; Isa. 51.9f.; Jer. 51.34, 36, 42; 50.2f.; Am. 9.2f.; Hab. 3.8; Job 9.13; 26.12f; 7.12; 38.8ff.; Ezk. 29.3ff.; 32.2ff. Cf. Gunkel, *Schöpfung und Chaos*, pp. 29ff.

[6] Cf. the term 'our maker', Ps. 95.6f. with vv. 7bff.; 100.3; 99; cf. 97.2–6.

[7] Cf. Isa. 30.7; 51.9; Pss. 87.4; 89.11.

[8] Ps. 114.1f.; Deut. 33.2–5.

in the enthronement psalms. This historical basis of Yahweh's becoming king is alluded to in Ps. 99.

In the poet's imagination this enthronement of Yahweh is an event which has just taken place, and the hymn of praise is sung to acclaim the new king. The enthronement psalms are principally hymns of praise with the usual character of such hymns, and with the free variations occasioned by their special theme: the enthronement and the great deed on which it is based together with the results for the whole earth. The main points are: the exhortation to praise, the mention of Yahweh's glorious presence and of the excellent deeds he has just performed or is about to perform:

> Yahweh has become King! Let earth rejoice;
> > let the many shores be glad thereof.
> Clouds and darkness are round about him;
> > equity and justice are the fundament of his throne.
> Fire blazes in front of him
> > and burns his enemies round about.
> His lightnings illumined the world;
> > till earth shivered at the sight.
> The mountains melted just like wax
> > before the Lord of all the earth. (Ps. 97.1–5.)

> Shout the homage-cry before the King,
> > with bugle and with cornet . . . ,
> Before Lord Yahweh, for he hath come
> > to reign upon the earth;
> To rule the world with righteousness,
> > the peoples with equity. (Ps. 98.6, 9.)

3

How are these psalms to be interpreted? What are the poets alluding to, and what is it they seek to bring out in their description of the 'enthronement' of Yahweh?

The most prominent feature of these psalms is, as we have seen, their actuality and contemporaneous character. There can be no doubt that the situation into which the poets have projected themselves, which forms the basis of their vision, and which they want the singer and the listeners to take part in, is this: that the people—the congregation—is now actually standing in the presence of the new king to salute him as the victorious king who has ousted his competitors and seated himself on the throne, has established his kingdom and inaugurated a beneficial reign over this people and the whole earth. In whatever way one may explain the circumstance that Yahweh, the Lord, who has through all time been God and

Ruler, can also be pictured as having just succeeded to the throne, there can be no doubt that it is the latter fact which the poets wish to convey: they see before them, and praise—and let the congregation praise—Yahweh as the king who has *now* taken over his realm.

In the Old Testament we also meet with the idea that Yahweh *is* the king of Israel.[9] 'The King' was in the East a very common title and name for the god of the country, or of the town. Marduk of the Babylonians, Asshur of the Assyrians, the Ammonite Milkom, the Tyrian Melkart, the Ugaritic Ba'al and many others—all were 'the King'. It was natural for the Israelites to conceive of Yahweh in the same way. But how is this idea related to the conception that he has at a certain moment *become* King? One might reason as follows: he became king when he chose Israel as his people; and certain psalms suggest this, as we have seen above. But this is evidently not the general idea of the enthronement psalms. As a rule, it is not an historical but a 'cosmic', 'mythical' act of salvation which is conceived of as the foundation of the kingship—in the first place, as mentioned, the Creation in its various aspects. How is this to be understood? What does it mean that the poet and the congregation, who are in these psalms acclaiming Yahweh, are, so to speak, contemporaries of the Creation?

Attempts have been made to interpret them historically, in connexion with some particular historical event, in which Yahweh had clearly proved himself king, e.g. the fall of the Chaldean kingdom and the return of the first 'Diaspora Jews' to Zion.[10] But this does not explain the universal, world-embracing character of these psalms. And why are there no definite references to actual historical events? Psalms like 46 and 48 are quasi-historical, but events like those described—the nations' attack on Jerusalem, and their rout and destruction there—never happened in actual history. And how to explain from an historical view-point the fact that Creation and the fight with the primeval dragon form the foundation of the kingdom? and how the part played by Nature in the exhortation to praise? The historical interpretation is as impracticable in the case of the enthronement psalms as in that of Pss. 46 and 48. They are not actual and historical, but 'mythical', unearthly events, to which the enthronement psalms refer;[11] when there occasionally is a reference to something 'historical' as in Pss. 99; 97 and 95 (and 81), it is a matter of happenings in the remote past.

Others have tried to interpret them eschatologically: the poet and the congregation sing in advance the poem regarding the final salvation, when Yahweh shall annihilate the power of evil and deliver his people and

---

[9] Isa. 6.5; 41.21; 43.15; 44.6; Pss. 5.3; 44.5; 74.12; 84.4; 24.7, 9 and other places.

[10] As eminent representatives of this interpretation may be mentioned Ewald, Cheyne, Baethgen, Wellhausen, Buhl, Davison. Even Olshausen gives a time-historial interpretation, but has realized more clearly than the above-mentioned the liturgical character of these psalms. In addition see *Ps.St.* II, pp. 10–13.

[11] Pss. 93.2ff.; 95.4f.; 96.10. Cf. 24.2; 29.3, 10; 100.3; 149.2.

establish the eschatological kingdom of God, when he wholly and absolutely shall become king and be recognized as such by the whole world.[12] True enough, these ideas are also to be found as elements in the restoration hope and in eschatology; the psalmists, however, did not get them from those sources, but vice versa, as we shall shortly see. When, for instance, Deutero-Isaiah describes the coming salvation as the enthronement day of a cosmic Yahweh,[13] he speaks in the psalm style, showing that these ideas belong to *psalm* poetry. And when the prophets at times break out in such 'anticipatory' salvation songs—as an expressive form of prophecy, and in certainty and joy regarding its arrival—it is always in some way suggested that they are speaking of a future matter: 'On that day ye shall sing and say' (cf. Isa. 12.1, 3f.; 25.9; 27.2; Jer. 31.6). The connexion in which the prophets' lyrical outburst is found proves that it is intended as a spectacular version of the prophecy itself, of which it is a portion.[14] In a separate individual psalm, on the other hand, there is no such 'connexion' indicating that it is to be applied to the future. The only thing that might suggest an eschatological character would be the content, which frequently tallies with eschatological ideas.[15] But the truth of the matter is, as we shall see later on, that eschatology here has drawn its ideas from the same source as the enthronement psalms, and has reinterpreted these ideas in its own way. As a matter of fact there are no properly 'eschatological' psalms in the whole collection.[16]

Everything contained in the enthronement psalms, then, gives the strongest impression of belonging to the actual present. It is not only in their imagination that the poets have witnessed Yahweh's arrival and ascent of the throne as a present event (which by its nature might belong either to the past or to the future); no, they refer to something objective and experienced outside themselves, but with which they have been contemporaneous. That which they are witnessing: that the Lord after certain acts 'goes up' and seats himself on the throne and is acclaimed as having taken the name of the king, is an act which already to the poet's vision is a 'myth', and might easily have been presented in the epic form of the myth. But it is noticeable that the poets never *describe* this enthronement as such; they merely refer to it in hymnal form as something real and well known, and which the audience also can understand. They do not need to describe it; they merely rejoice that it has now taken place. If it had been an image of the future, present only in their imagination, they could not have expected their audience to have understood what they were

---

[12] Cf. Additional Note VII.

[13] See *Ps.St.* II, pp. 190ff.; 238ff.; 251ff.; 256ff.; 273ff.; 282ff.; 292ff.; *GTMMM* III, pp. 188f.

[14] With this, Gunkel's reply (*Einl.*, p. 81) to my own and H. Schmidt's objections to his eschatological interpretation loses its force.

[15] This is certainly admitted by Gunkel, *Einl.*, p. 80. However, as he is likewise forced to admit that the same conceptions also belong in places outside eschatology, namely in an (earlier) cultic enthronement festival (see below, n. 21), his objections lose their validity.

[16] See Additional Note VIII.

talking about; we should then have expected them to describe what they saw and tell their listeners that this many-sided and portentous enthrone-ment was now taking place, or was going to happen. The picture of the enthronement is thus not simply a poetical conception which the authors have received individually and which they put before their listeners to make them also experience the event. They take it for granted that the series of events referred to is well known beforehand to those who are to hear or sing the psalm; they refer to a (mythical) conception which they share with a large group. The enthronement of Yahweh must to them have been an event which could be both presented and alluded to, because the group knew that it had now taken place. As we have seen, this event is connected both with the Creation of the world and with the Exodus from Egypt.

But at the same time, it is in these psalms presented as something belonging to the living present, something which all who hear or sing the psalm themselves have taken part in and are experiencing at the time, something on which the singing congregation's whole happiness and well-being—their salvation—would depend, and which they are at the moment praising and celebrating. 'O sing unto the Lord, for he is come, he is come!' it says in the enthronement hymn 98.9; and in another psalm, which belongs in fact to the same ideological group, the congregation declares: 'As we have heard, so we have seen' (48.9). But it is, on the other hand, true that there is something in these psalms that points beyond the mo-ment; they also express a hope and a certainty regarding the future, beyond human and political calculations. We shall come back to this later. But the essential point about these psalms is the rejoicing about something recently experienced.

We must ask: *where* are the historico-mythical 'acts of salvation' that are at the same time described as belonging both to the past and the present, and experienced as belonging to the present, with results decisive for the future? From all we know of religious life in its manifestations and especially in the more ancient 'primitive' civilizations, the answer can only be this: it is where religion and religious life unfold in a common experience and realization of 'the real' in all its creative and existential wealth and concrete presence, that is, in the congregational temple cult. In other words the only interpretation which is satisfactory both for the actual and the future, the historical and the cosmic, together with the primeval element (the Creation) in these psalms, and which at the same time tallies with the general view of the psalms which has been presented in the foregoing, is the *cultic* one.[17] That is to say, these psalms presuppose and, from their very nature have sprung from and belong to, a festival, which has, at least from one point of view, been celebrated as a festival of the enthronement of Yahweh.[18] At this festival the congregation has

---

[17] See Additional Note IX.   [18] See Additional Note X.

most vividly experienced the personal coming of the Lord to save his people—his epiphany.[19] In the cultic festival, past, present and future are welded into one.   It is an experience of this sort that lies behind the enthronement psalms, and which they express.[20] In fact, this cultic interpretation is the only one that can provide any support for the kernel of truth in Gunkel's eschatological interpretation.[21]

Let us recall what was said above about the essence of the cult. All cult is, from one point of view—as we have seen[22]—repetition, renewed experience of the fundamental facts of life and existence. It was a repetition, which to the ancient peoples did not mean simply 'in memory of', but a positive reality, in the same way as this notion still lives in the Easter greeting of the Orthodox Church: 'Christ is verily arisen!' That means, *now*, as it also rings in our Christmas and Easter hymns: 'Our Saviour has been born *to-day*;' 'Arisen is our Lord, the Christ ... who *Friday* died the bitter death' ..., 'Three women went *this morning* forth ...', and so on.[23]

To the ancients this renewed experience was still more real than it is to us; it was an actual repetition of the event. In the cult the creative and saving events took place again and again, in regular recurrence. Life is a constant struggle between good and evil powers, between 'blessing', and 'curse', between 'life' and 'death'. In this struggle the powers of good must be renewed and strengthened, otherwise the world would perish. This renewal takes place in the cult. At the festival the deity is called, and comes; through the cult, strength and blessing are drawn into human life; a wall is built against the powers of evil, and impurity and sin are washed away. Thus life, 'the World', is created anew. The bond made with the deity in the harvest festival causes the rains to return, so that the curse of drought and death is overcome, dormant nature revives and life awakens, to the benefit of mankind (cf. Ps. 65). In the language and spirit of the Yahweh religion: then the Lord comes and brings all this along with him, vanquishes the powers of evil—including (on principle) the enemies of his chosen people, for whom he 'maketh all things new'.

At the 'enthronement festival'—as we may preliminarily call it— ancient Israel witnessed Yahweh's arrival as king, when he literally founded his kingdom. They acclaimed and celebrated him as conqueror, creator, king of the whole earth, reformer of the people and its fortunes, as the king of Israel who repeats the acts of deliverance from Egypt and the Reed Lake, and who, by his mere coming, has set the world aright again and crushed every onslaught that the enemies might make on his

---

[19] See above, p. 94 and n. 42 to Chap. IV. That the idea of theophany is really connected with the cult and with an actual, regular, 'to all eternity' repeated cultic experience has also been realized by Weiser, who gives further reasons for it, *Festschrift für Bertholet*, pp. 513ff.

[20] See Additional Note XI.

[21] See below, Chap. V. 10, 11 and Additional Note XII.

[22] See above, Chap. I, pp. 15ff., cf. Mowinckel, *Religion und Kultus*, pp. 10ff.

[23] *M.B. Landstads Kirkesalmebok*, revised and added to, Nos. 114, 349.

city and his people—though all the kings of the earth were to combine
and to conspire together.

To the interpretation that the enthronement psalms on a special festival
state that Yahweh has become king, it is not a valid objection to say that
Yahweh had, according to the Israelite view, always been king.[24] The
latter statement is correct enough. The Old Testament often declares
that the Lord is king, 'King for ever', etc.;[25] he is Israel's king, king in
Zion, but sometimes also king over all the earth. The notion that the god
is the king (melekh, 'ādhōn) of the city or of the land and people, is no
original Israelite idea: in the wilderness, a king was unknown to the
nomad tribes. The ancient Semitic conception of the deity is that he is
the 'father' of the tribe or of the people, and he is therefore often identified
with the tribal progenitor.[26]

The conception of the deity as king was taken over by the Israelites from
the Canaanites,[27] who had received it from the great kingdoms on the
Euphrates and Tigris and Nile,[28] where it had been developed as early as
ancient Sumerian times.[29] When Israel was gathered into one state,
and acquired its chief national holy place in Jerusalem, Yahweh was
looked upon as the king of Zion. There is every reason to believe that the
conception of Yahweh as the king of the township derives from the supreme Canaanite deity in Jerusalem, El Elyon, whom Yahweh succeeded,
and whose throne and realm he won, with David's conquest of the city
and introduction of the worship of Yahweh as the official cult of the
kingdom; this becomes still clearer in the new 'royal temple' of Solomon.
That the royal title was linked with the pre-Israelite god on Zion, is seen,
from the name Melchizedek, i.e. malkî ṣedheq—'the god Ṣedeq is my king'.[30]

It naturally followed that Yahweh gradually came to be regarded as
king of the land and people of Israel, and, in religious lyrical poetry, as
'the King of all the earth', an idea which in the prophets acquired a
practical religious content. He is the world-ruler who uses all nations and
kingdoms as his instruments. For as long as Israel has existed as a nation—
such was at least the general conception in the time of the kings—Yahweh
has been its king (Num. 23.11; Deut. 33.5; Ps. 114); it was also declared
that since the creation of the world he has been its universal ruler (cf.
Mic. 4.13; Zech. 4.14).

But this did not prevent the view that Yahweh at a certain point of

[24] Thus, for instance, Eissfeldt, Eerdmans and others (see n. 21). This is in fact the only
'positive' argument of Eerdmans against the idea of the enthronement festival.

[25] All the authoritative passages attaching the epithet of melekh to Yahweh have been gathered
by Eissfeldt, op. cit., p. 89.

[26] See v. Baudissin, Adonis u. Esmun, pp. 39ff.

[27] Von Gall, 'Über die Herkunft der Bezeichnung Jahwes als König', in Wellhausenfestschrift,
pp. 147ff. See further Additional Note XIII.

[28] On this general oriental background of the ideas of the kingship of the god, see Eissfeldt in
ZATW 46, 1928.

[29] Cf. Gadd, Ideas of Divine Rule in the Ancient East; Frankfort, Kingship.

[30] See von Gall in Wellhausenfestschrift, pp. 155f.

time *became* the king of Israel, i.e. at the election, at the Exodus from Egypt (Ps. 114.1f.), or at the making of the covenant on Mount Sinai (Deut. 33.5). That Yahweh *became* king is bound up with the fundamental fact of salvation in the life of the people.

But in the cult the fact of salvation is re-experienced as a new and actual reality. Yahweh is ever anew witnessed as 'coming', 'revealing himself', and doing works of salvation on earth. The Israelite idea of God was not static but dynamic. Israel did not regard the Lord principally as sitting in calm possession and execution of his divine power,[31] but as one who rises and seizes the power, and wields it in mighty works. And this is as a rule concretely pictured; from the 'mythical' side this is seen epically and dramatically: at a certain time Yahweh *became* king. To the Israelite way of thinking there is no contradiction between this and that he is king for ever; such a contradistinction is modern and rationalistic. This particularly applies to the cult, as it re-experiences as a new reality the fundamental fact of salvation. From the modern point of view we should in such cases say that he has *again* become king, seized the royal power, or the like; the Israelite might have said the same, if his language had distinguished between the 'permansive' and the 'inchoative' act or event— but that is exactly what it does not do.[32] And in the cultic experience the whole attention is concentrated on that which is again witnessed as something actual; it is there conceived as something happening at that moment. The Lord, Yahweh, becomes king, he shows himself as king, and performs kingly deeds, and in the graphic conception and presentation of the cult this is all gathered up in the definite picture of his royal entry and arrival, invisibly mounted on the cherub-borne throne.

Exactly the same logically undeveloped mode of conception obtained in the Babylonian religion. There also Anu, or Enlil, or Marduk, or Ashur, *is* king; but the sources prove that the cultic feast celebrated him as the one *now becoming* king; the new year festival marked his enthronement. So also in Israel.

In the rites and psalms belonging to the festival of the enthronement of Yahweh this idea was mirrored, or, rather, presented, expressed, and experienced. A main event was evidently the great festal procession, the victorious coronation entry of the Lord, to which reference is made in Ps. 47.6. It must have had a strongly dramatic character,[33] with playing, singing and dancing.[34] The personal presence of Yahweh in the festive procession was most probably symbolized by his holy shrine (the ark). Both Ps. 24 and Ps. 132 were probably connected with this procession; but our hypothesis is valid even without these witnesses.

[31] As it finds expression for instance in the oriental statues of gods, which also present the god standing or enthroned, with the royal tiara and the royal staff and the like.
[32] See Birkeland, *Grunnriss*, p. 23. (Grammar ¶ 613).
[33] Pss. 68.25ff.; 132; 24. On the connexion of these psalms with the cultic enthronement of Yahweh, see below.
[34] Cf. 2 Sam. 6.5, 12–16; Pss. 42.5; 149.3; 150.4.

It is this appearance and enthronement day of Yahweh which originally was called 'the day of the Lord', 'the day of the feast of Yahweh'.[35]

4

Before taking up the question of the feast day to which Yahweh's enthronement festival may belong, we shall discuss the age of the enthronement psalms. In point of principle this question has two aspects: (a) How old is this form of poetry in itself, the type as such? and (b) How old are the actual enthronement psalms still extant?

Interpreters have always been aware of the close relationship between the enthronement psalms and Deutero-Isaiah, with regard to substance as well as phraseology. For contemporary interpreters it seems almost too obvious that they are dependent on Deutero-Isaiah. Even Gunkel (followed by Kraus) maintains this, though it actually does not agree with his fundamental view of the psalm types; for he admits that Jeremiah imitated the style of the psalms of lamentation and not vice versa, and that Deutero-Isaiah elsewhere imitated the forms and ideas of the hymns. When Gunkel therefore makes the enthronement psalms an exception to his principle, it is as a result of his insistence on the eschatological interpretation. Snaith has taken up the idea of dependence upon Deutero-Isaiah as an argument against tracing them to a pre-exilic new year festival, and tries to prove this by means of long lists of passages showing conformity between the psalms and Deutero-Isaiah.[36] But Johnson is perfectly right in saying that 'such a list may prove to be a two-edged sword, and that as a result quite the opposite conclusion is possible'.[37]

The fundamental question, however, is not concerned with the date of individual enthronement psalms, but with this type (Gattung) of psalm as such. A methodical comparison based on the history of forms and ideas provides clear evidence that instead of the now prevalent tendency to attribute to these psalms a dependence on Deutero-Isaiah, exactly the opposite is true. In the same way that Jeremiah is dependent on the traditional style of the psalms of lamentation with their particular elements of form and substance, and as Deutero-Isaiah himself takes up the forms

---

[35] Hos. 7.5; 2.15; 9.5.—That the 'day' of Yahweh originally indicated the day of his festival becomes quite obvious from Am. 5.17ff., which does not refer to an eschatological day of Yahweh (as supposed by Gunkel, Gressmann, Sellin, Dürr and many others), but where the 'day' is clearly and distinctly imagined as a festival day, see v. Gall, *Basileia*, pp. 25f. Akkadian *umu ili* is the 'festival day of the god'. But in Akkadian already the term has to a certain degree become detached from the cult, indicating in general a day when the god reveals himself in all his power in order to help his worshippers; thus for instance the term 'the day of (the god) Nusku' is used in prayers, see Hölscher, *Urspr. d. jüd. Eschat.*, p. 13. But the idea of 'revelation', 'epiphany', was also originally attached to the cult, see Weinreich in *HBKLA*, *Ergänzungsbd.*; this also applies to the typical epiphany formula 'I am . . .', see Norden, *Agnostos Theos*, pp. 207ff., 215ff.; Gressmann in *ZATW* 34, 1914, pp. 288ff. The epiphany psalm 50 (see *hôphîa'* v.2) according to tradition belongs to the festival of harvest and tabernacles.

[36] See Snaith, *Studies in the Psalter*, pp. 66ff.—Feuillet, too, champions the dependence on Deutero-Isaiah and the post-exilic date of the enthronement psalms (*Nouv. Revue Theol.*, 73), but without new arguments.

[37] *The O.T. and Modern Study*, ed. H. H. Rowley, p. 194.

and ideas of the hymn, so too is he dependent on the ideology and style of the enthronement psalms. That is to say, he has consciously imitated and used them as a pregnant expression of the message he is bringing.[38] The enthronement psalm as a special cultic type (*Gattung*) therefore is older than Deutero-Isaiah, and must consequently have existed even in the cult at the pre-exilic temple.

This agrees with the fact that other psalms which are closely related to the enthronement psalms as regards ideology and cultic situation, such as Pss. 132; 84; 68; 24, without doubt belong to pre-exilic times. We shall discuss the relationship of these psalms to the enthronement festival more closely below.

This fact does not exclude the possibility that *some* specimens handed down to us of this type, may be later, even post-exilic. From the history of form and cult, however, there is nothing to indicate that the so-called Exile marks any important line of distinction. After the restoration, about 520 B.C., the ancient temple service was certainly as far as possible restored with the old forms and according to traditions still alive both in the levitical families who had been carried away, and among those left behind who even during the 'period of exile' had maintained some kind of cult among the ruins of the Temple (cf. Jer. 41.5). And I feel convinced that it will not be possible to give cogent *proof* of the post-exilic origin of any one of the enthronement psalms. One might be tempted to take the reference to the 'commandments and laws' of Yahweh in Ps. 99 as an expression of the particular spirit of Judaism, namely 'legalism', but we find the same term for the revealed will of Yahweh even in the definitely pre-exilic royal thanksgiving psalm (Ps. 18.23). It is worth noticing that in Ps. 99, Moses like Aaron is included among those 'that call upon the name of Yahweh'. To 'call upon the name of Yahweh', *qārā' (bĕ)šēm Yhwh*, is a term used of cultic supplication, especially by the one who is performing the cult, a task in the first instance belonging to the priest (cf. Joel 2.17). So even Samuel is here considered to be a priest, and this agrees with the earlier tradition, where he is a priestly 'seer' (*rō'eh*), whereas the later tradition describes him as a 'prophet'. A divergent version of the Meribah tradition, earlier than the one in the Pentateuch, is presupposed in Ps. 81.[39] The reference to 'Yahweh's footstool', i.e. the ark, in v. 5 may also be taken to indicate a pre-exilic origin of Ps. 99. Ps. 93, too, may well be of pre-exilic origin.[40]

In favour of a post-exilic dating of the enthronement psalms Eissfeldt has urged that in no unquestionably pre-exilic passage is the kingship of Yahweh ever mentioned in connexion with creation,[41] so that this idea

[38] See *Ps.St.* II, pp. 195ff. That Ps. 93 is older than Deutero-Isaiah is maintained by Helen Jefferson in *JBL* LXXI, 1951, pp. 155ff.
[39] See Bentzen, *Salmerne, ad. loc.*
[40] See Jefferson in *JBL* LXXI, 1951, pp. 155ff. Whether Deutero-Isaiah has known this definite psalm or not, is of minor importance since the psalm-type as such undoubtedly is older than he.
[41] See Eissfeldt in *ZATW* 46, 1928, p. 103. Repeated by Kraus, *Die Königsherrschaft Gottes im A.T.*, p. 131.

must have been derived from Deutero-Isaiah. This is completely false. We find it—and moreover in a highly mythological version—in Pss. 74.12ff., and 89.10ff.; in the latter passage the word *melekh* is not used, but 'ruler' (*mōšēl*); but on the other hand we have here the 'homage-cry to the king' (*tĕrû'â*) as the characteristic mode of homage to Yahweh (v. 16). Doubt remains whether Ps. 89 must be dated from pre-exilic times; in this lament 'the Anointed', i.e. the king, utters the lamentation. And Ps. 74 may with just as much probability be referred to one of the great disasters during the later monarchy, to 598 or 587, as to an unknown conquest and spoliation of the Temple in post-exilic times—the age of the Maccabees is out of the question from reasons based on the history of the canon. So Deutero-Isaiah cannot possibly have a prior claim on the idea of creation as the basis of Yahweh's kingship. In fact he is here dependent on earlier tradition and style, and here, as in many other cases, he has simply drawn on the thoughts and style of the cultic psalms. The idea of creation as the great achievement of Yahweh and the idea of his kingship are both indigenous in the cultic lyrics; that is where the two ideas have been knit together, and that is where Deutero-Isaiah has found thought content as well as thought forms.

So, though one or another enthronement psalm may be of post-exilic origin, it is of no consequence for the problem as to the age of the type as such and of the cultic festival presupposed. In fact Deutero-Isaiah is a witness to the existence of the enthronement psalm type in pre-exilic days. And should this type of psalm presuppose a corresponding cultic 'enthronement festival', then such a festival must have existed in pre-exilic times. The following pages will make apparent so many features of the festival which are so closely connected with Israel's national existence as an independent state, and with the Davidic dynasty, that there can be no further doubt as to its pre-exilic origin.

5

No particular day named after the feast of Yahweh's enthronement is expressly mentioned in the texts. But the enthronement idea may, as shown above, have been only one of many ideas underlying the cultic festival which must be presupposed as the background of the enthronement psalms. This festival is likely to have been one of the well-known great festivals of the year. Let us try to find out which festival it was.

Yahweh's enthronement day is the day when he 'comes' (96.13; 98.9) and 'makes himself known' (98.2), reveals himself and his 'salvation' and his will (93.5; 99.7), when he repeats the theophany of Mount Sinai (97.3ff.; 99.7f.) and renews the election (47.5) of Israel, and the covenant with his people (95.6ff.; 99.6ff.). The mighty 'deed of salvation' upon which his kingdom is founded is the Creation, which is alluded to in a rather mythic guise (93.3f.). His coming means the renewal of the life of nature—this being the reason why the poets exhort heaven and earth and sea, field and stream, trees and mountains, to rejoice at the coming of the king. All these ideas will be dealt with at length below. The festival is, then, a festival of the epiphany of Yahweh[41a] in the literal meaning of this word. As just mentioned, there is reason to think that it—or one of its days—was called 'the day of Yahweh', i.e. the day of his cultic coming and revelation as king (Hos. 7.5); this day was the *yôm ḥagh yhwh*, 'the day of Yahweh's (special) feast' (Hos. 9.5).

Among the three great festivals of the year there was one which in ancient times was considered as '*the* (special) feast of Yahweh', or simply 'the feast', *heḥāgh*, and this was the 'Harvest festival' or 'feast of Tabernacles' in the autumn (Ex. 23.16; 34.22). It closed the agricultural year and opened the new one, which in ancient Canaan began with the rainy season and the awakening of the whole creation to new life (see above, p. 94). In somewhat later times[42] it was celebrated throughout eight days at full moon in the month of Tishri which, according to the Babylonian calendar used by the Jews from the Exile, was reckoned as the seventh. But there is reason to believe that in older times it was celebrated one month later, in the old month of Ethanim (the eighth month), i.e. October/November.[43] The olive harvest lasts this long,[44] and then the rainy season begins. To this festival belongs, without doubt, the public thanksgiving psalm (Ps. 65) with its allusions to the rain that the new 'year of goodness' has brought to the land. Cf. Zech. 14.17, for the connexion between the feast of Tabernacles and the coming of the rain. In Zech. 14.16–19 we are told expressly that this feast is the feast of Yahweh Sèba'oth as king.

Ps. 65 shows that this festival in older times, too, had regard to the annual revival of life. And it also shows that its 'cult myth' was that of Creation (and of the fight with the primeval dragon), and all that was connected with it. To the mind that sees the cult as a reality which liberates new forces and recreates life, this idea of the new year ceremony as

[41a] See above, Chap. IV. 3, p. 93.

[42] Mentioned for the first time in the law about the feasts of the Lord, Lev. 23.33ff., in the book of Ezekiel 45.25 and by P in Nu. 28.11ff. (The chronological relation between these three passages is disputed; I consider Lev. 23.33ff. the oldest.) That the feast started on the day when the moon was at her full is also seen from 1 Kgs. 12.33, where the critical remark about Jeroboam does not refer to the day, but to the month. 1 Kgs. 12.26–33 is handed down to us as written by the Deuteronomistic author, but is no doubt based on older material, in the last instance dating from the official annals of Jerusalem. Vv. 28, 30b and 32a at any rate are derived from the sources used by the author.

[43] Notice that the critical remark in 1 Kgs. 12.33, 'which he had devised of his own heart', is not mentioned in the note about the source of v. 32a. Apart from v. 33 there is no reason to refer the words 'like unto the *ḥagh* of Jerusalem' only to the date; the most natural interpretation is to refer it both to date and month. If so we here find testified that in earlier times even in Jerusalem the harvest feast (*he-ḥāgh*) was celebrated in the eighth month, that is to say in the month of Bul, not as was later the case, in the 'seventh' Ethanim. Nor is Jeroboam, when he wanted to introduce a festival in competition with that of Jerusalem, very likely to have chosen a date one month later than the latter; then we have far better reason to suppose that the festival of Jerusalem was later advanced one month in order to forestall Bethel. The choice of the month Ethanim would then probably indicate the desire to attach the feast to the time of the autumnal equinox.

[44] See the references above, Chap. IV, n. 43, p. 94.

a world-creation feast would come quite naturally. It is well known that
in later Judaism the new year time in autumn was considered as the time
of the renewal of the Creation. To the same harvest festival also belongs the
thanksgiving psalm (Ps. 67), with the idea of Yahweh's 'ruling' (*šāphaṭ*)
the nations of the earth and the consequent blessing of the year as the result
of this 'just rule'. The idea of the election and the covenant is alluded to
in Ps. 65.5. There is absolutely no reason to reject the tradition in Mishna
Sukka IV.5 that Ps. 118 belonged to the feast of Tabernacles. It is a
procession psalm and alludes to 'the day' of the feast (v. 24), to the procession up to and around the altar, and to the green branches with which
the altar was covered 'up to its horns', or, as read in Sukka IV.5, 'so
that their tops bent over the altar'. The psalm alludes also to the
Hosanna-cry of the procession, and to the light of the torches in the torch
dance on the first night of the feast, giving the rites a symbolic interpretation: 'Yahweh is our God who has brought us light' (v. 27).

It is also quite clear that already in pre-exilic times the harvest festival
was also that of the new year. Originally there was probably no specific
single day that was considered to be new year's day, as was the case in
later Jewish times. The whole seven to eight days of autumn or harvest
festival (*ḥagh hā'āsîph*, *ḥagh haqqāṣîr*) may in older times have been celebrated
as the new year's feast; it was expressly stated that the 'feast of ingathering'
was to take place 'at the year's end', 'at the turn of the year' (*bithĕqûphath
haššānā*, 'when the year has completed its round'), 'in the beginning of the
year' (*bĕṣē'th haššānā* Ex. 34.22; 23.16).[45] It is not rare in the time-
reckoning of ancient nations to find that a rather indefinite 'New Year's
Tide' precedes the later definite 'New Year's Day', or that several annual
new year festivals were celebrated, whenever one arrived at an important
new departure in the round of life and nature. This happened both in
Egypt and in Babylonia.[46] The idea is connected with the general conception of the need for special initiating and inaugurating 'transition-
rites' at all the important new departures in the life of society and of the
individual.[47] The important thing to remember here is that in Israel the
harvest thanksgiving was a new year festival. In Jewish times the harvest
festival was divided into three parts, following close upon one another:
the new year feast or 'the memorial of blowing of trumpets', on Tishri 1st;
the feast of the atonement, on the 10th, and the feast of tabernacles on
Tishri 15th to 21st; the items of the general festival being to a certain
extent distributed between these three.[48] Remembering the invariable

---

[45] See Wellhausen, *Prolegomena*[3] A, Chap. 3, pp. 109ff. (E.T., pp. 108ff.). The festival of
harvest and tabernacles always retained this character of new year even after a definite new
year day, *rō'š haššānā*, 1st of Tishri, had come into being; see Volz, *Das Neujahrsfest Jahwes*,
pp. 7ff.; Mowinckel, *Ps.St.* II, pp. 94ff. See Additional Note XIV.

[46] Cf. van der Leeuw, *Phänomenologie*, ¶ 56.2, p. 368 (E.T., p. 391); Nilsson, *Primitive Time-
Reckoning*, pp. 267ff.; Frankfort, *Kingship*, pp. 103f., 313f.; Mowinckel, *Zum isr. Neujahr*, p. 18.

[47] Cf. van Gennep, *Les rites de passage*.

[48] Lev. 23.23-36.—In *HUCA* I, III and X Morgenstern has tried to penetrate into the question
as to when and how this division took place.

conservatism of cults we find no reason to doubt that many of the ideas and ceremonies which are connected with the opening day of the year in later Judaism are largely derived from the older, more comprehensive celebration of harvest and new year, the feast of tabernacles.[49] All over the East these ideas have been connected with the new year cult, the greatest of all the annual celebrations.[50]

Our thesis then will be that even on the basis of the special group of 'enthronement psalms' in the form-critical sense, we shall be able to prove that the enthronement festival of Yahweh, presupposed by them, could not be a separate, as yet unknown festival, but must have been the old festival of harvest and new year, the 'feast of tabernacles'. We have not here a newly discovered festival, not referred to elsewhere in the Old Testament, but a hitherto unheeded aspect of the well-known and frequently mentioned feast of tabernacles in its character of new year festival.[51]

We have already seen that the enthronement festival of Yahweh and the feast of tabernacles and of New Year have in common the idea of Yahweh's 'appearance' and 'epiphany', of the renewal of nature and creation, of the repeated 'work of salvation' to be performed by him, and of Yahweh's universal dominion over the earth (cf. Ps. 65).

In addition there are further reasons. Jewish tradition affirms the enthronement psalm (Ps. 47), to be a new year psalm. There can be no reason to doubt that this liturgical usage corresponds with the original meaning of the psalm, particularly since the great procession which it implies is known to have been the usual oriental new year's rite. The Mishna tradition of course, refers to the later special new year's day on the 1st of Tishri, which dates back to earlier Judaic times and is a result of the independent development of a single aspect of an original festal complex of several days. The new thing about this new year day is that it has become a single day in advance of the main festival; its substance is derived from the earlier festal complex.

According to tradition as well as the explicit testimony of the psalm itself, Ps. 81 is also a new year psalm. But Ps. 81, both with regard to logical structure—the different items contained in it—and the cultic situation making up its background, is an exact parallel to the enthronement psalm (Ps. 95). In common with Ps. 95 it has the conception of Yahweh's appearance and the revelation of his nature ('name') and will—the epiphany concept—also the renewal of the covenant, and an admoni-

---

[49] For details see below in the text, pp. 135ff.

[50] Cf. Wensinck in *Act. Or.* I, pp. 158ff.; *id.*, *Arabic New Year.*

[51] That this is the meaning of the expression 'Enthronement festival' has been made perfectly clear already in *Ps.St.* II. Nevertheless, the objection has been made again and again (e.g. by Gunkel, *Einl.*, pp. 105f., Kraus, *Königsherrschaft Gottes*, pp. 21f., and lastly by McCullough in *A Stubborn Faith*, pp. 53ff.) that no such 'new feast' is known or mentioned in the O.T. The answer to this is simply—as the present author again and again has pointed out—that the feast of tabernacles, the old harvest and new year feast, is mentioned and hinted at very often in the O.T., as is well known to every Bible reader. An unfair objection does not become fair by being repeated (cf. below, n. 60).

tion to faithfulness thereto, with a reference to the fate of the Fathers. Ps. 50 follows the same train of ideas. If we may take for granted that Ps. 81 not only reflects a situation in the imagination of the poet, but a real cultic situation of dramatic character—and there is no reason to doubt this—then this psalm must belong to the same festal complex as Pss. 95 and 47, that is to say, to the complex of harvest and new year festival. But along with Pss. 47 and 95 must also go the whole group of enthronement psalms, properly so called; their cultic situation cannot be distinguished from that of Ps. 95, the first part of which is obviously an enthronement psalm.

To what has been said, may be added a series of other observations. Just as the harvest feast was 'Yahweh's festival', so new year's day on the 1st of Tishri was the special festal day of Yahweh: 'this day is sacred to our Lord' (Neh. 8.10).

New year's day is the day for the 'sounding of horns' (*yôm haššôphār*), a rite characteristic of the festal enthronement procession of Yahweh (Pss. 47.6; 98.6; cf. 81.4). It is also called the 'day for the cry of homage', *yôm hattĕrû'â*; the cry of homage (*tĕrû'â*) is at the same time characteristic of the psalms and of the day of enthronement (47.2, 6; 98.6); the cry of homage means 'royal homage', 'homage to the king' (*tĕrû'ath melekh*) for Yahweh; when this cry is heard in Israel it is evidence that 'Yahweh her God is with her' (Num. 23.21).[52]

These proofs and indications are supported by the Jewish tradition in the Mishnah. Here new year's day is looked upon as the day of creation, just as the feast of tabernacles, as well as the enthronement psalms, have a special connexion with creation. 'This day is the origin of thy works'.[53] It is also the day when Yahweh 'judgeth', i.e. decides all that is going to happen in the year to come, determines the fate of states and land, of mankind and of the crops of the earth.[54] To the lessons read in the synagogues first of all belong the so-called 'Malkiyoth', i.e. passages from the Scriptures speaking of Yahweh as a king, and the so-called 'Zikronoth', Scripture passages telling that Yahweh 'remembers' his creation.[55] We shall return to this in more detail below, and see that in fact many other psalms are closely related to the substance and cultic situation of the 'enthronement festival' and that they thus throw a new light on both.

The objection might be raised that the traditions of the Mishna are too late to prove anything with regard to Old Testament times.[56] But as long as the thought of creation is undoubtedly to be found in a psalm for the feast of tabernacles, like 65 (which beyond doubt also refers to the turn of the year), the connexion between the idea of creation and that of

---

[52] The parallelism shows that *melekh* in Nu. 23.21 can be nobody else than Yahweh himself.
[53] See Fiebig, *Rosch ha-schana*, pp. 45, 48f., 53f.
[54] Fiebig, *ibid.*, pp. 41ff., 77.
[55] Fiebig, *ibid.*, pp. 53ff. See *Ps.St.* II, p. 82.
[56] So for instance both Pap and Snaith; see also Johnson in *The O.T. and Modern Study*, pp. 193, 195.

the time of new year has been proved, even with regard to the Old Testament. Nor can the tradition of the Mishna about the connexion between new year's day and the kingship (and enthronement) of Yahweh be quite fortuitous; nor is it likely to be due to foreign influence, at a time when official Judaism tended more and more to isolate itself from anything extraneous. The ideas must have some relevance to an earlier Jewish conception of new year's day or the festal complex of new year. In fact, these very ideas play the leading role in the new year psalm (Ps. 47), which can on no account be dated later than early Jewish times.[57] Another fact is that several rites in the feast of Tabernacles, which are only mentioned in the Mishna, are much older and are actually referred to in the Old Testament.[58]

In the light of all these evidences and indications, increased emphasis must be laid on the fact that the ideas of the appearance and enthronement of the god and of the repeated creation and renewal of life were connected with the new year festivals in the whole of the surrounding orient. It is a fact that Israel's cult has not escaped strong influence from oriental cultic customs and ideas, with Canaan as the nearest and natural connecting link.

On the basis of a cultic interpretation of the enthronement psalms we may therefore state that they take for granted the existence of a corresponding festal day,[59] characterized by the same ideas, and that this festival had the feature of a new year festival.[60] In earlier times the new year festival in Jerusalem was the chief festival of the year, the feast of Tabernacles and of harvest; later, at any rate in earlier post-exilic time, a separate new year's day, rō'š haššānâ (Ezk. 40.1), detached itself and assumed a great many ideas that had hitherto been connected with the wider new year festival. This did not make the latter lose its old character, on the contrary it remained still very much alive in rites as well as psalms till the fall of the Temple, and was even known to the tradition of the Mishna. Amongst these conceptions was that of the kingship of Yahweh based on the creation and renewal of life. So, what has so far been called

---

[57] Snaith and Aalen deny that the idea of creation is found in the enthronement psalms. See, however, Additional Note XV.

[58] The festival of light (with the dance with torches) is referred to in Ps. 118.27, and so is the dance-like procession (ḥagh); the whole psalm has been sung at such a procession. The same thing applies to the crowning of the altar with garlands of green branches. Isa. 12.3 refers to the ceremony with pouring of water. Worth noticing also is that Isa. 12 and Ps. 118 are almost identical as to substance and partly even phraseology, just as Isa. 12.4–6 stands quite in line with the 'enthronement psalms' as to style, tone and ideas. In fact there is every reason to suppose that the two psalm quotations in Isa. 12 are derived from psalms belonging to the festival of tabernacles (new year) and enthronement. If we bear in mind the religio-phenomenological connexion of the said rites with the primeval 'primitive' rites of fertility, rain and life-revival, it is quite out of the question that they should be late Jewish innovations in the temple cult.

[59] On two new attempts to find another cultic situation behind the enthronement psalms, see Additional Note XVI.

[60] See above, n. 45.

'the enthronement festival of Yahweh' is, historically speaking, actually another aspect of the harvest and new year festival itself.

The question then is, whether the enthronement psalms belong to the detached new year's day or to the new year festival of the older complex. Did the very idea of enthronement, with the ceremonies attached to it, above all the great royal procession, in later time still belong to the festival of the older complex, or has it then been attached to the detached new year's day alone?

Ps. 81 mentions a special new year's day at the new moon besides 'the feast' (*haggēnû*), i.e. of harvest and Tabernacles, at full moon. It contains clear references to the 'cry of homage' and the 'sounding of horns', characteristic of new year's day, the 1st of Tishri, the 'day for sounding horns', the 'day for cries of homage'.[61] But side by side with the 'day of new moon' we are here told of 'the full moon on our feast day'.[62] It is therefore not easy to decide for which of these two days the psalm was composed. But the text at least shows that the author was fully aware that the two feasts belonged to the same set, that they were based on the same ideas, and distinguished in part by the same customs. Nor does the psalm deny that the detached new year's day received its content and rites from the earlier feast of Tabernacles.

The special new year's day is first mentioned in Ezk. 40.1, and for those who hold that the book of Ezekiel is written by Ezekiel himself, the question ought to be settled. The day is mentioned there in a perfectly matter-of-course way, as something well known and not as a piece of news. But even to those who, like the present author, consider the book to be a work of Ezekiel's disciples some time after the return (the restoration), its evidence is not without importance.

But even if we should abide by the impossibility of proving that a new year's day on the 1st of Tishri was pre-exilic, and that the 'enthronement festival' of the monarchy was part of, or an aspect of, the seven days' complex of harvest and new year, the question yet remains whether among the seven (or eight) days of the feast one particular day might stand out as the day of Yahweh's enthronement, to which the enthronement psalms would belong,[63] as was the case with the Babylonian feast of new year and enthronement.[64] If so, it would be natural to think of the seventh day, 'the last day, that great day of the feast', and to suppose that Yahweh's royal entry would take place on that day. In support of this hypothesis we might plead that the Mishna and Talmud refer the procession psalm (Ps. 118), to the seventh day of the feast. The 'last day' is likely to be the seventh; the eighth being considered a supplement to the seven days of the feast proper.

---

[61] See *hārīʿû* = 'cry *těrûʿâ*' = 'cry out' (cf. Humbert, *La 'Terouʿa'*, pp. 39ff.); 'blow the trumpets on the day when the moon is at her full'.

[62] *bakkese' yôm ḥaggēnû*. See Additional Note XVI.

[63] See above, n. 45.

[64] See Frankfort, *Kingship*, pp. 318ff.

If it be true that the enthronement idea is a pre-exilic aspect of the feast of harvest and Tabernacles, then we have to ask how old this connexion may be. How far back into pre-exilic times can we trace the concept of Yahweh's 'appearance' and epiphany at the harvest feast as a royal entry and an enthronement? Here we need to remember that the feast itself, the chief feast of the year, marking the end of the old year and the beginning of the new, had been adopted from the Canaanites. The ground for this statement is, quite simply, its nature as an agrarian festival. Its basic idea is connected with the cultivation of the earth, and this fact is clearly brought out by its ancient fertility rites, the green branches and the ceremony of water drawing. It was celebrated in Ugarit before the invasion of the Israelites,[65] and by the Canaanites at Shechem at the time of Abimelech (Jdg. 9.27). There is no reason to doubt that the Jebusites in Jerusalem, too, used to celebrate a similar harvest and new year feast. That the festival itself was adopted by the Israelites even before the monarchy will be seen from Jdg. 21 and 1 Sam. 1f.[66]

Everything seems to suggest that the Canaanites already celebrated the festival as an enthronement festival for the god as king. For Ugarit the texts give ample evidence. The resurrection of Baal (and his victorious fight against Môt) ends with his sitting down on the throne, receiving the homage of his people, and building his temple. Therefore it is very likely that the El Elyon feast in the Jebusite Jerusalem was celebrated as an enthronement festival.

On the other hand, the concept of Yahweh as a king would hardly be adopted by the Israelites until they themselves had got a king, and, with him, an obvious occasion to bestow on Yahweh this highest title of honour.

How early Yahweh came to be looked upon as a king in Jerusalem, it is impossible to tell with any certainty on the basis of the few and fragmentary texts handed down to us from earlier times.[67] But at any rate we know that Solomon had furnished the Temple with an (empty) cherub's throne, which was certainly understood to be the throne of Yahweh.[68] In the very old Ps. 110 Yahweh is the king, sitting on his throne and offering to his 'son', the earthly king, the seat of honour at his right side. In the likewise very old Ps. 68 the worshipper calls Yahweh 'his king and his god'. Therefore we have every reason to believe that the rich temple cult in Jerusalem, highly influenced as it was from Canaan, would also very early have adopted and given expression to the idea of Yahweh's royal entry and enthronement—and if so, it would naturally attach it to the chief festival of the year, 'Yahweh's festival'.

[65] See Hvidberg, *Graad og Latter*; Kapelrud in *NTT*, 1940, pp. 38ff.

[66] See Judges 21.19; 1 Sam. 1.3, 7, 20f. (the words *wayĕhî lithĕqûphôth hayyāmîm* v. 20 have to be placed before v. 21, see *BHK³*).

[67] See Additional Note XVII.

[68] See H. Schmidt, *Lade und Cherubenthron*, *Gunkelfestschrift*; Johs. Pedersen, Israel III–IV, pp. 246ff.; a little differently, Bellas in *Theologia*, 1930.

There is still another aspect of the feast of harvest and Tabernacles, to which the enthronement psalms refer. In Ps. 93.5 we read:

> Thy testimonies are very sure,
> holiness becomes thine house,
> O Yahweh, unto endless time.

In connexion with Yahweh's victory over the powers of chaos, and his enthronement we hear that his temple has now received the 'holiness' belonging to it. 'Holiness' is the numinous quality, which the Temple must have in order to be an abode worthy of Yahweh, and 'effective' for the purpose at which the cult there is aimed. The opposite is 'profaneness', in this connexion the same thing as 'impurity'. The 'holiness' which the Temple now possesses, is not (only) a consequence of Yahweh's entry into it; according to the conception of the Old Testament, certain cultic measures are required in order to consecrate and cleanse it from impurity; cf. Ex. 19. That is the idea behind the great annual 'day of purification'; even if the form in which we find it in Lev. 16, as a separate *yôm kippûrîm*, five days before the feast of Tabernacles, represents a later system, there can be no doubt that something like it, some re-inauguration, re-conse-cration of the Temple must have belonged to the preparations for the feast of Tabernacles even in earlier times.[69] This was the case with the Baby-lonian new year festival. Let us here anticipate slightly by pointing out that the festal hymn preserved for us in Ex. 15, but originally no doubt belonging to the cult, makes the description of the great achievement of Yahweh culminate with the story of the foundation of the Temple, where Yahweh is now enthroned as king:

> A sanctuary thy hands have formed, O Yahweh;
> now Yahweh is king for evermore.

That the Temple has been re-consecrated implies therefore that the whole cultic system is again fully effective as of old. There is a reference to this in Ps. 99 whose true meaning is exactly given in Moffatt's somewhat free translation:[70]

> His priests have still a Moses and an Aaron,
> his worshippers have still a Samuel,
> and Yahweh answers when they call to him,
> still, through the cloudy pillar, speaks to them.

---

[69] In this connexion it may be of interest to point out that the law of Lev. 16 gives the impres-sion of containing different strata; cf. Messel in *ZATW* 27, 1907, pp. 1ff., who claims to have found 3 different strata of laws in the chapter. The original connexion between the festival of tabernacles and new year and that of *Kippurîm* is also maintained with detailed arguments by Bellas in *Theologia*, 1930.

[70] The correct interpretation is given by Buhl, *Psalmerne*; in the second edition he adds a reference to Boehmer, *ZATW* 26, 1906, pp. 156ff.

A re-consecration is a repetition of the first consecration; it is an all but obvious conclusion that it would take place on the anniversary of the original consecration—or, to put it the other way about, from the traditional date of consecration and purification we may deduce that the original consecration must have been performed on that day. This was the line of argument followed in Israel as well. Therefore the first book of Kings (8.1ff.)—in this case probably with the annals of the kingdom for its source—tells us that Solomon consecrated his new Temple 'at the feast in the month Ethanim' (which means the feast of harvest and Tabernacles), and there is no reason to doubt that this is historically correct. The new year feast has been chosen as the feast of the consecration of the Temple! In this connexion it is important that in 1 Kgs. 8 the central act of the temple consecration consists in the ark being brought in a procession into the sanctuary as a symbol of the personal presence of Yahweh. The festal act of 1 Kgs. 8 is described as a repetition of the one in 2 Sam. 6. In this way a connexion has again been established between the enthronement psalms and the new year festival.[71]

The later tradition as it has been handed down to us in the book of Chronicles, traces this connexion to the age of David. When the Chronicler (1.16) in his version of 2 Sam. 6 relates that on the transference of the ark of Yahweh to Jerusalem, a hymn was sung which was composed of passages from the enthronement psalms (Pss. 96 and 97), and other closely related psalms, this cannot be free imagination on his part. There can be hardly any doubt that he conventionalizes his records of the age of David from the actual customs of the festal cult of his own day, in other words, he had a certain day in his mind as a model, the festal day to which the enthronement psalms belonged. Then, we must ask, does not the earlier tradition in 2 Sam. 6 also mean that the transference of the ark, and with it the official inauguration by David of the Yahweh cult in Jerusalem, took place in connexion with the festival of the year, the harvest feast? And as we are able to infer with all likelihood from the Ugaritic texts that the connexion between this festival and the victorious entry of the deity was traditional in Palestine even before the invasion of Israel, and as we consider the purposeful religious politics of David: to fuse the El Elyon cult into the cult of Yahweh and thus make it Israelite, it would be rather strange if he had not seized this opportunity of putting the stamp of Yahwism on this originally Canaanite festival. Even before the time of David it had become the chief festival of the Israelites, being celebrated as such in Shiloh (see above), the centre with which the ark had formerly been associated.

The idea of the purification and re-consecration of the Temple also involves—as can be seen from the law in Lev. 16 about the great day of purification—the idea of atonement for, and forgiveness of, all sins which in the course of the year may have covered people and land with guilt and

[71] See Additional Note XVIII.

impurity. The royal epiphany of Yahweh also means that he shall grace-fully forgive the sins of his people. There is even a reference to this in the enthronement psalm (Ps. 99). As at the time of Moses and Aaron and Samuel—and in conformity with the intentions of the psalmist, it is safe to add, ever after in the history of the people—so through the enthrone-ment of Yahweh it has again become evident that

> thou has been a forgiving God to them,
> hast (not) taken vengeance on their deeds. (v. 8)

Even the earthly king would grant an amnesty on the day of his enthrone-ment (1 Kgs. 1.51ff.; 2 Kgs. 25.57ff.; cf. 1 Sam. 11.12ff.).

Even here the enthronement psalms are in accordance with the thoughts of Judaism on the religious meaning of the new year. It is a well-known circumstance, which, for instance, finds expression in the prayer Abinu Malkenu, that to the new year feast belongs the idea that God shall then forgive the sins of his people, so that they may have a new start as 'new creatures'.[71a]

In 2 Sam. 6, as well as in 1 Kgs. 8, the king himself, David, or Solomon respectively, officiates as chief priest, performing the most important cultic actions with his own hand. This is in full agreement with the ancient Israelite view of the king as 'Yahweh's anointed', his 'son', his viceroy on earth.[72] It results from the nature of the case, that the earthly king would be a central figure in the cult of the new year festival. Of course this will not be brought out by the enthronement psalms, properly so called, in which the personal presence and kingship of Yahweh himself is celebrated. But there are other evidences of the close connexion between the religious aspect of kingship and the chief festival of the year.

First of all we shall draw attention to the term: 'in the beginning of the reign of N.N.' (rē'šîth mamlekheth N.N.) Jer. 26.1. As can be seen from the Akkadian rēš šarruti ša N.N., this is not simply an indefinite dating, but a technical term with a definite intention. In Akkadian it indicates the interval between the death of the old king and the actual assumption of power on the part of his successor and the official sacral installation of the latter at the following new year festival; this installation of the king was celebrated over again every year at the same time with solemn cultic ceremonies. There can be no doubt that the Hebrew term has been directly adopted and translated from the Akkadian. So there is every reason to believe that the phrase has the same technical meaning, though possibly with the difference that it came to indicate especially the very climax of the period: its solemn termination with the sacral installation of the king. Jer. 26 shows that at (the end of) the rēšîth mamlekheth of the king, a great cultic festival would take place. Everything seems to indicate that this festival was the chief one of the year, the feast of tabernacles and

---

[71a] Cf. Sjöberg in StTh IV, 1951, p. 57.
[72] See my book He that Cometh, Chap. III.2, and above, Chap. III.2-4.

new year. The speech made on that occasion by Jeremiah (see Jer. 7) takes as its starting-point precisely the main thoughts of the festival: the complete confidence of the people in the promises of Yahweh with regard to the existence and importance of the Temple. The basis of this becomes still clearer and the idea still more distinct if we consider it against the background of the thought in Ps. 93.5: the faith in the trustworthy promises, guaranteed by the re-consecrated Temple.

Here Ps. 132 may be brought in. It belongs without any doubt to a dramatic festal procession, Yahweh's entry into his palace, where homage is paid to him at his footstool, that is to say, with himself sitting on his throne. But the procession at the same time celebrates the remembrance of, and calls to life the transference of, the ark to Jerusalem and the inauguration of the cult of Yahweh in Jerusalem, i.e. the situation in 2 Sam. 6; and the king here literally plays the part of David. The festival, to which the psalm belongs, is here again proved to be celebrated as a repetition of the succession to kingship, by the grace of Yahweh, of a scion of the house of David; the very favour and the very blessings once secured to David and re-echoed in Ps. 88.20ff. and 2 Sam. 7, are now secured to the reigning king. We can hardly doubt that this episode had its place within the framework of the new year festival. As we shall see, below, there are other things to indicate that Ps. 132 belongs here. And attention must be drawn to the fact that the connexion between the festival of temple consecration and the covenant of David is explicitly mentioned in Solomon's prayer at the consecration of the Temple, 1 Kgs. 8.16.[73]

Together with 2 Sam. 6 and 1 Kgs. 8, Ps. 132 shows, then, that in the religious and cultic conceptions and arrangements the repetition of the covenant of David was connected with the inauguration of the cult of Yahweh in Jerusalem. In the festal complex, including the commemoration of the erection of the Temple and the annual re-consecration of it, 'David', the king, played a central role, both as the 'son' and representative of the deity, and as the 'father' and representative of the people. The king's person is a visible token of God's merciful and strong presence in the midst of his people—a thought and a 'prophecy' which becomes a higher reality in Christ the king, the son of God, and his presence in the midst of his own, both when two or three are gathered in his name, and when the congregation commemorate his work in church festivals.

Now we may sum up the result of this preliminary research based on the rather confined group of true enthronement psalms with occasional references to other texts.

From the very principle of cultic interpretation it is plain that a 'feast of Yahweh's enthronement' must have existed, the main foci of which must have been Yahweh's enthronement and his kingship, based on his victory over the powers of chaos and the primeval ocean, and the creation, repetition and re-experience of these 'facts of salvation' in and through the

[73] Kraus has rightly drawn attention to this, op. cit., p. 43.

festival, and further, the renewal of the historical 'savation': the election, the deliverance from Egypt, and the making of the covenant. The most prominent act of this festival was the great procession with its dramatic and symbolic character, the personal presence of Yahweh being symbolized by the ark.

This feast was originally one aspect of the old agricultural feast of harvest and new year, probably characteristic of a certain day in the festal complex, possibly the seventh; later on, great parts of its complex of ideas were passed on to the new special new year's day, the 1st of Tishri. The enthronement aspect of the feast of new year and Tabernacles can be traced back to the monarchic period.

Another aspect of the festal complex of harvest and new year was its nature as a repeated festival for the consecration of the Temple, commemorating the inauguration of the cult of Yahweh in Jerusalem; to the feast for the consecration of the Temple was attached an annual purification of the same.

The feast for the consecration of the Temple also had the character of a renewal of the covenant with David and the royal house; this idea is naturally linked up with the idea of a renewal of the covenant on Mount Sinai, completed by the covenant with David. Therefore the offspring of David, the king of Israel, would also play an important role in the rites and conceptions of the festal complex.

6

The whole of the harvest festival as an agricultural feast is of course not a legacy from the time in the desert but, as mentioned above, was taken over from the Canaanites after the settlement; and in the same way the conception of the deity as a king, and the annual celebration of his accession and enthronement are of Canaanite origin.

The ancient Canaanite harvest festival was a religious nature feast closely connected with agriculture and fertility religion. It was a question of calling the forces of nature to life again after the time of drought. The changes of the natural year were a manifestation of divine power. The life of nature was one with the life of the deity, his death and triumphant resurrection, which was communicated to the congregation. Life in general, the earth, the whole world, plants, animals and man were created anew with the awakening of the god. It was this that should be ensured by the potent rites of the cultic feast. This was effected through the representation and realization of the process in a dramatic-symbolical form. To ask which is the primary cause, the creative rites, or the recuperative powers of the divinities, is to put a modern, rationalistic question that is here out of place; each is linked with the others; the rites are sacred and divine and established by the deity to create and ensure life and blessing. To higher vision the deity itself would surely be 'the source of life'.

This original nature and fertility cult has left many traces in the old Israelite harvest festival, right down to the latest times—but charged with a new sense and significance. We may mention such things as the tabernacles (Lev. 23.40ff.), and processions round the altar with green branches and fruits (Ps. 118.27), which to the comparative history of religions appear not as originally a thanksgiving, but as an awakening and force-transferring ceremony.[74] The holy power is also to be transferred to the altar to sanctify it, so that it may radiate blessing—as is suggested in the formula which according to the Mishna was pronounced before the altar when the solemn procession touch it with their branches.[75] The same holds good with regard to the water pouring ceremony which is mentioned in the Mishna and referred to in Isa. 12.3; the ceremony was originally intended to secure rain and water for the coming year.[76] During the feast of Tabernacles the water was fetched every day in a solemn procession from the holy spring, Gihon, and poured over the altar. The rabbis were probably still aware of the connexion between this rite and the approaching period of rains;[77] the water is to procure 'salvation', i.e. peace and prosperity—hence the 'well of salvation'. A corresponding significance originally pertained to the wine-offering which was poured over the altar with a view to obtaining a rich vintage. The ritual lighting of a fire, the torch-dance and the light festival,[78] which are mentioned in late Jewish times and may be referred to in Ps. 118.27a, are also a reminiscence of an ancient sun and light ceremony.[79]

In Israel all these ancient rites were gradually reinterpreted as symbolical expressions of the prayer to Yahweh to come and create life and fertility and peace and salvation ('light');[80] but some of the old ideas shine through, right down to late Jewish times, and appear clearly when the presentation of tithes and first-fruits is connected with the festival (Deut. 26.1ff.; Am. 4.4f.). This presentation was, moreover, no mere thanksgiving rite; it was also a prayer for blessings on land and people (cf. Deut. 26.15).

This harvest and new year festival already in ancient times lasted for several days; we hear of this in the days of the Judges, as regards the temple in Shiloh, and in those of Amos regarding Bethel (1 Sam. 1.19; Am. 4.4f.). In Jerusalem it covered seven-plus-one days (Deut. 16.15; Lev. 23.34ff.). Already in Shiloh it was a *hagh*, its chief characteristic

[74] Cf. Nilsson, *Primit. Religion*, pp. 31, 33ff. Frazer, *Golden Bough* (1 vol.), pp. 118ff.
[75] *yōphî lēkhā hammizbēaḥ*, Bab. Sukka IV, 5; see *Ps.St.* V, pp. 25ff.
[76] Bab. Sukka IV, 5.—The pouring of water as a new year custom also occurs with the Persians and the Syrians, see Feuchtwang in *MGWJ* 1911, p. 60; likewise in Burma, see Bastian, *Völker d. öst Asiens* II, pp. 254f. (after Volz, op. cit., p. 57, n. 60); in the light of comparative anthropology: Patai, *Man and Temple*, pp. 24ff.
[77] Bab. Rosh hasshana 16a; Bab. Ta 'anit 2a.
[78] Cf. Hos. 9.4 and see Bab. Sukka IV, 9f., 48a, b, where the original idea is still alive; see Volz, op. cit., pp. 37, 59.
[79] Cf. Volz, op. cit., pp. 26ff.; Nilsson, op. cit., pp. 31f.; Frazer, op. cit., pp. 78ff., 609ff., 643ff., 647f.
[80] For 'light' as a symbol for life, happiness and salvation see Aalen, op. cit., pp. 63ff., 70f.

being the great dance-like procession. From all later custom in Jerusalem, as we see it in Ps. 132 and are able to judge it from the account of the festal procession in 2 Sam. 6, and from the ancient cultic verse, Num. 10.35,[81] we may safely conclude that already in Shiloh the centre of the procession was formed by the visible symbol of the personal presence of the Lord, his holy ark or shrine, from which the divine power radiated; the ark in Jerusalem was, according to official opinion, identical with that in Shiloh[82] which was associated with Moses himself.

But with Yahweh's shrine was linked the view of Yahweh as king. 'Yahweh Sebaoth who is enthroned on the cherubim' is the name he carries when he is represented by the ark (1 Sam. 4.4); but the meaning of the name is 'he that sits on the cherub throne', the sides and arm-rests of which are formed by two winged cherubim; the king on the throne is 'throned on cherubim'.

The conception of the god as king is, as before mentioned, older than Israel. But it is not only this general form of the idea which Israel has received from the Canaanites, it is the same with its cultic and epic expression of the enthronement of the god. In the religious texts from the town of Ugarit (Ras Shamra) in Phoenicia, the feast of the rains—the harvest and new year festival—signifies the revival and resurrection of the god Baal or Aleyan Baal, who, having conquered death (*Môt*), seats himself on the throne and is proclaimed king of gods and men. Together with the enthronement of the god goes the building and consecration of his temple.[83]

These performances were apparently common to the whole of Canaan, and not restricted to Ugarit. That they have been of importance for the development of the cult of Yahweh in Jerusalem cannot be doubted. We know that the god who in pre-Israelite times was worshipped in Jerusalem as the highest god was El Elyon, in our bible translated as 'the most high God' (Gen. 14.18ff.). Inscriptions prove that El Elyon was widely worshipped in Canaan and Syria.[84] The name is the same as the Ugaritic Aleyan. But the name El Elyon, and with it undoubtedly also features both of the cult and the concept, were in Israel transferred to Yahweh—it is Yahweh who is 'the most high god'. Other deities in pre-Israelite days worshipped in Jerusalem were Melekh (the King), Shalem (the Covenant) and Ṣedeq (Justice);[85] they were probably already in the pre-Israelite age

[81] See Additional Note XIX.
[82] See 2 Sam. 6 together with 1 Sam. 4–6, and Additional Note XIX.
[83] See Hvidberg, *Graad og Latter*; Mowinckel in *NTT* 1939, pp. 16ff.; Kapelrud in *NTT* 1940, pp. 38ff., particularly pp. 44ff.; Engnell, *Div. Kingship*, pp. 97ff.
[84] See for instance the Sujin inscription, Bauer *AfO* VIII, the translation p. 11; cf. *A.N.E.T.*, p. 504; cf. also Johnson in *The Labyrinth*, pp. 81ff.
[85] Cf. the names of the kings of Jerusalem: Adonizedeq = 'Zedeq is (my) lord' and Malkizedeq = 'Zedeq is (my) king', or, 'Zedeq is (the god) Adon', 'Zedeq is (the god) Melek'. Probably it is the name of the god Shalem that makes up the last part of Jerusalem, cf. the local name Jeru'el, 2 Chron. 20.16.—For Shalem in Ugarit see Bauer in *ZATW* 51, 1933, p. 99, W. F. Albright, *A.R.I.*, pp. 73, 79. For Zedeq (Ṣydeq) see Baudissin, *Adonis u. Esmun*, pp. 247f. and Index, ibid.

at least to a certain degree conceived as manifestations of El Elyon. El Elyon was also the sun god, whose rays at daybreak puts the evil powers to flight, and who overthrows the haughty who would occupy his throne (cf. Ps. 46.6; Isa. 14.12–15). In Israel Yahweh himself became both 'King' and 'Justice'. His temple was built as a temple of the sun with its opening towards the east, so that the sun at the equinoxes shone straight through the open gates in towards 'the Holy of Holies', where 'He would dwell in the thick darkness', according to Solomon's inaugural prayer.

Already in pre-Israelite times there were, without doubt, connected with El Elyon and Melekh and Ṣedeq certain notions as to how it came to pass that the god *became* 'the Most High', *became* 'the King', and the wielder of 'Justice'—a word which also means 'the royal power' and 'fortune'— and of 'the peace of the covenant'. It behoves 'the Most High God' and 'the King' to provide rain and fertility and crops, and also to protect the 'power', 'peace' and 'fortune' of his people. All this the Israelites transferred to the desert war-god Yahweh, who already before Moses was the god of law and justice, of the peace of the covenant, of markets and the roads.[86] A transference of this kind is quite natural, and in keeping with the character of a revealed religion. In these ideas from patriarchal times the Israelites found ready prepared just those conceptions which could serve as links to the highest vision of Yahweh as the god both of the chosen people and of the whole world. This transition becomes still more easily comprehensible if, as certain things indicate, David's new priest in Jerusalem, Zadok, was descended from the ancient race of priest kings, of whom Melchizedek was a representative.[87] David and his successors were professedly 'priests' after the order of Melchizedek ('for the sake of Melchizedek'), as we hear in Ps. 110.

When Yahweh, in the thought and belief of the Israelites, subjected also the countryside and its agriculture, and became Lord (*ba'al*) and king of the land, and the giver of growth and fruitfulness, the ideas connected with the agricultural and harvesting feasts were also transferred to him. It is well known that all the great annual feasts—excepting that of the passover—were originally connected with agriculture, and taken over from the Canaanites.

[86] Cf. the name 'En mishpāṭ—'the fountain of justice (or judgment)'—for Yahweh's holy fountain at Kadesh. Kadesh was the specific cult place of Yahweh already before the tribes of Israel came to Goshen, and was also their first goal when they left Egypt; here the holy mountain Sinai-Horeb was situated, see Mowinckel in Norsk Geogr. Tidsskrift IX, pp. 21ff., J. Gray in *VT*, IV, 1954, pp. 148ff.; Engnell's doubt as to the connexion between Yahweh and Kadesh (*Gml. Testm.*, I, p. 265, in which by the way he gives a rather inaccurate statement of my opinion) is groundless. In the stories of the Exodus this connexion is evident. When Engnell (and Nyberg) suppose the 'original' deity of Kadesh to be the goddess of the same name, this is nothing but mere conjecture. It might be observed that the *name* of the goddess Kadesh must be secondary as compared to the name of the sanctuary, just as the name of the god Bethel is secondary as compared to the local name; and Babylonian Ea, originally indicating the temple, is secondary as the name of the god; the real name of the god is Enki. The name of the goddess Kadesh has probably been shortened from something like Ba'alat Kadesh.

[87] See Mowinckel, *Ezra d. Skriftlaerde*, p. 109, n. 2; Hall in Peake, *The People and the Book*, p. 11; Bentzen, *Stud. o. d. zadok. Praesteskabs Hist.*, pp. 10f.; Rowley in *JBL* LVIII, 1939, pp. 113ff. and in *Festschrift für Bertholet*, pp. 461ff.

It is important that, in the Canaanite temples also, the appearance of the god before the rainy period was celebrated as a royal enthronement festival, at which Baal's death and resurrection, his struggle and victory, ascent of the throne, 'holy marriage', and also the foundation of his temple, which was both his house and symbolically the whole world, and from which blessing should flow, were all dramatically presented and followed by the congregation as a creative reality filling them, too, with the divine forces of blessing, life, and fertility. Together with this transfer or imitation of a Canaanite agricultural feast, and its conversion to a feast of Yahweh, the Israelites took over and Yahwistically reformed the ideas of the enthronement of the deity, of the royal character of the feast, and of the restoration of life in nature as the result of king Yahweh's victory over his enemies.

But it is also important to note that the king-god festival of the Canaanites was, in fact, only a particular version of a general cultic pattern obtaining throughout ancient oriental civilization, its fundamental features being traceable in most of the religions and cultic systems, although naturally stamped by different national and religious characteristics.[88] In several places the cult found its climax in an annual festival, which more or less clearly and completely contained the representation of the death and resurrection of the god, of the creation-myth, the god's fight with and victory over his enemies, his holy marriage and triumphant entry as king. It is principally from Babylonia and Assyria that we have our certain knowledge of these facts. Here was celebrated, in all the larger cultic centres—mostly in the spring, but in some places in the autumn—a new year festival which may be considered as the enthronement festival of the god—Anu, Enlil, Marduk, Asshur, etc.—at which all the features mentioned were in evidence, and at which hymns were sung which acclaimed the god as creator and king, and described the blessing that his victory and reign would bring to his land and people, and to the whole earth.[89] In a similar way the enthronement of Osiris and Horus was celebrated in Egypt.[90]

This idea of the arrival of the life-creating and renewing god as a king mounting the throne, culminating in a great festal procession then faced the Israelites from all quarters, as soon as they had settled in Canaan and started to adapt their cult to settled agricultural and urban conditions.

When the rains came and renewed their 'world' or 'country'—the Hebrew 'ereṣ has both meanings—the Israelites saw in this a sign that Yahweh himself had come to visit his people and had conquered the powers of chaos and death, and seated himself on the throne and re-established his kingdom, bringing peace and prosperity to his people.

[88] See Additional Note XX.
[89] Cf. Zimmern, AO XXXV, 3; Babyl. Neujahrsfest I and II; Pallis, Babyl. Akitu Festival; Gadd in Myth and Ritual, pp. 40ff.
[90] Erman, Aegypt. Relig.,[2] pp. 62ff.; Ps.St. II, pp. 30ff.; Blackman in Myth and Ritual, pp. 15ff.; cf. Frankfort, Kingship, pp. 181ff.

They then wanted to use the strongest expressions in praise of the Lord and found them in the symbols of the enthronement and the kingdom and the new creation.

In ancient Canaan as well, they spoke of the god's war with, and victory over, the sea and the monsters of the deep. But whether they considered this as an act of *creation* is uncertain; in none of the hitherto known texts does the dragon fight lead to any creation.[91] Baal is on the whole not envisaged as a creator; he is the life-force itself, the god of fertility in field, folk and cattle. It is El, the highest god, who in the Ugarit texts appears as the creator, Baal being identified with the awakening life-force in nature. Yahweh, on the other hand, is the sovereign Lord of the universe, who has conquered chaos and shaped cosmos from it. He is El, Baal and Adon in one, both God and Lord. Yahweh's struggle with chaos and the primeval sea leads to the act of creation.

The same was the case in Babylonia-Assyria, where the annual 're-creation' of life and nature consists in the fields rising from the primeval sea of the spring floods, which inundated the low alluvial plain for miles; there, naturally, the vernal equinox was the time of new year, and there the myth of the primeval sea and the fight with the dragon stood for the story of the creation: Marduk vanquishes Tiamat and creates the world.[92]

Now we find in many places in the Old Testament that in Israel poets and prophets imagined creation as Yahweh's victorious struggle with the primeval sea and its dragon, with Leviathan or Rahab or his 'proud Helpers'.[93] In a much modified and 'rationalized' form the same idea lies at the back of the later story of creation in Gen. 1. No doubt also Canaanite elements now entered into this poetic myth; the Ugarit texts also speak of a dragon, *Lotan* (i.e. Leviathan). But both the strong similarity with corresponding Babylonian religious poetry and the circumstance that it is particularly in the later time of the monarchy (when the connexion with Assyria-Babylonia was lively), that we meet with these ideas in the Old Testament, indicate that it is here a question of Assyrian-Babylonian influence in addition to that of the old Canaanite traditions.

Other features of the enthronement festival point to the same conclusion. First and foremost we may mention the close connexion between the idea of creation and that of the kingship of the deity. In the Babylonian epic of creation, which was the legend and text for the new year's day service, the god Marduk is made king at the council meeting of the gods; and this choice is repeated every year, when they foregather in the 'chamber of fate' in the temple of Marduk. Here fate is 'fixed' for the coming year. The gods 'judge' what the fate of the peoples and the countries is to be, as they 'set fate' ('set that which is determined') for the year.

<hr/>

91 See Additional Note XXI.
92 See Additional Note XXII.
93 Ps. 104.5ff.; Job 38.8ff.; Pss. 74.12ff.; 104.25f.; 89.10f.; Isa. 51.9f.; Job 9.13; 26.12; 7.12; (Ps. 44.20).

The Jewish tradition, too, as we have mentioned, holds that on new year's day, or in the course of the new year festival, Yahweh 'judges' how the new year is to be as to the harvest and the fate of land and people generally.

We may, then, conclude that both ancient Canaanite and Babylonian-Assyrian ideas and customs have contributed elements to the Israelite harvest, new year, and enthronement festival.

In its original form, then, the harvest festival is at the same time a festival of creation and of enthronement. It implies that the 'world' of the congregation is 'created' again, is renewed, and re-constituted a home for mankind, holding fruitfulness and blessing, and secured by the returning deity's apprehended strength and power. This character the feast retained in Israel. We may put it like this, that, when it was a matter of expressing the real religious experience of the festival in the poetical language of the epic myth, then the myth of creation is the original 'legend' of the festival, and this myth includes also that of the enthronement of the god Yahweh: he is made king because of the victory over the enemy, which is implied by the fact of the creation, and because he himself has created his kingdom, the world.

7

In Israel, however, the old, originally Canaanite festival has become something entirely new and *sui generis*. The Yahweh religion has taken over material from many sources. But it has always remoulded this material and made it the bearer of a new spirit.

With regard to the taking over and transforming of the conception of the god's ascension, we must first mention the most important 'negative' new form that Israel gave to it. The conception which was so characteristic of the Canaanite Baal, namely that the defeat, death and resurrection of the god precede his final victory and ascension, was wholly incompatible with Yahweh's essential character.[94] All representations and rites which directly expressed or referred to the death and resurrection of the god therefore had to disappear.

In recent times it has been maintained by several scholars that Israel took over the whole of this 'cultic pattern' more or less unchanged. Some have thought that just as in Canaan, Babylonia-Assyria and other places in the ancient orient, so in Israel, too, the death of the god was dramatically presented in the cult, and the king was regarded as divine, and one with the god; so that when the king in the cultic drama 'died' and 'rose again', he thereby made real the death and resurrection of the god. Through the effective cultic drama the king and the god mutually made each other alive again and gave each other new powers for the new

---

[94] Cf. Johs. Pedersen, *Israel* III–IV, pp. 441ff., cf. ibid., pp. 458, 466, 484, 737ff., 749; see also *Act. Or.* XVIII, pp. 1ff.; Hvidberg, *Israelitiske religion*, p. 71; Bentzen, *Sakrale kongedömme*, pp. 10ff. and *passim*.

beginning of life.[95] In such a case one could think of it either as a direct taking over of the whole 'cultic pattern' and its ideas, or that it was taken over in a more or less 'disintegrated' form, and in such a way that the customs and rites have only in part retained their original meaning, and have partly been reinterpreted or have disappeared.[96] It has thus been maintained that in the Israelite new year ritual it is not Yahweh himself who suffers, dies and rises again, but that this was transferred to a special fertility god, *Dōd*, who is supposed to have been' split off' from Yahweh, by one of the attributes of Yahweh becoming independent, and he is supposed to have been represented in the cult by the king: *Dōd* linguistically equals 'David', which was also a royal title in Israel.[97]

But this hypothesis, in all its different forms, is untenable. It is of course quite right that the temple cult of Israel to a large degree is based on Canaanite and, in the last resort, general oriental cultic patterns. This appears from what has been said above about the new year festival and is constantly confirmed by new archaeological results and text discoveries.[98] It is something which is self-evident, and also has long been recognized by all Biblical scholars.[99] But it is just as self-evident that this has not taken place without deep changes both of the thought and the cultic forms, due to the peculiarity of the Yahweh religion and its essential difference from the surrounding religions,[100] even though Israel only gradually became conscious of this difference.[101] It is unquestionably right that a fundamental thought both in Babylonian-Assyrian and in Canaanite religion was the death and resurrection of the god, represented as a struggle against the power of death and as the defeat and death of the god, succeeded by his resurrection and victory, the whole presented and experienced as a drama in the cult, a cultic play with actual and real effects.[102] But it is equally clear that Israel itself very early felt that there was a decisive difference between these dying Canaanite gods and Yahweh.

[95] See Johnson in *The Labyrinth*, pp. 71ff., joining Hocart, *Kingship*. Cf. Engnell, *Div. Kingship*, p. 170, n. 4, p. 210; Haldar, *Studies in the book of Nahum*, *passim*. See also n. 97, below.

[96] Cf. above, n. 62 to Chap. III.

[97] Engnell, *Kortfattat bemötande av Prof. Bentzens 'diskusjonsinnlägg' Det Sakrale kongedömme*, a manuscript submitted in connexion with the competition for a professorship in Lund, 1946; cf. H. S. Nyberg's critique thereon in 'Sakkunnigutlätande angäende ledigförklarade professorämbetet i exegetisk teologi', published in mimeograph by the University of Lund, 1947, 'Nyberg', p. 15.

[98] See for instance Hooke, *Origins of Early Sem. Ritual*—certainly with a tendency to construct and reckon with too many hypothetical factors—and the summing-up in Albright, *A.R.I.*

[99] See above, n. 57 to Chap. I, and cf. *Ps.St.* II, pp. 200ff.

[100] See references in n. 94 above, and in addition, Baumgartner, *ThZ* III, pp. 98ff.

[101] In spite of justifiable objections to a rigid schematic 'evolutionism', there is a 'development' within historical Yahwism, a development which to a great extent had the nature of a dramatic conflict between the old views of Israel and the religion of the Canaanites; and through which the religion of Israel became conscious of its inherent peculiarities and their potentialities, and expanded them. It is from this 'dramatic' point of view that Hvidberg's *Israelitiske Religions Historie*, for instance, has been written. Cf. also Cook in *The Modern Churchman*, November 1934. To grasp this dramatic history and the line of its development is important even from the point of view of 'revelation history'.

[102] See for instance Hvidberg, *Graad og Latter*; Engnell, *Div. Kingship*, pp. 16ff., 97ff., 143ff., and above, note 95.

While the expression 'the living God' applied to a Canaanite deity meant 'the god who again has become alive' it has, as applied to Yahweh, always meant: The God who always has lived, and always lives, and who, accordingly, everlastingly creates and sustains life.[103] Yahweh is, in the words of the prophet, 'The Holy God who does not die' (Hab. 1.12). That Israel, therefore, should have taken over a complete cult ritual, which implies and exhibits the suffering, death and resurrection of the deity is wholly excluded. Even in the modified form of the 'split-off' vegetation god, who in the person of the king dies and rises again, the theory is unacceptable. In the Old Testament there is no recognizable trace of the cult of such a *Dōd* in Jerusalem. Without doubt the worship of the vegetation god did make its way into many places in Israel, not the least in North Israel,[104] but wherever the Old Testament refers to it, it is in order to condemn it as paganism.[105]

In Canaanite religion—and partly also in Egyptian, but less clearly in Sumero-Babylonian religion—the real thought is that it is the god himself who is renewed in the cult, together with his visible representative, the king. The powerful acts of the cult give to both the god and the king new strength, new blessing, new life, and through his participation in the dramatic rites the king is so to speak (to carry the idea to its extreme) active in creating new life for the god, in order that he in turn should give new life to the fields, the cattle and the people. In Israel, i.e. in the circles who thought and felt in genuinely Israelite fashion, such an idea was unthinkable. For this reason Yahweh was also kept as far away from death and the realm of the dead as possible. Yahweh has nothing to do with the realm of the dead, where he makes no 'wonders'; the dead 'are torn out of his hand', a thought which is emphasized so strongly that logically it enters into opposition to the belief in the omnipotence of Yahweh, and which also led to the strange, unsemitic and non-Hebraic idea that the dead are unclean, and one must have no dealings with them. In Israel the king became, not the one who helps the god to get life and power, but just the reverse, the representative of the whole body of the people, who himself gets all blessing, power and 'life' from Yahweh, because he is Yahweh's 'anointed one', and 'son', who passes on to the people the blessing which he has received from Yahweh through his anointing, and which is renewed for him and the body of the people through the coming of Yahweh in the cult.[106]

This radical exclusion of the thought of the deity's death and resurrection has certainly made the thought of Yahweh's yearly repeated enthronement less logical, but at the same time more deeply religious and realistic.

---

[103] See v. Baudissin, *Adonis und Esmun*, pp. 450ff.

[104] Reference is made for instance in the Mesha' inscription 1.12 to some Israelite deity Daud or Dod and his cultic equipment. Text to be found in Lidzbarski, *Handbuch d. Nordsem. Epigr.* I, pp. 415f., II, Tafel I, etc.; translation by Gressmann, *A.O.T.B.*[2] p. 441. Differently by Albright in *A.N.E.T.*, 1950, p. 320; cf. Ullendorf in *Docts. from O.T. Times*, p. 198.

[105] Ezk. 9.4; Zech. 12.11. Cf. Baumgartner in *ThZ* III, p. 98.

[106] Cf. Johs. Pedersen, *Israel* III–IV, pp. 84ff.

Yahweh's own power and existence and kingship cannot really be threatened by any enemy; no one equals him either in heaven or on earth or in the underworld.[107] But time and time again the evil powers of existence may threaten his creation and bring his cosmos to the verge of destruction —as may be seen to happen in the droughts of summer, in the hostility of the gentiles against his people, and so on. Then on each occasion Yahweh in battle and victory sustains his honour, saves and restores his creation, secures his 'kingdom' and his people, thus maintaining and proving the kingship which is really his from the beginning of Israel and from eternity. This is what happens at his 'epiphany' in the new year festival, when he comes to be 'enthroned', when, after a new victory and a new creation, he sits again on his world-wide throne.

But on the positive side, too, something new was added to the ideological content of the festival in Israel. This derived partly from the contrast between Yahweh and the local deities of nature and fertility, and partly from the historical influence on Israelite religion of their experience of Yahweh in a decisive historical hour, which resulted in the making of Israel. From this experience emerged a vision, of which the prophets gradually became the greatest exponents: Yahweh works and reveals himself in living history.

On the whole this historical character is a really fundamental feature in the religion of Israel. That Israel had experienced Yahweh in history, and that the prophets ever more clearly continued to see him there, and to interpret real history as the truest revelation of him, or, in theological terms, that God actually 'revealed' himself to his witnesses and to his people through reality itself, that the facts of revealed history are his 'words', properly so called, receiving their full meaning through the historical person who was at the same time the 'Word'—this is what has made Israelite religion something essentially different from the 'natural' religions and 'nature-religions' of the Near East.[108] The aphorism about man as distinct from animals: 'man has no nature, he has only a history', eminently fits the religion of Israel.

This also means that in Yahwism the cult has been made into history, and history has been drawn into the cult. The reality re-experienced through the cult is no longer first and foremost the cyclical course and renewal of nature, but the historical 'facts of salvation'.

The facts of salvation, 'recalled' and repeated by means of the festival, were removed from the sphere of natural religion (fertility and so on) to the world of historical reality.[109] Creation itself was no longer considered an undatable phenomenon, but a mighty mythico-historical action taking place on a definite occasion, later 'recalled' and kept up ('renewed', 'preserved', in the language of dogmatics) through the coming of Yahweh

---

[107] Ps. 86.6–8; Isa. 43.11; 44.6; 45.5, 6, 14, 18, 21, 22; 46.9.
[108] On this cf. Elliger, *Bedeutung d. Gesch. Israels f. d. Kirche*; see also Birkeland in *SEÅ* XIII, pp. 44f.
[109] See Additional Note XXIII.

at the festival, and through his miracles there. And side by side with the creation and the re-creation of nature through the festival we have the recollection of the deliverance from Egypt, of the miracle at the Reed Lake and of the Covenant of Kadesh-Sinai and the victory over the natives after the settlement, in short *the election*. These were the elements brought to the fore as the true work of a king and the true saving action of Yahweh, cf. the words of the poet in Ex. 15.18; these are the happenings 'recalled' at the festival and 'repeated' there; for the coming and enthronement of Yahweh again guarantee that the election is still valid, and that the 'right' and supremacy (*sedeq*) over all enemies thus secured for as long as he shall keep the commandments of Yahweh, were again promised and confirmed to Israel.

From what has been said above (pp. 138f.) we are entitled to conclude that in all probability the enthronement idea has been combined with the 'feast of Yahweh' (*hagh* YHWH) in Jerusalem from the very time of the first institution of his cult there. Maybe the idea of Yahweh as king was admitted into Israelite religion even before that time, and if so, presumably at the temple of Shiloh, where the 'Ark of Yahweh Seba'oth' was the central cultic symbol. But we have no clear indications of the enthronement ideas in such early times.[109a]

It goes without saying that not all the ideas connected with the Jerusalem feast of Yahweh's epiphany were taken over at once. The adaptation of the Canaanite ideas to the spirit of the Yahweh religion must have taken time; of course a gradual development of ideas and cult forms has taken place. To this extent our picture of the festival in this chapter is an 'idealized' picture which may not have been fully realized at any particular point of time. A long history has been telescoped in our description. But the main ideas and rites have certainly been the same throughout all the pre-exilic period, and perhaps even much later.

8

As already mentioned, every cultic festival has its festal 'myth', i.e. the tale or 'message' about the 'saving', existential reality, which is being realized through the festival. Such a myth need not be fashioned as an elaborate epic tale, nor even have poetic form; it may be nothing more than a more or less fixed complex of religious concepts about what is taking place, and referred to by the festal songs in more or less detail. So the festival of Yahweh's enthronement naturally had a festal myth,

---

[109a] A. Alt, 'Gedanken über das Königtum Jahwes', *Kleine Schriften* I, pp. 345ff., has tried to find pointers for dating the idea of Yahweh's kingdom back to the period of the 'Judges' and has drawn attention to many of the points dealt with above (pp. 177ff., and other places). But I can neither subscribe to his early dating of the J-saga, nor to his concluding from the existence of the idea of the *benê 'ĕlohîm* in Gen. 6.1ff., the existence of the idea of Yahweh as king. Alt is right, however, in thinking that these ideas have been combined later on, as we can see from 1 Kgs. 22 and Job 1f.

expressing the prevailing ideas concerning what happened at the coming of Yahweh, what was the basis of his enthronement, and what it led to.

But before passing on, and trying to give a picture of the myths behind the festival, we must first explain why we have to draw on material beyond the range of actual 'enthronement psalms' in the strict form-critical sense of the words. Gunkel identifies the picture given by this specific group of psalms with the picture of the cultic situation underlying it, without always realizing that this situation may be, and often is, only part of a greater liturgical whole. So far as the enthronement psalms are concerned, he is content to give a description of the enthronement as the imagination of the poet pictured it, and he does not make any attempt to describe the content of the festival as a whole; he even rejects any endeavour to justify such attempts.[110] But every cultic festival reflects many sides of life; in it the basic fact of 'salvation' in all its complexity becomes experienced reality. The enthronement festival was the chief festival of the year, *the* feast of Yahweh at his personal 'coming' in the hour of deepest danger and need, and with all the 'salvation' and bliss which this coming includes, so that all the fundamental experiences, emotions and ideas of religion must have met together here.

It is certain therefore that at such a feast not only songs of praise or 'coronation hymns' in the definite form-critical meaning of the word were sung, but that all the emotions and overtones of religion as comprehended in this total experience would have to find expression, from lamentations and prayers of distress 'out of the depths', to rejoicing at the coming of the saviour-god with victory and salvation are as prophesied. To limit our picture of the festival to what may be deduced from a single, though typical, form-historically defined group of psalms, cannot be methodologi-cally correct. It is therefore impossible to draw a hard-and-fast line between psalms of enthronement and other psalms that belong to the new year festival and reflect its ideology.

But we also have to take into account that ideas of enthronement had an influence, too, on other psalms belonging to the 'enthronement festival', and not only on the 'coronation hymns' in the specific sense; just as the chief idea, the real 'message' and 'experience' of Christmas and Easter have had an influence on all hymns belonging to the Christian celebration of these festivals, regardless of the literary type and style of the individual hymns, whether they be hymns of petition or praise. When we are dealing with the 'enthronement festival' as an aspect of a more exten-sive festival—the epiphany feast of Yahweh—we must therefore also have recourse to such psalms as contain some of the main ideas of the enthrone-ment hymns, and give expression to such distinctive aspects as the idea of Yahweh's epiphany for (renewed) creation, his kingship, his kingly victory over the demons of chaos and primordial ocean, and particularly so if

---

[110] Gunkel-Begrich, *Einl.*, p. 104.—Krauss (op. cit.) follows Gunkel in his formalistic limita-tion of the material.

these and other features from the enthronement psalms are found combined in one psalm. The other possibility, to which Gunkel draws attention, that there may also have existed other festivals of Advent, is of lesser
importance, as long as we *know* that this Advent feast was pre-eminently
the feast of harvest and new year together with the enthronement of
Yahweh.

The most important of these other psalms are Pss. 46; 48; 75; 76; 81;
24; but there are others, which will be taken into account in the following
paragraphs.[111]

As already mentioned, the fundamental thought in the festal experience
and the festal myth is that Yahweh is coming (96.13; 98.9) and 'revealing
himself', 'becoming revealed' and 'making himself known',[112] appearing
as the one he really is, manifesting his works and his will. This is not
a mere idea, it is reality, visibly expressed through the symbols and
rites of the feast and the emotional reactions of the congregation to its
experiences. The festival, in short, is the *festal epiphany* of Yahweh.

> Yahweh hath 'made known' his salvation,
>   hath 'revealed' his saving victory. (98.2.)
>
> God is within her citadels,
>   hath 'made himself known' as a defence. (48.4.)
>
> God hath 'made himself known' in Judah,
>   his 'name' is great in Israel.
> In Salem is now his pavilion,
>   In Zion his abode. (76.2f.)

This idea was current in the orient generally, and was originally understood quite literally as a cultic reality. In Babylonia as well as in Egypt
it was considered to be a climax in the festival, when the idol was carried
out and the curtain drawn aside, so that the congregation might 'behold
the face of the god', 'see the god in his beauty' or 'grace'. Such terms
were also adopted in Israelite religion (cf. Ps. 27.4), but there they were
taken in a spiritualized sense about the way *faith* 'beholds'. But even in
Israel this 'beholding' was attached to a visible symbol, namely to the
holy ark of Yahweh, which to all appearance was a focal point in the
festal procession at the enthronement (Ps. 132; cf. 2 Sam. 6).

In the festal experience it is first of all through his works, his 'saving
works' (*tĕšû'ôth*, *ṣĕdhāqôth*) that Yahweh reveals himself, manifesting to all
the world who and what he is. They are the 'message' of the festival.
The term 'glad tidings' (*bšrt*) was already used in Ugarit about the
announcement that Baal had again become alive,[113] and in the same
terms the cultic festival announced to Israel the appearance of Yahweh

---

[111] On the pertinent material, see Additional Note XXIV.
[112] Ps. 98.2: *hôdhîa'*, *gillā*. Cf. also *nôdha'*, Pss. 48.4; 76.2; *hôphîa'*, Ps. 50.2.
[113] See Mowinckel in *NTT*, 1931, pp. 205ff.

as king and his enthronement (Ps. 96.2, cf. Isa. 52.7). But—and we shall return to this below—he also reveals his true being by revealing his will, through his laws and the commandments of his Covenant.

The epiphany of Yahweh is described with all the traditional features which, according to the usual oriental conception, belong to a theophany. Yahweh reveals himself with thunder and lightning (Pss. 97.2ff.; 29.3, 7ff.), with storm (29.5; 48.8), earthquake (29.6, 8; 46.7; 97.4), clothed in his wonderful armour, to which belongs also the girdle of strength (93.1). Against his enemies he raises his frightening and miracle-working voice into a war-cry (46.7; 29.3ff.; 76.7), manifesting his flaming majesty (48.6); the poison cup is ready to be drunk by his enemies.[114] The metaphors belong to the usual style of the theophany, indeed they are so conventional that they are used where no definite enemies are mentioned. They serve to depict the majesty of the divine revelation, creating in Yahweh's own worshippers awe and confidence, and smiting his enemies with horror. It would be a most rationalistic exegesis to find in such picturings any recollections of particular historical events,[115] just as in themselves they have nothing whatever to do with the eschatological appearance of Yahweh.[116]

If we start out from the power-charged epiphany of Yahweh, a special light is thrown on all ideas about his work as a king.

Even the special hymns of enthronement bring out very clearly that the fundamental myth of the festival is the *myth of creation* (see above, pp. 108f.). Yahweh has become king of the world, because he has created it. And as we have seen, these psalms do not refer to any abstract notion of creation, but to the same mythical and poetical idea which may be glimpsed behind the account of the creation in Gen. 1, but which is much more prominent in other passages of the Old Testament, namely the idea of creation as the victorious struggle of Yahweh against the dragon of the primeval ocean, or against the primeval ocean itself (*tĕhôm*).

In the enthronement psalms proper this rather mythical conception of creation is not very prominent. But in other psalms it is:

[114] Cf. Ps. 75.9. That this metaphor in itself has nothing to do with eschatology, even if taken up by the latter, will be seen from its use in Ps. 60.5, a national psalm of lamentation without any trace of eschatological ideas. Cf. *Ps.St.* II, pp. 330f., 339f.

[115] This applies for instance to the theory of Gunkel and Gressmann and Musil based on evidence that Sinai was once a volcano, so that the revelation there had something to do with an eruption. On the peninsula of Sinai there have been no active volcanos in historical times; but Sinai is closely connected with Kadesh on the Sinai peninsula. Of such geographical interpretations of the metaphors of theophany, Johs. Pedersen most rightly says that we may just as well search the map for the hills 'melting like wax at the presence of Yahweh' (Ps. 97.5).

[116] Gunkel, *Einl.*, p. 115, in these metaphors finds evidence proving that the enthronement psalms must be interpreted in an eschatological manner; the idea that Yahweh would appear in the eruption of a volcano and in an earthquake and the like, 'would be a strange thought at a festival'. The objection just shows that Gunkel has not realized the nature of cultic experience. At the epiphany festival all the thoughts connected with the conception of God and of the fundamental idea of the festival are being actualized; the enthronement psalms often emphasize that Yahweh's appearance is 'terrible' (*nôrā'*), Pss. 96.4; (97.9); 99.3, and a main point of the festal myth is that he comes and defeats his enemies.

> Thou, Yahweh, art my king of old,
>   working victorious salvation on the earth.
> Thou didst divide the ocean by thy power
>   and break the Dragon's heads on the waves.
>
> Thou didst crush the heads of Leviathan to pieces,
>   leaving him a prey to the folk of the jackals.
> Thou didst open springs and torrents,
>   thou didst dry up flowing streams.
>
> Thine is the day and thine is the night,
>   thou settest up the sun as light.
> Thou has set all the zones of the earth,
>   thou has made both summer and winter. (Ps. 74.12–17.)

The connexion between the primeval ocean and the dragons (Leviathan, Rahab), and between the victory over them, and creation and the kingship of Yahweh, is here quite evident. We see the same thing in Ps. 89.10–13:

> Thou art ruler, even if the sea rages,
>   as its waves tossed, thou didst still them.
> Thou didst crush Rahab as a profaned carcass
>   and scattered thine enemies by the force of thine arm.
>
> Thine is the heaven, the earth is thine,
>   thou has founded the continent and its fulness.
> The North and the South, thou hast created them,
>   Tabor and Hermon rejoice in thy name.

But sometimes the conception has been toned down to describe a fight against the ocean of chaos alone, which has been allotted its proper place and limits by Yahweh, so that an ordered cosmos has come into existence:

> Thou didst found the earth upon its pillars,
>   that it never more can be shaken.
> The ocean covered it as a garment,
>   the water stood above the mountains:
> but it retired at thy rebuke,
>   and hasted away at the sound of thy thunder;
> having scaled the mountains, it ran down in the valleys
>   to the place which thou hast determined for it;
> a bound hast thou set which it may not pass over,
>   it shall never cover the earth again. (Ps. 104.5–9.)

An echo of this fight is to be heard in the hymns of enthronement:

> The earth is now established, shall never be shaken;
>> from that time thy throne is established also,
>>> from all eternity hast thou (established it).

> The floods, they lifted up, O Yahweh,
>> the floods, they lifted up their voice,
>>> the floods, they lifted up their thunder.

> But high above the roaring billows,
>> high above the ocean breakers
>>> is Yahweh, glorious on high. (Ps. 93.1b-4.)

It has long been acknowledged[117] that this poetical myth of creation has been derived from the Babylonian one, where the god—Marduk, or whichever god was considered the chief god of that district—takes up arms on behalf of the other gods against the rebellious Tiamat (Hebr. *tĕhôm*), pictured as a female dragon of the primeval ocean. He captures her in his net, blowing his 'wind' into her jaws, cleaving her with his sword, and finally building up heaven and earth out of her body; the annual re-creation of the world, when the fields rise to the surface of the 'primeval ocean' of the spring flood, finds expression in this myth, and is each time made real again through the cultic rites connected with it. In all probability Israel did not take over these conceptions directly, but North Mesopotamian and Canaanite tales provided a connecting link.[118] The name Leviathan for the dragon of the ocean is now known from the Phoenician Ugarit texts, and possibly the name Rahab also has its origin there. And if the conceptions of the enthronement of the god and of the corresponding cultic festival of enthronement are based on a common oriental 'cultic pattern', Yahweh's achievement as a king, being the basis of the conceptions about his enthronement, must needs also—at least partly—be derived from the same sources.

Whether the Israelites before or in the age of Moses looked upon Yahweh as the god of creation, we do not know. But the conception of a supreme god being at the same time the god of creation, was known in Canaan as well as in the civilized countries surrounding it. So it would not be very long before this thought was transferred to Yahweh; Yahweh is El, he is El Elyon; he who comprises all divinity with his power and holiness, and to whom may therefore be attributed the plural Elohim, 'the gods', but according to its meaning a so-called abstract plural = the 'divinity', the 'divine majesty'. The common oriental conception of creation as the basis of the kingship of the god would therefore be a matter of course to the Israelites. We may presume that even in Israel the mythical conception of creation as a fight against *dragons* and against the

---

[117] See Gunkel, *Schöpfung und Chaos*; *Genesis.*[4]
[118] Cf. Albright in *JBL* LVII, 1938, pp. 230ff.; LVIII, 1939, pp. 91ff.; cf. *Studies in Prophecy* (Robinson festschrift), pp. 1ff.

primeval ocean must have belonged to the ideas of the festival of enthronement from the beginning.

But here the special character of Yahwism makes itself felt as a re-
moulding power. The growth of mono-, or heno-theism in Israel generally
is matched step for step in the cultic myths and psalms. In Israel the
universalistic character involved in the very conception of creation and
in the festival of enthronement was more and more emphasized. But at
the same time this God of creation does not become a pale 'power in the
background', standing aloof from the world, as is not infrequently the case
with the deities of creation in other religions;[119] but he remains a personal
God, actively willing, making plans and carrying them out, charged with
the moral energy of a personality, a concrete figure, who has revealed
himself throughout history and again and again appears in this historical
concreteness. Therefore neither the psalmists nor the prophets ever let go
of the mythical way of thinking about the primeval ocean and the dragon;
this myth was admirably fitted to bring out the concrete personal and
dynamic nature of Yahweh and to give an overwhelming impression of the
reality of his power and secure the confidence that 'blessed is the people
whose God is Yahweh'.

That Yahweh (again) creates, means that out of threatening chaos
(*tōhû wābhōhû*), he makes an ordered cosmos, an earth where men can
live (Isa. 45.18). He (again) establishes the 'right order', without which
heaven and earth cannot exist. It is this establishment of the right order
which the Hebrews express by the verb *šāphaṭ* and the noun *mišpāṭ*, usually
translated by 'judge' and 'judgment'. The words express His 'saving
activity', his *ṣedheq* or *ṣĕdhāqâ*, usually translated 'justice'. In the enthronement psalms we often hear of Yahweh's 'judgments', and the word
is used in many connexions and with many nuances of meaning. One of
them is the activity which we moderns express by the juridical term 'judge';
to the Hebrews, however, this juridical activity is only one side of the idea
of *mišpāṭ*. In the enthronement psalms the sense of (re-)establishment of
the right order and the right relation between the nations is generally
included in the word, whatever may be the relations alluded to.

The original comprehensive meaning of the 'judgment' connected with
the coming of Yahweh and the re-creation of the right order is still to be
seen in an idea which in later Judaism is very clearly connected with the
new year festival. In the Mishna we are told that on new year's day
Yahweh 'judges', i.e. determines what is to happen in the coming year,
both in nature and in the history of nations and the lives of individuals.[120]
In other words he lays down fate. This idea has older roots in the old
enthronement festival. In several psalms there are suggestions that at his
coming Yahweh shall 'turn the destiny' (*šûbh šĕbhûth*) of his people.[121] Like

---

[119] Cf. van der Leeuw, *Phänomenologie*, pp. 142ff. ¶ 18 (E.T., pp. 159ff.).
[120] Tosephta Rosh hasshana I, 13. Cf. *Ps.St.* II, pp. 74ff.
[121] Pss. 85.2; 126.4; 14.7; 53.7. See Additional Note XXVII.

most other ideas from the enthronement festival this expression has been taken up by eschatology, but in itself it is neutral and originally had nothing to do with the eschatological 'change'.[122] It means letting the thing in question return to its original starting-point in order to start afresh, so it is something like putting it in its original proper condition.[123] In the cult it refers to 'turning' things back to the starting-point in connexion with the 'turning' of the new year.[124]

When Yahweh comes he will change the destiny of his people, and the psalms of the festival ask him to do so:

> That those who are sowing now with tears
> may reap with shouts of joy. (126.5.)

Here we have a reference to the crops of the coming year, which are to be safeguarded by the harvest feast. But the thought goes further. The turning of destiny involves all conceivable happiness, in a moral as well as a material sense; when Yahweh shall again let 'his glory dwell in our land', says the harvest festival liturgy (Ps. 85), then:

> Kindness and faithfulness unite,
> right-order and welfare kiss each other;
> faithfulness rises from the earth,
> and kindness will look down from heaven.

> Thus Yahweh gives all that is good,
> Our land is yielding us its fruit;
> right-order marches before God
> and welfare follows in his steps. (85.11–14.)

In later times the thought of the national restoration of Israel would naturally come to the fore, when the psalms prayed for a 'turning of the destiny' (Pss. 14.7; 53.7), and the more so because the prophets of the return had used the term in this sense.

But as we have seen, it actually means the turning of destiny, the new 'laying down of fate', which would take place, when Yahweh would come at the new year's feast and take up the 'rule' over his people, 'judging' her destiny. This is also seen from the fact that even in Babylonia the same idea belonged to the new year festival. There the gods would meet in the 'room of destiny' (*ubšukagina*) and 'lay down destiny' (*sîm sîmti*) for the coming year, both for nations and kingdoms, first of all for Babylon itself, and for all individuals. To the ritual of the festival also belonged a

---

[122] See Additional Note XXV.

[123] In all probability the term *šûbh šĕbhûth* is formed on the pattern of Akkad. *sîm sîmti*—'fixation of the fixed', i.e. the fixation of destiny that takes place in the council of gods every year at the new year festival. See *Ps.St.* II, pp. 74ff.

[124] Cf. the expressions 'the turning of the sun'—*tĕqûphâ*—about the point at which, according to the antique view of the world, the sun would turn in the west and return to its starting point (Ps. 19.7), and 'the turning of the year'—*tĕqûphath haššânâ, tĕšûbhath haššânâ*—about the transition from the old year to the new (Ex. 34.22). Cf. note 45 above, and Additional Note XIV.

prayer for a 'merciful destiny'.[125] It is most likely that the Israelite expression has been modelled on the Babylonian pattern.

This idea of Yahweh's 'judgment' in its manifold nuances and applications has deeply influenced the other ideas connected with the festival, the different versions of the 'festival myth'.

We find this especially when we look at what the psalms have to tell us about Yahweh's relation to *the other gods*. His appearance is 'a horror to all the gods', these 'nobodies' (*'ĕlîlîm*) prostrating themselves before his face and paying homage to him. When he appears, he does so even as 'king over all gods'.[126] This very term points back to the way the concept of enthronement was expressed in the other oriental religions. In the Ugaritic myth Baal becomes the king of gods after his resurrection and victory over Môt. And in the Babylonian epic of creation and enthronement we are told that when Tiamat, the monster of the primeval ocean, revolted against the gods, none of them ventured to take up the fight, until Marduk offered to do so on condition that the other gods should make him king, and the crown of victory consisted in his being proclaimed king over all gods: *marduk-ma šarru*, 'Marduk has become king'. This implies the idea brought out in plain words by the Israelite psalms of enthronement, that the other gods have been 'put to shame'. But here the relationship between them and Yahweh has become a different one. In true Yahwism the other gods had been Yahweh's enemies ever since the struggles of the immigration and the fights for independence against the natives. The fusion of Israel with the natives after David's reign resulted in the identification of the great gods, El, El Elyon, etc., with Yahweh; they became merged in him; and so, also, the great host of gods and heavenly beings, *bĕnê 'ēlîm*, 'the divine ones', the 'divine beings', came to be looked upon as the servants of Yahweh, his household staff, his body guard and his army, and finally were identified with his 'messengers' or 'deputies', 'the angels'. The other national gods were considered as the governors of Yahweh, installed by him to rule over the other nations.[127]

But in spite of all this wholesale conversion to Yahwism some of the tension between Yahweh and the other gods continued to exist. The unlucky experiences suffered by Israel throughout the greater part of her history with regard to other nations and their oppression of Israel taught her that the rule of their gods, Yahweh's vassals, over the world was most unjust:

> Do ye indeed judge righteously, ye gods,
>   do ye reign over mankind with justice?
> No! evil deeds ye do on 'the earth',
>   your hands weigh up violence in the world,

---

[125] See Zimmern, *AO* XXV, 3, pp. 16f.; *Babyl. Neujahrsfest* II, p. 38.

[126] Pss. 96.4f.; 97.7, 9; 99.2f. (in v. 2 read with 3 Mss. *'ĕlōhîm* instead of *hā'ammîm*).

[127] Deut. 32.8 (G, now corroborated by the Qumran texts). For the 'sons of god', i.e. those of divine family, the divine beings, see Ps. 29.1; Job 1f.; cf. 1 Kgs. 22.20ff.

says the psalmist (58.2f.). And thus in the psalms of enthronement the 'gods' gradually move into the rank of evil enemies, 'put to shame' by Yahweh and 'judged' by him when he 'comes' and sits upon his throne. This actually means: they assume the place in the myth, which once belonged to the demons of the primeval ocean and of chaos; we have a *myth about the fight of gods* side by side with the myth about the dragon fight. The term is not quite adequate, for in the psalms we do not hear of any real fight against the gods. They are struck with horror at the very appearance of Yahweh, and tremblingly throw themselves down, paying homage to him. This also means shame and defeat to all 'image worshippers', who put their confidence in 'nothingnesses'. That is why we are told that the appearance of Yahweh puts all the other gods 'to shame' (Ps. 97.7). 'Shame' means defeat and destruction.[128]

It is the idea of Yahweh's 'judgment' in its more juridical sense which has been applied here to his relations to the other gods. And here too we notice the same exclusive tendency, as in the Israelite versions of the myth about the fight against the powers of chaos (see above, pp. 145f.).

The enthronement psalms often allude to Yahweh's righteous and luck-bringing rule after he has been enthroned. This is what is indicated by the words *mišpāṭ* and *dîn* and the corresponding verbs (96.13; 97.8; 98.9; 48.12), traditionally translated by 'judgment' and 'judge', but which do not merely indicate this judicial ('forensic') activity, but all activity on the part of king and leaders for the purpose of maintaining the balance and 'harmony' and 'peace' of society, and to secure to everybody what according to the covenant is his 'right',[129] i.e. what we would call to 'rule' or 'govern'. Thus when the king displays his 'judgment' and 'righteousness'—*ṣedheq, ṣĕdhāqâ*—it means his power to do the 'right' thing in all senses of the word, and create 'right order', i.e. blessing, peace, good morals and victory for his people—'justifying them' (*hiṣdîq*), i.e. creating for them the right social, moral and religious conditions. In this way Yahweh also is going to 'rule' or 'judge' his people. When the verb is used with Israel for its object, it first of all means: provide and secure, or restore, his happiness and welfare and power and 'peace' and 'salvation'; with the enemies for its object, it means conquering, crushing. Therefore can 'the villages of Judah rejoice over the judgments of Yahweh' (Pss. 48.12; 97.8) in the widest sense of the word 'judgment'.

But the mind might also fasten on the fundamental 'act of judgment' at the coming of Yahweh. And then the forensic aspect of the idea would become more prominent and result in the conception of a solemn act of judgment, at which Yahweh summons his antagonists before his judgment seat and judges them, just as this used to be the first act of government of an earthly king.[130] Ps. 76 suggests that when Yahweh revealed himself in

[128] Cf. Johs. Pedersen, *Israel* I–II, pp. 182ff.
[129] See Johs. Pedersen, *Israel* I–II, pp. 336ff.
[130] 1 Kgs. 1.49ff.; 2.13–38; 2 Kgs. 10.1ff.; 1 Sam. 11.12. Cf. Ps. 2.

Salem, he also 'caused judgment to be heard from heaven'; once he has taken his place on his throne in Salem he has 'arisen to judgment to save all the oppressed ones of the earth' (or of 'the land'). In Ps. 75 he speaks words of severe reproof to all the inhabitants of the earth; he is 'the judge (or ruler) who lowers one and lifts another' (v. 8). And the poet describes how Yahweh is standing with the poison cup in his hand, which all his enemies have to empty. Now that he has come to bind kings and nobles with chains and with fetters of iron (Ps. 149), he is 'executing upon them the judgment written'.[131] We are here dealing with a conception which may be called the *myth of doom.*

This myth also colours Yahweh's relationship to other gods. The poet of Ps. 82 describes how Yahweh 'stands out in the assembly of the gods', sentencing them to death for their unjust rule:

> God stands out in the council of the gods,
>   in the midst of the gods he speaks his judgment:
> How long yet will you rule unjustly,
>   (how long yet) favour the evildoers?
> Uphold the weak, the fatherless,
>   let the forlorn and poor have justice!
> Rescue the weak and the wretched ones,
>   pluck them out of the grip of the wicked!
> They know not, neither will understand;
>   all the foundations of the earth are shaken.
> But now I say: though you are gods,
>   all of you sons of the Most High,
> yet you shall die as men must die,
>   shall perish like the (earthly) princes.

As we have seen, the idea of a council (assembly) of gods belongs to the festival of new year and enthronement. It was in such an assembly of 'sons of gods' and 'saints', i.e. divine beings, that Yahweh once portioned out the nations amongst the 'sons of gods' whom he made governors over them.[132] A markedly Israelitic feature of this psalm, which probably belongs to a comparatively late time, is the close connexion between the idea of judgment and that of Yahweh's universal kingship: when the gods are sentenced it is because of their unjust and immoral rule, their want of 'moral sense' and 'understanding', of proper 'knowledge of God'. An essential feature in the Israelite conception of God, the tendency towards ethical monotheism, is here bound up with the historical way of thinking: iniquity in the history of mankind, of nations and states, is what forces Yahweh to interfere in history and pronounce judgment over the mighty

---

[131] Behind this expression may lie a rite corresponding to that of the Egyptian 'execration texts', see Bentzen in [D]*TT*, 1929, pp. 6off.

[132] Deut. 32.8f. (voc. *běhanḥîl* and *yaṣṣîbh* with 2 Mss. (Ken.) and Sam., and corroborated by a Qumran fragment, see P. W. Skehan in *BASOR* 136, 1954, pp. 12ff.; read *běnê 'ēl*, cf. G, L); and 33.2f. 'Holy ones' in the O.T. always means divine beings.

of this world, who serve evil and faithless gods. Under the rule of such powers Israel has become 'poor and needy and oppressed'; and this is reflected by the internal condition of the people, so that no justice is to be found either for 'widows or fatherless or common people'. But here we get a glimpse, too, of another essential and markedly Israelite feature, to which we shall return in detail below: the future lookingness of the ideas and experiences in the festival of enthronement. The congregation knows that even at the coming of Yahweh this judgment has been laid down, so to speak, only 'in principle'; it has not yet appeared in the visible reality of experience. Therefore this message closes with prayer on the part of the congregation that this may now happen:

> Up, O God, rule thou the earth,
> for to thee belong all the nations!

Yahweh gives judgment as 'ruler', as king. From being an assembly paying homage, as in the Babylonian epic, the assembly of gods has become a judgment hall: the homage-paying vassals, who together with the supreme god 'judged' the fate of the new year, have been changed into unfaithful vassals and have become the accused party, being themselves judged on account of 'crimes against mankind'.[133]

The 'historical' point of view is more prominent in another conception which finds expression in the enthronement psalms: that is, that Yahweh has secured his kingdom and his enthronement by coming and delivering his people and his city from a threatening attack by the united kings and nations of the world (cf. above, p. 109). This conception is to be found in Pss. 46; 48; 75 and 76. Here the idea of Yahweh's historic and ever repeated victory over the 'nations', and the confidence engendered by these experiences and the faith on which they were based, is presented as an epic tale woven around a mythically tinted happening. The 'happening' to which the psalms allude, along with its corresponding 'tale' is an attack on Jerusalem by all the kings and nations of the earth; but just when the distress is at its height Yahweh appears and crushes them all; so the walls of Jerusalem are safe, the 'City of the Great King' stands unshaken. This hardly refers to any single real historical event, as earlier interpreters of the psalms used to think, nor is it meant to be a description of what is going to take place in the 'latter days', in eschatological times. It is described as something just experienced, something the congregation 'itself has seen' (Ps. 48.9). But at the same time it is something it 'has heard of' before. Here, too, the explanation is that there is a reference to the realities of faith being re-experienced as repeated reality in the cult. What has taken place, and always will take place, in faith is presented by the cultic myth as an 'ideal' supra-worldly reality in the epic form of a once-only event. In an 'ideal' and real sense it is repeated whenever Yahweh appears as king, victorious in the festival. It is being ensured to

[133] See Additional Note XXVI.

faith as something that is also going to happen in political and empirical reality, should the 'nations' or any specific nation be so presumptuous as to attack Yahweh's city. Here we have a version of the 'cultic myth' of the festival, which we call the *myth about the fight of nations*.

Even this conception has some of its roots in the myth about the fight against chaos, and in the ancient conception of the state of need and chaos that the world got into before the coming of Yahweh, and from which he comes to deliver it at the last moment, just as the powers of death seem to be victorious. That it is the primeval ocean and the power of chaos which after all loom behind 'the nations', is brought out still more clearly by Ps. 46.2–4, 7f.:

> God is a stronghold and shelter for us,
>   as a helper in trouble always found.
> Therefore we will not fear though the earth be overturned,
>   though the mountains quake in the depths of the sea.
> Let (the ocean) roar, let its billows foam,
>   let the mountains shake under its haughtiness . . .
> The nations raged, the kingdoms were moved,
>   He lifted his voice, and the earth shivered.
> Yahweh, the Lord of Hosts, is with us,
>   the God of Jacob is our fortress.

In Ps. 68, a typical procession psalm for the new year festival—the feast of the 'coming' and 'epiphany' of Yahweh—we also have the identification of the actual and potential enemies of Israel with the chaotic powers. The enemies have now been scattered and destroyed by his mighty 'word' (v. 12).

But at the back of this conception about the repeated attack of the powers of chaos we find actual experiences from the life of nature and of men. For the distress from which Yahweh is coming to deliver man was originally and truly the distress arising because the world had been worn out, destroyed by the deadly powers of drought, and in danger of sinking back again into chaos; thus 'Death'—in Ugaritic mythology, Môt—as a supernatural and demonic being threatens God's world with destruction. This conception we also find in Ps. 68: Yahweh's coming is the salvation from 'the Death' (*māweth*, v. 21). Here the original Canaanite form of the myth, the victory of Baal over Môt is clearly reflected.[133a] The same idea we meet also in Ps. 48.15, Yahweh is our leader against the Death.

This mutation of the chaos myth into a myth about the fight against the nations is the place where the fundamentally historical point of view of Israelite religion breaks in and depicts the distress in a new guise. Israel was constantly experiencing threatened distress of this different kind: the enmity of all the surrounding nations, the 'gentiles' and their kings, constantly planning to destroy Yahweh's people—or, as it is ex-

[133a] See the author's *Der achtundsechsigste Psalm*, p. 48f.

pressed in the royal psalm (Ps. 2), again and again taking counsel against their righteous Lord, Yahweh, and against his Anointed, his vice-gerent on earth. This is the danger and the distress from which Yahweh comes to deliver his people by 'judging' all these enemies in one crushing act. But all the same the mythical way of thinking has always a tendency towards the epic. And in the cult the salvation which is going to be effected in time to come is experienced as concentrated present-day reality. Considering the manner of thinking of Israelite poets and the fullness of the cultic experience, it would be much too abstract to say, for instance, 'now that Yahweh has come we are safe with regard to all eventual enemies who might be expected to attack his city and his people'. To the cultic and mythical way of thinking all these possibilities are concentrated in a single concrete picture: the kings and peoples of the world *have* already taken counsel, and are besieging Yahweh's city; but in its last extremity, at the 'break of day', Yahweh comes, slaying and crushing them all and securing his city to all eternity, for now he himself is there as a victorious king on his throne, therefore it can never be shaken. 'Though the ocean roar and its billows foam—the God of Jacob is our refuge'.

This is the picture drawn for us by Ps. 48.5–8:

> For lo, the kings made a conspiracy,
>   and passed by together.
> They saw—and they were scared with panic
>   and, terrified, they took to flight.
> Fear took hold upon them there
>   like women in travail,
> (as) when the easterly storm breaks down
>   the (biggest) Tarshish-ships.[134]

And therefore the festal psalm (Ps. 76.2–6, see above, p. 142), rejoices over the 'appearance' of Yahweh:

> There (i.e. in Salem) he has broken the arrows of the bow,
>   the shields, and the swords, and all martial weapons.

In this way he 'judges' all his own and Israel's enemies:

> Thou lettest thy sentence be heard from heaven,
>   the earth feared, and was still,
> when God arose to judgment,
>   to save all the oppressed on earth. (76.9f.)

These 'oppressed on earth'—or 'in the land'—are the Israelites themselves.

[134] Read *ka'ăsher* and 3. s.f. *těšabbēr*—even if Tarshish also indicates the (earlier) Phoenician name of the town in Sardinia (see Albright in *BASOR* 83, 1941, pp. 21f.), in the O.T. it probably, as Albright also thinks, means Tartessus in Spain. In the expression 'ships of Tarshish' we probably have the proper name, used in the sense of 'distant travellers', 'ocean-farers', not the original appellative sense of 'smelting-boat', 'turret' (*tarshish* = 'smeltery', from Akkad. *rasâsu* = 'melt', see Albright, op. cit.).

Thus has Yahweh hitherto helped his people, not allowing them to be destroyed, in spite of all tribulations and well-deserved chastisements, and thus will he ever help them.

So in the myth of the fight of nations the cosmic and mythical meets with the historically orientated view of the basis of Yahweh's kingship and its consequences to the world.

In the oracles of doom against the enemies of Israel, these latter are always referred to in general terms, not mentioning any particular people—unlike the casual oracles in the psalms of lamentation (see below, Chap. VI.3). It is, however, very possible that a custom of pronouncing a series of oracles against different individual peoples may have developed out of the general oracles at the epiphany feast, and that we have here the 'cultic' background of such oracles as we find in Am. 1–2.[135] If this suggestion is true, we should be inclined to think that such oracles did not belong to the festal ritual proper, but that they mark extempore inspirations and improvisations of the cult prophet, only loosely connected with the festival, and taking place before the crowd, which was eating and drinking and playing in the temple courts.

On the basis of this historical orientation it is understandable that Creation and the rise of Israel should become one: Creation reaches its climax in the rise of Israel, i.e. the *election*, manifesting itself in the escape from Egypt. Egypt becomes the chaotic monster Rahab and the Reed Lake becomes the primeval ocean, Tehom (Isa. 30.7; Ex. 15.48); and just as in the beginning Yahweh 'divided' the waters, so did he also divide the waters of the Reed Lake for his people. Quite logically the thought would also arise that through this 'creative act' on the part of Yahweh, he became king of Israel. In a psalm of epiphany, now forming the frame of the so-called 'blessing of Moses' it says (Deut. 33.2, 4f.):[136]

> From Mount Sinai Yahweh came,
> from Se'ir he dawned on us,
> from Paran's range he gleamed out
> moving from Meribath-Kadesh . . . .

---

[135] See Würthwein's suggestion in *ZATW* 62, 1949–50, pp. 35ff.

[136] Deut. 33.2–5, 26–29 is originally an independent psalm, which the author of the 'Blessing of Moses'—a younger imitator of the 'Blessing of Jacob' in Gen. 49—has used as a framework for his own poem; v. 26 is the direct continuation of v. 5. Ideologically, the psalm belongs to the enthronement feast: note Yahweh's coming from Mount Sinai to his people, his epiphany (*hôphîa'*), his becoming King of Israel, his driving over the skies, the byname 'the primeval God', his blessing of the land with dew from heaven, the security of his people under his shelter, cf. Ps. 29.10f. See *GTMMM* I, pp. 421ff.; *Der achtundsechzigste Psalm*, pp. 75ff. The text of vv. 2–5 is very damaged; v. 2 read: *lĕ'ammô* (cf. *lānû* G, P, V) for *lāmô*, and *mimmĕribhath qādhesh*; v. 2e is to be connected with 3a; read *'ēš lappîdhôth* for *'ēš dath*; 3a read: *'aph sĕbhîbhô* (parall. *mîmînô*, v. 2e) *'ădhath* (or: *qĕhal*) *qĕdhôshāw* (athnach *to qedhôshaw)*; *lĕyādhô* (so with V) corresponds to *lĕraghlô*; the original text seems to have spoken about heavenly beings (cf. 'His holy ones', in the O.T. always used to indicate supernatural beings) standing 'at his hand', and 'at his foot', cf. Isa. 6.2, but the original wording we can only guess at. V. 4a is a gloss (the idea of Moses and the Torah has no connexion with this stage of the idea of enthronement); v. 5a has its original place before v. 4b.

> The congregation of Jacob became his domain,
>> and he became king in Jeshurun,
> as the chiefs of the people there gathered,
>> and all the clans of Israel.

Jeshurun is an honorific name for Israel. And in another psalm (114.1f.) it says:

> When Israel went out of Egypt,
>> the house of Jacob from the barbarous people,
> Judah became his sacred dominion,
>> Israel his kingly domain.

At that time he apportioned all the other nations among the 'divine ones' ('sons of the gods'), but he kept Israel for himself as his 'part' and his 'heritage' (Deut. 32.8.G). Then it was that he laid the foundation of his true historical 'kingship'.

The festal psalm put in the mouth of Miriam by a later saga writer, and describing the Exodus and the miracle of the Reed Lake and the first settlement in Canaan, ends with a comment on the founding of the sanctuary of Zion, and the proclamation of the kingship of Yahweh (Ex. 15.17f.):

> Thou tookest thy folk and plantedst them in thine own hill,
>> thou madest a shrine for thy dwelling, Yahweh,
> a sanctuary thy hands founded, O Lord:
>> now Yahweh is king for evermore.

What Yahweh has done for Israel in actual history forms the basis of his kingship, and is recalled when in the new year festival he takes his seat on his throne as the victorious king.

But election is bound up with the making of the *covenant*, which is maybe the most important innovation on the basis of the historical orientation of Yahwism. The idea in itself is not new; in ancient Israel all cult was in the nature of a strengthening of the covenant; 'life' just meant covenant. But what was originally thought of was the, so-to-speak, *natural* covenant, made up of family and tribe in connexion with the ancestors and the family god. To Israel after the time of Moses, 'covenant' means the historical covenant which Yahweh in his goodness 'granted' to his elected people. This is a fundamental idea in Israelite religion among the cultic officials as well as among the prophets of doom. At the festival of enthronement, with its 'commemoration' of the election, the idea of a renewal of the covenant would be a leading thought, with explicit reference to what Yahweh had done in history; at the festival he came to renew the covenant he had once made with the people at Kadesh-Sinai.

Through the renewal of the covenant were promised to king and people all the blessing, all the happiness, all the victory they might need in the year to come: a righteous, strong and victorious king, true priests, a pure temple, outer and inner power, a new happiness, a 'turning of the fate', paradisiac fertility, peace, dominion over the neighbouring peoples, victory over enemies, protection against demons and evil powers, and destruction of evil-doers and sinners.[137]

There is a reference to this in Ps. 99.6ff. Now that Yahweh is 'enthroned' on the cherubim and has 'established equity and executed judgment and righteousness in Jacob', the making of the covenant at the time of its foundation in the historical past is repeated:

> His priests have still a Moses and an Aaron,
>   his worshippers have still a Samuel,
> and Yahweh answers when they call to him,
>   Thou Yahweh, our God, Thou answerest them.
> In the cloudy pillar doth he speak to them,
>   when they obey the laws and rules he gave them.
> A forgiving God hast Thou ever been to them,
>   and one who has (not) avenged their evil deeds.

What is meant is this:[138] again there is a Moses, an Aaron, a Samuel, among his people; again he shall answer from the pillar of the cloud, whenever the leaders and intercessors of the people shall cry out to him. The covenant bringing happiness and help and forgiveness of sins to all who keep the commandments of Yahweh has again been established as a result of the enthronement of Yahweh.

That this is a reference to the covenant of Kadesh-Sinai will be seen from such psalms as 95 and 81. The very essence of the covenant is brought out by a stanza like this:

> Let us go in and worship and bow down,
>   kneeling before Yahweh who has made us!
> For he is our God, and we, we are the people
>   which he pastures and shepherds with his hand. (95.6f.)

But these psalms also prove the organic connexion between the idea of a renewal of the covenant and that of epiphany and of the statement of the commandments of the covenant. The first part of Ps. 95 is evidently an enthronement hymn. Now the king, Yahweh, creator of the world and of Israel, has come to take his seat on his throne and receive the homage of his people; in the second part of the psalm it is as a king renewing the covenant—through the mouth of the cultic prophet—that he recalls the

---

[137] For further details see *Ps.St.* II, pp. 150ff.

[138] For the interpretation of Ps. 99 and particularly v. 6, see Buhl, *Psalmerne*[2], pp. 629ff.; *Ps.St.* II, p. 152. Gunkel's interpretation: 'Der zweite Teil nennt die grössten Namen aus der älteren Geschichte, offenbar um zu sagen: sieht, solche Heroen standen in Jahves Diensten!' gives no real connexion between the two parts of the psalm: what would be the point of such a contemplation of the past as past, in a psalm dealing with present day events—much less in an eschatological psalm, as Gunkel makes it? As for the text, v. 8a must be replaced after v. 6b; in v. 8b the negative (*lŏ'*) is to be inserted.

first making of the covenant and the faithlessness of the people at Meribah and Massah, and warns against breaking the commandments of the covenant. And in the psalm of the new year festival, Ps. 81.11, he reveals himself to the congregation through the ancient 'formula of epiphany',[139] referring to the traditions of the Exodus and of Sinai:

> For I am Yahweh, I am your God
>   who brought you out of Egypt's land.

And here, too, we find the reference to the disobedience of the people at the spring of Meribah just after the making of the covenant:

> I tested you at the spring of Meribah:
>   'Open your mouth, and I will fill it'.[140]

The festival of harvest and new year became the festival of the renewal of the historical covenant; and among its 'festal myths' may also be mentioned a *myth about the making of the covenant*, in terms which bring out quite clearly that the word 'myth' may also indicate the religious and cultic conception and formulation of a historical fact.

The covenant of Sinai, according to later Jewish ways of thinking, is itself a renewal of the covenant with the first ancestors, which was fulfilled through the settlement in Canaan. The kingship of Yahweh rests on this coherent historical fact of salvation, and it is all brought to life again through his appearance and epiphany in the festival cult.[141]

Even Yahweh's covenant with David was considered to be a repetition of the covenant of Sinai itself. Therefore the covenant with David is also kept in mind at the festival of harvest and new year, as in Ps. 132.

As already suggested, the *covenant obligations* naturally enter into the thought of the making and renewal of the covenant in Israel, and so have also a place in the festival of the renewal of the covenant. Both Ps. 95 and Ps. 81, like Ps. 99, refer to the commandments and laws given by Yahweh at Kadesh-Sinai, and now repeated and reinforced by him, because both then and later they had been broken by the people. Here we are face to face with another important new development in connexion with the festival, deriving from the special historical nature of Yahwism.

As the ritual of the great annual feast of Jerusalem developed there occurred several points where the traditions about the making of the fundamental covenant and its conditions, the commandments, could link on. One such link was provided by the idea of Yahweh's epiphany. The announcement of Yahweh's epiphany in order to renew the covenant would lead to an emphasis on, and enforcement of, the fundamental

---

[139] For this formula of 'self-introduction' and its original connexion with the idea of the epiphany of a god, cf. Ed. Norden, *Agnostos Theos*, pp. 191ff., 197ff., 210ff.; Gressmann in *ZATW* 34, 1914, pp. 286 ff.; Mowinckel, *Le Decalogue*, pp. 126f.; Zimmerli in *Geschichte u. AT.*, pp. 179 ff,

[140] The isolated single cola vv. 8b and 11b obviously belong together; if 11b is replaced behind 8b we shall have quite regular stanzas throughout the whole psalm.

[141] See Additional Note XXVII.

commandments on which the covenant rested. In Pss. 95 and 81 we find just this presentation and enforcement. 'Today', Yahweh again admonishes his people, warning them to hear his voice (95.7)—'today', on the day when the covenant is renewed and the commandments announced, as they were at Sinai.[142] And whereas in Ps. 95 Yahweh's warning is against infidelity and grumbling, in Ps. 81.9f. he warns against the transgression of the fundamental commandments themselves:

> Listen, my people, to my warning,
>   O Israel, if you would only listen:
> You must allow no foreign god,
>   no worship of an outside god.

That these words refer to the very same commandments, which—with greater or smaller variations—were considered to be those of the Sinai covenant and had been formulated in different sets of 'decalogues'[143] is clearly seen from Ps. 81.11, quoted above (p. 157).

This verse is nothing but the traditional introduction to the Ten Commandments. It seems to have been usual to arrange the particular *leges sacrae* applicable to the sanctuary, as well as, later, also the commandments which were considered to be the actual laws of the covenant, as a set of ten (or twelve) commandments; first among these was always the fundamental law of worshipping Yahweh only. By their connexion with the idea of epiphany these collections got the traditional introductory formula referring to the appearance of Yahweh and—because of the historical idea of election and covenant—to the Exodus from Egypt,[144] which was originally considered as the election itself.[145] The influence of this 'decalogical tradition' is also clearly seen in Ps. 15, where the number of commandments making the 'laws of entrance', the 'conditions of admission' to temple and salvation, are precisely ten; this is certainly no mere accident.

The annual renewal of the covenant came to include the idea of commandments in general; not only this, but also of certain specific and definite commandments. We do not imply a recital of written law-books, but the reminder through the cult prophet's mouth of those commandments which at different times were considered to be the fundamental commandments of the covenant. As to which these were, opinions may have differed with changing times, just as have the opinions as to which were the ten fundamental commandments from Mount Sinai. But certain

---

[142] On the Sinai covenant and the Davidic covenant, see Rost in *ThLtz* 72, 1947, col. 129ff.

[143] Ex. 34.14ff.; 20.1ff.; Deut. 5.6ff. See Mowinckel, *Decalogue*, pp. 11ff., 19ff., 36ff.; *ZATW* 55, 1937, pp. 218ff.

[144] See Mowinckel, *Decalogue*, pp. 7ff., 24ff., 125ff. Against Weiser (in *Festschrift für Bertholet*) Bückers, 'Z. Verwertung d. Sinaitradition i.d. Pss.', *Biblica* 32, 1951, pp. 401ff. denies the influence of the Sinai traditions on the psalms and on the cultic festival, without making due allowance, however, for *Ps.St.* II and *Offersang og Sangoffer*, pp. 154ff. (above, pp. 154ff.).

[145] See Galling, *Die Erwählungstraditionen Israels*.

of them always appear to have been included, and foremost the commandment not to have other gods besides Yahweh.

In this rite as well as in the custom of advising the pilgrims and the partakers of the feast procession about the *leges sacrae* of the holy place (see below), we have the root of the later custom of the Jewish congregation reciting the law-book, i.e. Deuteronomy, every seventh year at the feast of Tabernacles.[146]

The *promises* of the epiphany festival are attached, above all, to this repeated revelation and enforcement of the commandments of the covenant. That a covenant with the deity would be a source of blessing was a matter of course to the early Hebrews as well as to the Canaanites. But in the Israel of historical times and in Yahwism it was not just a matter of course in the same way. A covenant with Yahweh is not a covenant between equals. To Israel it was a historical fact that Yahweh, of his own free will, had chosen the people in its hour of emergency and made a covenant with it. This covenant is something 'given' and 'stipulated' by Yahweh. In the idea of covenant which unfolds in the psalms Yahweh's sovereign superiority over the people and its king is very prominent. He always attaches *conditions* to it, namely the commandments of the covenant.[147] To Yahwistic Israel it was clear that it was not the vitality—the life power—of gods and men which was being renewed through the festival —as was the case with the Canaanites—but Yahweh's *promise* and *pledge* of blessing and power and life. In the liturgies of the festival and in the psalms reflecting them, such as Pss. 81 and 95 and others, we not only meet with a warning against breaking the covenant, but also with positive rich promises to people and king, if they should this time—'today'—keep Yahweh's commandments better than before:

> Oh that my people would listen to me,
>   that Israel would walk in my ways!
> Then I would soon subdue their foes,
>   and turn my hand against their enemies.
>
> Their haters then would cower before them,
>   their time (of submission) never end.
> But themselves I would feed with the finest wheat,
>   with honey from the rock I would satisfy thee.
>
> (Ps. 81.14–17.)

The blessing that shall ensue to king and people and land, if the king, and his sons after him, keep the commandments and laws of Yahweh is

---

[146] In his interesting paper in *ZATW* 62, 1949–50, pp. 44ff., Würthwein in my opinion antedates the cultic rite of reciting the law, and operates too much with the idea of written law texts in this connexion. This is, however, of no importance to his main thesis. The background of the message of Amos is not written codes of law, but traditional standards of right and morals in Israel, and, as Würthwein rightly stresses, among the circles of the temple personnel (in Jerusalem).

[147] See Galling, op. cit., pp. 5ff.

described in still more detail in Ps. 132, which also belongs to the festival of harvest and new year.

Such cultic promises are echoed by the prophet of re-establishment, Deutero-Isaiah, who describes what is going to happen after the pattern of the festival of enthronement, when he makes Yahweh say to Israel (Isa. 55.3):

> I will make an everlasting covenant with you,
> the favours promised faithfully to David.

Here again the covenant is a renewal of the old one; it is the covenant with David which is to be renewed, but this is in itself the renewal and the crowning of the Sinai-covenant. And even here in the prophet a description has been attached of all the blessings which Israel is going to receive as a free gift: 'corn without money, and wine and milk for nothing'.

Both Pss. 81 and 95 explicitly refer to the grave breach of the covenant of which Israel had been guilty even at Mount Sinai,[148] and warn them against the recurrence of any such thing 'today'. The idea evidently is that such has actually happened much too often; the warning has a present reference, backed up by the sad experience of many generations. The poets know that the future happiness of the people depends on whether it is going to keep the commandments of Yahweh from now on. The fact of the matter is that in the relationship of the people to the commandments of Yahweh they have found the sufficient explanation of its fate. Every year Yahweh renewed the rich promises of his covenant. But when year after year passed and the lot and fate of Israel often seemed to become worse and worse, when none of the expectations and promises of the festival seemed to come true in everyday reality during the ensuing year, then the prophetically inspired authors of the psalms knew the reason, and they did not hide it. It was not because Yahweh could not or would not keep his word. It was due to the *sin* of the people themselves, because in some way or other they always broke the covenant, as they had already done once upon a time at Meribath-Kadesh (Pss. 95.8; 81.8, 11). Like the prophets, the authors of the psalms also had to take up the *problem of theodicy*. In liturgies like Pss. 81 and 95 we indirectly find Yahwism vindicating the justice of God. Yahweh is in the right; we have sinned.

In this cultic *admonition* and rebuke of the transgressions of the people lies the root of the prophetic speech of rebuke and doom. Yahweh's claim to the complete surrender of the people to him as their one and only God,

---

[148] It is strange that they do not allude to the offence with the golden calf, but to the fact that through unbelief and grumbling and disobedience the people 'tempted' Yahweh at Meribah and Massah, Ex. 17.1–7; Num. 20.1–13. This is obviously an earlier tradition than that of the golden calf as the cause of the wanderings in the desert. The earliest traditions about the covenant are attached to Kadesh rather than Sinai, and Meribah or Meribat-Kadesh is the main watering place of these districts, = 'Ain qederāt (see Mowinckel in *Norsk Geografisk Tidsskrift* 9, pp. 21ff., cf. above, n. 86). It is characteristic of the conservatism of the cult that the earlier tradition has been kept up in Pss. 81 and 95, though both of them are comparatively late.

and the inherent ethical approach of the Yahweh religion, resulted in picturing the just judgment of his coming as a judgment not only of their demonic and historical enemies and of the sinners within Israel, but as judgment of *his own people* as well.[149]

The preaching of the great prophets has, in turn, strengthened this idea in the complex of ideas belonging to the festival. This idea of the judgment against Israel is clearly expressed in Ps. 50. According to a tradition in the Mishna this psalm belongs to the feast of Tabernacles, so many of whose old ideas and ancient rites survived even into late times. The psalm itself probably dates from comparatively late times; but its ideo-historical and liturgico-historical connexion with Pss. 81 and 95 and with the idea of the renewal of the covenant against the background of a severe admonition to the people is quite clear. With the enthronement festival Ps. 50 has in common the idea of the epiphany, of the Sinai covenant as the background of what Yahweh is now to say, of his commandments according to the 'decalogical tradition', of his judgment, and of his severe castigation of the sins of the people. The latter is characterized by the verbs *šāphaṭ* and *dîn*, 'judge'. The description of the epiphany is followed by an upbraiding of the congregation because of its laxity towards the sinners and criminals tolerated in its midst. But the idea of judgment is not very prominent here; the congregation is 'lectured' and admonished in prophetic wording, but it is left at that.

In the first instance the historical reference, to which the festal myths bear witness on all points, implies that the idea of Yahweh's kingship is once more limited to *Israel* in practice. But the universalistic feature from the very beginning inherent in the connexion of the idea of enthronement with that of creation could not be obliterated. There came to be a certain tension between the world-wide view involved in the idea of creation—Yahweh as creator and therefore king of the world—together with the prophets' 'practical monotheism' on the one side, and the idea of Yahweh coming to defeat the gentiles and bring 'justice' and salvation to Israel on the other. Side by side with the call for all the world to rejoice over the enthronement of Yahweh, there is an emphasis on the 'shame' this means to the 'nations' and their gods and the idea of the triumph thereby secured to Israel.

But in spite of all this, *Yahweh's universal dominion* nowhere stands out so clearly as in the enthronement psalms, and consequently also his superiority over all other gods. It seems as if the poets cannot help imagining that all the world would rejoice in this just as much as they themselves do. Thus these psalms point forward to the New Testament conception of the 'kingdom' of God, even if the Old Testament limits have not yet

---

[149] This side of the complex of ideas of the feast has also been observed and elaborated by Würthwein in *ZThK* 49, pp. 1ff. In the critical remarks against Würthwein by Hesse in *ZATW* 65, 1953, pp. 45ff., Hesse is right in maintaining that the differences between the ordinary cult prophets and the classic 'great prophets' are not to be blurred; but the first creative impulse came from the ideas of the cult prophets.

been exceeded. The exclusive kingship of Yahweh is not far from true monotheism; the other gods have been completely degraded, not only to the position of servants of Yahweh, but almost to evil beings, defeated by him, as we have seen, at his coming.

We have spoken above of the promises given to the congregation, when Yahweh appeared at the festival, promises certainly pronounced in Yahweh's name by one of the temple prophets officiating at the cult performances (cf. for details, Chap. XII). When Yahweh shall become king and again establish his 'kingdom', his 'kingship', he shall come with rich gifts. Even the earthly kings used to distribute gifts on their festal days (cf. 2 Sam. 6.19), but in the case of the coming of the deity this was something involved in the nature of things. For in the first instance the festival meant a re-awakening to new riches and blessing, and 'salvation' for land and cattle and men; the coming of Yahweh meant the coming of the rainy season, when streams of blessing would again pour over the earth, so that the fields would flow with cream and honey, an expression which is found in the ancient Phoenician cult songs referring to the resurrection and enthronement of Baal.

At Yahweh's festival of enthronement all this receives a more personal touch. The almighty creator is coming to his people, renewing the covenant and securing to them all the 'blessing' which belongs to 'life' and 'peace' and 'salvation'. All the *gifts of the 'kingdom of God'* may indeed be summed up in these words. In fact, to secure all this was the real intention of the festal cult. When Yahweh comes again to the feast from his primeval home in the far south he brings 'abundant rain' with him, and thus restores his suffering people (Ps. 68.8–11). Ps. 65, the thanksgiving psalm of the harvest feast, gives a magnificent picture of all the blessings promised and granted by the new victory over the powers of chaos, the new creation and the coming of the rainy season, in the following outburst of praise:

> who by his might raised up the mountains,
>   being girded with power,
> who stilled the roaring of the sea . . . ,
>   the tumults of its waves,
> so that the dwellers at the ends of the earth
>   were terrified by thy wonders;
> the gates of the morning and evening
>   thou madest to shout with joy.

As the poet is here speaking of the victory over the primordial ocean and of the creation, 'the dwellers at the ends of the earth' are obviously not the 'nations' in the remotest parts of the world—as the glossator in v. 8 thinks—but the demonic powers of the *tĕhōm* around the earth, 'the helpers of Rahab' (Job 9.3), whom Yahweh at that time conquered. This victory Yahweh at the preceding new year feast repeated, and re-established the world 'not as a waste (*tōhû*) but to be inhabited' (Isa.

45.18). The consequence of this 'right order' was the rain, that now yields all the blessings of heaven and earth, for which the congregation at *this* new year feast has to give thanks. The same victory and re-creation are also granted by Yahweh's 'coming' again *this* time, and so the thanksgiving psalm has in mind both the blessings of the year already past, and those to be expected for the year to come:

> Thou has visited now and watered the earth
>> with rains, and greatly enriched her;
> God's river is now full of water;
>> thou hast prepared their corn;
> her ridges hast thou watered well
>> and soaked all her furrows,
> with showers has thou softened her,
>> thou blessest all her growth.

> Thou now hast crowned thy year of bliss,
>> for thus hast thou prepared it.
> The ruts of thy carriage wheels flow with fatness,
>> the wilderness overflows,
> the hills are girded with shouts of joy,
>> they shout and sing for joy;
> the meadows now are clothed with flocks,
>> the valleys covered with corn.[150]

But all this blessing and 'salvation' may also be regarded from an ethical point of view, and the mind may dwell on the good social conditions which are to prevail in Yahweh's kingdom, when the fellowship ('loyalty', *ḥesedh*) and faithfulness of the covenant, when justice and right order shall prevail in the land like good angels, while at the same time the 'earth shall give crops' and 'Yahweh give that which is good' as it was described in the quotation above from Ps. 85.

How real and manifold these good gifts of Yahweh were imagined to be will be still more clear to us, if we read the promises of the festal psalms in the light of all the different forms of 'festal myths' discussed in the preceding paragraphs. With Yahweh's victory over the powers of chaos, over primeval ocean and demons—those who 'dwell at the ends (of the earth)' (Ps. 65.9)—'the world is (again) stablished, that it cannot be moved' (Ps. 93.1ff.); chaos and desert have been kept off; the 'river of God', which the mind located high up in the heavens, but which the eyes of faith might also see welling forth from the holy place itself,[151] 'is now

---

[150] As for the text: *hămōn lĕ'ummîm* (v. 8) is a rationalizing gloss to the mythological metaphor, giving the latter a historical application and making the verse-line (stichos, bicolon) too long. V. 10b also makes the line too long, but may be the half-line (hemistich, colon) lacking after v. 12a. Vv. 13b and 14 are of one set; as 14aα and aβ are of one set as parallel cola, both thought-rhyme and metre demand that 14b be placed in front of 14a.

[151] Pss. 46.5; 36.9f.; cf. Ezk. 47.1–12; Isa. 33.21.

full of water' (Ps. 65.10). Yahweh's appearance as king involves a promise; he has renewed the covenant with his people, which in itself guarantees that all such things are going to happen in the coming year of grace and goodwill (Ps. 65.10; Isa. 49.8; 61.2) as faith may expect from the god of the covenant. In Jerusalem the festival was celebrated before the rainy season—and, originally, to cause it; when Yahweh has come, faith knows that blessing and crops and wealth will come also, if king and people but keep the covenant. 'The fate has already been turned' to good things for his people, and the days to come shall prove this.

However, Yahweh's victory over the powers of chaos and death are also transferred to the historical conditions of Israel. His appearance also implies his victory over all the 'nations' and so guarantees that no earthly enemy shall be able to threaten his city or be a match for the people fighting in his power. Yahweh's kingdom is going to be a kingdom of peace, for Israel has already 'been justified'—has got its right granted—and shall have its rights in all conflicts with its enemies. The other nations and their gods have already been judged and 'put to shame'; 'the villages of Judah rejoice over his righteous judgments'. With the coming of Yahweh 'holiness again becometh his house' (93.5); it has again been cleansed and consecrated, and the sources of blessing may again flow from there so that the congregation

> May have their fill of the fatness of thy house
> and drink of thy delicious stream. (Ps. 36.9.)

The poet does not here speak only about what *we* call 'spiritual' goods, but about the 'material' ones as well—and in the first place; these two aspects of reality were still undifferentiated in the minds of the Israelites. The 'holiness' (*qōdhes̆*) that after the coming of Yahweh again 'becomes his house' (93.5) also includes the sources of the material goods, the 'blessing'. In the Israelite conception of holiness the idea of the 'powerful' is always an important element; as 'the Holy One of Israel' Yahweh shows himself both in destroying the enemies of his people (Deutero-Isaiah) and in punishing his own people (Isaiah) and in re-creating the world. How close to one another the ideas of 'holiness' (taboo) and of 'might' (mana) lay, may be seen in the above mentioned Ps. 65, whose main theme is the renewed fertility of the land:

> we have been satisfied with the good things of thy house,
> with the holiness of thy temple. (v. 5.)

The fertility of the land flows from the source of 'holiness' that now is in the Temple.

But even the *earthly king* of Israel has been renewed and strengthened through the commemoration of his first installation and the repeated promises of Yahweh's coming and covenant: he is going to be the true luck-bringing king, under whose government land and people shall prosper (Ps. 132.11ff.). Israel shall always have true priests and prophets and intercessors (Pss. 99.6f., 132.16), 'her priests are wrapped in salvation', and able to transfer salvation to the rejoicing people. From now on—and on the basis of the entire history of the people—they know that Yahweh is a god who forgives sins, who provides redemption for his people through the religious commandments and rules and the righteous priests he has given them (99.6ff., cf. 93.5). He hears prayers as in days of old, and gives trustworthy oracles and guidance through the revelations received by his temple prophets and priests from the cloudy pillar over his altar (99.7). 'Blessed be the people who has such a god!'

It is a manifold, and to modern feelings perhaps contradictory, picture which is produced by all the versions of 'festal myths' and complexes of ideas attached to them. Nor are they to be systematized. Israel at any rate had not—as had the Hellenes even in Antiquity—arrived at a point when scientific 'mythologists'—we should say, theologians—would try to give a consistent and rationalized epic form to the many apparently contradictory expressions of the religious experience in the cult—the 'myths'—or even try to arrange their ideas in a kind of religio-philosophical system, as for instance Philo of Byblos had tried to do with the Phoenician 'mythology' in his *Sanchuniaton*.

But we may ask whether the thinkers and poets of Israel serving the cult—her *homines religiosi*—ever tried to unite the different variants of the 'festal myth' in separate rounded-off epic versions.

If we realize that the myth is a more or less epic and actualizing conception, and a more or less suggestive tale of the reality 'taking place' and experienced through the cult, then it will be clear that it may, in fact, exist in many versions, right from what may be called its myth seed or myth embryo—the immediate conception at the moment of experience of what 'happens' according to its transcendental and existential meaning—up to the completely formulated and poetically modelled tale of gods, the myth-epic.[152]

When, in the preceding paragraphs, we have been speaking of the different complexes of ideas, such as the 'struggle against chaos' myth, the 'struggle of the nations' myth, the 'judgment myth', the 'myth about the making of the covenant', and so on, we do not necessarily imply that all these myths have existed as rigidly formulated epic tales, whether in verse or prose. Nor need such a tale have been recited at a certain point in the festal liturgies. The original and essential thing is not that the myth is recited, but that it is experienced; it is not told, it is 'acted' and it 'takes place'. That such and such a complex of ideas made up the myth of a festival need mean no more than that the reality expressed by it was reiterated and experienced at the festival. How the reality was to be expressed might, so to speak, be left to the individual. But of course a certain common skeleton is to be found in the more or less realistic or

---

[152] Cf. Mowinckel, *Religion und Kultus*, pp. 94ff.

symbolical ritual drama, actualizing what was 'taking place'. The myth may exist in the cultic drama and the ritual, and even in the allusions in hymns and prayers to what is 'taking place'.

For the myth to be stabilized in an epic form is a later phase. Its starting-point may have been the explanatory words accompanying the rites: 'this means that the god is doing such and such a thing'; or it may have been the hymns, as they picture the great works of the god, depicted in the rites as 'taking place'.

The development of the myth as epic may come about in different ways. In the first instance it probably happens spontaneously. Some person attached to the cult and acquainted with what is going to 'take place', and possessing the poetic power of 'seeing', and a poet's delight in fabulizing, begins to tell with primeval reality and power about the great happenings here and now, and those 'once upon a time' in the beginning. The wake-night before the great festal day, the intervals between the acts, the day of preparation when the tribes gather and the pilgrims pour in from all quarters, these are all suitable and obvious opportunities for such narrations. The pilgrims to the festival would gather round the narrator, listening and asking and wanting to know more. It would become a custom for such tales to be told. The person with a creative talent would soon find that he could make a profit from it; the audience would be quite willing to spare a gift for an exciting and stimulating bit of saga. What may be called an order of professional saga-tellers would grow into being, attached to the sanctuary in question; or this function would be taken over especially by the wandering 'men of god', the Levites, the seers and nĕbhî'îm, saints and miracle-workers, wandering from one sanctuary to another.

There would be co-operation between the saga-teller and his audience. The interest and the questions would goad the imagination and the delight in telling. Some things would please the audience and be constantly repeated, others would be forgotten. The saga-teller himself would want to hear other versions and new features from other 'wise men'. New features were added and combined with his own repertoire, variants were inter-woven and equated; by means of leit-motifs and additions the separate tales were connected into greater series and 'complexes of traditions'. In this way both the religio-mythical and the more 'secular' epic would come to exist, though in antiquity no epic ever became entirely 'secular' and the connexion with the cult and the cult places and with the wandering 'holy men' and minstrels was always more or less recognizable.

The close connexion existing between hymns and cultic drama makes it likely that the epic myth from its start would have had a poetic form and style. All the epic myths known to us from Babylonia as well as from Ugarit are in verse; they are mythical and epic poems. That attempts at earlier stages may sometimes have used plain prose is not to be denied; but we seem justified in maintaining that the true form of the myth was the poetic epic, the cycle of songs; the 'rhapsodist', the 'bard', the 'skald' was at the same time the 'mythologist'. That the myths, for instance about the origin of the world, about creation, about the oldest generations of gods (cosmogony, theogony) are in prose seems to be due to the fact that later 'scientists' used them as material for an extensive historical sketch or some other non-cultic purpose. Thus we have had handed down to us the prose account of the Babylonian creation epic as part of Berossos' 'Babylonian History', and the Phoenician theogony and cosmogony we have as part of Philo's cosmological and philosophical text-book, in which Phoenician traditions are quoted. In much the same way we have the tales of Norse mythology quoted and explained in prose in Snorre's text-book about skaldic art, 'Edda'. There are thus grounds for believing that the same thing happened in Israel.

That poetic accounts of the fight against dragons and chaos, creation, the first man, and so on, existed in Israel at a comparatively early time may be concluded with certainty from the way the psalmists and prophets adopted and imitated such epic pieces.[153] They probably had Canaanite patterns; the Old Testament Leviathan, the dragon of the primeval ocean, corresponds to the dragon Lotan in the mythology of Ugarit. There are also indications that an actual account of creation existed in verse as part of an epic, but without being couched in the form of a fight against dragon and primeval ocean; we seem to find some remnants of such a creation epic in verse underlying the story in Gen. 2–3.[154] And from Ps. 8 we may infer that to the festival also belonged a presentation of creation, which did not have the form of a myth about a fight against dragon and primeval ocean, but was more closely related to the conceptions of Gen. 1.

From the very beginning, however, there was to be found in Israel yet another tradition, which was to become an essential part of the myth, namely the historical tradition about the origin of the people, about Yahweh's miracle at the Exodus and about the making of the covenant. Through the festival Israel very early—perhaps already at the time of David and Solomon—experienced a repetition of the history of her origin. Here the story had become historicized tradition, saga, even before it became a cultic myth. But it was in connexion with the cult that the form and the leading religious ideas were stabilized;[155] and there this history was re-experienced as a real history of salvation, as *mythos*. But in the cult even this tradition became a formula of 'confessions' and of hymns containing versions of the historical traditions,[156] such as the Exodus hymn of Ex. 15.[157] But there are also traces showing that even this traditional material, this 'myth of exodus and settlement and covenant', has been

---

[153] See Pss. 74.12–17; 89.2–3, 6–17; 104.5–9; Isa. 42.10ff.; 51.9f.; Ezk. 28.11ff.; 29.3f.
[154] See Mowinckel in *ZATW* 53, 1935, pp. 146f.
[155] See v. Rad, *Formgesch. Problem d. Hexateuchs*, pp. 30ff.
[156] v. Rad, op. cit., pp. 3ff., 8ff., is hardly right in saying that the latter type is derived from the former; they are both co-ordinate ritualizings of historical tradition.
[157] See Additional Note XXIV.

made a subject of epic adaptation, an Israelite religious 'national epic'.[158]

If anything becomes a custom in connexion with cult and sanctuary, it naturally develops into a rite. Even the spontaneous and free, or the artistically formed poetical tale about something 'taking place' in some way or other becomes part of the ritual. But the mythical epic may also be composed expressly for the purpose of becoming part of the cultic ritual. This is probably the case with the Babylonian creation epic on seven tablets ending in a hymn to Marduk, in which all his fifty cultic names are specified. But it may also happen in another way, so that the mythic tale first comes to rank as canonical writing, and then it reacts on the cultic liturgy and replaces the earlier freer forms of what is 'taking place'; the tale becomes a cultic 'lesson' ('legend').[159]

Of whether the temple rites of Jerusalem included recitations of such poetic and epic festal myths, and what may have been their form and place in the ritual, we know nothing directly. That the laws in the Pentateuch say nothing about it is of no consequence; for neither do they mention the singing of psalms. But analogies from Babylonia and Egypt, as well as all the allusions in the psalms to the festal myths, make it likely that such epic features would have a part in the festal rituals.

Other things seem to point in the same direction. In so far as the passover festival is concerned, the allusions to the rituals to be found in the Exodus itself contain a piece of information which probably implies that it was part of the ritual to ask questions as to the meaning of the different ceremonies and that these questions were answered by references to the Exodus (Ex. 12.26f.; 13.8). At any rate, later Jewish practice understood it in this way and supposed the answers to be given in the form of a re-narration of the Exodus as we have had it handed down to us in the book of the same name. The fact that these tales contain not a few allusions to, and details from, the festal ritual, proves that in the last instance the form they have is due to the cult. With great certainty we may therefore infer that at a comparatively early time there existed a fairly fixed cultic form of the traditions about the Exodus, forming part of the cult of the passover festival,[160] even if it existed in different versions. This may then permit us to analogize with regard to the other great festivals. But if so, we must remember that we are dealing with versions which are older than, and form the basis of, those which are to be found in the Pentateuch—for instance the story of creation.

Even in Israel the prose versions of the story of creation and of the traditions of exodus and settlement appear as parts of a *saga*, a historical account based on religious and *historical* interests—just like the Baby-

---

[158] See Mowinckel in *ZATW* 53, 1935, pp. 130ff.

[159] Such was the fate of the 'kerygma', the history of the passion and resurrection in the primitive church: instead of the free 'presentations' and allusions in singing and testimony along with a symbolic dramatic 'realization' in the 'active' liturgy itself, we have the reading of texts from the gospels. Cf. my *Religion und Kultus*, pp. 113f.

[160] See v. Rad, op. cit., pp. 3ff., 18ff., 37ff., and see below, n. 163.

lonian creation story of Berossos. On the whole the reading of 'lessons' seems to have played an inconspicuous part in the temple service, even after Judaism had her Holy Scriptures. The only clear evidence seems to be the reading of the 'law of the covenant' (Deuteronomy) every seven years at the feast of Tabernacles (Deut. 31.10ff.), a custom which obviously originated from the cultic rite of announcing Yahweh's basic commandments as part of the ritual of the covenant (see above, pp. 156f.). Here we may find further evidence that 'Scripture' was replacing the earlier and freer cultic forms. This system also seems to have led to more extensive reading of the 'Law' at the festivals of harvest and new year; at any rate the most natural interpretation of the reading of the law by Ezra at the new year festival, is that it refers to a regular cultic practice, not to the introduction of any new law.[161]

Therefore it is most unlikely that any part of the traditions about early times and the time of the occupation, in the form in which they have been handed down to us in the Pentateuch, should ever have been used in the temple cult as a 'festival legend' in the true sense of the word. This applies, for instance, to the creation tales in Gen. 1 and 2[162] and to the saga about the Exodus in Ex. 1–15.[163] In the form known to us *now*, they are meant to be part of a saga, not a festal myth or legend. But they are derived from earlier forms evidently connected with the festal cult.

9

The enthronement psalms and the other psalms of new year and harvest often allude to different rites and ceremonies belonging to the festal complex; but it is not possible to make a complete picture out of them. We have only a few glimpses.

Here we must recall what was said above of the dramatic character of the cultic festival. The feast is a 'holy drama', where the contents of the festal myths are presented, and thus are embodied and re-experienced as

---

[161] See Mowinckel, *Ezra den skriftlaerde*, pp. 32ff., 72ff.

[162] Humbert's arguments in favour of ascribing Gen. 1 to the new year festival as a 'legend' (*RHPhR* XV, 1935, pp. 1ff.) only suffice to bring out the connexion between the very material of the tradition and the new year festival. Ringgren has also realized this, *SEÅ* XIII, 1948, pp. 9ff. Ringgren's own attempt at showing that Gen. 1 has been formed in conscious protest against a certain (Canaanizing) version of the new year festival, is not convincing. P—like J before him— wanted to write history, and as it was part of the learned and holy tradition that a saga ought to start with the origin of the world (cf. Ehrenzweig in *ZATW* 38, 1919–20, pp. 65f.), both of them had recourse to the material to be found in the cultic tradition, giving it the form and idea of a saga.

[163] Johs. Pedersen has maintained that the saga of the Exodus in Ex. 1–15 is 'a festal legend of the Passover' (*Israel* III–IV, pp. 728ff.,; *ZATW* 52, 1934, pp. 161ff.). If this is to be applied to the form in which it has been handed down to us, it cannot be correct; even if Ex. 1–15 contains many evidences of an earlier connexion between the material of the tradition and the cult, the intention of the form as at present is to be a saga (cf. the preceding note); in fact it has been composed from two literary sources, each of which claims to be a saga—and the argumentation of Pedersen has not been able to impair the force of evidence. See Mowinckel in *StTh* V, 1951, pp. 66ff.

something which is actually creating what is then coming into existence. Only we must not think that this 'presentation' was anything like a modern realistic play. It is just possible that most of the things 'taking place' were presented by means of suggestive symbols. We need to realize the part played by symbols in the cult.[164] The fundamental idea itself, the epiphany of Yahweh as a victorious king, was suggested by carrying the ark in the festal procession. Just as, for instance, the whole of the Christian salvation-drama is presented in the 'holy drama' of the Orthodox Church, so we may very well imagine that the whole of the 'festal myth' described above was in some way or other expressed through dramatic symbols during the seven days' festival of harvest, new year and enthronement.[165]

We have mentioned above the important part played by the festal processions in the ancient cult.[166] Likewise it has been mentioned that, if we are justified in analogizing from corresponding new year and enthronement festivals, for instance in Babylonia, it would probably be on the last day of the seven or eight days of the festal complex—'the last day, that great day of the feast' as it is called in the Gospel of John (7.37)—that the royal entry of Yahweh would take place, the grand procession when the king, Yahweh, was represented by his ark. Now there are many psalms which belonged to the complex of the harvest festival, in which such a procession is taken for granted. We *may* be dealing with different parts of one and the same procession; but there may also be references to several processions on different days of the festival. Therefore it will always be a doubtful undertaking to try to reconstruct the picture of Yahweh's royal entry on the basis of these psalms.

An impressionistic picture of the changing scenes and emotions of the procession is given in Ps. 68, undoubtedly a procession psalm at Yahweh's triumphal entry as king. Other obvious procession psalms are 132, 24, and 118; the two former evidently belong to Yahweh's royal entry itself and, like Ps. 68, allude to the entry of the ark as his visible representative. Whether all these psalms belong to the same procession is more uncertain; they may even reflect the ceremonies of different periods, though certainly the first three, and probably also Ps. 118, date from pre-exilic times.

A 'processional road' always belonged to the cultic processions at the great temples of the orient, a *via sacra*, as it was called by the Romans. Babylon's processional road, Aiburshabu, has been excavated; it was decorated with lions and inscriptions in blue and white faience.[167] But Jerusalem, too, had her *via sacra*; there is a reference to it in Ps. 84.6:

---

[164] Cf. E. Underhill, *Worship*, p. 20.

[165] Therefore the objection of Kraus does not hold good, when he says (op. cit., p. 23): 'Es muss schon ein kaum vorstellbarer szenischer Aufwand bei der von Mowinckel postulierten dramatischen Aufführung des Festmythus ... angenommen werden, um die Worte und Bilder der Thronbesteigungspsalmen als "Kulterlebnisse" zu verstehen.' It only shows that Kraus has a very vague conception of cult, just as he lacks understanding of the true essence of myth.

[166] See above, Chap. I, pp. 2of.; *Religion und Kultus*, pp. 73ff.

[167] See Weissbach, *AO* V, pp. 26f.; Ravn, *Herodots beskrivelse av Babylon*, pp. 75f. More detailed in Koldewey, *Wiedersteh. Babylon*,[4] pp. 25ff.

> Blessed the man whose strength is in Thee,
> in whose mind are the paved ways!

The 'paved way' (*měsillâ*)—the plural is amplificatory—on which the partakers of the festival have it 'in their hearts' to walk, and on which they intend to walk, is the holy way, on which the procession 'ascend' to the Temple. So the Greek translation is justified in paraphrasing this verse: 'with the "ascension" (i.e. festal procession) in their hearts'. And when, in the spirit, the prophet sees the dispersed Jews returning to Jerusalem with Yahweh at their head, he pictures a mighty procession approaching, and therefore speaks also of the wonderful 'paved way', the 'eschatological' *via sacra*, which will then be made through the desert:

> and there shall be a paved road
> its name 'The Sacred Way'. (Isa. 35.8.)

On the basis of the story told in 2 Sam. 6 as to how David took Yahweh's ark to Jerusalem, we may guess that the processional way started from a place called the house of Obed-Edom, outside the oldest part of the town, the 'castle of David',[168] and from there it ran on the outside (to the east) of, or through the royal castle and into the temple court through the eastern gate—probably the one also called the water-gate, perhaps because at the ceremony of water drawing the water from the spring Gihon would be carried in this way.[169] Ps. 118.19f. also speaks of a definite gate, the 'Gate of Righteousness' (*ša'ărê ṣedheq*), through which the procession would enter, the 'gate, through which the righteous (i.e. the Israelite congregation), shall enter'. Even the temple and procession gates of Babylonia had such symbolical names: the 'Gate of Allegiance', the 'Gate of Salvation', the 'Gate of Life', etc.[170]

The holy way played a central role in the festival. There would take place the 'pageant of my God and King', as the psalmist would call it—the 'ascension(s)' was the technical term.[171] The royal entry of Yahweh, at which he himself is present, symbolized by his holy 'ark', is the pre-eminent visible centre of the experiences connected with the enthronement festival:

> God is gone up amid shouts of homage,
>   Yahweh (has come) with trumpet blasts.
> Music of praise for God, sing music!
>   Music of praise now for our King! (Ps. 47.6f.)

---

[168] See Mowinckel, *Ps.St.* II, pp. 128f., giving a more detailed statement.

[169] The water gate is a temple gate, not a gate in the city wall, see Mowinckel in *Studier tilegnet Buhl*, p. 172. For the city gates of Jerusalem, cf. the article 'Jerusalem' in *BRL*.

[170] See Zimmern in *ZDMG* 76, 1922, p. 49, and below, note 191.

[171] This is no doubt the meaning of the psalm heading *shîr hamma'ălôth*, 'the psalms of ascent, i.e. of the festal procession', see below, Chap. XXIII.3 and *Ps.St.* IV, p. 3. Vb. *'ălâ* 'ascend' is used about the procession in Ps. 47.6.

If we agree that the three psalms 68, 132 and 24 belong to Yahweh's royal entry itself, then it is clear that 132 deals with the preparation for the transport of the ark from some place outside the sanctuary, whereas the first scene of 24 is played before and within the gates of the Temple itself. Ps. 68 seems to reflect the start of the procession, so that its situation partly overlaps that of 132. But Ps. 132 continues after the procession has passed through the gates. With the above reservation (p. 170) we must put the psalms 68, 132 and 24 in this sequence.

As Ps. 68 gives the most vivid general impression of the festival procession, it is best to deal with it first.[172]

That the psalm belongs to a festal procession is quite evident:

> Behold, everyone! the procession (hălîkhôth) of Yahweh,
>   the holy procession of my God and King;
> singers in front, musicians behind (them),
>   between, young girls with tambourines. (vv. 25f.)

Then the whole people comes by tribes: Benjamin, Judah, Zebulon, Naphtali, led by their tribal chiefs (vv. 27f.).

The poet speaks in the first person, but he speaks on behalf of the whole festal congregation. He speaks as one who is personally taking part in the procession—as no doubt he is. He gives us the programme of the procession, and describes the impressions made on himself and his fellow worshippers by what happens and what they are now all experiencing: the triumphal entry of Yahweh, their king, into his palace (v. 30), his sanctuary (vv. 18, 36) his 'ascension' to 'the height' (mārōm, v. 19)—here the poet uses the technical term 'ālâ for the procession up to the sanctuary.

The general character of the psalm is hymnal. But the impressionistic character in itself, the changing scenes with the changing emotions—and probably even voices—makes it most natural for us to describe it as a processional cantata. Yahweh is making his entry as king. That he is represented by his visible symbol, the ark, is seen from the introductory version of the ancient 'stanza of breaking camp' (Num. 10.35). He is coming as a victorious king, the festal procession being his rejoicing army. However, he is not only accompanied by his earthly host; in the procession are also his 'thousands upon thousands of chariots', the mythical hosts (v. 18).

Instead of the usual hymnal invitation to praise,[173] the introductory stanza, vv. 2–4, keeps in medias res and, in deference to the ancient invitation to 'break up' and start the procession, describes how Yahweh has once

---

[172] As for Ps. 68 the author was long in doubt whether it was a 'casual' song of victory (see Chap. IX. 1) or a festal hymn of praise belonging to the enthronement of Yahweh, see Ps.St. II, pp. 12, 332; VI, pp. 31, n. 3, 38, n. 9; Offersang og sangoffer, pp. 179, 279, here, pp. 182, 226, Years ago now, however, he became convinced that the latter interpretation is the right one (Offersang, p. 179, here p. 182), as H. Schmidt has already seen (Thronfahrt Jahves, pp. 13ff.), see now Der achtundsechzigste Psalm, 1953, with a discussion of Albright's hypothesis in HUCA XXIII, 1, 1950, pp. 1ff., and the writer's Real and Apparent Tricola, pp. 92ff.

[173] See above, Chap. IV. 1, pp. 81f.

more 'risen', scattering his enemies and creating joy and delight in his people, 'the righteous'; what has happened so often before has again become reality. The second stanza, vv. 5–7, goes on with a regular little hymn of praise to Yahweh 'the skyrider', an epithet adopted from Ugarit-Canaan preferentially to indicate Yahweh's coming to fight against the powers of chaos (cf. Ps. 18.11ff.). The congregation is called upon to praise the 'name' of Yahweh, which he has once more made known by his coming to help all those in distress and to destroy 'the rebellious'. In the situation of a festal psalm these general sentences must obviously be applied to Israel and her enemies. The third stanza, vv. 8–11, starts the broader hymnal description of the real theme of the psalm:

> O Yahweh, when thou 'wentest out' before thy people,
>   when thou didst march through the steppes,
> the earth was shaking, the skies were dropping
>   before Yahweh, the God of Israel.
> O Yahweh, thou didst pour out a generous rain,
>   raising up (again) thy weary property;
> thy household is (now) dwelling therein,
>   in thy goodness thou hast raised up the languishing people.

Here we are told how Yahweh personally led his people out of the desert to Canaan, by means of a simple picture, the picture of a triumphal procession. The term 'go forth' (*yāṣā'*) refers to the start of such a festal procession. The description, however, is not just meant to be an account of the events of the past; this 'act of salvation' is being 'remembered' and thus re-experienced as actual presence; the festal procession of the day is identical with the act of salvation of the past. Even today Yahweh comes, as he did before, from his original dwelling-place in Sinai (v. 18) and enters his 'abode', the Temple (v. 29), accompanied by his delivered people.

The re-experienced act of salvation is not here a mere mythical happening, but the historical experience, the Exodus, the wandering in the desert and the victorious settling in Canaan—just as in the psalm, Ex. 15.2ff. In fact, from the following fourth stanza, vv. 12–15, we see that the act of salvation, which is now re-experienced in the festival, is 'the myth about the victory over the nations'. The festal procession is also 'the mighty host of those bringing the good tidings' of the victory, and tells of 'the fleeing war lords', the slain kings and horses and chariots scattered over the field 'like snow on Black Mountain', and the abundant booty. In the sixth stanza (vv. 20–24) there may be an allusion to a definite people, perhaps Se'ir-Edom as Israel's actual enemy, to whom the myth has been applied (v. 20).

But in the background of this conception we find here too the chaos myth, Yahweh's victory over the primeval chaotic powers. This is not only seen from 'the myriads of chariots' (v. 18) and 'the skyrider' (v. 5), 'that rideth' or, rather, 'driveth on the primeval heaven' (v. 34), but also from the metaphors used in the eighth stanza (vv. 29–32) of 'the nations delighting in war' (v. 31c); 'the beasts of the reeds (or, marshes)', 'the herd of bullocks' are terms for the demonic monsters of chaos, which have been destroyed by Yahweh, and which he is repeatedly asked to destroy by his 'threatening'—the threatening word of power, with which in the beginning he had chased away the primeval ocean (and its monsters) (cf. Ps. 104.7), it is an indication in the same direction when the enemy is characterized as 'those with hairy scalps', *śāʿîr*, a word in which the Israelite must needs hear the by-meaning of 'demoniac' (*śāʿîr*). In v. 21 we are told in plain words that the victory of Yahweh is a victory over, and deliverance from, 'Death', by which here is not meant natural decease, but Death with a capital D, Môt, in Canaanite mythology the adversary of Baʿal, here of Yahweh, in the constantly repeated war between life and death, the Living God and the god of death, Môt. We find the same idea in Ps. 48 (see below, p. 182). That is why the poet can put the triumphal words into the mouth of Yahweh: 'I bring back again from the Dragon— *beshen*[174]—I bring back again from the depths of the Sea' (v. 23). Every year, as we have heard above, Death or 'Prince Sea'—*zebul yam*, as he is named in Ugaritic mythology—seeks to overthrow the land of the living, but every time Yahweh again conquers him, and 'brings back' from his realm.

As in Pss. 46 and 48 (see below) the poet glorifies the sanctuary on the 'mountain of God', the true Olympus (vv. 16f.). And in the eighth stanza (vv. 29–32) the congregation prays that from there (v. 30) Yahweh, who is dwelling there, may 'display thy strength which thou mightily prevailest for us from thy palace' (vv. 29f.), and (again and again) 'rebuke' (Moffatt: check) 'the chaotic powers in the shape of the nations delighting in war' (see above). If it be so, the congregation promises, even kings of the richest and remotest nations, Patros, Egypt and Kush, will bring gifts of gold and silver and other precious metals to this temple and 'stretch out their hands to him'.

In the last, the ninth stanza (vv. 33–35), the hymn of praise, as is often the case, returns to the beginning, and calls all the kingdoms of the earth to praise this mighty God of the heavens, the thunderer, who 'demonstrates his power in the clouds', who is also 'the God of Israel, who bestows power on his people—blessed be He!' This quite corresponds to the enthronement psalms when the cosmic aspect of the festal experience is expressed. To 'what happens' in the cultic drama corresponds what happens in heaven; he that sits enthroned in the Temple is the one who sits enthroned up there, and sends thunder and rain and 'renews the surface of the earth'—and with awe, all kings and peoples ought to recognize that he is at the same time the god of Israel!

Ps. 132 gives us the 'text' of a dramatic procession with Yahweh's ark. It has a markedly historical savour; the procession is here looked upon as

[174] See Albright in *BASOR* 46, 1932, p. 19, n. 16; *HUCA* XXIII, 1, 1950, p. 27.

a repetition of Yahweh's first entry into Jerusalem, when David laid the foundation of the cult of Yahweh there and introduced the holy ark as the centre of the cult and the symbol of the personal presence of Yahweh. That Yahweh's ark, the hub of the old cultic centre of Shiloh, actually did play a part at the institution by David of the cult of Yahweh in Jerusalem is known to us from the tradition in 2 Sam. 6, but it is also a self-evident deduction: David could not have indicated more clearly that his new kingdom was to be based on the traditions of the old Israel. And considering all we know about the way in which cult institutions and the foundation of a kingdom were celebrated in the ancient orient,[175] we may take it for granted that such a ceremony would be repeated as an annual festival; and then everything indicates that the festival of the institution of Temple and cult in Jerusalem was identical with the new year festival, the enthronement festival of Yahweh.[176] For when the Chronicler (2 Chron. 6.41f.) quotes part of this psalm as the festal song at the consecration of the Temple of Solomon in the month of Ethanim, we are justified in taking this as showing how the psalm actually was used, and in concluding that the harvest feast was also considered to be the celebration of the consecration of the Temple; the Temple of the new king was consecrated anew. The psalm proves that the festival of consecration was at the same time the festival of the institution of the cult of Yahweh on Zion under David.

We find a reflection of the ritual of this consecration festival in the description of 2 Sam. 6; of course the saga-writer had no contemporary reports about the festival from the time of David, so he described it on the model of the celebration of his own day.[177] Along with Ps. 132 the description of the saga teller gives us a picture in broad outline of this important part of the festival.

The whole thing has the character of a cultic and historical drama, in which the king, the Anointed, evidently plays the part of David. First we hear the intercessory prayer for 'David'—and so for the whole royal family—that Yahweh may remember the piety of the ancestor who swore never to indulge in sleep or rest till he had found the ark of Yahweh and brought it to its proper place. Here we probably have to imagine that David is waiting to hear from those whom he has sent out to seek for the ark, and that in the meantime the chorus representing the congregation is comforting and strengthening him by this intercession. At this moment

---

[175] See Dürr in *Theol. u. Glaube* 20.

[176] Solomon's consecration of the Temple took place at the 'festival' in the month of Ethanim, the old name for the month of the autumnal equinox Tishri (1 Kgs. 8.2). The central rite was here the procession with Yahweh's ark (8.1ff.), just as at the foundation festival of David (2 Sam. 6). The enthronement psalm 93.5 refers to the consecration of the Temple. Ps. 132 is the dramatic liturgy of the 'procession' at the festival of the foundation of the Temple; the centre is the ark of Yahweh (see above, n. 111). The Chronicler explicitly quotes Ps. 132 as the psalm sung at the festival for the consecration of the Temple under Solomon (2 Chron. 6.41f.). Cf. *Ps.St.* II, pp. 109ff. and above, n. 71, and Additional Note XVIII.

[177] Cf. Additional Note XVI.

a new chorus appears on the 'stage': the men return to say that the ark has been found 'in the precincts of the town of Ephratah', i.e. Kiriath-jearim,[178] whither, according to tradition, it had come from the land of the Philistines; now they are bringing it with them. Let us 'go into his tabernacles—the sanctuary, and (by implication), put the ark in its proper place—and worship at his footstool'; this latter name is that given to the ark itself; in the Temple it stood under the wings of the two giant cherubs, whose outstretched wings span the whole room; on it Yahweh was supposed to be enthroned unseen. Thereupon follows a version of the old 'stanza of breaking up', used when the ark was lifted up and moved forward (Num. 10.35) requesting Yahweh to go at the head of the procession. The priests are referred to as being now clothed in the beauties of holiness and having the proper inner quality, and the people of the covenant shout for joy before their king. Evidently the priests carrying the ark are speaking here. Whether what follows takes place while the ark is still standing in the same place, or a little later, is doubtful; the analogy with 2 Sam. 6.13 rather seems to suggest the latter, and that after having taken six steps they make a halt to offer up a sacrifice for the success of the undertaking. The following prayer for the blessing of Yahweh on 'his anointed', 'for (the ancestor) David's sake', would then be attached to the sacrifice. And as the prayer of vv. 11–18 is answered by a sonorous oracle of bliss to the royal house, to people and country, in the very same style as the royal oracles containing promises to David in Ps. 89.4–5, 20–38 and 2 Sam. 7, and evidently pronounced by one of the temple prophets (cf. Chap. XII.3); it is not unreasonable to imagine that this promise was formulated in connexion with happy auguries from the offering.

An important point strikes us when we compare this festal drama with the corresponding part of the Babylonian new year and enthronement drama.[179] In Babylonia the other gods would go out along with the king and the priests, etc., in a cultic procession to search for and deliver the lost, dead, or imprisoned god. In the cultic drama of Israel it is the king, 'David', who with his army marches out to search for the representative symbol of Yahweh, the holy ark; who finds it, and provides a permanent abode for it on Zion. The search for the god has become part of the *historically* orientated festival for the institution of the Yahweh cult and the erection and consecration of the Temple, Yahweh's 'resting place' or 'home'. This is the true gist of Ps. 132, not for instance the re-instatement of the king. All these national and religious historical memories become merged in the enthronement festival and are repeated through it, becoming a living reality again. Creation, Yahweh's victory over his enemies, is brought to an issue through the creation of his people, i.e. through the

---

[178] Thus Delitzsch in his psalm commentary, pp. 811f., with reference to 1 Chron. 2.50; Kiriath-jearim is a descendant of Hur, who according to 2.19 is a son of (Caleb and) Ephrath.
[179] See Frankfort, *Kingship*, pp. 321ff.

deliverance of the people and the covenant with them, which is again concentrated and renewed through the covenant with the house of David and reaches its climax through the foundation of the Temple and the worship of Yahweh there, an idea also present in the psalm in Ex. 15. Yahweh's victorious and royal entry also includes the entry into the renewed Temple, where from now on he shall 'sit enthroned upon the praises of Israel' (Ps. 22.4).

Ps. 24 gives us another picture of the festival. If Ps. 132 shows us the beginning of the day's procession as it started from a place outside the temple citadel, corresponding to the house of Obed-Edom—where the ark had stood for three months,[180] till David brought it to Zion—then Ps. 24 shows us what happened when the procession reached the temple gate. The psalm falls into three parts: the introductory hymn to the creator and ruler of the world (vv. 1–2), the dialogue between the leader of the procession and the gate-keepers as to who is allowed to enter the sanctuary (the 'conditions of entry'), with the assurance from the side of the pageant (the congregation) that they fulfil the demands (vv. 3–6), and finally the request for the gates to open to the One who is coming, 'the King of glory, Yahweh Zebaoth' (vv. 7–10).

What is of special interest in this connexion is the second scene: the question from the leader of the procession and the answer from the 'gate-keeper', who, in earlier times at any rate, belonged to the higher clergy: in pre-exilic times the 'three keepers of the door' ranked next to the chief priest, and so were second from the top (2 Kgs. 25.18).

This way of asking is no doubt old, and has a natural explanation. The many different sanctuaries, besides having general rules for purification and abstinence and preliminary dues,[181] had also their own special *leges sacrae* or 'laws of the sanctuary', their special rules and special demands as to the qualifications of those to be admitted. The pilgrims, perhaps people from afar, had to put questions about the special rules applying at that sanctuary, what conditions were made, what would be the 'rights' and 'customs' of the deity in that place. In the course of time these natural practices would, as so often happens, develop into a fixed form, a rite: in such and such a way people were to ask, and thus they were to be answered on given occasions, even if everybody knew the answer beforehand.[182] Originally, these laws of the sanctuaries were of an essentially ritual cultic and taboo nature, and concerned with external things; at certain sanctuaries for instance no admittance was granted to women. But certain gross crimes and all sorts of ritual impurity were also reasons for exclusion. It is a remnant of such old prohibitions that in Jerusalem the blind and paralysed were not admitted to the Temple.[183] But gradually the moral

[180] 2 Sam. 6.10f. See *Ps.St.* IV, pp. 44f.; *Ps.St.* II, pp. 107ff., 128f.
[181] Cf. 1 Sam. 21.5f., Ex. 19.10, 14f.
[182] Cf. Ex. 12.26f.; 13.8, 14.
[183] 2 Sam. 5.8, which is, in fact, an aetiological explanation of the custom. Later on this taboo was only applied to the admission to priesthood, Lev. 21.18.

commandments became more prominent. In this way religious and moral instruction about the fundamental laws of Yahweh would grow to be a permanent element of the cultic ritual. Such sacred laws are a universal feature at ancient oriental sanctuaries.[184] They may even be cut into a stone or engraved on tablets at the entrance of the temple.[185]

In Israel these commandments, quite naturally, gradually came to be looked upon as commandments of the covenant, and as commandments given by Yahweh at Kadesh or Sinai; the instruction as to the conditions of admittance became merged in the idea of the festival as being a renewal of the covenant and a commemoration of the great works of God and of his commandments, i.e. the fundamental happenings in the life of the people, as we meet them in Pss. 81 and 95; in both cases it is the supposed commandments of Mount Sinai and of Kadesh which are imposed on the congregation at the festival of epiphany.

Here we have a special form or application of Yahweh's demands, which has been called 'laws (*tôrôth*) of entry',[186] i.e. authoritative divine 'instruction' (*tôrâ*) through the priest as to what is demanded from those who are admitted to the sanctuary and cult and the blessing thereof. They may have the form of answers to questions on the part of the congregation, or as in this case, the procession.

In so far as the psalms are texts for the cultic rituals, the commandments of Yahweh and the enforcement of them find a place in psalmography. Ps. 24 gives us an example of this as an element in a larger context. The instruction about 'the conditions of admittance' here becomes part of the dramatically modelled liturgy of the procession at Yahweh's royal entry into his abode (the Temple) after having obtained glory through victory over the powers of chaos, and once more proved himself creator and saviour, and having obtained kingship over the whole earth.

The third element in this logical structure of questions and answers would obviously be a declaration on the part of those who want to attend the cult (the congregation) as to whether they are equal to the demands: I have kept these commandments, I am guiltless of these crimes (taboos). The pattern for this part of the liturgy would then be:

1. Who shall be admitted to the hill of Yahweh?
2. The answer of the priests: he that hath kept such and such rules; he that is of such and such a character.
3. The answer of the procession: we have kept and fulfilled all this.

[184] See for instance the texts translated by Sam Wide in *Främ. Relig.-urk.* III, pp. 213f.—The most important collection of classical *leges sacrae* is in Proht and Ziehen, *Leges Graecorum sacrae*, fasc. 1–2. Select pieces in Dittenberger, *Sylloge inscr. Graec.* III, pp. 105ff. See also Helbing, *Auswahl aus gr. Inschr.*, pp. 105–111.

[185] A remnant of this custom is the limestone tablet set up at the entrance to 'the court of Israel' in the Temple of Herod, enforcing the interdict against the access of all non-Jews; one of these tablets has been found in Jerusalem, see Dittenberger, *Orientes Graeci Inscriptiones Selectae* II, 1905, no. 538; Benzinger, *Hebr. Archäologie,*[3] p. 337. The tradition that the ten commandments were written on such tablets is an echo of such a custom.

[186] See Mowinckel, *Decalogue*, pp. 141ff.; *Ps.St.* V, pp. 107ff.; Gunkel-Begrich, *Einl.*, pp. 327ff., 408f., with literary references.

Such an answer may be detailed: I have not committed this and this and this. In Ps. 24 it is summed up shortly in v. 6: 'Such are the men who are in quest of Yahweh, who seek the face of the God of Jacob', i.e. we are confident of fulfilling the demands.[187]

So this part of the cult was developed into a means of religious and moral instruction. Ps. 15 is an independent parallel to the part of Ps. 24 which speaks of the conditions of admittance. Here quite a 'moral catechism' is put before the congregation, telling them what a man must be like, who wants to be 'the guest of Yahweh' and 'eternally blessed'.

We notice that ten conditions are mentioned here. This gives a hint of an important and interesting connexion in the history of liturgy and religion. For here we find the fundamental tendency of Yahwism, the approved tendency to keep aloof from the other religions and to have a moral conception of the essence and will and commandments of Yahweh; we find it conquering, so to speak, and filling the ancient—in itself pre-Yahwistic—pattern of the liturgies of entry. It is the same tendency that find expression in the traditions about the making of the covenant on Mount Sinai and in the commandments of the covenant, Ex. 34 and 20. The custom of announcing the 'sacred laws' of the sanctuary, and the tradition about the making of the covenant and the ancient Yahweh law from Kadesh-Sinai have mutually attracted each other, and in this way the old custom of putting questions as to the laws of admittance was filled with the spirit and essence of Yahwism.

This has been an important factor in the moulding and growth of the tradition about the commandments connected with the making of Yahweh's covenant. The enforcement of the fundamental commandments of the sanctuary, and the fact that these were considered to be derived from the making of the covenant and therefore identical with the law of Yahweh and the commandments of Kadesh and Mount Sinai, together with the tendency of Yahwism to get at the essence of God's demands as a whole, led to a definite tradition about these fundamental commandments, a tradition which—probably in keeping with the ancient practices of sanctuaries—would try to sum up the demands in the shape of ten (sometimes twelve) commandments, 'decalogues', and which we may therefore call the 'decalogical tradition' of Israel. So then, those commandments, which at the time were supposed to be the most important, would make up these ten fundamental commandments. Some of them, of course, would remain constant, e.g. the claim for the exclusive authority of Yahweh, and the rejection of cultic images.

The existing *tôrôth* of entry also belong to the decalogical tradition. The traditional figure 10 in such groupings of the fundamental commandments of the covenant ('the decalogues') is probably derived from the instruction of pilgrims: one commandment for each finger.

---

[187] On Pss. 15 and 24 cf. also Galling. He understands the context against the same background in *ZATW* 47, 1929, pp. 125ff.

At which of these two points within the ritual of the festival the deca-logical tradition first came in is a less important question.[188] The funda-mental commandments of the covenant of Mount Sinai encounter the congregation outside the temple gate, and they are also heard at a climax of the festal cult, at the renewal of the covenant. Two, by themselves independent, cultic ideas and customs: the announcement of the condi-tions of admittance to the sanctuary, and the renewal of the covenant with its conditions, both receive a new substance of ideas from the historical tradition in the religion of Israel. And this has probably happened under mutual influence.

In principle these fundamental religious and moral commandments are related to the congregation, to 'Israel' collectively, both in Pss. 81 and 95, and in Pss. 24 and 15. But in the 'liturgy of entry' the commandments are of such a nature that the challenge must be taken up by the individual, who is put fact to face with his personal responsibility, both for his own 'blessing' and for the future of the people. Imitations of this mode of speaking as an expression of the message of the prophets are to be found in Isa. 33.14–16 and Mic. 6.6–8.

Another procession psalm based on the same ideas and probably also used at the same festival is Ps. 118. This psalm, too, starts outside the temple gate and reflects the entry through the 'Gate of Righteousness'. This is probably the name of an actual gate, very likely the innermost temple gate,[189] through which only 'the righteous'—the congregation in a state worthy of the cult—are allowed to enter. It is just possible that Ps. 24 refers to events taking place outside the outer gate leading to the precincts of the whole citadel and Temple, whereas Ps. 118 refers to those taking place before and after the passage through the inner temple gate proper.[190] The psalm starts with a thanksgiving by the king or the leader of the congregation on behalf of the people both for the aid Yahweh has given them in all distress and danger throughout the ages, and because their enemies have been put to shame, and Israel, though certainly chas-tised, has not been given over to death, but is now able to rejoice over the great acts of Yahweh (vv. 1–18). The description of the history of Israel, so full of distress, is summed up in one concentrated picture: all the nations compassed her about, but in the name of Yahweh, the king has destroyed them; here the saga has been conventionalized on the model of the 'myth about the fight of nations' (see above). Then follows the request to open the Gate of Righteousness to the righteous, who are now coming (vv. 19–20), followed by a new thanksgiving psalm ending in an allusion to

---

[188] Details about this tangled plexus of ideas connected with the law of Yahweh in the festal cult, are given in *Ps.St.* V, pp. 107ff.; *Decalogue*, pp. 114–156.—In *Le Decalogue* the present author had fancied the 'torot d'entré' to be the origin of the promulgation of the commandments at the renewal of the covenant, but in fact we have to deal with two parallel cultic phenomena and developments of the Israelitic ritual.

[189] See above, p. 171. If so the gate is not the present 'Golden Gate', the eastern gate to Haram esh-sherif, as Morgenstern thinks, *HUCA* VI, 1929, pp. 1ff.

[190] Cf. the sketch plan in *BRL* col. 411f.; 'F' indicates the outer gate.

this festal day, created by Yahweh himself (vv. 21–24). The very fact that the congregation was allowed to enter through the Gate of Righteousness was at the same time a corroboration of its righteousness and an imparting of the power of 'righteousness' and happiness.[191] This thanksgiving psalm ends in a prayer of prosperity and happiness (v. 25), to which the priests answer with a blessing from the house of Yahweh on those who are now coming in the name of Yahweh (v. 26). While the procession is marching through the gate another short thanksgiving hymn is sung, with a reference to the 'festival of light' and a call to join in the festal dance up to (and round?) the altar (v. 27). Another thanksgiving hymn accompanies the attendance and finishes the psalm (vv. 28–29).

The 'myth about the fight of nations' has been mentioned above several times. It is the illustration of the idea that the enthronement of Yahweh guarantees victory over the enemies of Israel in the 'mythical' form of a destruction of the 'nations' en bloc outside the walls of Jerusalem. In several psalms this 'fight of the nations' is a central theme, especially in Pss. 46 and 48. Both these psalms refer to the congregation as having 'seen' the 'works' of Yahweh and his 'loving-kindness' (*hesedh*) towards his people (46.9; 48.10):

> Come, behold the works of Yahweh,
>   who endeth the wars all over the world:
> He hath broken the bow and snapped the spear
>   and burned the shields in the fire. (46.9f.)

> What once we heard of, now we have seen
>   within the city of our God:
> that God preserveth it evermore,
>   (it never shall be moved).
> We are now contemplating thy loving-kindness
>   within thy Temple, O God. (48.9f.)

Knowing how thoroughly the cult in ancient times was a 'drama' for the purpose of presenting visibly what faith knew to be happening,[192] and considering the prominent part played by ritual fighting games in the cult of ancient peoples,[193] we can hardly help interpreting the words in the above passages as references to ritual acts, through which was presented in a more or less realistic or symbolical way the victory of Yahweh over the united nations. Perhaps the sword dance, referred to in Ps. 149, had a connexion with this performance. It would be logical, considering the dramatic character of the festival, if these ritual fighting games were to

---

[191] In Babylonia, too, the different temple gates had names indicating the blessing received when entering: 'the gate of grace', 'the gate of salvation', 'the gate of life' and so on. The sick person for instance who is to be cleansed and obtain 'salvation' enters through the 12 gates of the Marduk temple, and for each gate he gets the blessing expressed by the name: 'In the gate of grace he gets grace, in the gate of salvation he sees salvation, in the gate of life, life is given to him.' See Zimmern in *ZDMG* 76, 1922, p. 49, and above, p. 171.

[192] Cf. *Ps.St.* II, pp. 19ff.; the article 'Drama' in *RGG²* I, 2000ff.; *Religion und Kultus*, pp. 73ff.

[193] See for instance *Myth and Ritual*, ed. Hooke, Index *s.v.* 'Combat, ritual'; Engnell, *Div. Kingship*, Topical Index *s.v.* 'Shamfight'.

take place some time *before* the triumphal procession described in the preceding paragraph, since this performance was also followed by a procession, a circumambulation about, or on, the walls of the city, as we can see from Ps. 48.13-15:

> Walk about Zion, go round about her,
>   and count up all her towers;
> mark you well her ramparts now,
>   and scan her citadels,
> that you may tell the age to come
>   that He is Yahweh himself,
> (he is) our God for evermore,
>   he shall guide us against Death.

Probably such a circumabulation was originally supposed to be a consecration of walls and city, by which power was transferred;[194] here it has been 'rationalized': it is meant to assure the congregation that the walls are unshaken, and to strengthen their faith that the city is now safe under the protection of Yahweh.

We can gather from this psalm that the fight of nations had not only earthly and political, but even cosmic dimensions. Behind the idea of Yahweh's coming as a victory over the historical enemies of the people, we find the idea of his coming as a victory over the evil cosmic powers, the dragon of the primeval ocean, the powers of chaos and of death—'Death' itself, or Môt, as the personified adversary of the god in the Canaanite cultic myth was called. The last lines from the quotation above imply this: From now on, the king, Yahweh, will be the guide of his people against 'Death'. All evil powers threatening land and nature and people have been destroyed through the coming and enthronement of Yahweh.[195]

This series of pictures from the rites of the festival gives an indication of their general character and of the unity between the rites and the thoughts and experiences of faith to which they are meant to give expression.

There are also allusions to other ritual festival customs; above (p. 181), we have already mentioned the 'festival of light', the illumination of Temple and city at night during the feast of tabernacles, which is mentioned in the Mishna (Sukka V) and hinted at in Ps. 118.27. Ps. 68 is a procession psalm for this festival, which contains many references, but, unfortunately, mostly to rites unknown to us now.

---

[194] Cf. Neh. 12.27ff., and see Additional Note XIX.

[195] Cf. Johnson in *The Labyrinth*, pp. 94f.—Rowley, *Rediscovery of the O.T.*, pp. 126f., 174, thinks that with such a conception of the creative nature of the cultic drama I must be of the opinion that the ritual had a 'magic' character. That this is not the right interpretation of my opinion ought to become evident from what has been said above of 'the gifts of the kingdom of God', pp. 161ff. That something really 'happens' in the cult does not make it into 'magic'; I doubt the legitimacy of using this notion in the world of religion. If the drama of the Israelite new year festival, as I have sketched it in *Ps.St.* II and in the preceding paragraphs, be 'magic' then the Orthodox, Roman, Anglican and in fact even the Lutheran cult must be 'magic' as well.

10

The enthronement psalms must be understood against the background of this festival, with all the rich experiences contained in it, experiences including past and future in a re-creating present. The psalms of epiphany and enthronement are hymns of praise and prayer which hail Yahweh as the king who has now returned and revealed himself to his people. They express the reactions of the congregation, in jubilant joy and in awe, to the great, constantly repeated and ever new experience. But they are also the congregation's confession of faith in the mighty covenant God, who has again revealed himself to do his work of salvation.[196]

There is every reason to believe that *the true enthronement hymns* in the strictest sense of the term belonged to that day in the festal complex considered to be Yahweh's own particular 'day', the day of his royal entry and triumph. They all take for granted that Yahweh has already gone up to his abode and is sitting on his throne.[197] This explains the calls to pass into his court and appear before him and kneel at his footstool worshipping him[198] and hailing him with the 'shout of royal homage'.[199] All the 'salvation' that finds expression in the festal myths is experienced here and now.[200] The psalms themselves are meant to provide the homage, which the authors call upon the congregation, the king's people, to pay to the king. They claim to be the 'new song' (96.1; 98.1) 'fit' (cf. 65.2) for the newly arrived king at the start of the new year on the re-created earth; they are themselves the songs of homage to the revealed, enthroned King and God, Yahweh.

Their contents may be summed up in the following list.[201] 1. In the usual hymnic introduction they first call for exultant homage to the king, who has now arrived and is sitting on his throne; the invitation contains characteristic peculiarities, connected with the nature and essence of the festival: because Yahweh is king of the world, this invitation is addressed to all nations; because his coming also means re-creation, all nature is called upon to rejoice; because the work performed by him is operative far beyond the borders of Israel, his congregation is called upon to take the message to all nations and make them take part in the homage. 2. As usual in the hymns, the invitation is motivated by short references to the great

---

[196] Cf. Weiser in *Festschrift für Bertholet*, pp. 524f.

[197] Pss. 47.6, 9; 93.2, cf. v. 5b; 96.13; 97.2b, 7b, cf. the description of the epiphany = procession of entry in vv. 3–6; 98.3b, 9b; 99.1.

[198] Pss. 47.2, 7; 96.7–9; 97.12; 98.1a, 4–8; 99.5, 9; cf. 95.1–2, 6–7.

[199] *těrû'ath melekh*, Num. 23.21. Cf. Humbert, *La Terou'a*, pp. 30ff.

[200] Pss. 47.4f., 10; 93.1c, 5b; 96.3, 6, 10, 13; 97.8, 11f.; 98.1b, 2, 3b, 9. Gunkel (*Einl.*, p. 113) is entirely wrong when he tries to explain this 'actual' character of the psalms mentioned —with the presentation of Yahweh's appearance and salvation as something just having taken place—by supposing that Israel was unable to express the idea of Yahweh's presence in an abstract form and would therefore imagine it to be a lasting state. The actuality is, indeed, the true form of the cultic psalm, which emerges from the cultic experience itself; it is literally meant; the authors do not seek to describe the permanent dwelling of Yahweh in the Temple, but his actual appearance.

[201] Cf. Gunkel-Begrich, *Einl.*, p. 113.

works which Yahweh has performed and which form the basis of his kingship, those 'works of salvation' expressed in the 'festal myth'. There are also occasional references to incidents in the cultic ritual reflecting a 'mythical reality': Yahweh's entry in procession at the head of his people. 3. To this are attached descriptions suggesting the state of things, which will now come about, or in an ideal sense has already come about, with the enthronement of Yahweh, the 'terrible' and 'holy' and 'exalted' and 'glorious one'; his enemies are going to be struck with awe, whereas his people shall rejoice in his righteous and luck-bringing rule.

What has been said above about the heart of the hymn of praise still more applies to the enthronement hymn. This is literally an 'epiphany hymn': now Yahweh has revealed himself as he really is, in all his power and glory, in all his terrible and condemning holiness, in all his saving 'righteousness', and *He* is king of Israel, and Israel is *His* chosen people. Their past and future may rest secure in his covenant faithfulness. For their sake the world has again been created, the powers of death and chaos have been put down, blessing and peace and victory are secured, all wishes and dreams fulfilled. Such another God and king exists nowhere, no people has experienced anything like it, no one can imagine anything higher. This very God is now enthroned as a king in the midst of his people! Should he not be 'enthroned upon the praises of Israel'? Could anything possibly be imagined or composed or said or sung that would be too high for his honour? Whatever the people may have experienced in days past has now become a new reality; 'Rahab' has been destroyed, the covenant renewed, everything now belongs to his people. And the eyes of faith behold him. His hand is full of good things; his Temple is full of holy power. He has been 'revealed in Salem'; we have seen him and all his glorious works, seen them with the eyes of faith, beheld them embodied in the symbols and scenes of the divine service. If the rejoicing at the enthronement of an earthly king would resound, 'so that the earth rent', what then would the shouts of homage be like in honour of King Yahweh! All creation, forests and mountains and valleys and rivers shall clap their hands, hailing him when he comes; his congregation shall fall down before his face in worship; from the newly saved people on the re-created earth the 'new song' shall rise to the King, who is visiting his people and dwelling in their midst. His enemies are trembling with horror, but Jerusalem and the villages of Judah rejoice at his work of righteousness and salvation.

II

But regarding the emotions to which the festal psalms give expression, we are justified in resorting to other psalms also, which have been composed on the basis of ideas drawn from the feast of the epiphany and belong to the complex of harvest and new year in a wider sense. We cannot possibly draw a hard-and-fast line between the 'enthronement festival' and the great festal complex of which it is only one separate aspect.

The experiences contained in the festival made up a spiritual totality and unity. The whole of the religious life in all its aspects and phases was expressed through the festival. Then we realize that not only hymns and thanksgiving psalms but even psalms of prayer and words of promise belong here. Each kind of psalm gives only one aspect of the total sum of experiences and emotions and ideas.

But this also means that the enthronement hymns proper, as is the wont of hymns, as a rule only refer quite briefly to important experiences and ideas which are characteristic of the festival and especially of the whole harvest festival complex. For instance we shall not be able fully to realize the emotions of poet and congregation when, in Ps. 93, creation is mentioned as the basis of kingship, unless we have also realized the actual re-experience of the saving work of creation through the growth and the crops of the blessed year, which is expressed by the authors of harvest festival thanksgiving psalms like 65 or 67. Nor shall we fully understand what the author of Ps. 93 is thinking of when he says that the world is stablished because Yahweh proved himself to be 'mightier' than the waves of the sea, until we have also grasped that aspect of the steadiness of the earth which the author of Pss. 46 or 48 has experienced, and describes by means of the picture of the uproar of the primeval ocean or the assault of all gentile nations on Jerusalem. And vice versa: it is because Yahweh has again appeared as king and has secured the earth against 'the waves of the sea', that Jerusalem may feel sure that even if all the kings and nations of the earth were to conspire against her, Yahweh would destroy them at the very last moment, 'as the east wind breaks the ocean-going ships'.

We have mentioned all this previously, when speaking of the gifts of the festival. But we also need to consider the emotions expressed in the enthronement psalms in the light of all these experiences and promises. If we include all the psalms which, with more or less probability, may be traced to the complex of the new year festival, we shall find that taken together they reflect the whole gamut of religious emotion.

First let us take the joy and rejoicing at the appearance and victory and mighty act of the glorious king. Its basis is the feeling of security at being under the protection of such a king—as clearly expressed in Pss. 46 and 48 and in 95.7; 97.10ff., cf. 125; nothing can, any more, seriously threaten Yahweh's city and people. Even sin will no longer separate them from him, for again he has proved himself to be 'a God who forgives sins' (99.8; 85.3f.; 130.3f.). Therefore gratitude breaks forth, partly in thanksgiving psalms for the good gifts of the passing year (Ps. 65), partly in the admiring contemplation of the work of creation (65.7–9; cf. 8) and the grateful retrospective glance at all the many times past when Yahweh had 'turned the destiny of Israel' (85.2ff.; 126.1ff.), and saved his people from

enemies of superior strength (Ps. 124). Hand in hand with gratitude goes
love. Quite characteristically, however, it is not the Holy One himself who
is described as the object of this love, but outward things, to which his
presence was attached and from which his blessing flowed: the cult, the
sanctuary, the city where he is now living (122; 84.2ff.). The religious
emotion reaches its climax in quiet worship (cf. 95.6; 96.9) without words
before the footstool of the One whose nature and name is 'Holy' (99.5).

However, the emotions of the festival have also another pole: fear, or
perhaps better, awe. Quite characteristically it is said of Yahweh: 'There
is forgiveness with thee, that thou mayest be feared' (130.4). The Holy
One not only calls forth ecstatic rejoicings or silent worshipping; he is also
the one who frightens, which in an ethical religion means: who demands.
At the festival the congregation is reminded of the commandments, the
fulfilment of which is the condition of blessing (24.3ff.; 15; 81.9f.; 95.7);
and at the renewal of the covenant Yahweh imposes on them obedience
to his commandments (95.7ff.; 81.7ff., cf. 132.12). But combined with
this, as we have seen (p. 160) was the knowledge that the covenant had
constantly been broken, and that this is the reason why the full effect of
Yahweh's coming can never eventuate. Grave misgivings mix with joy.
Is the turning of the destiny this time going to mean the great turning,
which the high hopes of the festival and the prophetic words of the rituals
promise? Then the people must clear itself from its sins, just as it and the
sanctuary have been cleansed from impurity through the introductory
ceremonies of cleansing (the day of expiation). All sinners must needs
dread and fear the devouring fire of the Holy One;[202] if anyone would
receive forgiveness of his sins he must repent and confess, as we hear in the
personal thanksgiving psalm, Ps. 32. Therefore, at this festival is heard
the repentant confession of sins on the part of the congregation (130.1ff.).
It is connected with the longing for Yahweh to come with forgiveness of
sins, happiness and blessing (130.6ff.), with deliverance from all disaster,
from sufferings, tormentors and enemies (123; 125). The prayer sometimes
rises to stormy impatience, an ardent longing for deliverance as in Ps. 123,
found side by side with humble silence in the certainty that with Yahweh
is comfort and the satisfaction of all need and all desire, as in Ps. 131.

But beneath all this lies the *expectation* of great things to happen; and
so finally we devote some words to that.

12

The festival of harvest and new year looked to both the past and the future;
it was a thanksgiving feast for the passing year—being celebrated with
delight and rejoicings, when the harvest of wine and olive was safely
home, and it was the foundation festival of the coming year.

---

[202] Cf. Isa. 33.14ff., where we find a new, eschatological reading of the cultic tora of entry
in Pss. 24.3–6; 15.

All its different rites stress the future aspect. These rites, which according to the original conception were power-filled, world-renewing, luck- and blessing-bringing, remained as sacramental symbols of the re-creation and blessing Yahweh will bring at his coming. Among such rites may be mentioned the water fetching: from the holy fountain of Gihon the priests would fetch water in solemn procession and pour it on the altar of burnt sacrifice. As can be seen from Jewish popular belief even in New Testament times, this was originally meant to be a powerful means of securing water and rain for the new year.[203] Isa. 12.3 refers to this custom. The festival was also celebrated as a night festival of fire and light with bonfire, illuminations, and torch dancing in the temple court.[204] Like the 'sun-fires' all over the world it was originally meant to re-create and secure sun and light and warmth in the year to come. That the altar was crowned with green branches after the festal procession,[205] and the people lived in 'tabernacles' during the festival,[206] is not only a survival from the stay in the vineyard during the grape-gathering, but is connected with the 'May-branches', the well-known restorative of fertility in nearly all parts of the earth. Even the procession to the Temple and the circumambulation on the walls of the city (Ps. 48.13f.) and around the altar (see above), are originally powerful dramatic cultic customs; they represent the new life and thereby create the same. Looking forward is an essential characteristic of the festival; it can be seen in the psalms in the idea that, from his enthronement onwards, Yahweh will reign as 'eternal king' (Isa. 29.10; Ex. 15.18)—an idea which strictly speaking contradicts the notion of his annual 'coming' and enthronement. But such is the nature of religious experience; the experienced present has 'eternal' importance; and 'eternal' here is not our rationalistic endless temporal line, but rather a quality of value, an eternal present, beyond which our sight does not pass. In other psalms, however, the idea of his 'eternal kingdom' has more of the character of a rationalized general tenet (145.13), expressing the conviction that he will always protect his people against all evil powers (10.16; 146.10; cf. Jer. 10.10).

The festival is the experience of an all-embracing 'Now' that includes the future—the 'eternal Now'. Therefore the *expectation* of the great thing that is to happen is a fundamental emotion at the festival as well as in the enthronement psalms. 'Yahweh has come to rule the earth', to tend his people and establish justice on earth, and 'Zion is glad and the villages of Judah rejoice because of his judgments' (98.9; 97.8; 48.12). When on his 'day' he renews the covenant and turns destiny, disperses darkness, and lets his 'light be sown for the righteous', he also fulfils whatever his

---

[203] See Billerbeck II, p. 804 n. o. For the ceremonies as a whole see ibid., pp. 799–805; further Moore, *Judaism* II, pp. 44f.; Scheftelowitz, *Alt-Paläst. Bauernglaube*, pp. 93ff.
[204] Cf. Moore, op. cit., II, pp. 46f.
[205] Cf. Ps. 118.26, and see Billerbeck II, pp. 793–799.
[206] Billerbeck II, pp. 774ff.

people, according to tradition, had a right to expect from their righteous, faithful, victorious God, the maintainer of the covenant.

This applies to material blessings as well as to national security and greatness, and to spiritual, religious and moral goods. 'The river of God is full of water', and the rain shall let the corn grow in the valleys and clothe the pastures with little lambs (65.10ff.); 'the streams thereof shall make holy the abode of the Most High' and protect his people against all dangers (46.5), 'He shall subdue the nations under us and provinces under our feet' (47.4); if all the kings on earth were to assemble and march forward together, the very sight of the great king on Mount Zion would suffice to strike them with horror and crush them (48.5ff.). His laws and promises are true and trustworthy; power-filled, protective and blessing-full 'holiness' belongs to his house for evermore (93.5). From now on he will again tend his people (95.7). 'In his hands are the deep places of the earth, and the peaks of the mountains are his also', for he made them all (95.4f.), and now that the waves of the ocean have again been conquered (93.3f.; 46.4; 65.8), so that 'the world is stablished that it cannot be moved', where Yahweh has raised 'his throne' (93.1f.; 29.10), it is a good and safe thing for men, and especially for his people, to live under his protection. His coming will strike with terror all 'idols and them that serve graven images', and the evil shall tremble before his judgment (97.7-10). Now he has laid the foundation of 'salvation and victory'—both these elements are implied in the Hebrew word *yěša‘*—for Israel, and revealed his self-asserting and covenant-maintaining 'righteousness' and his 'faithfulness' towards his people (98.2f.); from now on he 'preserveth the souls of his saints and delivereth them out of the hand of the wicked' (97.10). He forgives the sins of his people and will hear the prayers, which are sent up by 'his priests' and prophets (99.6ff.). This is all implied in the word 'judge', and that is what Yahweh has now come to do (98.9).

Consequently *prophetic promise* forms part and parcel of the festal liturgies. There are allusions to this in the enthronement psalms, when speaking of the firm promises of Yahweh (93.5). And we find the word of Yahweh, with a particular inversion of the idea, in the enthronement liturgy of Ps. 95 and its parallel Ps. 81, where the promise is conditional upon the faithfulness of the people to the commandments of Yahweh's covenant and thus receives a highly admonitory character. More general and comprehensive promises, in accordance with the expectations just quoted, are to be found in other psalms connected with the festival of harvest and new year or composed on the basis of its ideas and conceptions.[207]

So it is quite easy to understand that whenever the people was in need and danger, it would look forward to the coming 'Yahweh's day', when Yahweh would come and take care of the cause of his people and change darkness into light—as we hear even at the time of Amos (Am. 5.18ff.). In this way the idea of a day of Yahweh with salvation and victory might be

[207] Pss. 46.11; 75.3f.; 82; 85.9ff.; 132.11f.; cf. 50.5ff. For details see Chap. XII.

separated from its cultic basis and, so to speak, start living its own life in the minds of the people as a belief in and a hope for such a Yahweh's 'day of epiphany' to turn the destiny, to restore, avenge and save, whenever Israel was in distress.

13

If we consider the experiences and ideas of the festival of enthronement and new year, we shall be better able to understand the origin of the *hope for re-establishment* and of *eschatology* in Israel—or, rather, from whence this hope derived its conceptions.[208] When attempts have been made to interpret the enthronement psalms as eschatological poems, it has been as a result of the observation that what Yahweh's coming is said to have brought about, or is supposed to bring, in all essentials corresponds to the main items in the prophetic promises of re-establishment and in eschatology.

The strongest reason for the Israelite hope for the future is to be found in the character of revealed religion itself, i.e. in the experience of a God who is so real and so great that he cannot and will not drop his plan and reduce his election and his covenant to mere words. From a historical point of view this hope developed into a conscious hope of re-establishment as a result of the evil destiny of the people and their extinction as an independent kingdom and nation. Then the 'prophecy of re-establishment' took up the idea of the re-establishment of Israel, which became reality in the fullness of time through the New Testament people of God.[209] This hope for the future received its form and a great part of its substance from the experiences and thoughts of the 'day of Yahweh', when he was to appear and become king and establish his kingdom and thus secure justice and a future for his people. Just as the essential notion in Jewish and Christian eschatology has always been the 'kingdom (kingship) of God', so the message about the kingdom was always introduced by some such phrase as: the kingdom of God is at hand! or, in more Old Testament terms, Yahweh has become king, and has come—or shall come—in order to 'judge' on earth. The salvation to come is looked upon as an enthronement day of Yahweh with cosmic dimensions—such in short is the substance of the prophecy of re-establishment and later also of eschatology. That was how Deutero-Isaiah preached it (Isa. 52.7), and he gave the tone to later prophecy. He largely imitates the forms and ideas of the psalms of enthronement and harvest in order to express what was at hand:[210] the victory of Yahweh over all hostile powers and his taking

---

[208] For the following see *Ps.St.* II, Part II.—The connexion between the new year festival and eschatology has also been realized—simultaneously with and independently of *Ps.St.* II— by Wensinck, *Act. Or.* I, 1923, pp. 159ff.

[209] For details see my *He that Cometh*, Chap. V.

[210] See *Ps.St.* II, pp. 49f., 195–199.

possession of the world empire, with the renewal of the covenant with his chosen people and its royal house, and with endless happiness and greatness for his worshippers. It is not, as earlier interpreters of the psalms used to think, the character and style of the enthronement psalms which are modelled on Deutero-Isaiah as a result of poetic concentration on his sayings, but the other way round: prophecy has here, as is so often the case, borrowed forms and expressions from cultic lyrics.[211] In the prophetic descriptions of salvation, accents and motives from the enthronement festival and the feast of Tabernacles are re-echoed, as is clearly seen in Isa. 52.1, 7f.:

> Awake, awake, Jerusalem,
>   put on your bravery,
> put on your finest garment now,
>   O holy city Zion! . . . .
> Look! The herald of good tidings
>   hastening over the hills,
> with glad, good news, with tidings of relief:
>   Your God has now become king!
> Hear, all your watchmen are shouting, hear
>   their joyful triumph cry,
> for they see now Yahweh face to face,
>   returning to Zion again.

'And then the survivors of all the nations which once came against Jerusalem (cf. Ps. 48!) shall "go up" (as in a procession) every year to fall down before king Yahweh Zebaoth, and celebrate the festival of booths. But if any race on earth will not go up to Jerusalem to worship king Yahweh Zebaoth, no rain (the primary natural gift of the festival to land and people) shall fall upon that race' (Zech. 14.16f.).

The Danish poet, Brorson, strikes a truly biblical note when he speaks of the eternal feast of booths by the river of the water of life, the lamb of God being at once host and guest. So was Yahweh on Mount Zion, when the 'river of God ran full of water',[212] the blessing of the new year.

Just because hope for the future and eschatology were conceived after the image of Yahweh's enthronement and the establishment of his kingdom, and described with relevance to psalms and conceptions which considered the enthronement to be a repetition of creation and its original acts of salvation, it became a fundamental motif of eschatology that the last things would be a repetition of the first, a 'turning' back to what originally existed. 'Behold, I shall make the last things like the first', says the early Christian letter of Barnabas.[213] As the earthly king was one of

---

[211] For details *GTMMM* III, pp. 188f.; *Ps.St.* II, pp. 195ff.

[212] Ps. 65.10. For the divine 'river' flowing from the sanctuary and from Heaven, see Hylander in *NTT*, 1931, pp. 1ff.

[213] Epistle of Barnabas 6.13. Cf. *Ps.St.* II, pp. 229f. Gunkel was the first to draw attention to this fundamental motive in his *Schöpfung und Chaos in Urzeit und Endzeit*.

the most important gifts of Yahweh at his 'coming', so in post-exilic and later Judaism the future king, the Messiah, became the most eagerly expected blessing of Yahweh at his last, eschatological coming. To this extent it may be said that the Messianic hope has its root in the cultic festival of Yahweh's epiphany and enthronement.[214]

The forward look of the enthronement psalms and the new year festival, and on the whole the ancient conception of the festival as involving the belief that full 'salvation' was at the door and already in the making, resulted, in turn, in the idea of Israel's full re-establishment being included in the programme of festival and psalms. The future-mindedness made it natural for those in later times, already living in the Jewish hope of re-establishment, to attach the thought of re-establishment to the hopes of the harvest festival.[215] From the experiences and the certainty of the festival the psalmists sometimes, too, look beyond the coming year to the re-establishment of Israel and the eschatological fulfilment, making the latter an object of prayer. In this way—and only in this way—do the psalms obtain an eschatological character.[216] But this happens more in certain psalms for the harvest festival and the feast of Tabernacles, such as Pss. 126 and 85, and in some of the psalms of lamentation and prayer of the congregation (see Chap. VI.5, 6), than in the actual enthronement hymns proper.

In this way the ancient form of the cultic psalm—the praise of the great work of salvation and re-establishment which Yahweh has performed in principle on his coming—also becomes the expression of the expectation and faith of the congregation. Similarly the same thoughts and forms appear in the latest, non-cultic, 'learned' psalmography (Chap. XVI), and in post-canonical legends,[217] not so much as praise for what has already been guaranteed, but as a doxological expression of the faith in the work of salvation, which the Lord certainly will perform as soon as he actually comes. This forward looking witness of faith is given by Sirach in connexion with an admonition to do justice to everyone, because God is a just judge (Sir. 32.24–26). The way the justice of God is referred to, in the usual phrases of the hymns, leads the mind on to the last great day of judgment, when the Lord shall remember his oppressed people and break the tyranny of the unrighteous 'nations', 'plead the cause of his people, giving them victory and joy through his salvation'. Here we find a faint echo of thoughts and forms from the psalms and promises of the enthronement.

---

[214] See the author's book, *He That Cometh.*
[215] Cf. Volz, *Neujahrsfest Jahwes*, pp. 46f.; Riesenfeld, *Jésus transfig.*, pp. 20ff. Riesenfeld has greatly exaggerated the eschatological element in the feast of tabernacles and the eschatological, symbolic interpretation of the cultic rites; see Kümmel's critique in *Symbl. Bibl. Upsal.* 11, pp. 49ff.
[216] On the question of psalms and eschatology, see Additional Note VIII.
[217] 1 Sam. 2; Jonah 2; Dan. 2.20–24; Tob. 13; Judith 16; Prayer of Manasses (addition to 2 Chron. 33 in G); Dan. 3.26–46 G (prayer of Azariah); Dan. 3.52–90 G (the hymn of thanksgiving sung by the three men in the furnace); for details see Chap. XVI.

The last offshoots of the forms and ideas of the enthronement psalms in their eschatological aspect appear among the young Christian congregations, as expressions both of the experience of the Kingdom that has come with the Messiah Jesus—as in the anthems of praise put in the mouths of Mary and Zacharias—and of the eschatological hope, as expressed in the hymns on the enthronement of the Lord and the Lamb.[218]

[218] For details see below, Chap. XVI, and the author's article in *NTT* 51, 1950, pp. 39ff.

CHAPTER VI

National Psalms of Lamentation

Just as the hymn pre-eminently belongs to the great fixed festivals, as an expression of joy and gratitude and praise, so does the national lament or congregational psalm[1] belong to the days of humiliation and prayer, which were 'proclaimed' on special occasions of crisis, and might be called the 'casual' or *ad hoc* cultic festivals.

I

When war, defeat, imprisonment, epidemics, drought, famine, locusts, and similar public disasters occurred or threatened,[2] a public *fast-day* would be 'proclaimed'.[3] The whole people, great and small, would assemble at the sanctuary. Through different ceremonies the congregation would consecrate themselves; in particular they had to abstain from certain things during the time of humiliation: food and drink, anointing with oil, sexual intercourse and other manifestations of normal life. Humiliation and mourning imply a state of impurity, because disaster, 'curse' has befallen the soul of the person concerned. People would rend their clothes, smite upon their breasts and hips, cut their skins with knives, shave or pluck off hair and beard, put on sackcloth, put dust and ashes on their heads, roll in the dust, fall on their knees or prostrate themselves on the ground, raise their hands in prayer towards the heavens.[4]

The disaster proves that the wrath of Yahweh has been roused because of some sin in the people or their leading men, or at least that Yahweh has not yet roused himself to come to the rescue of his people, now that evil powers or enemies have overtaken them. All these *penitential rites*, originally intended perhaps for the purpose of averting the disaster or protecting against it, and atoning for and cleansing from impurity, in Yahwism became a token of penitence and 'self-humiliation' before Yahweh in order to temper his wrath and rouse his compassion. Other *cultic rites* belonging to the fast-day have the same purpose: sacrifices and the 'pouring out of water before Yahweh' (offering of libation), burning

---

[1] Cf. Gunkel-Begrich, *Einl.*, pp. 177ff.; Widengren, *Accad. and Hebr. Pss. of Lamentation*; Birkeland, *Feinde d. Indiv.*

[2] Deut. 9.18; Josh. 7.6; Jdg. 20.23, 26ff.; 1 Sam. 7.6; 1 Kgs. 8.33ff.; Jer. 2.27; 14.2; Hos. 7.14; Joel 1.13f.; 2 Chron. 20.9.

[3] *qārā*, 1 Kgs. 21.9, 12; Jer. 36.9; Joel 1.14.

[4] Details about rites of penance and fasting with references to sources, in Gunkel-Begrich, *Einl.*, pp. 117–119.

upon the altar, and other measures.[5] From the whole congregation would be heard weeping and loud lamentations and crying, or low, unceasing wailings and sighing.[6]

The prayer of the priest[7] or of some other intercessor, for instance the king, is expressly mentioned. The fasting shall be 'heard' as well as 'seen' (Isa. 58.2f.); the rites come more and more to be interpreted as an emphasizing of the prayer, both when real disaster has actually occurred, and also before some dangerous enterprise, a long journey or some such thing (Ezra 8.21ff.).

That the prayer of humiliation and fasting would in time—at any rate at the larger temples—be moulded on the model of the *psalm* is self evident, and in Israel it may have been so from the very beginning; in Babylonia as well as in Egypt, laments on such occasions are very old.

2

The popular or congregational laments handed down to us belonged to these public fast-days.

Such unquestionably communal or national laments, which are recognizable partly by the use of 'we', partly by the occasion which produced them are Pss. 12; 14; 44; 58; 60; 74; 79; 80; 83; 89; 144; Lam. 5. But actually there are also a great many written in the first person singular which also were occasioned by some public event; we shall return to these below in Chap. VII. And as structure, thought and style are much the same in the 'I-psalms' as in the 'we-psalms', the former, too, will be considered in the following exposé.

From the point of view of style history, the *we-form* is probably later than the *I-form*. This seems obvious from the fact that the style of Israelite psalmody is directly or indirectly derived from Babylonia (see below, Chap. XX.3), and in the Assyro-Babylonian psalms of lamentation such a we-form does not seem to occur; there it is in the I-form that the king represents the people, even in public distress. On the whole this representation through an individual leader, who *is*, or pretends to be, the totality, is the earlier and more primitive idea, as we have seen in Chap. III.1.

So the we-form witnesses to the fact that the people as a fellowship of personal individuals is more prominent in the religion of Israel than in the despotisms of Babylonia and Assyria. It proves, as has been said, that in Israel, there is a *congregation* in the background of the service in a way different from that in Babylonia. Such a self-awareness on the part of the congregation became natural because, as has been mentioned above (Chap. III.6), religion was individualized and became more democratic.

---

[5] 1 Sam. 7.9; Jer. 14.12; Jdg. 20.26; 21.4; 2 Sam. 24.22; Ps. 4.6; also 1 Sam. 7.6; Lam. 2.19; and Num. 17.11ff.
[6] Jdg. 20.23, 26; Mic. 1.8; Jer. 14.12; Isa. 15.2ff.; Hos. 7.14; Isa. 29.4.
[7] Joel 1.13f.; 2.17; 1 Kgs. 8.28ff.; Jer. 7.16; 11.14; 2 Chron. 20.6ff., *et al.*

So far, it might seem more natural to speak first of the laments in the I-form. But since this form may really imply public as well as private occasions of lamentation, and thus two different kinds of psalms—or, in other words, because it partly expresses an old and partly a more modern way of thinking—it will be best to start with the we-psalms. From the point of view of form and style they are the most obvious and at the same time give expression to something characteristically Israelite.

3

Even in the laments there is a close connexion between *form and substance*, which are determined by situations and intentions. The people in its distress comes to the God, whose might and power and loving-kindness and faithfulness to the covenant were praised in the hymns, asking him to help. They know, and have often seen, his benefits; now they have also experienced his wrath, which is weighing heavily on them. He has turned away, he has 'hidden his face', and who can know 'why' and 'how long'. So the aim is to get to speak with him, make him hear and see, 'cry unto him', lay the distress before him, complain how hard it is, describe the horror of it. The people must try to find a way to touch the heart of Yahweh, where he will be susceptible to the prayers of men; they must rouse his compassion, appeal to the faithfulness of his covenant and to his loving-kindness, to his honour and power, so that he 'may again be moved with compassion for us'; they must remove whatever might displease him, ascribe honour and righteousness to him by confessing sins, asking for forgiveness and help, appeasing his wrath, invoking his love. For he is great, and we are small; he can do everything, we can do nothing; nobody else can help, and if he does not save, it will be the end of us, but we confide in him. The lament sprang up on the basis of these spontaneous human and religious thoughts and reactions, it was a call for help to a particular God in a particular situation—wherever it may have found its literary patterns.

Even the first word of the lament contains an *invocation of Yahweh's name*, a turning to God in prayer, with a preceding or following word of prayer in the imperative: 'Hear us!' 'Listen to my voice!' or the like—or right out: 'Give me my right, O Lord' (see below). Israel knows to *whom* she has to turn, among all the many 'gods and holy ones' in the world.

When the name has been mentioned, not infrequently some *hymnal attributes* are added, containing an appeal to the close relationship between Yahweh and his people, to his power and willingness to help, 'O Shepherd of Israel', 'O God of our salvation', 'O Judge of the earth', 'my God'.[8]

Let us give some examples: (*a*) the invocation is immediately followed by a cry for help:

---

[8] Pss. 83.14; 79.9; 85.5; 80.2, 8, 15; 94.1f., *et al.*

> O Yahweh, keep not thou silence,
> hold not thy peace, and be not still! (83.2.)

(*b*) To the invocation are added hymnal words, appealing to Yahweh:

> O shepherd of Israel, hear us, thou,
> who leadest Joseph like a flock!
> Thou that thronest upon the cherubs
> shine forth for Ephraim and Manasseh! (80.2.)

or (*c*) it is immediately followed by the plaintive question:

> O God, why hast thou discarded us for ever,
> why dost thou fume in anger at the flock of thy pasture?
>
> (74.1)

But the invocation may be missing, and the psalm start with the lament (the description of the conduct of the wicked), as in Ps. 14, or in Ps. 58, where the lament has the form of an accusation in the second person plural, directed against the gods of the oppressors. Or the psalm may start with an elaborate motivation expressing the confidence of the suppliants (see below), as in Ps. 44.

Sometimes this invocation may be developed into a complete hymn of praise, in which the psalm gets a *hymnal introduction*, appealing to the earlier great works of Yahweh and his saving benefactions to his people, calling to mind how he has thereby pledged his honour, and trying thus to make him rise to the rescue.[9] In such cases the hymnal sayings are usually expressed as independent sentences: e.g.

> Age after age, Lord, thou hast been our home,
> from all eternity hast thou been, O God. (90.1.)

Or, and this time entirely hymnal:

> I will always sing of Yahweh's love
> and tell all ages of thy faithfulness. (89.2.)

This cry of supplication indicates the motivation which expresses the real aim of the psalm. This is then followed up in detail in the main part of the psalm, containing *lamentations, prayers*, and *motivations of the prayer*. There is no definite sequence; these different items alternate in any order, and often recur several times.

In the true psalms of lamentation the character of the whole is fixed by the *lamentation*. It consists of a longer or shorter *description of the distress*, which is painted in the deepest colours, with regard to both its external and its mental aspect. Israel presents herself as being 'oppressed, distressed, miserable, in need of help'—all these shades of meaning are implied in the Hebrew word 'ānî or 'ānāw, generally used here.[10] This description is

---

[9] Pss. 44.2–4; 80.2; 89.2–17; 106.1f.; cf. the 'I-psalms' 9–10; 27; 40.
[10] Pss. 12.6; 74.19–21; cf. 68.11; 76.10; 149.4. Cf. below, pp. 229ff.

in itself aimed at getting the prayer heard: it is intended to rouse the compassion of Yahweh and make him help.

As a rule the national psalms of lamentation are concerned with national and political distress: defeat in war, attack and ravaging by external enemies, who are sometimes named.[11] But we also hear of days of humiliation and fasting with laments for droughts and plagues of locusts, as in Jer. 14 or Joel 1–2.

The background of such a psalm is some definite historical event. The enemies are real and historical; they are the 'nations' who have attacked and invaded Israel (or Judah), and now are oppressing it. In Ps. 83 the names of the enemies are explicitly mentioned: Edom, Moab, the Ishmaelites and the Hagarenes, Gebal, Ammon, Amalek, and the inhabitants of Tyre, and 'Asshur also is joined with them'. The people (or king) complains of the hostility and mockeries of the 'neighbours', i.e. the other Palestinian nations. (See below on the situation in Pss. 44 and 74, and cf. Chap. VII.6.)

As a rule, however, it is not possible to tell which peoples or rulers are intended by 'the enemies' in the psalm in question. The reason is that in ancient Israel, as also in the Akkadian literature, there existed a traditional 'pattern', according to which the 'evil-doers', rĕšā'îm—the enemies are always rĕšā'îm—are described. Consequently we have a stereotyped monotony in the description of the enemies, with very few individual traits.[11a]

The distress also has its mental aspect. This is owing to the wrath of Yahweh: his 'anger smokes', he has 'hidden his face' and 'cast off his own people'.—Can such a thing really be possible? Because the distress cannot be understood—'Why, Lord?'—it is increased. Is injustice really going to triumph?—To this bewilderment is added the old Israelite idea that disaster and defeat mean 'shame',[12] which makes the people wince at the sneers of their neighbours.[13] Their mental distress receives a deeper

[11] Pss. 60.11; 83.7–9; 137. For the mention of political and national afflictions: 44.10–17, 20, 23–25; 60.3–5, 12; 74.4–11; 79.1–4; 80.5–7, 13f.; 83.3–9; 85.6; 89.39–46; 123.3f.; Lam. 1.9f.; 3.42–51; 5.2–18. Cf. the imitation of the style in the lamentations of the prophets on behalf of the people, Isa. 26.14, 15f.; 33.7–9; 40.27; 49.14; 63.17–19; 64.5f., 9f.; Jer. 10.25; 31.18; Hab. 1.13–16.
Willesen (in *VT* II, 1952, pp. 289ff.) finds as the cultic situation of Ps. 74 (and 79) two cult-dramatical scenes, which were repeated every year, perhaps at the new year festival, the first showing the profanation of the Temple by the powers of chaos, the second the victory of Yahweh and the re-purification of the sanctuary. It is, however, impossible not to see real terrestrial beings in the enemies who are destroying the Temple with axes, hammers and fire; there are no demoniac traits in this description. Willesen also fails to take into due account the role of the hymnic 'motivation of the prayer' in the psalms of lamentation; amongst others, Ps. 89 shows that Yahweh's primordial fight against the powers of chaos is an important motif in [these 'motivations', though even here the enemies are earthly political foes. Cf. below, Additional Note XXXI.
[11a] See Birkeland, *Feinde d. Indiv.*, pp. 59ff.; *The Evildoers in the Pss.*, pp. 23ff. The same observation can be made at the description of the *nābhāl* ('the fool') and the *rāshā'* in Proverbs; it is not easy to say in every case to which definite persons or social classes these terms are applied by the wisdom authors.
[12] Ps. 80.17f.; cf. 2 Sam. 19.4f.; Ezk. 36.30; Ps. 40.15f. See Johs. Pedersen, *Israel* I–II, pp. 239ff.
[13] Pss. 44.14ff.; 79.4; 80.7.

religious meaning through the fact that other nations, 'the gentiles', will take it as a proof of Yahweh's powerlessness, and will blaspheme the God of Israel: 'Where is now thy God?'[14] All this tends to intensify the problem involved in the suffering of 'the righteous'—for Israel as a whole are 'the righteous', the people of the covenant, such is the usage of the psalms. The question 'Why?' becomes a big issue, as likewise the impatient 'How long?'.

Looked at in detail, the laments complain of the violence and injustice and abuse of power on the part of the enemies, their faithlessness and arrogance and godlessness—they do not worship Yahweh; the poets take for granted that they ought to do so, accordingly they are 'apostates', 'playing false'; their religion is nothing but 'sorcery'. They are described as completely corrupt people, false, lying, sinners, criminals, 'sorcerers' ("*āwen*-makers').[15] Compared with them Israel is always right, her enemies are always wrong; even if the congregation may confess their sinfulness before Yahweh (see below), her enemies are persecuting her 'without cause'.

Particularly when disaster has befallen the very Temple of Yahweh there is every reason to describe it in as gloomy colours as possible, in order to appeal to the honour of Yahweh himself. The following description (Ps. 74.3–9) enters into considerable detail:

> Turn thy steps to the long-standing ruins:
> > all has the foe destroyed in the sanctuary!
> Thine enemies roared inside thy festival hall,
> > total destruction have they made therein.
> They have cut down as woodmen bringing home brushwood,
> > brandishing their axes in the thicket of the wood.
> They smashed all the carved work therein,
> > with hatchet and hammer they broke it up;
> They set thy sanctuary ablaze,
> > profaning to the ground the abode of thy name.
> They said to themselves: 'Let us root them out'.
> > They burned all houses of God in the land.
> We see no signs concerning us, there is no prophet,
> > and no one among us knows how long.[15a]

The lament may be directed at Yahweh himself, because he has allowed such things to happen: has he really forgotten his covenant with the house of David? e.g.

---

[14] Pss. 74.10, 18, 22; 79.10, 12. Cf. the I-psalm 42.11.

[15] With more details and references to sources in Birkeland, *Feinde d. Indiv.*, pp. 59–66. For '*āwen* see pp. 199f., *Ps.St.* I, pp. 34ff., and Additional Note XXVIII.

[15a] V. 4b, 'they set their signs as signs' yields no sense; '*ôth* never means 'emblem' and the conquerors would not set up their own religious or military emblems in a house which they were going to set ablaze; read *šāmû šammôth ûmē šammôth běthôkhāh* (cf. Ps. 46.9; Ezk. 23.33; 33.38f.; 35.3). *yd*' in v. 5 is not 'know', but imperfect of a stem *d'y*, 'destroy', see Driver in *JBL* LXVIII, 1949, p. 58; rd. *yidh'û*; pronounce the following words *kiměbhî'ê lāmô 'āleh*. In v. 6 a verb is missing; rd. *hittěthû* for *wĕ'attâ*.

Thou hast abhorred the covenant with thy servant,
   and profaned his crown down to the ground.
Thou hast demolished all his walls,
   his strongholds hast thou laid in ruins;
the passers-by all plunder him,
   he is a butt of all his neighbours.
Thou hast allowed his enemies to triumph,
   giving delight to all his foes;
Thou hast turned back the edge of his sword,
   and hast not upheld him in battle.
His splendid sceptre hast thou broken,
   and cast his throne down to the ground;
the days of his youth hast thou shortened,
   and thou hast covered him with shame. (89.40–46.)

But, as a rule, the lamentations are directed against the enemies of the people.

The *evil and audacious words* of the enemies play a distinct part in the lamentations and the descriptions of the distress. They are not only blasphemies against Yahweh (see above), but also evil plans, and scornful and cursing words against Israel, tending to destroy her honour and paralyse her soul. All such words were considered to be powerful and fatal 'curses',[16] and were even used by the ancients in war, or before a battle, in order to strike the enemy in a way just as effective as the use of sword or spear.[17] That was why, before a war, they would send for the seer or the *nābhî'*, that his powerful words might enervate the enemy, so that the army might defeat him, as we hear for instance in the story about the seer Balaam.[18] In the eyes of those who are the objects of such words, they are naturally looked upon as *evil* curses, unlawful supernatural harmful words and operations, 'sorcery' and 'devilry'. This is what is meant by words like 'guile', 'falsehood', 'delusion', 'mischievous words' and the like, and especially by the word *'āwen*.[19] It indicates the evil 'power', or power used for evil ends, and its effects, and the means of starting it; but also the things and beings filled with this evil 'power'. Above all *'āwen* is used of *words* having such power and such effects. It need not have anything to do with 'sorcerers' and 'magic words' in a technical and, so to speak, professional sense, with people who themselves know that they are practising sorcery, and have established themselves as masters of that art, so to say. According to ancient opinion, *all* words were powerful in

---

[16] Pss. 12.3–5; 44.17; 74.8, 10, 18, 23; 79.10, 12; 80.7; 83.4ff.; and in addition the 'I-psalms'—really 'national psalms'—10.4, 6f.; 42.11; 55.4; 59.8, 13; etc. Cf. n. 17 to Chap. VII and Johs. Pedersen, *Israel* I–II, pp. 437ff.

[17] Pss. 74.8, 23; 83.5, 13; cf. 58.5 (I-psalm).

[18] Num. 22–24; cf. 1 Kgs. 22.11–13; Jdg. 5.12, and see *GTMMM* III, p. 11; Birkeland, *Feinde d. Indiv.*, pp. 62, 73–76.

[19] Pss. 14.4; 125.5; cf. Isa. 29.20; 31.2. Then also in consideration of Chap VII: Pss. 7.15; 10.7; 53.5; 55.4, 11; 56.8; 59.3; 94.23 *et al.* For *'āwen* see Additional Note XXVIII.

proportion to the 'power' of the speaker; evil words, curses, abuse, threats, sneers, evil wishes, 'the evil eye', jealous thoughts, scornful or threatening gestures and looks and symbols—in the eyes of the Israelites and of all other ancient orientals all such things were powerful, and would do harm to the soul and happiness of those against whom they were directed. All the powerful means of the gentile enemies, their plans and threats and sneers, the 'curses' of their prophets and priests, and all their accompanying ceremonies, in short all their religious and cultic measures and acts and words, in the eyes of the Israelites seemed to be sorcery, 'āwen; when used for the gods of the gentiles the word actually means 'demons', 'devils', 'trolls'.[20] What to one person is cultus, to the person on the other side appears as sorcery. Such powerful words on the part of the enemy are 'falsehoods', 'deceitful words', because they call up the 'false', pernicious power in life, 'the curse', draining and laying waste blessing and happiness. But they are also 'falsehoods', because they will make righteous people 'scoundrels', and because, by Yahweh's help, they shall turn out to be unreal and of no effect, injuring only the mischief-maker.

The psalms complain of such false, mocking 'curses' on the part of their enemies:

> Guile do they speak one to the other
>   with flattering lips and double mind, . . .
> They say: 'In our tongues we have our strength,
>   our lips are with us, who shall master us?' (12.3, 5.)

The congregation complains of such liars in the service of gentile gods:

> They have in them a venom like a viper's venom,
>   like the deaf adder that stops her ear,
> that will not listen to the charmer's voice,
>   to the most cunning sorcerer's spell. (58.5f.)
> His mouth is full of curse and deceit,
>   under his tongue is oppression and craft. (10.7.)
> They pour forth (curses) from their mouth,
>   upon their lips are sharp swords. (59.8.)

The climax of the distress often seems to be the mockery and sneers of enemies and neighbouring nations:

> Thou hast made us the butt of our neighbours,
>   a scorn and derision to all around.
> Thou hast made us a byword among the nations,
>   a shaking of the head among the peoples.
> All day long the disgrace is before me,
>   the shame of it overclouds my face
> at the sound of taunters and scoffers,
>   at the sight of the vengeful foe. (44.14–17.)

[20] Isa. 41.29; 66.3; 1 Sam. 15.23; Hos. 10.8; cf. Am. 5.5. In Babylonian-Assyrian texts the political enemies of the king are sometimes called 'evil demons' (devils) see Ps.St. I, p. 69.

The *prayer* as a rule is couched in general phrases which constantly recur: 'hear', 'look here', 'arise', 'plead our cause', 'turn our destiny', 'have mercy upon us', 'seek our their wickedness', 'cease from anger', 'do not cast us off for ever', 'forgive our trespasses', 'redeem us', 'help us'.[21]

But after all, of course, form and substance of the prayer depend on the nature of the disaster and of the situation. When defeated and oppressed, the people ask to be rescued from death and distress:

> Do not leave the lives of thy worshippers to destruction,
>   forget not thy poor people for all time. (74.19.)

They pray for the shame to be taken away from them:

> Let not the oppressed be ashamed again,
>   may the weak and wretched have good cause to praise thee!
> (74.21.)

And that the people may be raised up again:

> O God of hosts, restore us to power,
>   Let us see the light of thy face, that we may be saved. (80.4.)

And for revenge on their enemies:

> Let the pagans know—and may we see it!—
>   thy vengeance for spilling the blood of thy servants.
> May the moan of the prisoners come before thee,
>   by thy mighty power release those that are in peril of death,
> and render sevenfold unto our neighbours
>   the taunts that they have heaped on thee. (79.10–12.)

Yahweh must not forget how the enemies have mocked at himself and at his people:

> Arise, O God, to vindicate thy cause,
>   remember how the fool scoffs at thee all the day,
> forget not the clamour of thy enemies,
>   the endless din that rises from thy foes. (74.23.)

After the defeat the king prays:

> Remember, O Yahweh, the taunts thrown at thy servants,
>   the insults of the nations we have to bear,
> the taunts of thine own enemies, O Yahweh,
>   taunting the heels of thine anointed. (89.51f.)

'The heels' is a hint at the flight of the king after the battle. May the enemy meet the fate that such 'sorcerers' deserve:

[21] Ps. 80.2; Isa. 37.17.—Pss. 74.20; 80.15; Isa. 37.17; 63.15; 64.8; Lam. 1.9, 11, 20; 2.20; 5.1—Pss. 44.24; 9.20; 10.12; 44.27; 74.22; 82.8; 94.2.—Ps. 72.22.—Pss. 80.2; 94.1.— Pss. 10.12; 74.2–18, 23; 89.48, 51; 106.4; 137.7; Lam. 5.1.—Pss. 80.4, 8, 15, 20; 85.5.— Ps. 126.4.—Ps. 106.4.—Ps. 90.13; 123.3.—Ps. 79.8f.—Pss. 85.8; 80.4; 8, 20.—Pss. 44.27; 79.9, 11; 106.47.

> Shall they not rue it, all these sorcerers,
>   those who devour my people? (14.4)

> Pay them back for the sorcery they have done,
>   let the nations fall by (thine) anger, O God! (56.8.)

The prayer may be fierce, impatient, accusatory:

> Awake, why sleepest thou, O Yahweh?
>   Arise, cast us not off for ever.
> Why dost thou hide thy face before us,
>   forgetting our distress and woe?
> Our soul is bowed down to the dust,
>   our body lies low on the ground.
> Arise and come to our rescue
>   and save us for thy love's sake. (44.24–27.)

As well as prayers couched in the imperative we sometimes come across a *wish* (in the jussive mood, designating desirability):[22] 'may the moanings of the prisoners come before thy presence'; 'may Yahweh cut off all flattering tongues', and so on. This wording is used above all when speaking of the destruction of the enemies. The last example proves that in these 'wishes' we are dealing with terms of cursing and blessing. According to the Hebrew way of thinking something more is involved in such sayings than what we mean by the word 'wish': they are words with operative power. In ritual the operative word is often older than the prayer, and we can see how in the cult in Israel these words in the course of time develop into prayers: the aid of Yahweh is called on by means of the old powerful words. More details about this will be given in Chap. XI.

Prayers and wishes for the destruction of the enemy naturally claim much space in the national psalms of lamentation. Just as natural is that here, particularly, the ancient *formula of cursing* is used: 'may the gentiles be put to shame', 'be destroyed', 'may the culprit go to Sheol' (Hades), 'may Yahweh cut off all flattering lips', and so on.[23] The last is a transition form to actual prayer. In some of the psalms these curses dominate the whole; see, for instance, the detailed curse in Ps. 58.5–10. And see, likewise, the prayer in Ps. 83.14–17, where we only need to omit the reference to Yahweh and replace the imperatives by the subjunctive ('jussive') in order to get the wording of a cursing formula such as, for instance, the king of Moab would have had Balaam speak against Israel.

The aim is to strike at the root of the disaster: the operative evil words and tricks and intrigues of the enemy; and so, by means of the cult and the ritual curses of the psalm (see Chap. XI), the congregation tries to parry the curse words of the enemy. But we are not justified in concluding from this that the psalmists thought that without the will and help of

[22] Pss. 9.18a; 12.4; 74.21; 79.10f.; 83.16–19; 90.16f.; 125.5; cf. 104.35.
[23] Pss. 12.4; 74.22f.; 79.6, 12; 83.10–15, 17; cf. 31.18; 35.4, 26; 40.15f.; 56.10; 68.31; 71.13; 86.17; 109.29; cf. also 119.78; 140.10; Jer. 17.18.

Yahweh the word of cursing by itself could deliver them from the enemy; at most we have the lingering remains of the old style. Rather more frequently than the directly cursing word, we find the prayer for Yahweh to slay the enemy by means of his 'ban': *his* operative word, his 'threats' shall destroy them.[24] Even if we find an echo of the old 'magical' formula in many terms, and even if corresponding thoughts *may* at any time be attached to the sacred words of religion, the laments can claim to be true prayers to God, and no magical formulas. Yahweh has to interfere, if the malice of the enemies is to be struck at the root, and brought home to themselves:

> Let the evil of the wicked come to an end,
>   and let the righteous man stand firm!
> For He that trieth hearts and reins
>   is a God who vindicates the right.
>
> My protecting shield is Yahweh himself,
>   who saveth those whose hearts are right;
> yea, Yahweh is a righteous judge,
>   a God indignant every day.
>
> Surely he whets his sword again,
>   he bends his bow and takes aim,
> but his deadly darts and fire-tipped arrows
>   he has made ready against himself.
>
> He's alive with witchcraft, has conceived
>   mischief, and brings forth only deceit;
> he has digged out a pit, and made it deep,
>   but he shall fall into it himself.
>
> His mischief returns on his own head,
>   his violence drops on his own crown.
> But I shall thank Yahweh for his justice,
>   and praise the name of the Most High God.   (7.10–18.)

'I shall thank'—i.e., I shall one day have the opportunity of thanking him for the experienced salvation from this particular trouble. The psalms of lamentation trust God to do great things, and expect great things from him. Without him no rituals and 'sacred' words are of any use.

The *prayer for revenge* will often occur in a way which does not agree with the Christian way of thinking.[25] But here we have to remember two things. In the first place, revenge and dread of the joint responsibility of the tribe as against the *gō'ēl* would be the only means of keeping passions in check, and securing a certain legal system in the primitive social conditions under which Israel were living as nomads, and in great measure

---

[24] Cf. the 'I-psalms' (Chap. VII) 52.7; 69.25; 109.15; 139.19.
[25] Ps. 79.10; cf. Nah. 1.2; Pss. 58.11; 91.1; 149.7; 18.48; 106.4.

also after settling down. The request for revenge denotes that the sense of justice is alive, and may not be violated; it is a substitute for the punishment by the society.[26] And in the second place, prayer to the 'God of revenge' must be taken to express the knowledge and the faith that God will not allow justice to be violated. Side by side with the prayer for revenge stands all the time the prayer for God to 'provide justice', to 'still the enemy and the avenger' (Ps. 8.3), to prevent justice from being violated.[27] But even if the scope of the law was confined to Israel, still it was there. And the very fact that the idea of justice is attached to a God, who came gradually to be considered the God of the whole world, guarantees that it will some time break through the national limits—as we can see already in Amos.

Accordingly we find that the prayer against the gentiles takes a more religious turn: 'may they know that thou, Yahweh art God—even thou only' (2 Kgs. 19.19, cf. Ps. 46.11).

The lament as well as the prayer aims to 'smooth the face of Yahweh', i.e. mollify him, and touch Yahweh's heart. This is still more clearly brought out by the motivations of the prayers. In different ways the psalmists try to provide Yahweh with reasons for hearing them and granting their prayer.

We have already seen that the lament involves such a motivation; it seeks to rouse the pity of Yahweh, and thereby make him interfere and help. That is why the distress is painted in sombre colours, while the helplessness of the people and their dependence on Yahweh are called to mind: 'we are brought very low'.[28] When the congregation emphasizes that no one but Yahweh can help them[29] and that nobody else is to be trusted,[30] then the situation is shown to be truly desperate;

> O! help thou us against our foes,
>   for men's help is in vain. (Ps. 60.13.)

Especially in the later congregational psalms of lamentation of Jewish times this motive will recur. Thus originally naïve and selfish motives have been deepened into a religious recognition of complete dependence on God.

Rather more in keeping with old Israelite ways of thinking is the appeal to the *honour of Yahweh*. It is directly emphasized that Yahweh's own cause is at stake: '*thy* people', '*thine* inheritance', '*thy* possession', '*thy* congregation', 'the sheep of *thy* pasture', '*thine* anointed', '*thy* sanctuary, '*thine* enemies', and so on.[31] In Pss. 74 and 79 the lament starts with a description of the way Yahweh's Temple has been laid waste; then only do we hear of

---

[26] See Johs. Pedersen, *Israel* I–II, pp. 378ff.; Nyström, *Beduinentum und Jahwismus*, pp. 31ff. cf. 109ff.

[27] Cf. the 'I-psalms' 26.1; 7.7f.; 17.2; 35.1; 43.1, and Hab. 1.12f.

[28] Pss. 79.8; 89.48f.; cf. Isa. 64.7.

[29] Ps. 60.13; cf. Isa. 37.16; Jer. 3.23; 14.22; 2 Chron. 14.10; 20.6; Sir. 33.5 (G).

[30] Ps. 44.7f.; cf. 10.14; 33.20–22; Jer. 14.8; Dan. 9.18; Pss. Solom. 7.6–9; 9.19 (10).

[31] Pss. 74.1f.; 79.9, 13; 83.4; 89.39, 52; cf. 94.5; Isa. 63.18.

the sufferings of the congregation. Yahweh must help for the sake of his name and his honour:

> Help us, O God our saviour,
>   for the glory of thy name.
> Deliver us, purge away our sins
>   for thy name's sake, O God.
> Wherefore should heathen peoples sneer
>   and say: 'Where is thy God?' (79.9f.)

Surely the God who has done such great things in times of old and conferred such blessings on his people,[32] cannot possibly 'sleep' nor 'forget his people'[33] nor, still worse, allow the heathen to blaspheme his name? Shall the gentiles believe that the God of Israel is a powerless, a defeated, an insufficient God?[34]

> How long, O God, is the foe to be scoffing?
>   is the enemy always to blaspheme thee? (74.10.)
> He says to himself: 'God has forgotten,
>   he hides his face and never sees'. (10.11.)

How could Yahweh 'forget the roaring of his enemies' (74.23) and their sneering words? Certainly, he must interfere!

Closely related to the appeal to Yahweh's honour is the *hymnal motive*: in a naïve way the congregation will try to appeal to the grace of Yahweh by 'giving him honour', calling to mind all his great works from the days of creation, Exodus, or covenant, until now. Sometimes this motivation, like the introductory invocation of his name, may extend to quite a hymnal section,[35] as, for instance, the hymnal introduction to Pss. 44, 89, and others (see Chap. IV.5).

But even here the original utilitarian motive has been superseded by a purely religious one; the fear and awe of a mighty and exalted God has been called to life, and makes the psalmist want to approach God with praises; the thought of God's great works inspires confidence in poet and congregation, and makes them dare to approach him in the belief that he will hear their prayers; in the honour and eulogy motifs they find comfort and confidence for themselves.

The appeal to the great benefactions of Yahweh in times past, to his *kindness* ('favour') and 'covenant-mindedness' (*ḥesedh*) and to his 'helpful righteousness' (*ṣedheq*), is not only heard in connexion with the honour motif, but also as comprising an independent motivation for his readiness to hear prayers. How should Yahweh forget his own covenant:

[32] Pss. 44.2–4, 8; 74.2; 80.9–12; 89.50; 125.3; 2 Chron. 20.7; cf. Ps. 115.1; Isa. 63.11–14.
[33] Pss. 44.24f.; 74.19; cf. the 'I-psalm' 10.12.
[34] Pss. 12.5; 74.8, 10, 23; 79.12; 83.3, 5, 13; cf. 94.7; 10.4, 6, 13; 115.2; Isa. 37.17.
[35] Pss. 74.12–17; 77.14ff.; 90.1ff.; cf. the 'I-psalm' 139.1f.

> Remember the community thou didst buy long ago,
>   whom thou didst rescue to be thine own people. (74.2.)

The congregation expects him to be no less 'loyal' (*hāsîdh*) and merciful and faithful to the present generation than he used to be to the Fathers,[36] and by this thought their own faith is strengthened.

All these things go to make the basis of the *confidence* of Israel in her God. The congregation trusts in Yahweh's 'loyalty' to his covenant (*hesedh*). His faithfulness to the Fathers, his righteousness and the demands of his own honour can alone justify Israel in appealing to all these things. But confidence itself also appears as a separate motivation for hearing prayer, giving us then the 'confidence motif' so often urged by the congregation.

> Thou art the Holy (God of Jacob),
>   enthroned upon the praises of Israel.
> On thee our fathers did rely,
>   relied, and thou didst rescue them.
> They cried to thee, and were delivered,
>   they trusted and were not put to shame. (22.4–6.)

The congregation pleads that it is trusting in Yahweh—so did the Fathers, and they were not put to shame, the present generation must do the same— it is trusting in him who is the only Mighty one and the only Helper;[37] surely Yahweh will not disappoint such confidence!

> Who is my champion against evildoers,
>   who sides with me against such sorcerers?
> If Yahweh had not been my helper,
>   I should soon have dwelt in the silent land.

> If I must say: 'My foot is slipping'—
>   thy goodness, Yahweh, holds me up;
> when fearful thoughts are crowded within me,
>   thy comforts will delight my soul. (94.16–19.)

Thus the motif of confidence develops into a confession of faith, as in the first part of Ps. 44.

But the psalm may also call to mind the *cause of the distress*. Then we are told either that Israel is 'righteous' and has done nothing to outrage Yahweh, or that the wickedness and hate of the enemies are responsible for everything; such is the tone of psalms like 44 and 74. The congregation, 'the righteous' (see below) may plead their *innocence*—'the innocence motivation—and, where this is the case, we may talk of *laments of innocence*.

> All this has come upon us, yet we have
>   not forgotten thee nor failed they covenant. (44.18.)

---

[36] See n. 32, and Pss. 77.14ff.; 89.18ff.
[37] Ps. 44.7f.; cf. 33.20–22 and the 'I-psalms' 10.14; 13.6; 26.1; 31.7, 15; 55.24; 56.4; 143.8; 16.8; 62.2; Dan. 9.18; Jer. 14.8.

In the earlier national psalms of lamentation this is the most usual attitude. Of the we-psalms mentioned above, only Ps. 79 clearly preserves a different attitude. Even in the I-psalms where an individual is speaking on behalf of the congregation (Chap. VII), we are often assured that he is 'guiltless', 'has not transgressed thy commandments', and that therefore the enemies 'hate him without a cause',[38] or even because of his piety (69.10). So, among others, such psalms as 5; 7; 12; 26.

In this connexion we may be justified in considering a little more closely the term ṣaddîqîm—'the righteous'—frequently used in the psalms, and particularly so in contrast to rěšā'îm, 'the evil-doers', 'the wicked', 'the ungodly.' These two terms have often been taken to indicate two 'parties' or 'tendencies' within the Jewish congregation: the piously obedient to the law, and the ungodly apostates or wordly-minded. And certainly the two terms—especially in the singular—may be used to indicate the law-abiding Jew on the one hand, and his wordly-minded and—at any rate in the eyes of the more rigorous party—'apostate' countryman, who has emancipated himself from the law and from the 'tradition of the Fathers' and their conceptions of religion, on the other. Such is the case in the introductory poem to the whole psalter, Ps. 1, and probably also in some other late psalms, belonging to the 'wisdom poetry' (see Chap. XVI), such as Pss. 37 and 73 and others.

But Birkeland has proved beyond all contradiction that the two terms in the psalms do not as a rule indicate two different parties, representing conflicting 'tendencies' within the Jewish congregation, but, oftener than not, point to national antagonisms—which, on account of the way of thinking within the old national religion, would certainly also involve *religious* contrasts between the worshippers of Yahweh and 'the gentiles'. This is evident from a national psalm of lamentation like Ps. 125. Here the congregation first of all expresses its faith that Yahweh will protect those 'who put their confidence in him', 'his people':

> Those who trust in Yahweh are like Mount Zion,
> the unshakeable, that stands for ever;
> as mountains are round about Jerusalem,
> so is Yahweh round about his people.

And then the same thought is expressed again with reference to the actual situation of Israel under the supremacy of the gentiles:

> He will not let the sceptre of the wicked
> rest upon the lot of the righteous,
> lest the righteous put out their hand
> to do some wickedness.

I.e. Yahweh will prevent 'the ungodly' from having any longer the supremacy over 'the righteous', so that the latter shall not be led astray into

---

[38] Ps. 86.2; further, 17.3–5; 26.4; 35.7, 19; 59.10; 5.8; 26.6–8; cf. 69.10.

apostasy or heathenism. The prayer that this deliverance may become
reality is then added:

> O Yahweh, do good unto those who are good,
>   to those who are upright in heart.
> But to those who are wandering crooked ways
>   will Yahweh give the sorcerers' fate.

That this alludes to the contrast between Israel and gentiles is confirmed
by the final wish, making a kind of refrain to the psalm: 'May Israel
prosper!'

The same thing can be seen from Ps. 58. 'The wicked' are 'estranged
from the womb'; they stand outside the fellowship of the covenant. In
this psalm the lamentation takes the form of an accusation against the
strange 'gods', who really ought to be the loyal governors of Yahweh
over the nations, over whom he had appointed them to rule (Deut. 32.8),
but they were instead ruling with injustice and violence, cf. Ps. 82. The
'strange evil-doers' filling the earth with violence are in the service of
these gods.

In the psalms we find other passages, where it is quite obvious that
the 'evil-doers', rĕšā'îm, indicate the gentile enemies and oppressors of
Israel.[39] The lamentation in Ps. 58 is caused precisely by the fact that
these 'evil-doers' are also oppressing Israel, and the gist of the prayer is
that 'the righteous' shall 'see vengeance' and 'wash their feet in the blood
of the wicked'. There can be no doubt whatsoever that 'the righteous' in
this case indicate Israel as a nation—rĕšā'îm in the psalms does not
signify any single group of men, but all those who act as the enemies of
the worshipper. They may be either national enemies or treacherous
countrymen or such as practise some sort of witchcraft. But mostly they
are the national enemies of Israel, or 'the heathen' oppressors and their
helpers within Israel.

The words ṣaddîq and rāšā' express the two main notions in the ethical
view of life of an Israelite. Ṣaddîq,[40] in our translation of the Bible usually
and rather mechanically rendered by 'righteous', actually indicates that
a person or a thing is 'right'—is what it ought to be; for instance it may
be used of 'fair weights', the 'right way' as distinguished from the wrong
way, and so on. The 'right' man is a man who according to the moral
concepts of Israel is as he ought to be, the 'ideally normal' man. According
to the old Israelite notion with its 'corporate' view of the individual and

---

[39] Pss. 82.2, 4; 28.3. Cf. Birkeland, *Feinde d. Indiv.*, pp. 44f., 59ff. Marschall, *Die 'Gottlosen'
des ersten Psalmenbuches*, has seen that *rĕshā'îm* is capable of many interpretations, but his definitions
of the latter are often erroneous. Much the same must be said of Ridderboos, *De 'Werkers der
Ongerechtigheid'*.
[40] For this idea see especially Johs. Pedersen, *Israel* I–II, pp. 260ff.; Leivestad, *Guds straffende
rettferdighet*, pp. 9ff. A good, perhaps somewhat too systematized, examination of the ideological
content of the terms 'righteous', 'righteousness' is given by van der Weijden in *Die 'Gerechtigkeit'
in den Psalmen*, but curiously enough, he does not touch the religio-sociological question, *who* 'the
righteous' in the psalms are.

fellowship, he can only be such a man within the fellowship of the covenant, and if he leads the life of a 'normal', 'good' man in mental and social fellowship with his family and people. It involves the right relationship to the society in which he is living, with its customs and morals, and 'law', and to its god and its religion. As long as he remains within the fellowship of covenant and cult, and has done nothing to exclude himself from this fellowship, he is ṣaddîq, and belongs to the ṣaddîqîm. Through the cult his being 'right' is confirmed; through it he is cleansed from eventual trespasses and promised accession to the fellowship of 'the righteous'. In the Old Testament 'righteousness' does not signify the highest virtue, but a social and religious relationship; 'righteous' is he who answers the demands made on him by the fellowship to which he belongs. A man is either 'righteous', or he is not; there is nothing between.[41] But the term often involves an inner power as well. To the 'normal' righteousness of such a man also belongs the possession of the power and the will to 'succeed' in being united with his fellows; the 'right' man is the 'man of luck', who possesses 'blessing' and the power of good luck. Because of his covenant with Yahweh, Yahweh makes him 'succeed'; 'whatsoever he doeth shall prosper'. But it also means that he creates happiness and the 'right conditions', 'unity' or 'peace' (šālôm) in his surroundings; he is able to uphold himself and those belonging to him; the 'right' person is also the 'righteous' one. He is 'firm' and 'trustworthy'. That is why, above all, it is so important that the chief and king should be 'right', should possess the 'righteousness' that preserves society and vindicates its order, and sustain and help those in need of it, as it is described, for instance, in Chaps. 29 and 31 of the poem of Job.

Just because being 'right' was so bound up with the 'fellowship of the covenant' it was a matter of course to the ancient Israelite that true righteousness could be found only within the covenant, i.e. within the Israelite fellowship of the covenant. Its members only could be expected to be 'right' and 'righteous'. Obviously a person who had broken away from the social order would thereby 'make himself an evil-doer' (rāšā'), and that the outcast 'has been made an evil-doer' would in those days go without saying. And so, 'right' and 'righteous' would be the natural terms for members of the Israelite covenant fellowship, for Israel itself as a people and a congregation.

To the religious way of thinking the focal point of being 'right' would obviously be the right relationship to Yahweh; the 'right' man is he who does what is 'right in Yahweh's eyes'; 'the righteous' are 'the God-fearing'; but in the psalms this term too nearly always indicates the fellowship of Yahweh's worshippers, that is to say Israel as contrasted with other nations that worship 'other gods'. Like all ancient moral notions the term ṣaddîq has of course a religious element; but it is not from the start specifically religious, nor has it the same meaning as in the nomistic

[41] For details see von Rad in *Festschrift für Bertholet*, pp. 418ff.

Judaism of later days. Only after the development of the typical Jewish law-abidingness did 'righteousness' come to indicate a definite behaviour in accordance with the Jewish way of life under the 'Law', such as for instance in Ps. 1. But as has been said, in the psalms the word very seldom has this sense; the psalms represent the earlier, rather more 'inclusive' view of 'righteousness'; after all, 'the righteous' is here a term for Israel as a nation. It gives expression to the naïve self-estimate of the ancients: one's own nation are always the 'right' people; the others are 'strangers' or 'barbarians'. But the word has a full concrete substance as well; it is the most characteristic expression of the old Israelite view of life and morals with its religious undertone.

Closely related to the conception of 'the righteous' in the psalms is that of 'the pious', the *ḥăsîdhîm*, which would be better translated: 'the loyal' or 'the faithful'. In the psalms this term, too, indicates the people and congregation of Israel.[42] This is brought out with perfect clarity in, for instance, the festal psalm for new year, Ps. 149.5ff., where the congregation is rejoicing at the victorious power with which Yahweh's appearance at the festival has filled the people:

> The faithful now exult in glory,
>   and shout for joy here on their benches;
> the praise of God is on their lips,
>   two-edged swords are in their hands;
> to execute vengeance upon the nations
>   and punishment on (all) the peoples,
> to bind their Monarchs with chains,
>   their nobles with iron gyves,
> to execute upon them the written doom—
>   that is the honour of his faithful ones.

What is said here refers to the people as a whole, and not to any 'party'.[43] The traditional translation 'the pious' ('the saints') is misleading; it does not express what the term primarily implies, namely the connexion with the fellowship of the covenant.[44] The term *ḥāsîdh* is closely related to *ṣaddîq*, only that the emotional aspect of the fellowship of the covenant becomes more prominent. The 'right' man has a warm feeling towards his fellow member of the covenant, and 'does *ḥesedh*' towards him, sides with him, takes care of him, and helps him, when in distress; according to the covenant, *ḥesedh* is the proper way of feeling and acting towards one's fellows; the *ḥāsîdh* is a man who feels and acts as a member of the

---

[42] Pss. 50.5; 79.2; 85.9; 89.20; 97.10; 132.9, 16; 149.1, 5, 9; 145.10. See Birkeland, *Feinde d. Indiv.*, p. 98.

[43] The earlier critical interpretation to the effect that here and elsewhere in the psalms we have the party of 'the pious', the Chasidim, in the Maccabean period, has been decisively refuted by Birkeland, *'Ani und 'anaw in d. Pss; Feinde d. Indiv.*, pp. 94ff.; cf. Additional Note XXIX.

[44] See Nelson Glueck, *Das Wort hesed;* A. R. Johnson in *Interpretationes ... S. Mowinckel ad Septuagenario missae*, pp. 100ff.

covenant, inwardly as well as outwardly. Those who take seriously the way of acting and disposition proper to the brotherhood of the covenant are, '*ḥesedh*-men', true members of the 'brotherhood of the covenant'.

Israel is conscious of being such a people of Yahweh's covenant, just because she exists as a result of Yahweh's elective love and covenant. And this 'righteousness' is fully meant. As a covenant community which stands in the right relationship to Yahweh, and has its righteousness renewed in the cult, Israel knows that she can plead her 'right' in relation to Yahweh; the same is true also of the individual who approaches Yahweh to get his 'right'. The righteousness is based upon Yahweh's cultic and moral demands, and these demands can be fulfilled by a 'right', normal, man—that is the basic assumption in the old Israelite conception of life and of religion, cf. Deut. 30.11–14. The unavoidable failure—'sins of weakness', and 'unwitting sins'—can be remedied in the cult. Therefore as a people Israel are 'the right ones'.[45]

This therefore is what the congregation pleads in her prayers for help in the laments: her members are 'the righteous', 'the fellows of Yahweh's covenant'. Because Israel are the righteous, standing in a relationship of 'devotedness' to Yahweh, Yahweh must help them in his 'favour' (*ḥesedh*).

And so much the more so as their antagonists are 'wicked', 'evil-doers', *rĕšā'îm*. This word, in our translation of the Bible, is sometimes rendered by 'ungodly' but always means rather 'evil-doer'. What is characteristic of *rāšā'*, 'the wicked one', is not that he is an 'atheist', or that he has no religion at all, but that he is not 'right', that he is not a 'normal' man with a normal soul and normal abilities; he is 'crooked' and 'loose' and 'lax' instead of 'right' and 'steadfast'. He does not possess the power of luck, he is one who 'fails' and misses his aim—this gives us roughly the primary sense of the word. He neither feels nor thinks nor acts nor reacts like a 'normal', 'right' man. He is 'bad', a 'fool', intellectually as well as morally. Objectively speaking he is not to be trusted: something in him 'gives way', just like a slack bowstring. He does not acquit himself well in the fellowship of the covenant; he is a danger and a source of misfortune; he is an outsider—and must be one, as he will otherwise bring bad luck upon the fellowship. He is a failure and doomed to fail, and his apparent 'power' is a negative, injurious one, which will finally bring him to his end. His 'fruit' is destruction and death. Later on when hard facts proved that 'the wicked' might and did prosper, while 'the righteous' were defeated, the great moral and religious problem arose, of which Ps. 73 and the poem of Job complain, and on which they ponder. He who in some way or other breaks with the fellowship of the covenant and its customs and laws, 'makes himself an evil-doer', and the fellowship cannot but make him an outsider, and, according to the 'corporate' view of life, he will then have no true existence. Anything may be expected from him.

---

[45] See Pedersen, *Israel* I–II, pp. 336ff.; Mowinckel, *Diktet om Ijob*, pp. 7ff. Cf. von Rad in *Festschrift für Bertholet*, pp. 418ff.

Whatever he may do is 'wrong'; 'evil-doer' and 'sinner' are synonymous; the imminent 'injurious power' of the evil-doer is 'impurity' and 'sinfulness'.

Of course there are degrees of 'badness', just as there are degrees of 'righteousness' and 'blessing' and 'luck-power'. *Rāšā'* may be used of the one who loses a law-suit; in this case he will be the 'wrong man', and his counterpart the 'right man'; to adjudge a man to be 'wrong' was called 'to make him an unrighteous one' (*hiršîa'*). If such a man does not take upon himself to pay the penalty, 'atone for his unrighteousness', to his adversary, possibly even do penance before Yahweh, then the 'unrighteousness' will spread in his soul, and he may become quite filled with 'unrighteousness'.

But life also involves the danger for a 'right' man falsely 'to be made unrighteous'. Not only a wrong decision on the part of society may make him an outsider, or an oppressor may take away his 'righteousness' and his 'honour' and make him 'weak' and 'oppressed'—a pariah on the outskirts of society—but demons and evil men may, by means of 'black magic', put 'weakness' and 'impurity' and 'sinfulness' into the soul of an 'honest man', so as to make him lose health and purity and luck-power and honour and normality, and become just as charged with disasters and full of 'curse' as the 'evil-doer' himself. In a later chapter we shall see what society was able to do by way of retrieval in such cases.

'The righteous' of the psalms find themselves in this most paradoxical situation: though they *are* righteous, evil powers have 'made them unrighteous' by robbing them of their 'peace', and hurrying them to destruction. Such a state of things cannot continue; it is existence on the edge of a knife, poised between life and death. Yahweh settles it by interfering, and maintaining and establishing the righteousness of the righteous one.

As time went on and religion in Jewish times became more individualistic and the 'law' of Yahweh the fundamental religious reality, about which the individual had to make up his mind and to which he had to adjust himself, the same thing happened to the notion *rāšā'*, that happened to *ṣaddîq*: it came to express a definite view of life and an attitude to life, which alas! was also to be found within the community itself; the 'wicked one', the 'evil-doer' was the man who broke away from the law of Yahweh and from the manners and customs and traditions of the Fathers to imitate the manners and customs of the gentiles, and to join them; 'the publican' in the pay of the gentiles was considered to be the 'sinner' above all others. He is the 'apostate', who in the opinion of the righteous ought to be put outside the fellowship of the covenant, even if political conditions as a rule made it impossible to give effect to this claim. But the pious comforted themselves with the thought that in the end Yahweh was sure to smite the apostates, 'the wicked'. And as the distinguishing mark of the latter was considered to be the disregard of Yahweh's law and the claims of the covenant, the disaster befalling him was consequently looked upon as the just punishment of Yahweh, even if the ancient concept of disaster as the mechanically inevitable 'fruit' was still alive, side by side with the more rationalistic idea of the chastising interference of Yahweh. We find this later, more Jewish than Israelite, conception of 'the wicked' in some of the latest psalms, such as Pss. 37; 49 and 73.

But in the psalms the earlier conception is predominant, and it is in full accordance with it that 'the wicked' as a rule indicate the national and political enemies of Israel, the 'gentile' nations, that have attacked or oppressed her. As indeed all righteousness and 'happiness' was considered to be attached to the 'normal' life in the fellowship of the covenant, and the 'evil-doer' was the person who had made himself or been made an outsider, early Israel would logically conclude or rather immediately feel as a reality that anyone who did not belong to the fellowship of the covenant, i.e. to Israel, must be 'wicked'. To a primitive outlook anybody is wicked if he has an unfriendly disposition towards, or means a danger to, one's own society; in ancient Israel a 'stranger' meant an 'enemy'. That is why the author of Ps. 58.4 says of the oppressors of Israel, worshipping and representing the 'unrighteous' other gods, that

> The wicked are estranged from the womb,
>   go astray from their birth and speak (only) lies.

Their religion, like their whole conduct, is a 'falsehood', a deceitful imposture, a 'venom of asps', which, although it may badly hurt 'the righteous', shall yet in the end overtake the wicked themselves.

Such conduct is most hateful to Yahweh. He really must interfere against such 'evil-doers'! Therefore the lament justifies the prayer by pointing out that Israel are the 'righteous members of the covenant', while her enemies are oppressors and 'wicked evil-doers'. Characteristic in this respect is the prayer in Ps. 58.7ff. which follows on the picture of the enemies as venomous asps and beasts of prey, and with the wording of a curse side by side with prayer:

> Break the teeth in their mouth, O God,
>   break out the young lions' molars, Yahweh!
> May they vanish like water that runs away,
>   be trodden down like grass, and wither!
> Like a snail that melts away into slime,
>   an untimely birth, a mole, unseen by the sun!
> May their tents become jungle before they feel it,
>   may they be taken by the storm like dust from the threshing floor!
> The right men shall rejoice at seeing vengeance
>   and bathe their feet in the blood of the wicked!
> 'Yes', shall men say, 'the right men get their due,
>   there is indeed a God who rules on earth'.[46]

---

[46] For ḥiṣṣâw kĕmô v. 8 read kĕmô ḥāṣîr; ydrk may be a passive form yiddārĕkhû or yĕdhôrĕkhû. V. 9: nêphal and 'êsheth asyndeton. V. 10 rd. sukkôthêhem and môs miggôren; yis'ārennû imperson.: 'it storms him away'.

Practically all the above mentioned national psalms of lamentation are 'psalms of innocence'. The congregation, the people of Israel, are 'the righteous', 'the covenant minded', Yahweh's (true) 'worshippers', those who 'have never forgotten thee and never proved false to thy covenant'. The enemies are 'deceitful', 'oppressors', 'wicked', 'evil-doers', 'sorcerers', 'fools', 'faithless', 'robbers', 'lions', 'vipers full of venom'. How, then, can Yahweh have 'forgotten' his people, 'hidden his face from them'? How can it be explained that his 'anger is ablaze against them', that he 'has accounted them no better than sheep to be slaughtered', 'discarded them', 'crushed them in anger', 'given them hard times and a cup to drink that has dazed them', 'abjured the covenant with his anointed', 'not upheld him in the battle', 'made them fly from the archers', allowed the foe to 'cut down and burn the vine that he himself has planted', to 'plunder him' and to 'triumph over him'?

But the congregation may also admit that it has sinned, whatever sin it may be that it has committed (Ps. 79.8f.; Lam. 1.18, 20; 3.42); it may admit that Yahweh is right (cf. Ps. 51.6) and thereby do him honour, and make itself as small and miserable as possible; it humbles itself and does penance for its sins. In this way we get a *penitential lament*,[47] dominated by the motives of *penitence*, confession of sins, and humility.[48]

> Remember not against us our fathers' sins!
> May thy compassion hastily meet us—for we are low indeed! . . .
> Do thou deliver us and forgive our sins
> for the sake of thy (holy) name! (79.8, 9b.)

Here the motives of penitence, compassion and honour go together.

Actually in very many psalms the motive of penitence is not dominant. Certainly the feeling of penitence may be there, even if it does not find expression in words and confessions of sin; it is to be found in the penitential rites themselves (see above), which also give expression to an inward feeling of guilt and to the knowledge that the wrath of Yahweh must be appeased, although it may also imply a great deal of primitive, naïve calculation: by making oneself out to be small and miserable, one may rouse the compassion of Yahweh and 'make him great', and thus be restored to his favour. Meekness was no permanent part of the piety of ancient Israel; the main concern of the ancient Israelite was to maintain honour and justice.[49] But very early Yahweh had become so great to the mind of an Israelite that a man could not think of 'maintaining himself' (*hiṣtaddēq*) before him. It is for Yahweh to maintain the 'righteousness' and 'justice' of his people; Job demands from Yahweh that *he* shall

---

[47] Ps. 79; cf. the I-psalms 51; 130; The Prayer of Manasses. The group does not coincide with the traditional group of 'penitential psalms' of the church; most of the latter are not typical penitential psalms. In Bernini's book, *Le preghiere penitenziale*, the approach is more theological and doctrinal than literary.

[48] Pss. 79.8f.; 90.8; cf. the 'I-psalms of lament' (Chap. VII).

[49] Cf. Johs. Pedersen, *Israel* I–II, pp. 363ff.

maintain and prove and restore his 'righteousness'. The very words which
the ancient saga-tellers put into the mouth of David show what strict
Yahwistic circles considered to be the proper attitude to Yahweh, when
he had permitted disaster to strike the righteous one. 'If I shall find favour
in the eyes of Yahweh, he will bring me again and show me his face and
his habitation: but if he thus say, I have no delight in thee; behold here
am I, let him do to me as seemeth good to him'. David also refuses to
let Abishai cut down Shimei, who heaped curses on him in his distress:
'If he curseth, it is because Yahweh hath said unto him, "Curse David".
Who shall then say, Wherefore hast thou done so?' (2 Sam. 15.25f.;
16.5ff.). The disaster proves that the wrath of Yahweh has been roused
over something; then the best thing is to make oneself small and un-
noticed 'till his wrath hath passed by'. Therefore it was a wise and pious
thing to hold one's peace when struck with disaster.[50] To admit that
Yahweh is in the right—even if one does not understand it—means to
'give honour to Yahweh'; then it is to be hoped that he will again see to
the miserable one. Therefore it is necessary to 'humble oneself under the
mighty hand of God, that he may exalt one in due time'.

During her long and mostly unhappy external history, Israel learnt
that Yahweh possessed all power and all rights, and that the very existence
of the people was entirely dependent on his grace. She had no other help
to fall back upon. The help of man was not to be trusted; all assistance
had to come from Yahweh. Comparatively early this note is struck in the
psalmography,[51] and it is founded on the historical experiences of Israel
ever since the days of the Exodus and the miracle of the Reed Lake. It
is part of Yahweh's character to take care of those who are 'helpless', 'in
distress', 'lowly'[52]—even this belief is connected with the experiences of
the Exodus and of Yahweh's character as the God of ordeals (mišpāṭ),
and oracles (tôrâ), and fair peace (cf. the Treuga Dei) at the ancient cult
place Kadesh with the 'Spring of judgement' and the 'Court-well'.[53] The
emphasis on humility receives a personal touch and ring from the prophets' personal experiences of their complete dependence on God, and of
God as absolute holiness and overwhelming majesty.[54] They experienced
God as the one who had their minds as well as their bodies in his power,
and who overwhelmed them, so that they could but do what he wanted
them to, even if it hurt.[55] They also experienced him as the sublimely
holy and pure one, so that the knowledge of their own impurity and sin
was brought home to them (Isa. 6). And they declared pride to be the real
and central sin—that is to say: wanting to be something in oneself, and

[50] Ps. 39.3, 10; see below, Chap. VIII.7, II.11.
[51] Pss. 44.7f.; 62.9f. (royal psalm); cf. 118.8f.; 146.3. Cf. the references in n. 30.
[52] Pss. 9.13, 19; 10.17; 18.28; 14.6; 22.25, 27; 34.3, 7; 35.10; 68.11; 69.33; 76.10;
82.3f.; 140.13; 147.6; 149.4; 113.7; 1 Sam. 2.8.
[53] Cf. Mowinckel in Norsk Geogr. Tidskr. IX, pp. 21f.
[54] Cf. Mowinckel, Profeten Jesaja, pp. 88f., 123f.
[55] Cf. Jer. 20.7ff.; 15.15ff.; Isa. 20.

trusting the wisdom and strength of oneself and of other people.[56] Such piety considers lowliness and humility to be the proper attitude to God. A new *religious ideal of humility* grew into being and became a determining factor in Jewish piety. The terms 'lowly', 'distressed', 'helpless' tend to imply 'religiously humble', which again approaches the sense of 'pious'.[57]

The ideal of humility is in itself of a personal nature. On the one hand the condition of Israel as a nation most of the time was to be 'oppressed' and 'distressed', so that she felt she had a special right to reckon with the aid of him who takes particular care of those in distress; this helped to make the feeling of dependence and lowliness and humility be regarded as the proper attitude of people and of congregation too, an attitude which ought to find expression in public worship. On the other hand, the ideal of humility tended to call forth humility—in actual reality—even with regard to the demands made on Yahweh on behalf of the people, as we can see for instance in Ps. 90; even the congregation must learn not to ask for too great things,[58] but be content to wait humbly, but trustingly, for God, until it should please him to re-establish Israel.

Ps. 123 gives fine expression to this humble feeling of dependence:

> As the eyes of the servants are fixed
>   on the hand of their lord,
> as the maid's eyes are fixed
>   on the hand of her mistress,
> so our eyes look to Yahweh, our God
>   till he take pity on us.
> Take pity on us, Yahweh, take pity,
>   for we have our fill of contempt,
> our souls have more than their fill
>   of the scorns of the proud.

This humility has found its clearest expression in Ps. 131, which is certainly spoken by an individual, but on behalf of the congregation. Therefore the psalm ends by calling upon Israel to 'wait for Yahweh' quietly and humbly, patiently and confidently—salvation shall come about in due season.

But, as we have said: neither the note of penitence nor the ideal of humility is very prominent in the national psalms of lamentation, but they come somewhat more to the fore in the congregation's prayers of Jewish times (see below). In the psalms as a whole it is the motive of innocence which is predominant, not that of penitence. Even if Israel be 'distressed', 'oppressed', she is also 'righteous', 'faithful to the covenant'.

To the prayer is often added as another main item *the vow*. Here is an example, which is admittedly taken from a psalm in the I-form:

---

[56] Cf. Mowinckel, *Profeten Jesaja*, pp. 104ff.
[57] Cf. Mowinckel, *Jesaja*, p. 98.
[58] Ps 90.17; 126.5f.; 128.5f. Cf. Proverbs 30.8.

> Freehandedly will I sacrifice to thee,
>   and confess thy name, that it is good,
>   that it has delivered me from all my woes
>   and let me triumph over my foes. (54.8f.)

As in this case so in all others also, originally the vow would relate to a thanksgiving sacrifice,[59] or to some other pious work to be performed when Yahweh has rendered aid. A vow in connexion with prayer for help was so usual that the ordinary term for making a vow to the deity (*nāzar*) in Hebrew, as well as in Aramaic, received the sense of praying to the deity, calling upon his help.[60] Perhaps it is no mere accident that in the extant 'we-psalms' the vow is not very prominent, whereas in the 'I-psalms' we find it much oftener; a vow is by its very nature a personal matter. That it also has a place, however, in the national psalms will be seen from the reference in the public thanksgiving psalm (Ps. 66), as well as from the fact that a great many of the I-psalms handed down to us are actually collective psalms in which an individual is speaking on behalf of the congregation.[61]

In connexion with the aim of the psalm even the vow becomes a motivation of the prayer;[62] sometimes the prayer itself suggests that God might give the suppliant a chance of thanking and praising him, that is to say of celebrating with a thanksgiving festival after deliverance from distress.[63] We meet with this development especially in laments (and thanksgiving psalms) in individual form (see Chap. VII), and in the individual psalms, properly so called. We shall return to this below.[64]

As a rule the psalm *ends* by expressing the *confidence of being heard* which is felt by the congregation (or the suppliant). This is not merely a motivation of the prayer, like the declaration of confidence found in the body of the psalm; the confidence is sometimes expressed in such strong language that it gives the effect of a thanksgiving for help already received, as if it were an anticipatory thanksgiving psalm; the style as well as other significant details of the thanksgiving psalm are prominent.[65] An instance of such an expression of confidence may be given:

> Through God we shall do valiantly,
>   for He will trample down our foes. (60.14.)

(cf. also 58.11f., quoted above, p. 213.)

This anticipatory confidence and thanksgiving cannot merely be explained psychologically, by saying that through his prayer the suppliant

---

[59] See Ps. 66.13ff., a public thanksgiving psalm (Chap. IX), and cf. Pss. 54.8; 22.26f.
[60] Cf. Ps. 61.6 and see Ginzberg in *Louis Ginzberg Jubilee Volume*, pp. 159ff.
[61] See below, Chap. VII, and for the promise, VII, 4 (pp. 234f.). A detailed treatment of 'the promise' in the O.T. and in Judaism is given by Wendel in *Das israelitische Gelübde*.
[62] Pss. 79.13; 80.19; 144.9f.; cf. 20.6; 21.14 (royal psalms).
[63] Pss. 79.13; 80.19; cf. 51.15–17; 142.8.
[64] See Chaps. VII. 4; VIII. 7; X. 2; cf. VIII. 11.
[65] Pss. 144.12–15; 12.7f.; 60.13f.; 79.13; cf. 58.11f.

has now achieved confidence and assurance. The confidence is based on objective grounds. For the psalms handed down to us show that it was part of the very ritual of the penitential festivals that (the priest or) the temple prophet would promise the suppliant salvation and the granting of his prayer by means of an *oracle* or a *promise* to that effect. A few such promises have been handed down in the texts: Pss. 12.6; 60.8–10; 108.8–10. We shall return to this in a later chapter (Chap. XII.2). From a psalm like Ps. 12 we can also see that it was part of the ritual, that the suppliant after having received the promise should answer by a thanksgiving declaration of confidence, expressing the positive assurance which he had now had imparted to him that his prayer had been heard and that (soon) he would experience its actual realization. The declaration may have the character of an anticipatory thanksgiving psalm in the usual style with perhaps an explicit reference to the promise:

> Those words of Yahweh are precious words,
>   sterling as silver seven times purified.
> Thou Yahweh wilt guard us against evildoing men
>   and ever save us from such a race. (12.7f.)

From its place in this part of the ritual the declaration of assurance was then transferred to the psalm of lamentation where it came to be the usual ending:

> O God, I will sing thee a new song,
>   and play to thee on the ten-stringed lute—
> O thou who makest (thy) kings victorious
>   and (ever) savest thy servant David. (144.9f.)

'David' means here the reigning king of Judah.

To faith, aid was secured and made real as a result of the promise. And so the stylistic and style-historical basis for this feature in the structure of the psalms becomes merged with the purely and wholly religious one: that it is in the nature of prayer to bring forth confidence and assurance that God will help. To what extent this will be the case depends on the willingness and power of the suppliant to resign himself totally into the hands of God and pray with the intention of receiving help for this most important aspect of being heard; a prayer with the qualification that God's will be done and not the suppliant's own, will always be a means of obtaining the peace of heart and the confidence in God's real help, which makes up the assurance of faith. But at this very point Old Testament religion and prayer had narrow limits; they never quite got beyond a personally selfish and nationally this-worldly utilitarianism. Therefore a purely religious and psychological explanation of this standing item in the laments—the confidence of being heard—is not sufficient; the style-historical explanation given above is a fundamental necessity.

Now, if a psalm of lamentation falls into two distinctly separate parts: first, the lament and the prayer, and then a more or less regular thanksgiving or an expression of absolute assurance of being heard, as in Pss. 6; 28; 31; 62, urging something the suppliant has just learnt (62.12; 20.7), the explanation is, that in between the two parts something has happened, on which the assurance is objectively based, namely the promise of salvation uttered by the priest or temple prophet; God's promise, his 'word',[66] is the objective basis of that confidence. As a result of this liturgical pattern it has become usual for the psalm of lamentation to end with an expression of confidence as to being heard, more or less in the style of the anticipatory thanksgiving psalm. The final note of the psalm is one of confidence and thanksgiving, as if the help had already been received.

4

Among the national psalms of lamentation there is a distinction which has to be mentioned. One group of them gives a rather general description of the distress or disaster which the enemy *has* already brought upon land and people and king (Pss. 44; 74; 89). They were no doubt occasioned by a day of prayer and fasting after one or more lost battles, or perhaps the sack of the town. These are the psalms of lamentation proper. With these also belong a series of I–psalms, which apparently are quite personal, but in reality are national (congregational) psalms, such as 9–10; 13; 31; 35; 42–43; 55; 56; 59; 69; 94; 102; 109; 142 (see below, Chap. VII).

Then there are others, which do not contain any description of the distress beyond a reference in general terms to the nature and character of the enemy at large. Consequently they contain a lesser amount of specific complaints or none at all. See Ps. 83, 'the royal psalms', 144 and 20, and others. Evidently they came into existence *before* the distress had become acute, that is to say not as a result of a disaster which had already occurred, but in the middle of, or before some threatening danger. From the story of Naboth and the legend about Samuel as a judge (1 Kgs. 19.14ff.; 1 Sam. 7.5ff.) we can see that days of prayer and fasting with all the cultic acts and words belonging to them were kept when it was announced for instance that the enemy had declared war or was already on the march, or before the king of Israel himself entered upon a military expedition. This other group of psalms belongs to such days of antecedent prayer and fasting. As distinguished from the psalms of lamentation they have therefore been called *protective psalms*:[67] they pray for the protection of Yahweh against an imminent danger.

But as Israelite mentality as well as the very purpose of the day of prayer and the style tradition of the psalms would tend to have both distress and danger painted with as gloomy colours as possible (cf. 'the

[66] Pss. 12.7; 56.11; cf. 68.12; 107.20.
[67] See Birkeland, *Feinde d. Indiv.*, pp. 104ff.

motive of compassion'), it is not always easy to distinguish between protective psalms and psalms of lamentation properly so called. Indeed, in later times they may have been used indiscriminately.

Beyond this we shall only mention that a whole series of such protective psalms are to be found among the national congregational laments in the I-form; e.g. the 'royal psalms' 28; 61; 63, but also some other I-psalms, e.g. Pss. 3; 5; 7; 11; 26; 27; 36; 52; 54; 57; 62; 64; 71; 77; 86; 139; 140.

The tone of the protective psalms is brighter than that of the psalms of lamentation. Above all, the confidence and assurance of getting help is more prominent in them; in some of them—especially in those which according to their form are individual—it is altogether predominant. Such have been called 'psalms of confidence'. But if we consider the psalms from a cultic point of view and divide them into groups according to their place in life, the 'psalms of confidence' are no separate category, but only a somewhat marked group within the protective psalms.

In these psalms of confidence the original connexion between hymns and psalms of prayer (see above, Chap. IV.1, 4) can still be easily distinguished. When confidence is to be expressed it will naturally be in the form of a rather hymnic eulogy: Yahweh is praised for the aspects of his being and for the works past and present on which the worshipper is building his confidence and faith; and that is just why they have a more personal note and form. A good example is the first part of Ps. 27. But this means that they are approaching the 'thanksgiving psalms' (Chap. X.2) with regard to substance and tone. It is significant that it has been discussed whether the psalms of confidence have been 'derived from' psalms of lamentation and prayer, or from thanksgiving psalms,[68] and whether a pure psalm of confidence like Ps. 23 is to be counted in the main group, 'psalms of prayer', or to be considered a thanksgiving psalm.[69] But this way of putting the question is irrelevant. This 'mixing' of eulogy and thanksgiving and confident prayer is in fact an inheritance from earlier times, when the different kinds of psalms had not yet been distinguished from each other and separately cultivated according to their special uses in the cult. And at the same time it is evidence of the fact that the total religious experience of the Holy One and the religious attitude to the deity are spontaneous and do not distinguish between the different elements of which they are made up.

5

A state of distress might last a long while. If such a thing happened, the result might be that the day of penance was repeated more or less regularly. In this way we may get psalms which do not refer to a single attack on the part of a gentile power, but to the foreign nation or the

[68] The former has been maintained by Gunkel, the latter earlier by the present author in Ps.St. I.

[69] See Ps.St. I, p. 126; Birkeland, Feinde d. Indiv., p. 253.

foreign ruler in a general complaint. So for instance Pss. 12; 14; 58; 82; 90; and others. Such psalms may possibly derive from the period of the later monarchy, when Israel (Judah) was for a long time under the supremacy of Assyria or Babylonia. Later on, Judaism had a series of annual days of public penance and fasting in remembrance of the great disasters associated with the fall of the kingdom and the destruction of city and Temple (Zech. 7.5; 8.19). On these occasions they would complain of the permanent distress, of the degradation of Israel and the oppression and dishonour of gentile supremacy and ask for deliverance, revenge and re-establishment. To this category probably belong for instance Pss. 90 and 137.

Such a *regularly repeated psalm of lamentation* borders on the ordinary psalm of prayer (see below).

In the eyes both of the prophets of re-establishment[70] and of pious people, gentile supremacy over God's people would often appear to be the cause of all misery and sin to be found among the people. Thus the prayer for deliverance from foreign supremacy would involve prayer for the salvation and re-establishment of Israel in general, a 'turning of the destiny'.

Such Jewish laments, with prayer for the national, moral and religious re-establishment of Israel, for their rights over their enemies and for an undisturbed and happy future, are—in addition to those above mentioned —Pss. 106; 123; 125; and there are others. Like the ancient psalms of lamentation, Ps. 137 in particular, has the character of a lamentation over an actual enemy (Edom), but apart from this it is an example of the introduction of an original and personally felt feature into the traditional style.

The idea of a *turning of destiny* in some of these psalms connects them with the prayers usually heard at the festival of harvest and new year (the enthronement festival).[71] As in those psalms the congregation is here looking forward into the future, towards the 'completion', and prayer finds rest in the faith in re-establishment, full salvation, the coming of the 'kingdom'. In such psalms, therefore, late Judaism could find an expression of the eschatologically tinctured hope in which she lived. A fine example of such a forward-looking congregational lament, in which an individual is speaking on behalf of the community, as the person whose heart is especially loaded with the sufferings and the pressure of his time (see Chap. VII), is Ps. 102.

6

According to *our* conception of divine service we should have expected *ordinary psalms of prayer*—asking for whatever the congregation at any time might be in need of—to have belonged to the regular festal service from the very beginning, just like hymns of praise. But this does not appear

---

[70] See *GTMMM* III, p. 24.
[71] See Chap. V (pp. 161ff.; 186f.; 190f.).

to have been the case. The Psalter does not contain many ordinary psalms of prayer, and none of them can be traced back to very early times. As not infrequently happens it seems that here, too, the mind first of all fastened on the special case, that calling for special attention. As far as the regular and daily benefits which the cult aimed at securing are concerned, it seems as if belief in the creative power of cultic acts dominated the field for a long time, either consciously or unconsciously; here, more than anywhere else, the prayer and psalm to a freely creating and gracefully giving God was slow in penetrating. We have thanksgiving psalms for the blessings of the year (see Chap. IX.5) but no real prayer-psalms 'for peace and a happy year'—as the old Norse expression runs. For a long time worshippers seem to have contented themselves with the words of general prayer, with which the festal hymn sometimes ends (see above, Chap. IV.3).

Evidently the psalms of prayer for ordinary use gradually evolved out of the increasing habit of repeating on the regular days of prayer psalms of lamentation composed for specific occasions, and out of the Jewish situation indicated by the custom. Of the psalms mentioned above (p. 221), Ps. 90 and to a certain extent Ps. 82 have this general character, possibly also Ps. 58. Ps. 82 prays for the restoration of justice and for the deliverance of the depressed and the improvement of social conditions, which will be the result of the collapse of the tyranny of pagan gods. Ps. 90 in general terms prays that the congregation may see the great works of Yahweh and experience his favour after the long years of suffering, so that every man may have the benefit of the work of his hands in peace. The backbone of it is the deliverance and re-establishment of Israel; all the other benefits follow on from the prayer for deliverance from foreign tyranny. Therefore these psalms, like the later ones of new year and enthronement, are closely connected with the Jewish hope of future re-establishment. The eyes of poet and congregation are turned towards the future, praying for the fulfilment of Israel's hope, 'the turning of the fate' (*šûbh šĕbhûth*). In accordance with the Jewish ideal of humility (see above, p. 216), we may also find the prayer expressed as a gentle wish, a sigh from longing hearts:

> O that the salvation of Israel
>   would come from Zion (soon)!
> When Yahweh turneth his people's fate
>   shall Jacob exult for joy. (14.7)

To this extent we may speak of an eschatological element in these psalms also.

Psalms 123; 130 and 131 are also of the same character. An individual ('I') speaks on behalf of the congregation, identifying himself with its distress: he is, in fact, the liturgical representative of the congregation—the chief priest, or somebody similar.

Two psalms of prayer (Pss. 85 and 126) can most naturally be interpreted as prayers for peace and a happy year, and most probably they belonged to the festival of harvest and new year; at any rate they have the idea of a 'turning of the destiny' in common with this festival; for this term originally indicates the 'turning' which every new year means and is expected to involve. Especially in Ps. 126 it is most natural to take the mention of sowing and reaping as referring to real life, and not merely as a metaphor for 'salvation' in general, the hoped-for restoration. Referring both to the experiences of the past and to the realization of its hope for the future the congregation prays:

> Turn, O Yahweh, our fate again,
>   like streams in the dry south;
> let those who are sowing now in tears,
>   reap with shouts of joy! (126.4f.)

Both psalms mentioned justify the prayer for a 'turning' by referring to a particular occasion known to everybody, on which God had turned the destinies of the people; this probably is a reference to the restoration after the Exile.

That these psalms are related to the psalms of lamentation is seen when what lies behind the prayer is described. Strong colours are used as if referring to a state of acute need and distress. Consequently scholars have been apt to interpret these two psalms as *ad hoc* laments and psalms of prayer, intended to be used on a special day of penance and prayer occasioned by threatening drought and a bad year. That is not necessary. The Old Testament mentality and poetry do not distinguish between need and disaster; the need of something is in itself disaster, distress.[72] The enthronement psalms and other new year psalms show that conditions as they regularly are before the coming of the new year and the rainy season were looked upon and described as a state of acute distress; the powers of chaos have already obtained the mastery, and if nothing happens, if Yahweh does not 'come' and interfere, 'the world' and mankind must perish. That is why the prayers for a new and blessed 'year of goodwill' or 'grace' (Isa. 61.2; Ps. 65.12) receive the character of laments, describing in the most gloomy colours what would otherwise happen, and as if it had already occurred.[73] But even in these two psalms the thought

---

[72] Westermann (in *ZATW* 66, 1954, pp. 44ff.) states that 'the lament' becomes much less prominent in later psalms of supplication and finally disappears, or develops into a literary species (Gattung) of its own (as e.g. in Jer. 20.14–18). In the Psalter, however, there are no pure 'psalms of supplication' without an element of 'lament', and Westermann seems not to have seen the 'cult-functional' difference between those two not strongly defined types. Nor does the transmitted source material allow for Westermann's theory that the most ancient way of addressing God in danger and distress consisted in laments only; the 'original' prayer was rather the 'cry for help'.

[73] Cf. here the sense of the words 'āni and 'ānaw, which mean being insignificant, poor, lowly in general; as well as being for the moment broken-hearted, distressed, oppressed, deprived of one's 'right'. See Birkeland, 'Ani und 'Anaw; Feinde d. Indiv., pp. 317ff.; and below, p. 229, and Additional Note XXIX.

advances; especially in Ps. 85 it is obvious that what, after all, the author is alluding to is the fulfilment of the Israelite hope of re-establishment, and that is what the congregation is including in its prayer.

7

One special kind of prayer is *intercession*.[74] Such, too, has its place in an ordered public worship. This is especially so with regard to the intercession for 'those having authority from God amongst us', i.e. for the person on whom the welfare of people and congregation depends more than on anyone else, above all the king, who in Israel was at the same time the representative of God before the people and of the people before God (see Chap. III. 1–2). Ps. 72 is just such a congregational intercession for the king on the day of his anointing, wishing him all the luck-power and righteousness and piety needed for him to be a king after Yahweh's heart and in conformity with the prevailing ideal of kingship. Ps. 21 belongs rather to the festivities at the annual celebration of the day of anointing and enthronement; it starts with a 'motive of confidence', in the style of the thanksgiving psalms, bringing to mind all the previous blessings which Yahweh has bestowed on the king, and the good wishes for the king end in a prayer for Yahweh to be with the king with his powerful works, so that the congregation in the future also may be able to praise his great works. The first part of Ps. 20 is an intercession for the king before a war or a battle, with a prayer for the victory and renown of his people ('we'); the second part expresses an assurance of being heard in the shape of an anticipatory thanksgiving psalm, and ends by summing up everything in a prayer for help 'to-day'.

Ps. 20, as well as Ps. 21, is partly addressed to the king himself, and in these psalms, as well as in Ps 72, the intercession is distinguished by piling up words of blessing (see Chap. XI); an evidence of the religious and style-historical connexion between the prayer and the word of blessing, which is the cultic origin of the intercession.

In the opinion of the ancient Israelites there was no great difference between the blessing word and the intercessory prayer. They are both to some degree efficacious words, creating what they are expressing. There are also close connexions between such words and the prophetic word, which is also a word filled with creative power. These stylistic and material connexions point, as we shall see later on, to an important element in the old Israelite cult, namely the role of the cult prophet as the intercessor on behalf of the congregation and the king.

[74] On intercession in the O.T. see Eichrodt, *Theologie d. A.T.* II–III, pp. 121ff.; for Jeremiah: Hertzberg, *Prophet und Gott*, pp. 146ff.; cf. also F. Hesse, *Die Fürbitte im A.T.* None of these authors are sufficiently aware of the part played by intercessory prayers in the cult; the view of de Boer in OTS III is more correct.

CHAPTER VII

National Psalms of Lamentation in the I-Form

I

Among the national and congregational psalms of lamentation mentioned in the preceding chapter (p. 194) there are several in which 'I' and 'we' alternate (see 44.5, 16; 74.12; 83.14; 123.1; 60.11). In two of them, Pss. 89 and 144, the lament is put into the mouth of one—in Ps. 89 occasionally referring to himself in the third person singular—who is no doubt the king of the people; 'the Anointed' is what he calls himself in 89.39; and in 144.10 he identifies himself with 'David', thus actually indicating that he is a descendant of David, cf. the 'seed of David' used of the worshipper himself in 18.51. There can be no doubt whatsoever that the distress complained of in Ps. 89 is of a national and political nature: enemies have demolished all the walls of David's descendant and laid his fortresses in ruins and cast his crown into the dust and overthrown his throne. In Ps. 144, too, the king is surrounded by foreign invaders and liars and threatened by 'the sword of evil'.

So, evidently, the national lament may have an individual and personal form. As we have seen, the king acts as the representative and the incorporation of the people: the cause of the people is his cause, and vice versa (see Chap. III).

It would hardly be correct to say that here the national psalm of lamentation has been influenced by the form of the individual lament. The fact is rather that here we still find the earliest form, in this case having two roots: first the collective way of thinking of the ancients, which would look upon the plurality as a totality, a person; and then the official royal style, which would be more interested in the king himself than in what he represented. This has been discussed in detail in Chap. III.3.

The question then presents itself whether other apparent I-laments also may not in fact be royal laments, speaking of national and political disasters and dangers. The answer to that question is in the affirmative. It must be emphasized in this connexion that we are not dealing with possible royal psalms in which the distress is private and personal, for instance illness; such poems belong rather to the true individual psalms of lamentation.

2

Psalm 20 is certainly a national psalm of intercession for the king before he goes to war (see Chap. VI.7), with a very pronounced 'assurance of being heard', behind which lies the explicit promise of the cultic leader (v. 7). So it must belong to the 'protective psalms' (Chap. VI.4).

In Ps. 63 also it is the king who prays; and he does so in a strain of confidence; as yet the emergency is only just on the horizon. Early in the morning the king appears in the Temple to offer up sacrifices and prayers for help against the threatening enemies. Ps. 61, too, must be understood in a similar way, as a prayer accompanying the offerings before the battle, far away from that capital and Temple which the king hopes to see again before long.

Accordingly we must be prepared to find that other I-laments, and particularly such as use martial terms and metaphors (cf. Chap. III.7), are actually national psalms of lamentation speaking of national and political conflicts,[1] the speaker being the king of the people or one of the leading men of the congregation, such as the High Priest, or the governor, or the chairman of the council (the 'prince' of Ezk. 45).[1a]

This explanation readily suggests itself, for instance, in psalms in which Yahweh is called upon to interfere against the 'peoples' or the 'nations' (as in 7.7f.; 56.8; 59.4, 6, 9) or in which there is an emphasis on Yahweh's power as lord and judge of the earth and of the peoples,[2] or on his being God and lord of Jacob, or Israel, as for instance in 22.4f. Or again, the psalm may indicate that the salvation of the worshipper is to have world-wide consequences: all the world shall call it to mind, and all tribes shall come and fall prostrate before the face of Yahweh (22.28). Or the psalm may describe the relationship in which the worshipper stands to Yahweh as being so intimate that it goes beyond what in ancient Israel would be said of a common man, and actually refers back to the old conceptions of the close relationship of the king to the national god. Thus, when the worshipper describes Yahweh as his accoucheur and foster-father (22.10f.), this is a feature belonging to the 'king ideology' of Babylonia as well as of Israel.[3]

---

[1] See Chap. III. 1, and cf. for this problem about congregational psalms in the I-form, Smend, 'Über das Ich der Psalmen', *ZATW* 8, 1888; Buhl, *Psalmerne*,[2] pp. XXXVIff.; Linder, 'Indiv. och kollet. pss.', *Kristendomen och vår tid*, 1928, pp. 45ff.; and now especially Birkeland, *Feinde d. Indiv.*, pp. 114ff. Gunkel was in fact on the right track when, following Balla, he observed on Ps. 44.9, 15 that the singular in this 'we-psalm' alludes to 'the person of the leader and intercessor' (*Die Psalmen*, p. 185). What has prevented both Balla and Gunkel from a full understanding of the phenomenon is (a) their lack of a distinct cultic approach, and (b) the mechanical distinction between I-psalms and we-psalms. It is therefore obviously a step backwards when Westermann in his rather formalistic and not very fruitful paper in *ZATW* 66, 1954, adheres to this merely formal distinction without discussing in principle the textual facts pointed out by the present author in *Ps.St.* and in this chapter (*Offersang og Sangoffer*, pp. 227ff.), and by Birkeland in *Feinde des Individuums*. The weakness of Westermann's position is seen from the fact that without any grounds he declares the vv. 16–17 of Ps. 44 to be 'a fragment of an individual psalm of lamentation'; nor does he make any attempt to deal with the undoubted identity of the 'I' and 'we' in Ps. 89. What we do learn from Westermann's paper is that we can attain no further results if we restrict ourselves to Gunkel's one-sided, formal use of the form-typological point of view ('Gattungsforschung').

[1a] See Chap. III. 6–7.

[2] Ps. 9.6–13, 16–20. See also Ps. 59.14; cf. 58.12; 57.10–12; 94.2, 5, 7, 14 and the evidently congregational psalm 82.8.

[3] See Labat, *Royauté*, pp. 5ff.; Engnell, *Div. Kingship*, p. 16, n. 7, and above, p. 54.

Among such psalms Ps. 94 has a first section which in no respect differs from the complaints and prayers of the national laments, whether it has for its background a single disaster (defeat and occupation) or some more lasting subjection under alien rule, abetted by internal traitors (v. 8). The individual ('I') appearing in the second part and complaining of (the same) distress must then be the representative of the congregation on the day of penance, most likely the king.

Similarly Ps. 102. In the first part (vv. 2–12), the speaker laments over his miserable state of disaster, in the same style and phraseology as a king defeated by his enemies, or a sick person seeking cleansing and health by the ritual ceremonies of the Temple. The second part (vv. 13–18), however, shows that the real point and purpose of the psalm is the prayer for the deliverance and restitution of Jerusalem and Israel, the state of which is described as a permanent oppression by the (heathen) 'nations'. The worshipper prays on behalf of his people, and describes himself as, so to say, suffering on behalf of Jerusalem and Israel. Certain allusions to the ideology of the new year festival (vv. 13f.) seem to indicate that the psalm belonged to this festival, among the prayers for Israel's restitution (see above, pp. 219f.).

Ps. 77 is really also a national psalm of lamentation; the whole people has been struck by disaster; the poet's motivation of his prayer is a reference to the benefits conferred on the people by Yahweh in days of old. The speaker is the representative of the people, whose own disaster is identical with the one which has befallen his people, the congregation of Israel.

Many other psalms make the same point: Pss. 7; 9–10; 54; 42–43; 3; 27 and others.

Several of these psalms are 'protective psalms' ('psalms of confidence'; see Chap. VI.4), not psalms of lamentation properly so called; as yet the emergency is but a threatening danger. That is why we get no such descriptions of the demeanour of the enemy as for instance in Pss. 44 and 74, where the description indeed leaves no doubt that here we have to do with political conflicts and enemies.[4]

3

Some psalms complain of *evil tongues and words*, and more definitely of *false charges* and *mendacious accusations* from 'lying lips' and 'deceitful lips', 'violent lips', and so on:

> They are devising deceitful words,
>   and widening their mouth against me. (35.20b, 21a.)

> False witnesses are risen up against me,
>   breathing out violence (upon me). (27.12.)

---

[4] See above, pp. 197ff. and below, ¶ 6, pp. 241ff. That in these psalms we are dealing first and foremost with national and political enemies and antagonisms, so that to this extent the earlier exegetes were on the right track, has been proved by Birkeland (*Feinde d. Indiv.*), even if he somewhat exaggerates his point of view. See also Additional Note Chap. XXVIII.

The last line refers to the magical blowing of the sorcerer.

> Malicious witnesses have risen up,
> charging me with crimes I know nought of. (35.11.)

We have seen above (Chap. VI.3) that even in the purely national laments, in which the disaster is war and defeat, the evil and injurious 'lying words' play an important part. Words are active instruments of disaster. But the 'lying words' may also contain specific references.

Side by side with complaints of the evil curses and soul-impairing and 'demoniacal' injurious words and sneers and intrigues we hear of evil-minded slanders and false charges (27.2, 12; 35.11). In other psalms Yahweh is called upon to help against the adversary in some lawsuit, or to judge righteously in such a case (35.23f.; 43.1; 7.9; 26.1; 54.3). Or the worshipper rejects an imagined or real accusation (7.4). Besides this, too, the same psalm may speak about the danger of war and hostility on the part of whole 'nations' (7.8; 27.3; 35.1f.; 69.51).

Here again it is the king or the leader of the people who is praying.[5] We know that during the greater part of her existence Israel-Judah was under alien rule; we know also that such a vassal king or governor was always exposed to more or less justifiable (or unjustifiable) accusations before his lord on the part of other, envious neighbouring vassals (as we are told by the governor Nehemiah (6.5–8), or on the part of suspicious superior officials (as we are told about the period after the first return from the Exile (Ezra 4.5ff.; 5.5ff.)), or on the part of subordinates aspiring to a ruler's position. Even the supreme lord himself might find reason for suspicion, and threaten to send an investigating commission or a punitive expedition. The Amarna letters, containing communications from the vassals of the Egyptian king in Syria and Palestine in the fifteenth and fourteenth centuries B.C., give examples of this. Every now and then such a vassal king would be summoned before the supreme king, and this might easily result in deprivation of office and imprisonment; but as in the instance of Manasseh, we see that there might also be hope of pardon (2 Chron. 33.10ff.). Something of the same kind is recorded about Pharaoh Psamthek's father Neku, who was a kinglet in the delta of the Nile, and an Assyrian vassal.[6]

In such disaster and danger the king or governor of Judah does what Manasseh did: humbles himself, and turns to Yahweh with the usual rites of fasting and penance and with psalms. He protests his innocence and prays for help against the mendacious accusations and false lips of deceitful

---

[5] H. Schmidt, *Gebet des Angeklagten*, has tried to prove that we have in these psalms private individuals who have been accused before the authorities of Israel and who are now in ritual forms praying to Yahweh for an acquitting oracle, perhaps by successfully passing some sort of 'ordeal'. Schmidt's hypothesis has been accepted by Bentzen (*Indledning til de gml. t.-lige Salmer; Fortolkning til Salmerne*), Leslie (*The Psalms Translated and Interpreted*) and others. But Birkeland (op. cit.) provides clear evidence that we have here national problems and relations with foreign rulers. See also *GTMMM* IV, introductory remarks on Pss. 7; 26; 35; 54 and others.

[6] Rassam-Cyl. I, 90ff., II, 8ff. See Streck, *Assurbanipal*, pp. 11f., 15f., cf. pp. CCLXXVIIf.

enemies. When the protective psalms speak of 'lying words' and 'lying enemies' they may in many cases refer to enemies of this kind.

These national psalms in the I-form, as well as the real individual psalms to be discussed in the following chapter, have frequently been interpreted as giving evidence of religious and social antagonisms and party disputes inside Israel or the Jewish congregation itself. Above all, this conception has been attached to the terms 'the oppressed' ('suffering', 'poor', Hebr. '$\bar{a}n\hat{\imath}$ and '$\bar{a}n\bar{a}w$), often occuring in these psalms,[7] and taken to indicate the socially inferior and oppressed 'tendency' or 'party' of the pious within the congregation; the enemies in these psalms, the 'ungodly' (the 'wicked' —$r\check{e}\check{s}\bar{a}'\hat{\imath}m$) were then supposed to indicate the wordly and well-to-do upper class or a movement that did not take the law too seriously, and would oppress the 'poor', pious people.[8]

This interpretation has proved to be false.[9] Neither religious and social party disputes, nor any 'class struggle', form the background of these psalms, but national-religious antagonisms and external political events. The 'oppressed', or 'humble'—the above mentioned Hebrew may mean either—are no party nor class, but Israel, or her representative men in times of emergency 'oppressed' by external enemies, 'helpless' in their own power, 'in need of help', and 'humbly' hoping for the interference of Yahweh. That the external enemy may in some cases be supported by traitors inside Israel itself, and that 'the enemies', 'the ungodly', and so on, may sometimes include even some Israelite 'quislings', is another matter, and does not alter the general picture of these psalms.

4

Between the national I-laments and the normal national psalms of lamentation ('we'-psalms) the only essential difference of form and content is that which results from substituting the first person singular. Structure and substance are the same: *the invocation*, generally one of the first words of the psalm,[10] and as a rule without any hymnal amplification,[11] but often with additional words emphasizing the relationship of the worshipper to Yahweh: 'my God', 'the God of Israel', and so on;[12] then *the complaint*[13] about the distress, not forgetting its mental aspect, described by means

---

[7] Complete statistics in Birkeland '*Ani und 'Anaw*, p. 1.

[8] See Additional Note XXIX.

[9] See n.8.

[10] Pss. 3.2; 5.2; 7.2; 13.2; 16.1; 17.1; 28.1; 35.1 and other places. Later in the psalm: 42.2; 120.2; Isa. 38.14.—A second invocation at the beginning of a new section: 3.4, 8; 5.9, 11; 7.4, 7; 13.4; 17.6, 13; 43.1; 69.4, 7; 71.13, 17; 77.12; 86.12, 14, etc.—Repeated at the end: 3.8; 43.4.—At other places within the psalm: 4.9; 5.13; 17.18; 27.11; 54.7; 59.13; 69.30; 71.4f., 14f.; 140.8f. and many other places. Cf. Chap. VI. 3. (Statistics after Gunkel).

[11] Such a hymnal addition is found in Jer. 17.12ff.; Prayer of Manasses.

[12] Pss. 3.8; 7.2, 4; 13.4; 16.1; 17.1; 30.9; 35.23; 43.4; 59.12; 86.4f., 8, 15; 69.7, etc.

[13] Pss. 3.2–5; 5.10; 10.1–11; 13.1–3; 27.10; 22.2f., 7–9, 15–19; 31.10–14; 42.2–4, 7–12; 43.2; 54.5; 55.4–6, 10–12, 13–15, 19–22; 56.3; 57.5; 59.4, 7f.; 64.4–7; 69.1b–5, 8–13, 20–22; 102.4–12, 24f., etc.

of many different metaphors,[14] and about the enemies,[15] about mockery
and sneers,[16] about evil words and sorcery on the part of ungodly and
deceitful enemies and about contemptuous malevolent rejoicing on the
part of neighbours and former friends;[17] in addition questions as to
'why?' or 'how long?';[18] next, the *prayers for help*,[19] supported by *motivations of the prayer* (Chap. VI.3); the 'motive of confidence' is particularly
prominent, and in many forms;[20] side by side with it may occur 'hymnal
motives',[21] 'motives of compassion', such as the brevity and troubles of
human life,[22] the 'motive of honour',[23] of 'innocence',[24] and of 'penitence',
with confession of sins;[25] finally the *promise* of sacrifice,[26] and expression
of thanksgiving,[27] and the *assurance* that the prayer will be heard[28] with
more or less marked anticipatory thanksgiving,[29] and reference to the
predictions of the priest or temple prophet.[30]

A few examples may serve to illustrate these different elements. *The
invocation* and the *complaint*, especially of deceit and treachery, are brought
out by this introductory stanza:

> Help, Yahweh! for loyalty (*ḥesedh*) is no more,
>   fidelity has vanished now from mankind.
> They speak falsity one to the other,
>   with flattering lips and double minds. (12.2f.)

---

[14] Pss. 42.5; 31.10; 13.3; 40.13, 18; 42.6, 12; 43.5; 102.1.

[15] Pss. 3.2f., 8; 5.9; 7.2f., 6f., 13–17; 13.3, 5; 17.4–14; 27.2f., 6, 11f.; 35.1–8, 11–21, 24–26; 40.15f.; 55.4, 13, 19–22, 24 and many other places, even in the 'account of the distress' in the thanksgiving psalms, for instance 27.2f.

[16] Pss. 22.7f.; 27.11; 31.12, 19, 21; 35.16, 19, 21; 40.16; 42.10f.; 43.2; 54.7; 55.13; 69.10, 20; 109.25; 142.5. Cf. Job 17.2; 19.14f.

[17] Pss. 3.3; 22.9; 35.21, 25; 40.16; 41.6, 9; 42.4, 11; 64.6f.; 71.11. Cf. Jer. 11.19; 17.5; 18.18; 20.10. See above, Chap VI. 3 and n. 16 and 19, and for details, Chap. VIII. 2, 4.

[18] Pss. 4.3; 10.1, 13; 22.2; 42.10; 43.2.

[19] Pss. 4.2; 5.2f., 9, 11; 7.2, 7, 9; 13.4; 16.1; 17.1ff., 6–9, 13f., and many other places; complete statistics in Gunkel-Begrich, *Einl.*, p. 218, n. 7, and for the different kinds of prayers ibid., pp. 219ff. Cf. above, Chap. VI. 3.

[20] Pss. 13.6; 16.1f.; 26.1; 31.7, 15; 55.24; 56.4; 57.2; 62.2.—Pss. 5.5; 23.4; 27.1; 56.5, 12; 59.9, 11.—Pss. 7.2; 11.1; 16.1; 31.2; 42.2; 57.2; 59.10; 61.5; 63.2; 71.1; 130.6; 143.6.—Pss. 3.4; 31.4; 22.10; 71.5; 42.3, 9; 27.1, 9; 22.5f.; 70.6; 102.15–23; 143.5, etc. For details, Gunkel-Begrich, *Einl.*, pp. 232–236.

[21] Pss. 7.11; 22.4; 25.6, 8–10, 14; 31.4; 86.5, 8.

[22] Pss. 89.48; 109.23; cf. the psalms of illness, 6.6; 30.10; 39.5.

[23] Pss. 10.13; 69.8, 10; cf. Jer. 15.15.

[24] 5.5–8; 7.4f.; 17.3–5; 26.4–8; 35.7, 19; 59.4; 69.10. Cf. the psalm of illness, 38.21.

[25] Pss. 25.11; 40.13; 69.6; prayer of Manasses, vv. 6f. Cf. Ps. 51.5–7, and the psalm of illness, 39.9f., 28. See Chap. VI. 3.

[26] Pss. 27.6; 54.8; 56.13; 61.9.

[27] Pss. 27.6; 54.8; 61.9.—Pss. 7.18; 13.6; 22.23ff.; 26.12; 27.6; 28.6f.; 31.8f.; 35.9f., 27f.; 42.6; 43.4f.; 52.11; 54.8; 56.13f.; 57.8f.; 59.17; 63.3, 6; 69.31ff.; 71.8, 14–16; 86.12ff.; 109.30; 119.171f., 175; 140.14; 142.8; 144.9. Cf. 51.15f.; 119.7 and the psalm of illness, 39.9f., 28. See Chap. VI. 3.

[28] Pss. 3.8; 5.13; 7.11–14; 13.6; 16.10f.; 26.12; 27.13; 36.13; 52.10; 55.24; 56.10–12; 57.7; cf. the psalm of illness, 6.8–11. See Chap. VI. 3.

[29] Pss. 22.24ff.; 56.14; 69.34ff.

[30] Pss. 56.10; 140.13.

The worshipper complains of *suffering* and *distress*:

> I am wearied with crying, my throat is dried,
> mine eyes are weak with waiting for my God. (69.4.)

and of threatening *enemies*:

> For strangers are risen up against me,
> oppressors are seeking now my life. (54.4.)

or of the *sorcery* and *deceit* of his enemies:

> He's pregnant with witchcraft, alive with malice
> (against me)—but shall bring forth deception;
> a deep pit he has digged out—
> and shall tumble into his own pitfall. (7.15f.)

> He is sprinkling witchcraft over me,
> and sets upon me furiously. (55.4b.)

and of *mockery* and *sneers*:

> I chasten my soul with fasting—
> they only jeer at me;
> I wear sack-cloth as my garment—
> and have become their byword;
> they that sit in the gate talk of me;
> I have become the beer-drinkers' song. (69.11–13.)

In all this need and trouble the sufferer *prays for help*:

> O Yahweh, listen to my words,
> consider my recital,
> hearken unto my cry for help,
> O thou, my King and God! (5.2f.)

> O Yahweh, my God, I trust in thee;
> deliver me from all my pursuers,
> lest he tear me like a lion,
> devouring me with none to rescue! (7.2f.)

The worshipper pleads *grounds for granting his prayer*. Not only a description of his wretchedness and need, but also, and not infrequently, his *confidence in Yahweh*:

> In Yahweh do I take my refuge.
> How dare you say, then, to my soul:
> 'Flee to the mountains like a bird,
> for wicked men have bent their bow'. (11.1f.)

For Yahweh would take care of the helpless:

> For thou beholdest toil and grief,
> thou seest the helpless and fatherless;
> he leaves his case in thine hands,
> thou art his helper, thou (alone). (10.14.)

Therefore the worshipper appeals to his *compassion*:

> But I am a worm, and not a man,
>> derided by men, by my relatives despised. . . .
> My soul is now poured out like water
>> and all my bones are out of joint;
> my heart has now become like wax,
>> is melted here within my breast;
> dry as a potsherd is my throat,
>> my tongue is cleaving to my jaws.
> I can count every bone in my body,
>> (my foes) are gloating over me.
> They've laid me down in the dust of death,
>> and bound my hands and feet (with grave-cloths);
> They are dividing my clothes among them,
>> Are casting lots for (all) my garments.
>>> (22.7, 15, 16a, 18, 16b, 17b, 19.)

He *does penance and confesses his sins*, as Yahweh would demand from the trespasser:

> O God, thou knowest my sinful folly,
>> No fault of mine is hid from thee. (69.6.)

So far the suffering has been deserved:

> My transgressions have overtaken me,
>> I cannot bear them any more.
> They are more than the hairs of my head,
>> and my heart has failed me now. (40.13.)

And so he must *ask God's forgiveness*, and do penance:

> O Yahweh, for the sake of thy name,
>> pardon my guilt, for it is great! (25.11.)

But more often the suppliant feels guiltless in relationship to his enemies, and pleads his *innocence* as the ground of the prayer:

> O Yahweh, my God, if I have done it,
>> if there be iniquity in my hands,
> if I have rewarded evil to my ally,
>> if I have plundered my foe for no cause. (7.4f.)

> Trying my heart, searching me out in the night,
>> testing me—thou shalt find no shameful deed.
> My mouth did not trespass at the (wrong) deeds of men,
>> the words of thy lips I have (always) heeded.
> In the paths of the robber [I never walked,
>> on the roads of the wicked I never wandered];
> my footsteps have steadfastly followed thy track,
>> they have never faltered [on thy paths]. (17.3–5.)

And in any case it will *add to the honour of Yahweh*, if he shows that he is going to help his faithful servant, who trusts him and depends on him:

> For thou art my rock, thou art my castle,
>   [where I can hide myself]
> and, Yahweh, for the sake of thy name,
>   Thou wilt lead me and guide me—Thou! (31.4.)

> It is for thy sake that I suffer taunts,
>   that shame now covers my face. . . .
> Zeal for thy house has eaten me up,
>   taunts against thee fall upon me. (69.8, 10.)

Here also we meet the question '*Wherefore?*':

> Wherefore shall the wicked disdain God,
>   thinking that thou wilt never punish? (10.13.)

The confident appeal to the honour and faithfulness of Yahweh sometimes takes the form of a hymn (cf. above, Chaps. IV.3; VI.3):

> But Yahweh is within his sacred palace,
>   Yahweh is enthroned in the heavens,
> his eyes behold [the whole earth],
>   his glance tests all mankind. (11.4.)

> My shield that covers [me] is God,
>   who saveth the upright heart;
> God is a judge who maintaineth the right,
>   indignant every day. (7.11f.)

> Thou, Lord, art kind, and ready to forgive,
>   rich in love to all who call on thee. . . .
> There is no God like thee, O Lord,
>   there are no deeds like thy deeds.
> All nations shall come and bow down before thee,
>   glorifying thy name, O Lord.
> For thou art great, thou workest wonders,
>   thou, only thou, art God. (86.5, 8–10.)

As in psalms in the we-form the *vow* originally referred to a thanksgiving sacrifice:[31]

> I will offer sacrifices of joy within his shrine,
>   and sing praises unto Yahweh. (27.6.)

But in the psalms before us it generally has reference to a thanksgiving feast with thanksgiving psalm and hymns 'in the midst of the congregation'. In fact, the thanksgiving sacrifice is involved in this vow as a matter of course; we can see this, for instance, from the reference to it in the vow of a thanksgiving song in Ps. 22.23ff. But the psalmists stand for

[31] See above, n. 26.

an estimate of the various elements of the cult, different from that of the priests; they rank the hymn above the sacrifice and the other elements of the cult: they consider the thanksgiving psalm better than the sacrifice, indeed it is the essential part of the sacrifice, the real sacrifice. That is why this element is emphasized in the promise:[32]

> I will give thee thanks in the great congregation,
> I will praise thee in the throng of worshippers;
> and all day long my tongue shall talk
> of thy justice and thy praiseworthiness. (35.18, 28.)

> I will praise thee, Yahweh, for evermore,
> because thou has showed (kindness to me),
> I will proclaim thy name, how good it is,
> in the presence of the men of thy covenant. (52.11.)

Trusting all these reasons ('motivations') why Yahweh should grant the prayer, the worshipper's *assurance of being heard* is a standing part of the psalm of lamentation:

> Surely I believe that I shall see
> the goodness of Yahweh, in the land of the living. (27.13.)

> I lay me down and sleep (secure),
> I waken, for Yahweh doth uphold me;
> I fear not an army of (many) myriads
> ranged against me all around me . . . .
> For thou breakest the cheekbone of all mine enemies,
> and crushest the teeth of the wicked (foes).
> It is Yahweh's to bring salvation,
> Thy blessing is upon thy people. (3.6–9.)

Sometimes there is a reference to the *oracle* on which the assurance rests:

> Blessed be Yahweh, because he has heard
> my voice of supplication!
> Yahweh is my strength and shield,
> my heart is trusting him. (28.6f.)

> Then shall mine enemies turn their backs.
> This is what I know: that God is for me.
> Through God I then shall praise the word,
> through Yahweh I shall praise his word. (56.10f.)

The statement of assurance not infrequently is expressed as an assurance that the worshipper will soon have reason to sing a thanksgiving psalm

---

[32] See above, n. 27.

to Yahweh in the congregation. While 'the violence of the wicked shall drop on his own head',

> I shall have to thank Yahweh for his salvation,
>> and sing praise to the name of the Lord most high.
>>>>>> (7.18.)

Here the promise is included in a more indirect form:

> So I shall praise thee on the lute
>> for thy loyalty, my God,
> and sing thy praises on the lyre,
>> O Holy One of Israel!

> My lips shall ring with joyful praise,
>> as I sing and play unto thee;
> even the life which thou hast saved
>> [shall praise thy grace unto me]. (71.22f.)

But often the poet would sing about his assurance in an *anticipatory thanksgiving psalm*, for with the oracle the prayer is already granted:

> I am under vows to thee, O God,
>> I will pay thee my sacrifice of praise.
> For thou hast saved my life from death,
>> hast saved my feet from stumbling,
> that I might walk before God's face
>> in the brilliant light of life. (56.13f.)

The difference from the we-laments which may be observed is natural, considering the different points of view: the we-laments look at the distress or danger from the point of view of the people and all the individuals, whereas the I-psalms look at everything from the point of view of the leading person, the king. That is why the former speak much more about the ravaging of land and city and temple, of the lost battles of 'our armies', and as motivation of the prayer will use the promises God had given to the Fathers and the benefits he had bestowed on them, the aid experienced from him in the history of the people. These elements are not completely wanting in the I-psalms either, see for instance 89.41f.; 22.4ff. But particularly important here, as already mentioned, are the complaints resulting from the uncertain position of the vassal king: the complaints of deceit and intrigues and false accusations and such 'violent conduct'. And on the whole, hostility, lying words, curses and sneers are all related to the praying king (leader of the people) himself, as being *his* disaster and as an attack on *him*; the suffering is what he personally feels, *he* is the one to be attacked and sneered at, the disgrace is the loss of honour that he himself has suffered; sometimes it is even emphasized that the success and triumph of the enemies, and his own defeat and disgrace have made him ill (69.21).

But this does not mean any essential difference in the nature of the distress or the enemies; in a whole series of I-psalms the distress, as we have seen, is of a political nature and the enemies are foreign foes and (or) internal traitors. The chief difference is that in the I-psalms we hear more often of attempts to get at the king personally and to remove him from his office, than of real battle tactics. But even where it is a matter of war—in the protective psalms about threatening attacks—everything is related to the king's own person. This royal egocentricity is just as evident in an undoubtedly national lament like Ps. 89, and we find it again in the royal thanksgiving psalm, Ps. 18, where, too, the background is war with its dangers. In short, the characteristic feature of the public I-psalms as distinguished from the we-psalms is the *oriental king-Ego style*, so well known from the old royal inscriptions with their royal I-form: the cause of people and state is looked upon as the personal—so to speak private— cause of the king himself; the whole picture is dominated by the king, so as to make him overshadow the totality he is representing.[33]

Of course this leads to a certain differentiation of detail. Hence the prayer will sometimes have a more personal character, since the very destiny of the people is dependent on the personal relationship of the king to Yahweh (Chap. III). False accusations and intrigues are included in the complaint. The prayer seems to become more fervent: 'I call out to thee', 'I cry', 'I implore thee'.[34] The suppliant calls attention to his personal situation and state of mind.[35] And because the disaster of the people is often occasioned by the sin of the king (the leader), the petition for forgiveness of sins and averting of the punishment will be more pro-minent.[36] Or the king will plead his personal righteousness and blameless-ness.[37] He will also ask for preservation from sin, and for God's guidance to walk righteously.[38] The prayer for help and salvation takes on the form of a prayer for an opportunity of singing psalms of thanksgiving to Yahweh.[39] Even the prayer for the destruction of enemies will sometimes have a more personal nuance.[40]

The *wish form* is more prominent in the prayer than in the pure we-psalms,[41] especially the cursing wish against the enemies.[42] It is signi-ficant that in the I-psalms the cursing wish, which is the older form, is

---

[33] Mowinckel, *Statholderen Nehemia*, pp. 124ff.; *Gunkel Festschrift, Eucharisterion* I [*FRLANT* 36], pp. 278ff.

[34] Pss. 5.4; 17.6; 27.8; 28.2; 57.3; 61.3; 63.2; 69.4; 77.2; 102.6; 130.1; 141.1.

[35] Pss. 5.4; 7.2; 17.1; 37.2; 42.2f., 9; 71.1; 77.3.

[36] Ps. 143.2; prayer of Manasses, v. 12; cf. Pss. 25.18; 51.3f., and the psalms of illness, 6.2; 38.2.

[37] Pss. 26.1f., 9; 7.9; 35.24; 43.1. Cf. 139.23f.; Jer. 12.3.

[38] Pss. 5.9; 25.4; 27.10f.; 90.12; 141.3f.; 143.8, 10; cf. 51.12–14.

[39] Pss. 5.12; 20.6; 31.8; 35.9, 28; 40.17; 43.4; 51.10, 16; 52.8; 63.6; 69.7; 71.14–16; 109.30; 142.8.

[40] Pss. 5.11; 7.7, 9; 10.15; 28.4; 35.1, 3; 59.6; 69.24f., 28; 109.6; 143.12. Cf. Jer. 12.3; 15.15; 18.21, 23.

[41] See references in n. 36.

[42] Pss. 7.10; 9.18; 31.18; 34.4, 8, 26; 35.8, 19, 24f.; 40.16; 54.7; 55.16, 24; 56.8, 10; 57.5; 59.13; 63.10f.; 64.9; 69.23, 26, 29; 71.13; 86.17; 109.9ff., 29.

much more frequent than the prayer for the destruction of the enemies; this confirms the conjecture that the I-psalm as a style of writing is older and more original than the we-psalm (see above, p. 194). The fact that Yahweh is not often named as the subject of these wishes for punishment points in the same direction; as a rule the old cursing formula belonging to the idea of the self-active word has been retained.

There is a certain difference, too, with regard to the *motivation of the prayer*;[43] even the latter becomes more personal, when the king himself is in the foreground, and distress and salvation are looked upon as something which in the first place concern him. This applies for instance to a special kind of 'motive of honour'; the suppliant points to the fact that Yahweh will lose a faithful servant, eager to praise him, if he allows him to go under; it is taken for granted that Yahweh wants to be praised and honoured, but the dead, having been 'plucked out of his hand' cannot praise him; in Sheol there are no sounds of praise![44]

> For Sheol does not sing thy praise,
>   Death does not celebrate thee;
> and those who have passed down to the pit
>   have no hope of thy love. (Isa. 38.18.)

So also in the 'private' sickness psalm (Chap. VIII):

> Dost thou work wonders for the dead,
>   do ghosts arise to sing thy praise?
> Do they recount they love in the grave,
>   thy faithfulness in the world below?
> Can thy wonders be known in the land of darkness,
>   thy saving help in the land of oblivion? (88.11–13.)

This note is heard even in a purely congregational psalm:

> The dead, they do not praise Yahweh,
>   nor any who sink to the silent land.
> But we, we will bless Yahweh
>   from this time forth and for evermore. (115.17f.)

As we have seen above (Chap. VI.4), the national psalms of lamentation in the I-form also can be divided into psalms of lamentation proper and *protective psalms*; in fact, the latter type is comparatively frequent. It belongs to the very nature of the protective psalm that the worshipper will emphasize his confidence in Yahweh, that he is not going to fail him when in danger. The accent is more confident because distress is as yet only threatening. This tends to strengthen the personal touch, often found in these psalms; evidently it is easier for the poet to find expressions for it when he is able to identify himself with the individual in whose name the

---

[43] See notes 20–25 and Chap. VI. 3.
[44] Pss. 115.16f., and the psalms of illness, 6.6; 30.10; 88.11ff.; Isa. 38.18f. Cf. Sir. 17.27f.; Bar. 2.17f.

psalm has been composed.[45] So it is significant that most of the psalms
called 'psalms of confidence' are to be found among the national psalms
in the I-form. We can easily understand this if the suppliant is supposed
to be king of Israel, Yahweh's anointed and 'son', having a particularly
close relationship to the god of the people, and able to rely on 'the everlasting promises of faithfulness to David' and to his offspring.[46] This feature
of warm personal confidence becomes prominent especially in cases where
the prayer part of the psalm is preceded by a hymnal thanksgiving, as in
Pss. 27 and 40. We may quote the first part of Ps. 27, where he who prays
is no doubt a king in the typically bad situation of a vassal king, as described above, pp. 238f.:

> Yahweh is my light and aid;
>   whom should I fear?
> Yahweh is the fortress of my life;
>   whom should I dread?
>
> When wicked men set upon me,
>   with slanders devouring me,
> 'Tis they, my enemies and foes,
>   who stumble to their fall.
>
> Though an host should encamp against me,
>   my heart would have no fear;
> though war should rise against me—still
>   would I be confident.
>
> One thing alone I ask from Yahweh,
>   one thing do I desire . . . ,
> to behold the beauty of Yahweh,
>   and inquire in his palace.
>
> For he hides me in his pavilion
>   whenever trouble comes;
> he shelters me within his tent,
>   takes me up upon his rock.
>
> Then shall my head be lifted up
>   over all my foes around,
> I shall offer sacrifice of joy
>   and sing praises unto Yahweh. (27.1–6.)

The 'inquiry' mentioned in v. 4 is the ritual examination of the omina
in connexion with the festal sacrifices (see below, II.53). To 'behold
the beauty of the god' is an old cultic expression also found in Egypt,

---

[45] We shall see below in Chap. XVII 2, that in a certain sense we have to distinguish between
the author and the pray-er ('the worshipper') of the psalms.
[46] Isa. 55.3; cf. Pss. 89.20ff.; 132.11f.; 18.51.

which originally meant the corporeal vision of the unveiled statue of the god at the festivals, as the highest religious experience. In Yahwism it has become a metaphor for the more spiritual experience of the grace and benevolence of Yahweh manifested especially at the festival of his personal 'epiphany' in the Temple. The verse obviously alludes to the position of the king as the sacral leader of the festal cult; his highest desire is to hold this position with its personal relation to Yahweh also in the future.

5

We shall here draw attention to a particular feature in the description of distress, which in the nature of the case could only occur in the I-psalms, but does so both in the properly national laments and in the authentic individual laments (Chap. VIII), namely the description of the distress not only as a deadly danger but as a real *state of death*.[47] The suppliant finds himself in the underworld (Sheol, Hades), in the 'pit', the 'well':[48]

> For trouble fills my soul to the full,
>   my life draws near unto Sheol;
> I am reckoned among those who sink to the pit,
>   I am like the man who has no strength. . . .
> Thou hast laid me in the lowest pit,
>   in the darkness, in the ocean's deep;
> thy wrath lies heavy upon me
>   and all thy waves overwhelm me. (88.4f., 7f.)

The worshipper feels he is about to be submerged by 'the waters of the underworld', by its 'floods and breakers', he has sunk into the 'mire', 'the sorrows of hell compass him about; the snares of death prevent' him:[49]

> Save me, O God, for the waters have
>   come up unto my throat!
> Now I have sunk deep in the mire
>   where foothold there is none;
> I have fallen into waters deep,
>   and floods sweep over me. (69.2f.)

Nothing worse could happen, for down there Yahweh performs no more miracles, and nobody will have an opportunity there of praising him for his help;[50] if a man has really descended there, he 'shall never again see Yahweh in the land of the living'.[51] Behind this there is the probably

---

[47] Pss. 102.12, 24f.; 109.23; 22.19; 41.6, 9 (psalm of illness); 13.4; 143.7; 51.16.
[48] Ps. 88.4; cf. in the thanksgiving psalms 103.4; 107.20; Jonah 2.7; Isa. 38.10; further Pss. 28.1; 30.10; 69.16; 88.5, 7; 143.7.
[49] Pss. 42.8; 18.5; Jonah 2.4; Pss. 40.3; 69.2f.; 18.6.
[50] Pss. 115.16ff.; 28.1; cf. the psalms of illness 6.6; 30.10; 88.11ff.
[51] Isa. 38.10f.; cf. Pss. 42.8; 130.1; 143.7.

Babylonian conception of the underworld as the depth of the ocean, the primeval ocean under the earth.[52] In keeping with this the sufferer is saved from the danger of death, as Yahweh descends, cleaving the depths of the ocean, stretching out his hand, and drawing him out of the pit, the mire, the foaming waters, and setting his feet upon a rock.[53]

This does not mean that death has actually occurred in our sense of the word. 'Life' to the Israelite means a full and happy life in health and welfare, in the 'light', in the 'land of the living'; 'death' means 'darkness', including any impairment of 'life' in this wide sense.[54] From the Israelite point of view the sick person, or the man who is in danger of death and marked by fear and despair, already carries death about with him, or death has him in its jaws: his soul has left him (cf. 1 Sam. 30.12). Therefore Yahweh must pull him out before it becomes too late. For God can do such a thing, even if according to the ancient faith the realm of the dead lay outside the domain of Yahweh, so that a man who was there, had been 'plucked out of his hand' (88.6; see above, p. 237). We are here dealing with a conception which naturally can only be applied to an individual. Originally it was probably a transfer to the king of the conception of the deity's 'descent into the nether world', of the dying and rising deities of fertility and, in so far, is of foreign origin; we also come across it in Babylonian psalms.[55] It may originally have been transferred to the king as the 'representative incorporation of the people' in the rituals of penitence, and it has as its background the ritual role of the king as the dying and rising partner of the Mother Goddess (cf. above, p. 136). In Israel the conception has been taken over unaware of this original meaning.

Since the thanksgiving psalm (Chap. X) praises Yahweh for having already pulled the unfortunate person out of Sheol, it is evidently no question here of salvation into another life after death, but of deliverance from imminent danger of death into health and happiness and freedom on this earth. According to the Israelite way of thinking, sickness, weakness and dissolution mean 'death', whereas strength and health mean 'life'; 'life' is not mere existence, but full, rich, happy life in 'entirety' and 'welfare' (šālôm).[56] Neither Israel nor early Judaism knew of a faith in any resurrection, nor is such a faith represented in the psalms. Of course the almighty Yahweh *might* every now and then call a dead man back to

[52] See Pedersen, *Israel* I–II, pp. 453ff.; *GTMMM* I, p. 351, n. *a* to Deut. 4.18.

[53] Pss. 9.14; 40.2f.; 71.20; 144.7; and cf. the thanksgiving psalm 18.8ff.; Job 33.28; Sir. 51.2ff.

[54] See Johs. Pedersen, *Israel* I–II, pp. 151ff., 179f.; A. R. Johnson, *The Vitality of the Individual,* and *Studies in Prophecy,* ed. H. H. Rowley, pp. 82ff. See also Gierlich, *Der Lichtgedanke in den Psalmen,* a handy collection of material but lacking a sufficient consideration of the cultural background and the ancient Israelite way of thinking; Aalen, *Licht und Finsternis,* pp. 63ff., 70f.

[55] See Sellin, *Zwölfprophetenbuch,*[2] p. 295; Jeremias, *A.T. im Lichte d. A.O.,*[4] pp. 723ff.; v. Baudissin, *Adonis u. Esmun,* p. 409.

[56] Cf. Gunkel-Begrich, *Einl.,* pp. 185ff.; Wheeler Robinson in *The Psalmists,* pp. 57ff.; Birkeland in *SEÅ* XIII, 1948, pp. 43ff.; the same in *StTh* III, pp. 6off. A. R. Johnson, *The Vitality of the Individual,* pp. 88–107.

life, or give his prophets the power of raising some one from the dead, as we hear in connexion with both Elijah and Elisha. But normally he would do no such thing, and practical religion did not take it into account. The religion of the psalms possesses every qualification for the development of a belief in resurrection, were the 'catalysing' impulse but added, but this came only as a result of the influence of Persian ideas.[57] When the psalms speak of the distressed worshipper as if he were already in the realm of the dead, *we* should call that a 'metaphor'; but to the ancients it meant something more: the concept of the permanent war between the powers of Life and Death, and the faith in the omnipotence of Yahweh, able to deliver a man, even if he was already between the jaws of death.

When a man is struck with disaster or illness, his life literally hangs in the balance. He is alive, and yet he is dead. This is but another expression for the paradoxical position in which the 'righteous one' finds himself when evil powers and impurity have 'made him unrighteous' (see above, pp. 207, 216). It is, so to speak, a matter of split seconds: Yahweh has to interfere immediately and prevent death from making the righteous man unrighteous—for such a thing would be not only logically absurd, but morally and cosmically unmaintainable as well, a break of the covenant and of the very order of the world and its laws instituted by God.

Expressions like those in Pss. 16.10; 17.15; 49.16; 73.23ff. must be understood against this background. Here also the intention is to express assurance that Yahweh will never fail his pious ones, but will save them from mortal peril and deliver them from an evil and sudden death—till they die, some time, 'old and full of days'.[58] That this firm faith deepened and broadened in later Judaism and in the light of Christianity is not our concern here. Ps. 73 shows how near even ancient Israel might approach to it: the bliss of communion with God becomes the highest value, going on beyond life and death.

6

The preceding exposé has proved that in the national psalms of lamentation, as well as in those I-laments which are actually national (congregational), we have real *historical conditions* and happenings; the needs and dangers are disasters which either have already befallen or else threaten people and king from actual, foreign enemies, partly supported by internal traitors—this is so, even if the psalms in most cases use such indefinite, general and conventional terms that we cannot now identify the historical

---

[57] See the short but excellent statement by Birkeland in *SEÅ* XIII, 1948, and in *StTh* III, pp. 6off. That the psalms of lamentation and thanksgiving know nothing of a faith in resurrection has also been noted by Chr. Barth, though in *Die Errettung vom Tode* he presents his thoughts in a form which is rather unscriptural and too much of the nature of subtle German philosophy, without the proper cultic perspective needed in order to understand the psalms fully (see the review by Kapelrud in *SEÅ* XIII, 1948, pp. 55ff.). De Groot, *De Psalmen*, goes much too far in finding belief in a future life in the psalms.

[58] See Additional Note XXX.

happenings and enemies to which they may refer.[58a] In no less than
five 'I-psalms' the enemies are expressly called '(foreign) nations', *gôyîm*,
'ammîm, *zārîm*.[58b] That we meet the 'nations' as the enemies of the king
when he is speaking on behalf of the whole people is only what we should
expect.[58c] Other psalms of this type presuppose alien domination.[58d] The
sufferer is the butt for the mockeries of the neighbouring peoples in the
royal psalm, Ps. 89. 42, 46, 51, as is the whole people in the national
psalms of lamentation, Pss. 44.14; 79.4, 12; 80.7. About the reality of
the historico-political situation of such psalms there can be no doubt.

It may be seen from the allusions to temple and cult found in some of
them[59] that these psalms too had a place in the cultic operations of the
Temple, made necessary by distress or threatening danger. But in some
cases the psalm was evidently supposed to be recited somewhere far away
from capital and Temple, e.g. we hear of the king 'crying from the end
of the earth' (61.3); in Pss. 42–43 he turns to Yahweh 'from the land of
Jordan and of the Hermonite hills'; perhaps it is meant to be taken
literally, when in Ps. 120 the suppliant says that he 'must sojourn as a
guest (*gûr*) among archers in the tents of the tribe of Kedar'. Obviously
this does not mean that the psalm in question must be a non-cultic poem
by a private individual living in exile, as for instance Gunkel holds; even
here the worshipper is the representative of the whole people; in Ps.
61.7, he calls himself 'the king' in plain words; in Pss. 42–43 he is looking
back on all the times he used to lead the pageant up to the Temple of
Yahweh. From a study of such passages we come to the conclusion that
during the period of the kings any place might be consecrated as a place
of sacrifice for the performance of the necessary cultic acts in wartime—
and in these psalms we are dealing with warfare (1 Sam. 14.33f.)—just
as the Assyrian kings used to take a transportable altar along with them
when making war. That such cultic acts were performed and psalms
recited on the battlefield even in late Jewish times may be concluded from
one of the Dead Sea Scrolls (IQM), where certain rituals and hymns for
cultic field services are found. Certainly the book speaks about the last,
eschatological, battle against the Sons of Darkness,[60] but as these are to be
found in the historical people, the Kittim, the cultic scenes, too, may have
been modelled after the pattern of real customs and rituals, as e.g., those
in the wars of the Maccabees.

Quite lately, however, a theory has sprung up, to the effect that in the
royal psalms of lamentation we do not have real dangers and sufferings,

---

[58a] See above, pp. 196f., 226f. with references to Birkeland.

[58b] Pss. 9.9, 18, 20; 10.16; 43.1; 54.5; 56.8 (cf. v. 2); 59.9. Duhm's conjecture: *gē'îm* for
gôyîm is absolutely groundless; see *i.a.* Birkeland, *The Evildoers*, pp. 12ff.

[58c] See Pss. 18.44f., 48; cf. v. 28 (thanksgiving psalm); 20.8f.; 21.9ff.; 89.51; 144.2, 7, 10.

[58d] E.g. Pss. 12; 14; 58; perhaps 83.

[59] Ps. 20.3f., 7 (the allusion to the oracle of reply); 63.3; 54.8; 3.6 (the incubation); 27.4,
8b–11 (the prayer for an oracle); 27.14 (the promise of the cultic servant). See below, II.20
and references there.

[60] See M. Burrows, *The Dead Sea Scrolls*, pp. 208ff.; Ginsburg in *BASOR* 112, 1948, pp. 19ff.

which have befallen the king; and that the king is not here really suffering, but only 'suffering in the cult', that is to say he is taking part in a cultic 'play' or drama, where he suffers, only to be later exalted. This view is a corollary of the theory mentioned above, that even in Israel the deity was presented in the cult as dying and rising again, and that in the cultic drama the king would play the part of the god, and die and rise along with him; such a performance could also be looked upon as the king's vicarious suffering and death on behalf of the people.[61] This interpretation, it is said, must be applied to the I-psalms discussed in this chapter, as well as to the 'psalms of illness' to be discussed in the next. It is maintained that we have here the adoption of a common Babylonian-Assyrian-Canaanite 'cultic pattern', even if in Israel it has become more or less 'disintegrated' and has therefore partly lost its original meaning.[62]

Accordingly, the 'enemies' of the laments could not be historical and human enemies, but only the mythical and demonic powers of chaos and death, attacking the god-king and defeating him. And the 'metaphor' of the lament, telling of the descent of the distressed one into the nether world and of his sojourn in Sheol, could not be intended to express an actual tangible state of distress and danger, but was to be understood 'literally'—admittedly in a mythical sense—as something experienced in the mythical and cultic 'drama', and so the same kind of 'distress' as is found behind Yahweh's 'appearance' in the enthronement psalms.

We have seen above that the assumption on which this theory was based, does not hold good. In Israel, that is to say in the legitimate Israelite cult of Jerusalem with which we have to deal, Yahweh was never conceived as dying and rising again, so the basis for any ritual, any cultic drama, presenting the king as one who suffers and dies in a cultic and mythical sense, fails. Nor is it very likely that in Israel the king would have appeared in the guise of Yahweh, however much his person may have been deified; the difference between Yahweh and a human being, however great, was too strongly felt for that (see Chap. III.3).

In spite of the central part played by the king in the cult, of which many instances have been given above,[63] the texts do not afford a single clear instance of his taking Yahweh's place in the cult. Even Ps. 110, in which the king receives the seat of honour on the right hand of Yahweh distinguishes clearly between Yahweh and the king. If in the cult the king had actually been made God, it would be most strange that, for instance, Ezekiel, who makes so many accusations against the kings of Judah (Ezk. 17; 19; 34) should not also have accused the king of making himself God; but the worst sacrilege of which Ezekiel can find the kings guilty is their having placed their graves close to the Temple, thus defiling the house of Yahweh (Ezk. 43.7ff.).

[61] See Chap. III, esp. pp. 66ff., and Additional Note XXXI.
[62] See n. 95 to Chap. V, and Additional Note XXXI.
[63] See Chap. III. 3; V. 3, 9; VII. 1-2.

Of course there is some truth in saying that the very picturing of the sufferer as descending into the nether world and sojourning in Sheol, must after all, at any rate partly, be derived from the common oriental, especially Sumerian and Babylonian concepts and myths about the god of vegetation descending thither (see above, p. 75). But to say that one who suffers and is threatened by death 'carries death around with him' and is already 'between the jaws of death', is to use expressions that might be applied to anybody in those circumstances. There is nothing here which is characteristic only of the god of vegetation or of the king taking part in the cult; death and danger of death remain the same thing, whosoever is struck or threatened by them. So there is nothing remarkable about the fact that the condition of the one who is threatened by death is described by means of the same metaphors, whether he be the dying god of vegetation, or a king in the tumult of battle, or any sick person. On the other hand, however, it is but natural that there should be a piling up of drastic descriptions in the myth which describes how the god of life must descend into the domain of death. But then it should also be easy to understand that the authors of the psalms of lamentation, wanting to rouse the compassion of Yahweh by making the distress appear as great and cruel as possible, would preferentially resort to known metaphors from the myth of the descent into the nether world, since this style of writing, like so many others, would spread and be adopted by Hebrew psalmography, that of Canaan possibly acting as the connecting link.[64] Therefore when these descriptions occur in laments and thanksgiving psalms they can never be used to prove the 'cultic descent into the nether world' of the king of Israel.

Another possibility is that parts of old oriental rituals concerned with the sufferings of the king have been taken over by Israel and re-expounded as the vicarious expiatory punishment of the king for the sins of the people. In Babylonia it was part of the festal ritual of new year, that the king was stripped of his regalia and arrayed in penitential clothes and treated by the priest with humiliating rites, such as boxing his ears or striking his cheeks.[65] In itself this rite has probably nothing to do with his sufferings as the representative of the gods, but is an expiatory ceremony on behalf of the whole community before the renewed enthronement of the king at every new year festival. Something like this might have been the case even in Jerusalem; only we have nothing to prove it, and in the royal laments nothing can be found to show that they refer to such sufferings.

On the other hand there are plenty of passages showing that they do speak of real human and historical enemies and real actual sufferings. In the plainly national laments, the 'we-laments', the background of human history is generally quite clear.[66] But even in many of the I-laments,

[64] See above, V. 7.
[65] See, for instance, L. Dürr, *Ursprung u. Ausbau*, pp. 135ff.
[66] See above, Chap. VI. 1-2, 3, 4.

the royal laments, the historical and human background is also quite evident. On the whole the enemies are described, as we have seen, in the same terms and metaphors as in the obviously national psalms. The enemies and antagonists of the king and of the leader of the people are 'nations' and no demonic beings;[67] in Ps. 118.6 we are told in plain words that they are 'men'. The sojourn of the suffering person in the realm of the dead, as we have seen, is neither a mythical nor a cultic reality, but a mode of picturing illness and danger of death (Chap. VII.5).

If the king in the laments were to represent the suffering and dying deity, how could he then possibly call to Yahweh for deliverance from the 'realm of the dead', and for help against his enemies? The Jerusalem cult did not allow any other cultic gods within the scope of Yahweh's festival— although at times other gods were worshipped in the Temple of Yahweh. And how could the king in such a case count on the possibility of human help—as he does for instance in Ps. 116.11[68]—if his sufferings were of a mythical cultic character? If we are dealing with a mythical cultic play, how then can the king complain of the enemies that they 'have broken down all his walls, and laid his fortresses in ruins': and how can it be that the 'wayfarers' 'plunder him' and his 'neighbours' 'sneer at him', if his suffering merely means that he has been put in Sheol in the mythical struggle against demons?[69] That here we have quite matter of fact human beings in historical political conditions must be obvious on any sober-minded and unprejudiced interpretation.

Another hypothesis, more in keeping with the essence of Yahwism, has been put forward regarding the king's playing the part of Yahweh.[70] A varying number of royal laments are interpreted as evidence that the king is there acting on behalf of Yahweh in the cultic drama—the 'sham fight' of the cult—presenting Yahweh's struggle and victory over the powers of evil; then the lamentation and the description of the distress refer to the troubles of the king in this drama, until by the aid of Yahweh he defeats all evil powers and in particular wins the victory over all the other nations who are supposed in the cultic drama to attack Jerusalem and Yahweh's anointed. According to this theory we would here have a cultic presentation of the 'myth about the fight of nations', where the king does not act as Yahweh himself, but as Yahweh's representative, his 'son'. That such

---

[67] It is particularly Birkeland, *Feinde d. Indiv.*, and *Evil-doers in the Pss.*, who has seen and proved this, and so corrected the great one-sidedness from which my statement in *Ps.St.* I was suffering; cf. my discourse as opposer to Birkeland *NTT* 134, pp. 1ff., and above, n. 19 to Chap. VI.

[68] This psalm—which by the way is no 'passion psalm' but a thanksgiving psalm—Engnell (*Div. Kingship*, p. 210, n. 2) would interpret as dealing with 'the king suffering in the cult'. The way Engnell apportions the text to the king (vv. 1–4, 6–14) and the chorus (vv. 5 and 15) conflicts with the obvious stanza division, which shows that v. 5 is closely connected with v. 6, and v. 15 with v. 16. In Ps. 118 we also meet with enemies obviously human, but Johnson (in *The Labyrinth*) would refer this psalm to the apparent sufferings of the king in the cult; see Additional Note XXXI.

[69] Ps. 89.41f. This psalm, too, is interpreted by Johnson (*The Labyrinth*) as referring to the apparent suffering in the cult. See Additional Note XXXI.

[70] This more modest and sympathetic version of the theory of the king as the sufferer in the psalms is represented by Johnson in *The Labyrinth*. See, however, Additional Note XXXI.

a dramatic presentation of the defeat of all the nations outside Jerusalem actually had a place in the old Israelite enthronement festival cult seems fairly certain; Pss. 46 and 48 testify to such a 'ritual sham fight'. We do not know, however, that this ritual fight was presented in the more or less realistic manner found in Egypt and Babylonia; in all probability it was presented by means of symbolic rites, the intrinsic merit of which went far beyond anything the eye could see. Nor is there anything to indicate that in Israel this cultic fight should have been looked upon and presented as a suffering on the part of the king, much less as his cultic death and sojourn in the realm of the dead, and that these laments must be read as the texts for such a cultic drama.

So there is no reason for us to give up the natural interpretation of the sufferings mentioned in the royal laments as real, historical troubles, brought about by actual (as a rule) political, conditions, in which the king is threatened either by hostile neighbouring nations or by a punitive expedition on the part of his foreign lord; some times it may be a genuine case of illness.

7

That a great many psalms of lamentation in the I-form are actually national laments, in which the king or the leader of the people is speaking on behalf of the whole community is confirmed by the fact that this is the undoubted rule in the *Babylonian-Assyrian laments*.[71] There the use of 'we' to indicate the worshipper does not seem to occur,[72] it is everywhere the 'I' of the king who speaks; the psalms are 'royal laments',[73] and very often on a national and political subject.

This point of resemblance is so much the more significant because of the close relationship between the biblical laments and the much older Babylonian-Assyrian laments, in both style and substance (see Chap. XX.3). Therefore the interpretation of the I-laments, which agrees with the use of this style of writing in Babylonian-Assyrian poetry, is likely to be correct: very often in the biblical laments also we do not have the troubles of private individuals, but public distress, with the king as the spokesman of the congregation.

[71] See Birkeland, *Feinde d. Indiv.*, pp. 350–379.
[72] Gunkel-Begrich, *Einl.*, p. 123.
[73] Cf. Gunkel-Begrich, *Einl.*, pp. 124, 127, 128, 129, 132; Jastrow, *Relig. Bab. u. Assyr.* II, pp. 1ff.